Reading Hemingway's *Winner Take Nothing*

READING HEMINGWAY SERIES

MARK CIRINO, EDITOR

ROBERT W. LEWIS, FOUNDING EDITOR

Reading Hemingway's
Winner Take Nothing

GLOSSARY AND COMMENTARY

Edited by Mark Cirino and Susan Vandagriff

The Kent State University Press

KENT, OHIO

© 2021 by The Kent State University Press, Kent, Ohio 44242
All rights reserved
Library of Congress Catalog Number 2021005740
ISBN 978-1-60635-423-0
Manufactured in the United States of America

Library of Congress Cataloging-in-Publication Data

Names: Cirino, Mark, 1971- editor. | Vandagriff, Susan, editor.
Title: Reading Hemingway's Winner take nothing : glossary and commentary / edited by
    Mark Cirino and Susan Vandagriff.
Description: Kent, Ohio : The Kent State University Press, [2021] | Series: Reading Heming-
    way series | Includes bibliographical references and index.
Identifiers: LCCN 2021005740 | ISBN 9781606354230 (paperback) | ISBN 9781631014512
    (epub) | ISBN 9781631014529 (pdf)
Subjects: LCSH: Hemingway, Ernest, 1899-1961. Winner takes nothing. | Hemingway,
    Ernest, 1899-1961--Criticism and interpretation.
Classification: LCC PS3515.E37 W537 2021 | DDC 813/.52--dc23
LC record available at https://lccn.loc.gov/2021005740

25 24 23 22 21   5 4 3 2 1

For his guidance and kindness, this book is dedicated to
Larry Caldwell

CONTENTS

ACKNOWLEDGMENTS

We would like to thank the excellent editorial team of ENGL 399 at the University of Evansville: Natalie Beaumont-Christy, Charlie Ericson, and Samantha Wallisch.

Thanks to the Hemingway Letters Project for its generosity and support, particularly Sandra Spanier and Verna Kale.

We greatly appreciate Stacey Chandler and Stephen Plotkin at the John F. Kennedy Library in Boston. We were honored to receive the John F. Kennedy Library Research Grant, which was so valuable to our work.

We benefited from the dogged interlibrary loan departments at the University of Evansville and the Kraemer Family Library.

Thanks to the team at Kent State University Press for their loyalty and support, particularly Will Underwood and Susan Wadsworth-Booth.

Mark Cirino would like to acknowledge:

The friendship, insight, and support from Mark P. Ott, Michael Von Cannon, Rob Elder, Mike Roos, and Matt Bolton.

The timely research assistance from Alex Vernon and Martina Mastandrea. Much appreciation to Isabella Giacometti at the Museo Francesco Baracca in Lugo.

Thanks to Michelle Lehman and Lesley Pleasant.

Thank you, Dr. Colin G. Crosby.

And as always, my love and appreciation to Kristen, Luca, and Noah.

Susan Vandagriff would like to thank:

Claire Carles-Huguet for her help in resolving a geographic quandary. I am also indebted to Bill Hemminger for "being that someone that knows some French" and checking my translations. I'd also like to thank Larry Caldwell for his expert advice on the medieval inspirations for the book's epigraph.

Finally, and most importantly, my thanks to Julie and Loyd Vandagriff for their love and support and their willingness to listen to more Hemingway trivia than parents ever should.

INTRODUCTION

Mark Cirino and Susan Vandagriff

Winner Take Nothing is a collection of short stories about loners and losers and misfits and ne'er-do-wells. Its characters are ill, tortured, maligned, and frustrated by Hemingway's world. Like the characters it depicts, *Winner Take Nothing* is also a misfit in Hemingway's career, a volume of short stories that, as of this writing, is not even in print. Its more popular predecessors, *In Our Time* (1925) and *Men Without Women* (1927), are held up as iconic collections in the American short story tradition. The grotesqueries of these fourteen stories are outcasts in Hemingway's corpus and have been virtually from the beginning.

In his review for *Esquire* in early 1934, Burton Rascoe joked that "Ernest Hemingway wrote as though he had so much hair on his chest that he had to do it up in curl papers every night" (86). Although Rascoe apologized for the joke only lines later, it is indicative of one of the major points of critique for *Winner Take Nothing*: Hemingway's brutish, masculine public persona as a writer now preceded him. Expectations for *Winner Take Nothing* were high: *The Kansas City Star* heralded Hemingway's return to the genre in the headline of its review, "Hemingway's First Book of Fiction in Four Years," and Sinclair Lewis and Isabel Paterson both named the book on their to-read lists for the *New York Tribune* and the *New York Herald Tribune,* respectively, in September 1933. After two novels, one novella, two short story collections, and *Death in the Afternoon* (which most reviewers seemed at least willing to forgive, if not praise), Hemingway was a known entity with a reputation for his singular style and form.

Several reviews began as Henry Canby's did, by commenting on just how well known; Canby noted that Hemingway's "staccato style has had the compliment of much imitation" (217). For good or ill, all reviewers remarked on Hemingway himself and his literary celebrity. Lewis Gannett went so far as to explicitly confuse the author with his work in his review, writing, "Hemingway's stories, even more than other writers', seem always to be about himself" (15), and many critics proposed that Hemingway did not create so much as he reported in this collection. As Lawrence H. Martin observed of the critical response to *Winner Take Nothing,*

"Hemingway now found himself to be a victim of his own invention" (362), as reviewers demanded Hemingway move beyond the hallmark style and subjects that had made him famous.

Although *Winner Take Nothing* has a reputation for a negative critical reception, the reality is mixed, with few reviewers giving wholly negative reviews (though, even fewer gave wholly positive ones). The main complaints center on the work's perceived repetitiveness, not only self-contained, but of Hemingway's other works. Canby wrote the stories "are repetitive with the slow pound, pound of a hammer upon a single mood" (217). His critique focused on the relentless pessimism of *Winner Take Nothing*, but others like the *New York Times*'s Louis Kronenberger, wondered, "can any writer go on and on writing about the same things when they are merely things he has observed?" (BR6). Similarly, John Chamberlain questioned Hemingway's emotional effectiveness: "the danger of repeating the patterns is that they may become a mannerism—Hemingway may go on writing of death, death, death, but no longer in a way that quickens your sympathies" (17).

Another frequent sticking point for criticism was that "death, death, death" subject matter, which managed to be at once shocking ("the grisliest," according to Chamberlain [17]) and also tired and overdone ("things which smell of the early 1920s," wrote Clifton Fadiman [58]). In his review for *The Brooklyn Daily Eagle,* John Erskine ran down the book's characters as "derelicts and waifs and ne'er do wells" and "abnormal and subnormal" (17). There is a temptation to dismiss the critiques of the subject matter as relics of a more conservative time, but most critics' dislike went beyond simple bigotry and prudishness.

Many felt that Hemingway was growing sentimental in this collection, a view that seems initially at odds with critics' disdain for tales of violence or complicated and frustrated sexuality. However, this focus on the dark, forbidden, and tragic, reviewers like Kronenberger found, gave Hemingway "the right to despise" the world (BR6). And to what end, Kronenberger asked: "As Hemingway presents his hard, stupid, aimless, greedy people they imply little more than the truth that they exist" (BR6). Critics read *Winner Take Nothing* as a book that harkens back to a better past though its lurid, disgusting, or disheartening depictions of the present. Among its only champions, Frank Getty defended the subject matter as Hemingway's challenge to "our predilection for sissy literature" (SM10). William Plomer, too, saw the subject matter as "cutting right across the muscle of the arm of Convention" and as "a protest against old conventions and an effort to escape from them" (184).

Others are less kind. Chamberlain saw the stories as devoid of "genuine emotion" and felt Hemingway "straining as he has not strained before" in this collection (17). Canby compared Hemingway to Rudyard Kipling and liked Kipling the better as "[h]e never is so sorry for himself as this man who records struggle where the winner gets nothing" (217). T. S. Matthews speculated this self-pity that Canby disliked is what made Hemingway popular to begin with but concluded that it has begun to work against him: "he expressed his generation's bitter adolescence in a way that even grown-ups had to take seriously. But what we are now beginning to see is that it was, after all, an expression of adolescence. We see it more clearly because Hemingway continues to express it" (24). David Garnett viewed the collection at its core as nostalgic longing for a simpler, truer time and the deliberately blunt style and shocking subject matter simply a means to "hide sentimentality or somehow nip it in the bud" (192).

Given most critics' dislike of the more scandalous storylines, their favorite stories from the collection may be unsurprising, despite most falling into modern obscurity. "After the Storm" was the most frequent favorite, with *Time* noting its "eerie atmosphere" (66) and T. S. Matthews calling it "almost magical" (24). Fanny Butcher and John Chamberlain appreciated the humor in "Homage to Switzerland." Unusual among reviewers, Butcher also liked "A Natural History of the Dead," calling it "life burned to the quick" (16). Plomer, too, was singular in his praise for "A Natural History" and "God Rest You Merry, Gentlemen," which the reviewer felt Hemingway treated with "that technical skill, that economy, and that peculiarly American kind of sophistication" Hemingway was noted for (184). "Wine of Wyoming" was repeatedly praised for its unique characters and dialogue and "Mr. Hemingway's talent for communicating the simpler pleasures" (Glendinning 90). "The Gambler, The Nun, and the Radio" was also popular with several reviewers, including William Troy who, in his only praise, called it "the most successful in the book" (570). Of the stories better known to modern audiences, "Fathers and Sons" was a favorite with Chamberlain and Garnett, and Garnett also praised "A Way You'll Never Be" as the "finest picture of shell-shock I've read" (192).

Fanny Butcher, William Plomer, and Horace Gregory offered the most praise for *Winner Take Nothing*. Several other positive reviews remain focused on Hemingway himself, such as the *Los Angeles Times* review that praised Hemingway as "a law unto himself" and "without peer in the realm of the short story" (A6), but gave minimal attention to *Winner Take Nothing*. In her review for the *Chicago Daily Tribune*, Butcher agreed with many critics that Hemingway had fallen into a predictable style, but she enjoyed the results enough not to mind. Although she qualified that "*some* of the stories" will be a part of Hemingway's greater legacy (16, emphasis added), she had no real complaints. Many critics felt the collection showed masculinity performed to a ridiculous point, but Butcher disagreed: "it is no more destined for men alone than life or birth or death are wholly male experiences" (16).

Plomer's review, while not uncritical (he does note that, in places, "Hemingway is content just to express disgust" [184–85]), celebrated what most critics viewed as weaknesses. The nihilism Plomer attributed to "Mr. Hemingway's vitality" which "quickens his eye and shapes his style" (185). Plomer did not question Hemingway's darker choices of subjects but accepted these "episodes of violence" as another part of the human experience. He concluded by describing Hemingway as "[v]ivid, adroit, and an expert in brevity" who can "put more point into an anecdote than many writers can into a novel" (185).

Horace Gregory was the most effusive in his praise, calling Hemingway the "spokesman of a lost generation" even as it enters middle age. Gregory preferred this collection's darker tone and more jaded worldview. He was untroubled by the stories he saw as "recalling the earlier, familiar Hemingway" (E5), including "A Way You'll Never Be," "God Rest You Merry, Gentlemen," "The Light of the World," and "A Clean, Well-Lighted Place," but was delighted by "Wine of Wyoming" and "The Gambler, The Nun, and the Radio," which show "a sudden expansion of Hemingway's range" (E5). Gregory alone found the more mature Hemingway that critics were seeking, directly contradicting many critics in his belief that the writing was "no longer an overflow of adolescent emotion" (E5).

By contrast, William Troy's review, "Mr. Hemingway's Opium," was arguably the harshest. Troy responded directly to Gregory's praise and called it an attempt to "let the champion down as easily as possible" (570). The collection was broadly dismissed, with even critical favorites like "Wine of Wyoming" and "Fathers and Sons" criticized as "a recurrence of all the old nostalgias" (570). For Troy, the collection showed both a "lack of growth" and "growth along what is for Hemingway a new and unfortunate direction" (570). Hemingway, Troy wrote, relies on "action as catharsis," and the results are "monotonous repetition" and "an increasing fondness for subjects and characters which are usually distinguished by the label 'special'" (570). It was, according to Troy, "the poorest and least interesting writing he has ever placed on public view" (570).

Clifton Fadiman was also disappointed. He felt that Hemingway had nothing new to say and resorted to retreading familiar territory without improvement or innovation. Although Fadiman admitted that these are "good stories" (58), he demanded better ones. In "A Letter to Mr. Hemingway," Fadiman wrote that Hemingway could no longer get by on "honesty and skill" alone (58), sharing the assumption of other critics, like Kronenberger, that Hemingway reported rather than created his stories. Fadiman echoed other critics' complaints of redundancy ("strong echoes of earlier work" [58]) and deliberately shocking subject matter ("third-position exercises in the macabre" [58]). Fadiman was clear that his disappointment stemmed from what he felt was Hemingway's untapped potential, and his review was by no means the cruelest or most pointed. Yet Fadiman's critique stands out because Hemingway chose to respond to it personally.

Hemingway, Baker writes, "mixed scorn and pride" in his letter back to Fadiman, where he decried the growing critical consensus that he was unimaginative and self-repeating (*Ernest Hemingway* 246). He responded not only to Fadiman's critiques, but others like "T. S. (Chickenshit) Mathews" [sic] (*Letters vol. 5*, 557). He dismissed the critique that he is repeating himself: "In stories I try to write only once about anything" (557). Hemingway also evinced his belief that *Winner*

Take Nothing was before its time and that this initial dislike would one day give way to appreciation. "I told Max Perkins nobody would like the book, but that it was anybody's $2.00 worth <u>if they would re-read them</u>," he writes (558, emphasis Hemingway's). His bluster with Fadiman (whom he informed of his prowess as a lover, progenitor, and war survivor, in addition to threatening to break a critic's jaw each year [556–60]) must be countered with his somewhat anxious tone with Maxwell Perkins in the same month. "This happens to be a book <u>you</u> have to do a little work to push," he chastised Perkins (541, emphasis Hemingway's), after noting the lack of advertising *Winner Take Nothing* seems to have.

Frustrated by claims that he only reported what he saw without any imagination or creativity, Hemingway complained to Perkins, "If I write about <u>anybody</u>—automatically they label that character as me—when I write about somebody that cant [sic] possibly be me—as in After The Storm ... Mr. Chamberlain says it is unusually imaginative or more imaginative than anything I've attempted. What shit" (*Letters vol. 5*, 541, emphasis Hemingway's). Although he admitted, "I write some stories absolutely as they happen"" (naming "Wine of Wyoming," "One Reader Writes," "A Day's Wait," "After the Storm," "The Mother of a Queen," "The Gambler, The Nun, and the Radio" as stories he recorded as experienced or as they were told to him) (541–42), "others I invent completely" (542). He went on to berate his critics' demands for growth, expressing his frustration with confining expectations to those his previous works have created. He wrote to Perkins, "I can't write better stories than some that I have written ... because you can't write better stories that those—and nobody can. . . . God damn it there can't be better ones" (542).

Like the book of short stories it analyzes, this *Reading Hemingway* volume is somewhat unorthodox. Since it would be virtually impossible for one person to hold particular expertise in a collection as diverse as *Winner Take Nothing*, the editors have assigned each story to a scholar with an insight that is compelling and authoritative. Readers will see, then, a by-line for each chapter of commentary. Through these fourteen disparate and even idiosyncratic examinations, a coherent product emerges. Just as Hemingway's fourteen stories combine to form a unified work of art, these scholars offer generous exegeses that will illuminate a previously darkened corner of Hemingway's work.

WORKS CITED

Baker, Carlos. *Ernest Hemingway: A Life Story*. Scribner's, 1969.
Butcher, Fanny. "Short Stories Still Live as Works of Art." *Chicago Daily Tribune*, 28 Oct. 1933, p. 16.
Canby, Henry Seidel. "Farewell to the Nineties." *Saturday Review of Literature*, 28 Oct. 1933, p. 217.

Chamberlain, John. "Books of the Times." Review of *Winner Take Nothing*. *The New York Times*, 27 Oct. 1933, p. 17.

Erskine, John. "The Hollow Life." *The Brooklyn Daily Eagle*, 5 Nov. 1933, p. 17.

Fadiman, Clifton. "A Letter to Mr. Hemingway." *The New Yorker*, 28 Oct. 1933, p. 58.

Gannet, Lewis. "Books and Things." Review of *Winner Take Nothing*. *The New York Herald Tribune*, 27 Oct. 1933, p. 15.

Garnett, David. "Books in General." Review of *Winner Take Nothing*. *The New Statesman and Nation*, 10 Feb. 1934, p. 192.

Getty, Frank. "Ernest Hemingway and Dorothy Parker." *The Washington Post*, 10 Dec. 1933, p. SM10.

Glendenning, Alex. "New Novels." Review of *Winner Take Nothing*. *The Times Literary Supplement*, 8 Feb. 1934, p. 90.

Gordon, Donald. "The Literary Lowbrow: Bookmarket Flashes." Review of *Winner Take Nothing*. *Saturday Evening Post*, 20 Jan. 1934, p. 43.

Gregory, Horace. "Ernest Hemingway Has Put on Maturity." *The New York Herald Tribune*, 29 Oct. 1933, p. E5.

Hemingway, Ernest. *The Letters of Ernest Hemingway: Volume 5 (1932–1934)*. Edited by Sandra Spanier and Miriam B. Mandel. CUP, 2020.

"Hemingway's Tales." *Springfield Republican* [MA], 26 Nov. 1933, p. 7e.

Herschell, Brickell. "Literary Landscapes." Review of *Winner Take Nothing*. *The North American Review*, vol. 237, no. 1, 1934, pp. 88–96.

"Incandescent Brilliance." *Los Angeles Times*, 5 Nov. 193, p. A6.

Kronenberger, Louis. "Hemingway's New Stories and Other Recent Works of Fiction." *The New York Times*, 5 Nov. 1933, p. BR6.

Lewis, Sinclair. "American Fiction," *New York Tribune*, 24 Sept. 1933, p. F5.

Martin, Lawrence H. J. "Crazy in Sheridan: Hemingway's "Wine of Wyoming" Reconsidered." *New Critical Approaches to the Short Stories of Ernest Hemingway*, edited by Jackson J. Benson. Duke UP, 1990, pp. 360–72.

Matthews, T. S. "Fiction by Young and Old." Review of *Winner Take Nothing*. *The New Republic*, 15 Nov. 1933, p. 24.

"New Novels." Review of *Winner Take Nothing*. *The Times*, 9 Feb. 1934, p. 9.

Paterson, Isabel. "Picking the New Fall Books Sight Unseen: A Rich and Varied List That Promises to Be Interesting." *New York Herald Tribune*, 24 Sept. 1933, p. F1.

Plomer, William. "Review of *Winner Take Nothing* by Ernest Hemingway." *Ernest Hemingway: The Critical Heritage*, edited by Jeffrey Meyers. Routledge, 2009, pp. 183–85.

Rascoe, Burton. "Esquire's Five-Minute Shelf." Review of *Winner Take Nothing*. *Esquire*, Jan. 1934, p. 86.

Review of *Winner Take Nothing* by Ernest Hemingway. *Kirkus Reviews*, 15 June 1933.

"Stiff Upper Lip." *Time*, 11 Nov. 1933, p. 65.

Troy, William. "Mr. Hemingway's Opium." *The Nation*, 15 Nov. 1933, p. 570.

ABBREVIATIONS FOR THE WORKS OF

ERNEST HEMINGWAY USED IN THIS BOOK

ARIT — *Across the River and into the Trees.* Scribner's, 1950.

BL — *By-LineErnest Hemingway: Selected Articles and Dispatches from Four Decades.* Edited by William White. Scribner's, 1967.

CP — *Complete Poems.* Edited by Nicholas Gerogiannis. U of Nebraska P, 1992.

CSS — *The Complete Short Stories of Ernest Hemingway: The Finca Vigía Edition.* Scribner's, 1987.

DIA — *Death in the Afternoon.* Scribner's, 1932.

DLT — *Dateline: Toronto. The Complete "Toronto Star" Dispatches, 1920–1924.* Edited by William White. Scribner's, 1985.

DS — *The Dangerous Summer.* Scribner's, 1985.

FTA — *A Farewell to Arms.* Scribner's, 1929.

FTA–HLE — *A Farewell to Arms: The Hemingway Library Edition.* Edited with an Introduction by Seán Hemingway. Scribner's, 2012.

FWBT — *For Whom the Bell Tolls.* Scribner's, 1940.

GHOA — *Green Hills of Africa.* Scribner's, 1935.

GOE — *The Garden of Eden.* Scribner's, 1986.

IIS — *Islands in the Stream.* Scribner's, 1970.

JFK — Ernest Hemingway Collection, John F. Kennedy Presidential Library and Museum, Boston, Massachusetts.

Letters vol. 1 — *The Letters of Ernest Hemingway: Volume 1 (1907–1922).* Edited by Sandra Spanier and Robert W. Trogdon. Cambridge UP, 2011.

Letters vol. 2 — *The Letters of Ernest Hemingway: Volume 2 (1923–1925).* Edited by Sandra Spanier, Albert J. DeFazio III, and Robert W. Trogdon. Cambridge UP, 2013.

Letters vol. 3 — *The Letters of Ernest Hemingway: Volume 3 (1926–1929).* Edited by Rena Sanderson, Sandra Spanier, and Robert W. Trogdon. Cambridge UP, 2015.

Letters vol. 4 — *The Letters of Ernest Hemingway: Volume 4 (1929–1931).* Edited by Sandra Spanier and Miriam B. Mandel. Cambridge UP, 2017.

SERIES NOTE

All page and line numbers reference *The Complete Short Stories of Ernest Heming-way: The Finca Vigía Edition*. All references to *Winner Take Nothing* stories are given a page and line number, separated by a colon. A reference to the third line of page 17, for instance, would be 17:3. A reference to the first three lines of page 40 would be 40:1–3.

TITLE, EPIGRAPH, AND DEDICATION

Susan Vandagriff

Title: Winner Take Nothing

On 7 June 1933, Hemingway wrote to editor (and creator of *Esquire* magazine, which would publish its first issue in three months) Arnold Gingrich to ask for his thoughts: "The title I have for the book is Winner Take Nothing" (*Letters vol. 5*, 401). Hemingway went on to explain, "The title is not meant to be tricky—any more than Men Without Women was—It has the same sort of application to the contents" (*Letters vol. 5*, 402). He asked Gingrich his thoughts on the title and epigraph. "Pauline, my wife, likes it but we have both been wrong before," he explained (402). Gingrich's response was positive when he wrote back later that month, calling it "a swell title" and noting that "it fits—at least the stories I've read—like a glove" (403n). As George Monteiro notes, the title also fits its time period. The stock market crash in 1929 ended an age of winners, and, in the Great Depression "[e]verybody became a 'loser,' it seemed, even the so-called winners" (87).

The phrase "winner take nothing" derives from the book's epigraph and is an ironic inversion of the traditional "winner take all." Its sport and gambling connotations reinforce the tone of brutal masculinity that many reviewers and critics noticed throughout the book. However, the concept of a winner who receives no reward also reflects the nihilism of many of the volume's stories. The titular nothing echoes the prayer of the older waiter in "A Clean, Well-Lighted Place" ("Our *nada* who art in *nada, nada* be thy name," 291:10–11), the diagnosis by Doc Fischer in "God Rest You Merry, Gentlemen" ("There is nothing wrong with your body," 300:13–14), "The Mother of a Queen" narrator's lament about Paco ("Nothing, nothing can touch them," 319:17–18), Schatz's fever in "A Day's Wait" ("nothing to worry about," 334:2), and the subject of the doctor and the artillery officer's fight in "A Natural History of the Dead" ("In time of war we dispute about nothing," 341:24–25). Even where nothingness is not directly referenced, it pervades a collection filled with grim depictions of disappointment and the worst human tendencies.

The title also evokes the last line of Hemingway's friend and contemporary Archibald MacLeish's poem "The End of the World": "Of nothing, nothing, nothing—nothing at all" (l. 14). In MacLeish's poem, the end of the world comes to a circus, where the routine of an eccentric cast of characters is abruptly brought to a harsh, explosive, and meaningless end. The poem's narrative shares many parallels to the stories of *Winner Take Nothing,* whose own characters, often living outside "normal" society, come to violent, empty ends or struggle to make meaning of the senseless tragedies they face. (For more on MacLeish, see Dedication entry below).

Epigraph: Unlike all other forms of lutte or combat the conditions are that the winner shall take nothing; neither his ease, nor his pleasure, nor any notions of glory; nor, if he win far enough, shall there be any reward within himself.

Hemingway refers to the epigraph in his letter to Gingrich as "the quotation," yet presumably Hemingway wrote the faux medieval epigraph himself (*Letters vol. 5,* 402). Hemingway would later write a similar epigraph for Martha Gellhorn's novel *A Stricken Field* (Moreland 40). Similar to Hemingway's claim that the epigraph of *Winner Take Nothing* is a quotation, in Gellhorn's novel the epigraph is attributed to "a Medieval Chronicle" (Gellhorn n.p.) In *A Stricken Field,* Hemingway's phrasing closely echoes the description of "many of the younger Spaniards, who had never been present at a stricken field" and "Jean de Rye an aged knight of Burgundy" from *A History of the Art of War* by Charles Oman (650). However, the inspiration for the *Winner Take Nothing* epigraph is less clear.

In his discussion of the epigraph, John McCormick notes its distinctive religious mood, describing it as a "profoundly religious sentiment, not the religion of popular Christianity, but the purer conception of an Augustine or a Loyola" (56). Looking at his previous works, it is possible that Hemingway returned to Ecclesiastes for inspiration,[1] having used it for the title and the second epigraph of *The Sun Also Rises.* Several verses in the King James Bible echo the sentiment of Hemingway's epigraph:

> "Then I looked on all the works that my hands had wrought, and on the labour that I had laboured to do: and behold, all was vanity and vexation of spirit, and there was no profit under the sun." (2:11)

> As he came forth of his mother's womb, naked shall he return to go as he came, and shall take nothing of his labour, which he may carry away in his hand. (5:15)

> For the living know that they shall die: but the dead know not anything, neither have they any more a reward, for the memory of them is forgotten. (9:5)

The epigraph's style is less biblical than medieval in its discussion of this unnamed form of combat's spoils Others have pointed to Hemingway's evident interest in medieval romances and the Middle Ages (see, for instance, Kim Moreland's "Hemingway's Medievalist Impulse," or Michael Reynolds's *Hemingway's Reading, 1910–1940*). Hemingway's epigraph has more syntactical similarities to medieval gaming rules, such as those described in Castiglione's *The Book of the Courtier*[2]:

"But if anyone is anxious to wrestle, to run or to jump with peasants, then he ought, in my opinion, to do it casually, out of *noblesse oblige,* so to say, and certainly not in competition with them; and he should be almost certain of winning, or else not take part at all, for it is too sad and shocking, and quite undignified when a gentleman is seen to be beaten by a peasant, especially in a wrestling-match." (Book II, p. 117)

Instead of the mockable superficiality of *The Book of the Courtier,* the rules of Hemingway's "combat" are steeped in ecclesiastical pessimism, self-denial, and severity. McCormick praises the epigraph as "perhaps the finest and most accurate brief description of Hemingway's heroes, of what he set out to do in his best work and what in the main he accomplished" (56). This reading suggests that the characters of *Winner Take Nothing* (and Hemingway's other works) struggle in the face of certain futility and that hopeless struggle is where their heroism lies. The façade of its medieval context allows the epigraph to allude to and refute older conceptions of heroism such as knights that win favor and glory in combat. *Lutte* is French for "struggle" or "fight" and is used specifically for the sport of wrestling. Given the themes of the collection, it is possible that this "form of lutte or combat" refers to love or marriage or even war itself, as the modern versions of these struggles no longer permit the clear and simple victories that appeared in earlier romantic depictions.

Dedication: To A. MacLeish

The dedication "To A. MacLeish" refers either to Archibald MacLeish, who, was a close friend of Hemingway's at this time, or to his wife Ada Hitchcock MacLeish. Archibald MacLeish (1892–1982), an American poet and writer, would, under President Franklin Delano Roosevelt, become librarian of Congress and assistant secretary of state for public affairs (Everett 329–30). Despite being seven years older than Hemingway, the two shared many similarities. Both grew up near Chicago (Everett 329), and MacLeish also served as an ambulance driver (and later an artillery officer) in World War I (Donaldson 93). MacLeish and Ada relocated to Paris in 1923 (Smith 1), only two years after Hemingway and Hadley Richardson had done the same. Hemingway met the MacLeishes in the late fall of 1924 (Baker 137). In 1930, MacLeish even visited Hemingway in the hospital that would serve as the setting and inspiration for "The Gambler, the Nun, and the Radio" (Baker 218).

A month later, Hemingway would write to editor Maxwell Perkins that MacLeish was "writing the best poetry written in America" and informing Perkins that he had convinced MacLeish to switch over to Scribner's (*Letters vol. 4,* 434). "You couldn't get a better name, a better writer, or a better guy for your list of what ever I may call them, and his future is ahead of him instead of behind him," Hemingway effused (434), going on to call MacLeish "the biggest favour I could do you" (435). In May 1932, Hemingway's response to a survey declared MacLeish's *Conquistador* the "most important book of poetry" published during the year (Cirino 32). This good opinion was clearly unchanged in 1933 when *Winner Take Nothing* was published and dedicated to MacLeish.

Hemingway jokingly wrote to MacLeish in November of 1933, shortly after the book came out, that Ada Hitchcock MacLeish was his intended recipient, referring to "Ms. MacLeish (to whom [I] recently dedicated a book but forgot to insert the Hitchcock" (*Letters vol. 5,* 545). However, he goes on to explain the dedication as a friendly defense of MacLeish, who had recently published *Frescoes for Mr. Rockefeller's City* to poor reviews. "No I thought they were treating you dirty. The critic boys and it was a good time to show fealty and allegiance to a pal," Hemingway writes (545). MacLeish had shown similar loyalty himself by vehemently defending Hemingway to Max Eastman after Eastman published a review of *DIA* that accused Hemingway of "lacking masculinity or courage" (399n). The English edition (published in 1934) avoids any confusion with a dedication that reads, "To Ada and Archibald MacLeish" (547n). MacLeish was flattered by the dedication, writing to Hemingway: "Deeply gratefully affectionately moved magnificent book unworthy dedicatee incommunicable sentiments" (Reynolds, *1930s* 153).

NOTES

1. In 1943, Hemingway wrote Maxwell Perkins that Gellhorn was having trouble coming up with a title for what would eventually be *Liana* and hinted at his own process by adding, "I think we ought to start Marty digging into Ecclesiastes or Proverbs where there are still very valuable properties buried" (*SL* 548).

2. There is no record that Hemingway read *The Book of the Courtier;* however, the book was known by other modernists, such as James Joyce who had read it at college (Curran 120.)

WORKS CITED

Baker, Carlos. *Ernest Hemingway: A Life Story.* Scribner's, 1969.

The Bible: King James Version with the Apocrypha. Edited by David Norton. Penguin, 2006.

Castiglione, Baldassare. *The Book of the Courtier.* Translated by George Bull. Penguin Books, 1967.

Cirino, Mark. "The Nasty Mess: Hemingway, Italian Fascism, and the *New Review* Controversy of 1932." *Hemingway Review,* vol. 33, no. 2, 2014, pp. 30–47.

Curran, Constantine. *James Joyce Remembered.* OUP, 1968.

Donaldson, Scott. *Archibald MacLeish: An American Life.* Houghton Mifflin, 1992.

Everett, Nicholas. "MacLeish, Archibald." *The Oxford Companion to Twentieth-Century Poetry,* edited by Ian Hamilton, OUP 1994, pp. 329–30.

Gellhorn, Martha. *A Stricken Field.* University of Chicago Press. 1968.

Hemingway, Ernest. *The Letters of Ernest Hemingway: Volume 4 (1929–1931)*. Edited by Sandra Spanier and Miriam B. Mandel. CUP, 2017.

———. *The Letters of Ernest Hemingway: Volume 5 (1932–1934)*. Edited by Sandra Spanier and Miriam B. Mandel. CUP, 2020.

———. *Selected Letters 1917–1961*. Edited by Carlos Baker. Scribner's 1982.

MacLeish, Archibald. *Collected Poems of Archibald MacLeish*. Houghton Mifflin, 1962.

McCormick, John. *American and European Literary Imagination, 1919–1932*. Routledge, 2017.

Monteiro, George. *The Hemingway Short Story: A Critical Appreciation*. McFarland, 2017.

Moreland, Kim. "Hemingway's Medievalist Impulse: Its Effect on the Presentation of Women and War in *The Sun Also Rises*. *Hemingway Review*, vol. 6, no. 1, 1986, pp. 30–41.

Oman, Charles. *A History of the Art of War: The Middle Ages from the Fourth to the Fourteenth Century*. G. P. Putnam's Sons, 1898.

Reynolds, Michael S. *Hemingway: The 1930s*. New York: Norton, 1997.

———. *Hemingway's Reading, 1910–1940: An Inventory*. Princeton UP, 1981.

Smith, Grover. "Archibald MacLeish." *American Writers: A Collection of Literary Biographies*. Edited by Leonard Unger. Vol. 3. Scribner's, 1974, pp. 1–25

AFTER THE STORM

Kirk Curnutt

Winner Take Nothing opens with one of the collection's strongest stories—if not *the* strongest, according to a handful of important critics. The most public advocate of "After the Storm" in the 1930s was Edmund Wilson, who praised it in a pair of influential critiques of the arc of Hemingway's career, which at that moment seemed in precipitous descent. In the first piece—*The New Republic* review of the African-safari memoir *Green Hills of Africa* (1935)—Wilson complained that the writer's "publicity legend" had infected his narrative voice to the point that he had "become his own worst-drawn character, and . . . his own worst commentator." "After the Storm" was the rare recent exception to this degeneration; as Wilson insisted, this "simple anecdote of a man who goes out to plunder a wreck and finds that he cannot even crack open the port-hole" was, "with its implications of the irreducible hazards and pains of life and the code of honor which one must evolve to live among them . . . more than worth the whole of *The Green Hills of Africa* [sic]" ("Review" 218–19). Unlike other efforts from the decade of the Great Depression, this variation did *not* belie "the apprehension of losing control of oneself which is aroused by the getting out of hand of a social-economic system, as well as of the fear of impotence which seems to accompany the loss of social mastery" (Wilson, "Gauge" 303, 304). In other words, for Wilson "After the Storm" embodied the old grit Hemingway had displayed in the early vignettes of war and bullfighting that had made *In Our Time* (1925) feel so devastatingly modern. Contemporaneous efforts, by contrast, seemed "fatuous and maudlin" ("Review" 218).

The second critic who felt the story stood out in *Winner Take Nothing*—although his carefully couched praise was circulated in private—was Hemingway's editor at Scribner's, Maxwell Perkins. The original title for the collection was "After the Storm and Other Stories," although superior quality was not necessarily what elevated it in Hemingway's eyes. As Perkins was painfully aware, nearly a third of the texts slated for inclusion were previously unpublished, which made a story collection a dicey proposition for readers in the early 1930s hesitant to spend $2.50 on unknown quantities. Another third had appeared in *Scribner's Magazine*, the publisher's medium-circulation literary magazine, where they had failed to make much of a splash. By contrast, "After the Storm" had appeared originally in the May 1932 issue of *Cosmopolitan,* a glossy periodical with a circulation approaching two million readers. Hemingway had a long and complicated relationship with this William Randolph Hearst-owned outlet, denouncing the magazine to friends as a "stink" when the story hit newsstands (*Letters vol. 5,* 98). His judgment seems a little ungracious considering that *Cosmopolitan* paid him $2,700 for the piece, a hefty amount (nearly $50,000 in 2021) amid the economic collapse of the period. In Perkins's eyes, "After the Storm" was the collection's highest-profile piece and for good reason. It possessed elements attractive to general readers that both he and Hemingway knew the accompanying stories did not.

As the author confessed to his editor on 8 April 1933,

> At present I know that the book needs one more simple story of action to balance some of the difficult stories it contains. . . . Stories like Fifty Grand, My Old Man and that sort are no where near as good stories, in the end, as a story like Hills Like White Elephants, or Sea Change. But a book needs them because people understand them easily and it gives them the necessary confidence in the stories that are hard for them. (*Only Thing* 188)

"Simple" or not, "After the Storm" is undoubtedly the template of the "story of action" to which Hemingway here refers; the only other *Winner Take Nothing* entry that comes anywhere close to that description—the Nick Adams war story "A Way You'll Never Be"—was intended as one but turned during the composition process into a more literary exercise. Perkins certainly assumed that Hemingway was talking about "After the Storm" as the example of the more dramatic, plot-oriented story he needed more of to offset the "difficult" efforts that submerged the central conflict, á la the writer's famous iceberg image, forcing readers to infer the causes of inherent strife. Three months later, when the writer submitted the table of contents, his closest confidant at Scribner's recommended that "After the Storm" lead the collection rather than the author's own choice, "The Light of the World." That story, which features several blowzy prostitutes, would "[u]tterly enrage those who do get enraged in the most hateful way about those things" (for example, disreputable issues like prostitution). Instead, the "conspicuous position" of an opening story inevitably meant that reviewers would "give it tremendous emphasis," and the collection frankly needed a piece that could gratify such attention. Perkins agreed that "After the Storm and Other Stories" was a bland title and waited patiently until Hemingway came up with the phrase *Winner Take Nothing.* Yet he was adamant that his star writer rethink the running order of the collection. Perkins admitted to Hemingway that "A Clean, Well-Lighted Place" was "one of the best of the stories," but it, too, would be "of that kind . . . which not many people would respond to." That left only one obvious choice as a kickoff if Hemingway wanted to sell books: "I think 'After the Storm' is really the most popular sort of story" (*Only Thing* 195).

Hemingway, somewhat reluctantly, conceded the point. Accordingly, this accessible, dynamic, and deceptively anecdotal Key West tale stepped to the forefront.

Perkins was proved to be wrong: reviewers did *not* give "After the Storm" "tremendous attention." As Robert W. Trogdon has shown, *Winner Take Nothing* received shockingly "scant notice" for an author whose previous work of fiction, *A Farewell to Arms* (1929), had been a blockbuster only four years earlier: "Only nine reviews appeared in major American newspapers and magazines," Trogdon writes, "only three of which were published within a week of [the collection's] publication. . . . Hemingway's scrapbooks contain only about thirty clippings or notices [from smaller regional papers and modest-circulation periodicals] for the book" (140). This curious indifference suggests just how deep the disregard for Hemingway was in 1933. The reviewers who did critique the collection tended to harp on its faults and fixate on the weaker entries, such as "The Mother of a Queen" or "One Reader Writes."

Only on rare occasions was "After the Storm" even mentioned—although when it was, reviewers hailed it as the collection's bright spot. John Chamberlain in the *New York Times* wrote, "'After the Storm,' which is more imaginative than anything Hemingway has hitherto written, is another story that should be three-starred by Edward J. O'Brien,[1] when he reads the short-story honor roll for the year. The remaining bits, however, are, by and large, trivial exercises in Grand Guignol" ("Books" 17). Louis Kronenberger in the *New York Times Book Review* lamented that the story's excellence only made the rest of the collection more disappointing: "One reads a story like the first and finest in the present book . . . and one deeply regrets that in the main such incomparable equipment as Hemingway's goes off so many times with a proud and clean report—and hits nothing" (143–44). *Time's* anonymous reviewer, meanwhile, declared, "For sinister atmospheres Hemingway has never been better than in 'After the Storm'" ("Stiff Upper Lip" 144). Otherwise, the chorus singing the story's praises was select.

The neglect would continue for decades. Rare was the occasion when a commentator such as Stanley Edgar Hyman, reviewing the 1953 compilation *The Hemingway Reader*, declared, "After the tough economy of 'After the Storm' it is embarrassing to read the same thing done less well in *The Old Man and the Sea*" (425). As Audre Hanneman documents in her invaluable 1967 bibliography, the story was translated into French, Danish, and Swedish and reprinted widely in story anthologies aimed at both general readers and college students (177, 213, 216, 231). In the mid-1950s alone, it was included in titles as diverse as *The Fourth Round: Stories for Men* (Grayson 1–5) and *The Types of Literature* (Connolly 148–50). Yet few academics found the piece worthy of explication. Across four editions of his influential *Hemingway: The Writer as Artist* (1952–1972), Carlos Baker never saw fit to mention "After the Storm" in more than a bibliographical note on its publication in *Cosmopolitan* (414). Baker did discuss the story's inspiration in his 1969 biography, noting that Hemingway's Key West fishing guide, Captain Eddie "Bra" Saunders, told him the tale of a Spanish ocean liner called the *Valbanera* that sunk near the Dry Tortugas in September 1919 (*Life* 194). Yet both Baker's passing comments and James McLendon's subsequent claim that "After the Storm" was "taken from the true story" of Saunders's failed attempt to plunder the ship's cargo diminished the story's reputation *as fiction* (McLendon 83). Critics took Hemingway's claim to Perkins that "Storm" was "word for word as it happened, to Bra" (*Letter vol. 5*, 542) at face value and assumed it lacked any catalytic element of authorial invention. As a result, during its first fifty-five years in print, the story inspired fewer than a dozen critical analyses.

Only in the late 1980s did the situation even hint at changing. The turning point was Susan F. Beegel's treatment of "After the Storm" in her *Hemingway's Craft of Omission: Four Manuscript Examples* (1988). Beegel demonstrates two salient facts that dispelled the notion that the tale was "Bra Saunders's story" (Baker, *Life* 141). First, drawing from long-forgotten newspaper sources, she documents the circumstances behind the *Valbanera* disaster, cataloguing numerous details in the historical record that do not align with the fiction, thereby proving Hemingway had created a range of elements to suit his thematic purpose. More important, she analyzes two very different drafts of the story that preceded the final published version, showing how extensively the author had experimented with narrative structure and point of view before he was satisfied. (These differences are discussed below in the glosses rather than summarized here.) In the end, the breadth of changes Bra Saunders's anecdote went through during the composition process revealed that biographers and critics had fallen for the very trick Hemingway boasted of pulling on readers who underestimated his creativity: "The point is *I want* them [his stories] all to sound as though they really happened. Then when I succeed those poor dumb pricks say they are all just skillful reporting" (*Letters vol. 5*, 542). As Beegel concludes, "Hemingway's assertion to Perkins that he told 'After the Storm' 'word for word as it happened to Bra' [was] itself a carefully crafted fiction, designed to augment his short story's compelling illusion of verity" (88).

Two years after Beegel's analysis, Ben Stoltzfus demonstrated that "After the Storm" is intriguing in ways beyond its historical backdrop and composition history. Stoltzfus's "Hemingway's 'After the Storm': A Lacanian Reading" proves that the text is amenable to applications of the sophisticated, sometimes impenetrable poststructuralist theory that dominated literary studies throughout the preceding decade. Drawing from the work of psychoanalyst Jacques Lacan, Stoltzfus argues that "[i]n this story almost every detail reveals a latent meaning" reflecting the narrator's suppression of desire: "The storm is a metaphor of shipwreck, actual as well as psychological. Not only is the title a metaphor for tragedy and trauma, the story itself is a metaphor of repression, death, and desire: a death of the self, a death wish against the father (the Law), and desire for the mother" (53). In this reading,

Hemingway's narrator is not a man struggling against hostile nature but a psyche struggling to survive its own fracturing, making the story more about interiority than exteriority. So complex and frankly ingenious is Stoltzfus's analysis that Paul Smith, reviewing criticism extant in 1990, claims that the essay "serves to raise 'After the Storm' close to the rank of a major story, or at least to suggest why stories like it both trouble and transfix our gaze" (Benson 390).

Close is no cigar, however. Thirty years on, "After the Storm" remains overshadowed by more famous and canonical Hemingway stories. Nevertheless, the criticism it has inspired since Beegel's and Stoltzfus's essays demonstrate its textural richness and its intertextual affinities with other significant works of American literature. In a 1994 *Hemingway Review* article, Nathaniel Philbrick—a future winner of the National Book Award—pointed out intriguing correspondences between the story and Herman Melville's "The Grand Armada" chapter in *Moby-Dick* (1851). Critics had long suggested Hemingway channeled at least a bit of Joseph Conrad's seafaring sensibility when writing his wrecker story, but Philbrick argues persuasively that "After the Storm" poses a powerful contrast to the assimilation into nature's order that Ishmael feels when he peers beneath the ocean's surface (25–35). Michael Crowley's 2009 essay "Reexamining the Origins of 'After the Storm,'" meanwhile, builds upon Beegel's analysis by parsing several conflicting accounts of the Key West fishing expedition where Hemingway first heard the story from Saunders; Crowley's piece does us the immense favor of clearing up the chronology, demonstrating that the trip took place in 1929, not 1928 as most sources claim. "After the Storm" also inspired a movie adaptation in 2001 starring Benjamin Bratt of television's *Law and Order* fame. The production, though flawed in its melodramatic effort to fill in its running time with an adultery subplot, was notable for employing a teleplay first drafted in the 1950s by Hemingway's controversial crony A. E. Hotchner, later author of the bestselling-but-unreliable *Papa Hemingway: A Personal Memoir* (1966).

Until "After the Storm" receives its due, it will likely remain overshadowed by *Winner Take Nothing's* most-analyzed entry ("A Clean, Well-Lighted Place") and its two Nick Adams stories that play important roles in the character development of Hemingway's alter-ego ("A Way You'll Never Be" and "Fathers and Sons"). Yet even if the text's critical reception does not recognize the story's importance, its author certainly did. "After the Storm" offered Hemingway a new direction that, unfortunately for the reputation of *Winner Take Nothing,* he failed to pursue until after unenthusiastic reviews of the collection cemented the public perception that his talent had waned. The story marks Hemingway's earliest use of the culture and atmosphere of the Florida straits he discovered upon moving to the southernmost point of the United States in April 1928. Since the founding of Key West a century earlier, the fiction and art of this region had shown a marked preference for action and adventure over the concerns "literary" culture was apt to explore, themes like alienation and moral uncertainty that Hemingway plumbs in more modernist-affiliated efforts such as "A Clean, Well-Lighted Place." Accordingly, "After the Storm" crackles with a salty aura of piracy and roguery. In spirit, it is more akin to James Fenimore Cooper's *Jack Tier, or the Florida Reef* (1848) or Mary Stanbery Watts's *Van Cleve* (1913) than to the stoicism of the author's war fiction or to the emotional blankness of his stories about family and romantic relationships. Thanks to both its setting and sense of propulsion, "After the Storm" marks a preliminary trying-out of several popular-fiction elements Hemingway would synthesize in the most hardboiled story he ever wrote, "One Trip Across" (1934). That piece appeared in *Cosmopolitan* exactly two years after its predecessor (20–23, 108–22), earning its author a whopping $5,500 ($88,000 in 2019) and rapturous praise from both Perkins and F. Scott Fitzgerald (Curnutt xxiv–xxv). The shoot-'em-up in turn became the opening section of *To Have and Have Not* (1937), a novel widely considered a failure, but one that nevertheless in the Hemingway oeuvre stands as a bold, unique experiment in form and style. As such, "After the Storm" plays a pivotal, catalytic role in the direction that Hemingway's writing took in the mid-1930s.

Title: As Robert Paul Lamb writes, "Hemingway's best titles are sometimes allusions that enrich the story" (137). Examples include several stories in *Winner Take Nothing*: "The Light of the World" (John 8:12), "The Sea Change" (Shakespeare's *The Tempest*), "God Rest You Merry, Gentlemen" (the traditional Christmas carol), "A Natural History of the Dead" (the work of several nineteenth-century naturalists, most notably W. H. Hudson), and "Fathers and Sons" (Ivan Turgenev).

"After the Storm" is an exception to this rule. The title is also relatively rare in that, unlike other Hemingway stories, it neither aligns with what Lamb describes as "denotative" titles that refer to "a character or characters" ("The Battler," "The Killers"), to a "symbolic object" ("Cat in the Rain"), or to "a resonant location" ("Big Two-Hearted River") (136–38). Instead, the title marks a temporal moment, which is rare in Hemingway. Arguably, the only other comparable titles that refer to time besides "Now I Lay Me" are *Men Without Women*'s "Today Is Friday," *Winner Take Nothing*'s "A Day's Wait," and a later Spanish Civil War story, "Night Before Battle." The reason Hemingway did not employ more temporal adjectives in his titles probably has to do with his inclinations as a modernist. Because early twentieth-century writers generally saw themselves as reaching back beyond what T. S. Eliot called "the immense panorama of futility and anarchy which is contemporary history" (177) to rediscover what they felt (or hoped) were universal human truths buried in classical myth, legend, and literature, they tended to avoid references that locked their narratives or images into a chronology. Instead, they aimed to arrest time, turning a poem or a prose work into an object akin to a sculpture—an *objet d'art,* in essence, or, in critic William K. Wimsatt's famous image, a "verbal icon" (x). Their basic goal was for writing to immerse the reader in a continuous present, a time-lessness that adverbs such as *after, before,* and *since* would interrupt.

That said, an underappreciated tradition has existed throughout modern and contemporary literature of titles beginning with *after*. The evocative power of such works indeed lies in the idea that the texts dramatize the consequences of a decisive shift in mindset, manners, or mores: a "post-" period. One thinks of Jean Rhys's 1931 novel *After Leaving Mr. Mackenzie,* but the quintessential example might be Arthur Miller's *After the Fall* (1964), where the event has symbolic value, imply-ing a postlapsarian state. The titles need not apply to fictional efforts. In 1951 liter-ary critic John Aldridge brashly called his study of contemporaries such as Nor-man Mailer *After the Lost Generation,* implying a decisive break in sensibility from the Hemingway/Fitzgerald/Faulkner template, while North Carolina critic Tony Buttitta's titled a memoir of meeting F. Scott Fitzgerald at that writer's nadir *After the Good Gay Times* (1974). One thinks of comparable titles in other art forms: Neil Young's classic LP *After the Gold Rush* (1970) or the 1980's cult band Lone Justice's "After the Flood" (1985) both root their poignancy in the power of that inaugurat-ing adverb to convey either an irreparable passage or a sense of loss.

To date, the only critic to explore this tradition even indirectly is James Plath. His 1994 essay "'After the Denim' and 'After the Storm': Raymond Carver Comes to Terms with the Hemingway Influence" explores how the author of *What We Talk About When We Talk About Love* (1981)—in which "After the Denim" appears (67–78)—sublimated the obvious influence of Hemingway within his trademark themes and abbreviated style.

283:2 **and then we started fighting:** "After the Storm" begins *in medias res* with a fistfight that "wasn't about anything, something about making punch" (283:1–2)—presumably alcohol punch. The violence recalls the opening of "The Battler," when a "lousy crut of a brakeman" knocks Nick Adams off a caboose for hopping a freight train chugging into the Michigan woods (*CSS* 97). The fight also foreshadows the bloody shootout that opens "One Trip Across." After a short conversation between Harry Morgan and a trio of Cuban revolutionaries in a Havana bar, a carload of thugs on the payroll of dictator Gerardo Machado rolls up and opens fire: "The first thing," Harry reports, "a pane of glass went and the bullet smashed into the row of bottles on the [bar's] show-case wall to the right. I heard the gun going, and, *bop, bop, bop,* there were bottles smashing all along the wall" (*CSS* 383, *THHN* 6).[2] The opening of "After the Storm" directly foreshadows this gruesome massa-cre, which leaves all three revolutionaries dead in the streets. *Cosmopolitan* seems to have recognized the implicit connection, for the opening illustrations to both stories vividly emphasize the violence. The voice in both stories, moreover, demon-strates Hemingway's awareness of pulp gangster and detective fiction whose popularity had steadily grown since the mid-1920s, culminating in the novels of Dashiell Hammett—including *The Dain Curse* (1929), which Hemingway references in *Death in the Afternoon* (181)—and in two Al Capone *romans à clef, Little Caesar* (by W. R. Burnett, 1929) and *Scarface* (by Armitage Trail, 1930).

283:2 **I:** Readers never learn the name of the narrator of "After the Storm," nor much of anything about his biography, making him a universal figure. In both idiom and cadence, his voice is virtually indistinguishable from the down-on-his-luck charterboat captain Harry Morgan, the protagonist of "One Trip Across" and, later, *To Have and Have Not*.[3] As Philip Young writes, so similar are the narrative voices that the narrator of "Storm" can be considered "an exact working-sketch for Harry" (91).

The distinctive voice of "After the Storm," however, came to Hemingway only after the story's first draft. In its original form, the story was narrated by an interlocutor on a deep-sea fishing charter with two friends, "Dos" (John Dos Passos) and "Waldo" (Waldo Peirce), whose captain, Bra—clearly Bra Saunders—regales them with the story of discovering the sunken ship. As Beegel writes, the narrator of this initial draft is "presumably Hemingway speaking in his own persona" (75). In this regard, "After the Storm" resembles the earliest attempt at *The Sun Also Rises,* which featured the names of real-life people later transformed into fictional personages. Throughout the preliminary attempt at "After the Storm," Bra's three clients interrupt the tale, peppering him with questions. The presence of the three members of "the Mob" (as Hemingway called his Key West entourage when they visited) is sometimes called a storytelling frame by critics, although, technically, that term does not apply to the story as it was first staged: a storytelling frame usually surrounds an interpolated tale, appearing at the beginning and the end but not weaving in and out of the main story. A more accurate term, one Beegel employs, is "a tale-within-a-tale" (79). The Hemingway-I of the original version differs markedly from the eventual "I" of the published version: his "standard English contrasts sharply with Bra's Conch dialect," and, more important, the naiveté of his point of view offers an ironic contrast to the captain's more experienced knowledge of the ocean's dangers: "To the Hemingway-narrator who does not have to earn a living on the water, but who fishes solely for pleasure, the sea shows only her tranquil aspect" (Beegel 79).

The story's second draft does away with the three sports fishermen and transfers the "I" to the Bra character without mentioning that name (which appears in the first version). As a result, "After the Storm" evolved from a tale-within-a-tale into a dramatic monologue. For decades, these two initial drafts of the story were only available in the Hemingway collection at the JFK Library in Boston. In 2017, the writer's grandson Seán Hemingway included them in the Hemingway Library Edition of *The Short Stories of Ernest Hemingway* (302–14), allowing general audiences to examine the difference between all three versions.

283:2–3 I slipped and he had me down kneeling on my chest and choking me with both hands: In addition to the opening shoot-out of "One Trip Across," this fight scene resembles another violent moment in Harry Morgan's rumrunner story, one that has proved even more shocking to readers past and present. In a scene in this second *Cosmopolitan* tale (it appears as Chapter 4 of *To Have and Have Not*), Harry agrees to smuggle Chinese illegals into Key West for a nefarious trafficker named Mr. Sing. When the pair rendezvous in their boats, Harry grabs the criminal and, during a short scuffle, snaps his neck.

The main difference is that "After the Storm" depicts its hero at a momentary disadvantage: the narrator is the one being choked. Nevertheless, the precision with which the choreography of both fights is narrated demonstrates how adept Hemingway was at describing bursts of physical action. The cracking of Mr. Sing's neck is one of the most shocking moments in Hemingway's fiction. Instead of the traditional Hemingway hero who stoically preserves his moral code, Hemingway experimented in the 1930s with *anti*-heroes, men who survive by doing what the moment demands. "After the Storm" is his first attempt at just such a more morally suspect character, one who will quickly whip out his knife and slash his attacker's arm muscle so he can wrestle free (283:6–8).

283:13 Well, I went out of there: The vague adverb should remind readers that Hemingway has declined to tell us where exactly this fight between the two men occurs. An earlier line—"Everybody was too drunk to pull him off me" (283:5–6)—indicates the setting is a bar. *Cosmopolitan* illustrator Dan Content interpreted it that way, picturing the two brawlers stretched out in front of a foot railing and spittoon.

Although the story never mentions the name "Key West," readers knowledge-able about Hemingway's hangouts in the island city likely assume the floor where the narrator's head is being hammered belongs to Sloppy Joe's Bar. Yet at the time the story was published, Sloppy Joe's did not yet exist (at least not in Key West; a famous haunt in Havana had opened under that name in the early 1920s). Instead, Hemingway's preferred drinking establishment was a speakeasy on Front Street operated by Joe Russell, who, in April–May 1932 as "After the Storm" hit newsstands, introduced Hemingway to Gulf Stream fishing on his charter boat *Anita*. Not until the end of Prohibition in December 1933 would Russell take over a nearby location on Greene Street called The Blind Pig and sometime thereafter redub it Sloppy Joe's. Legend insists Hemingway advocated for the name change due to his fondness for the Havana watering hole—though, like many Key West legends, proof is fleeting. Sloppy Joe's would not move to the current landmark location to which tourists flock on Duval Street until May 1937, about five months before the publication of *To Have and Have Not*. In picturing the opening battle royal then, Hemingway was likely imagining Russell's original "hole in the wall" on Front Street (Reynolds, *Homecoming* 173).

The Gulf of Mexico setting has led some critics to pose a basic question, one voiced recently by Eric Gary Anderson and Melanie Benson Taylor: Does "After the Storm" qualify as Southern literature? As Anderson and Taylor point out,

> The Companion to Southern Literature (2002) includes twenty-eight references to Hemingway (in a book that runs to one thousand pages), while The Oxford Handbook of the Literature of the U.S. South (2016) has a grand total of one mention of Hemingway. If anything, scholarly willingness to entertain Hemingway's circum-Caribbean Souths appears to be diminishing rather than expanding, even as the New Southern Studies and other movements in southern studies provocatively open the floodgates to new approaches, new maps. (332)

There is resistance against reading Hemingway as "Southern," even as the definition of that term has expanded beyond referring to the American South. The resistance is one reason that "After the Storm" and To Have and Have Not have received relatively little critical attention.

283:15 **he said somebody killed a man up the street:** The story of the fight spreads rapidly through Key West; here the narrator learns from an encounter with a stranger only moments later that the man he slashed has died, leading him to steal a skiff and head to his boat, which is moored offshore. The story of the murder appears in the first draft as well, implying that Bra Saunders claimed to Hemingway and friends that he had killed a man in a brawl (SS-HLE 303). As Beegel writes, however, no evidence exists to suggest that the real-life charterboat captain "was ever a fugitive from justice, involved in a barroom stabbing, or suspected of murder" (84). In fact, no evidence, she adds, suggests that any murder took place during the historical period the story borrows key events from (111).

283:17–19 **there was water standing in the street and no lights and windows broke and boats all up in the town and trees blown down and everything all blown:** Hemingway had not yet experienced a hurricane in Key West when he described here the damage and destruction to which the island city is annually exposed from Atlantic Ocean weather patterns. Although "After the Storm" is not specifically set in September 1919, the tropical cyclone that sank the Valbanera and led to Bra Saunders's story battered the Florida Keys with what today would be measured as Category 4 winds. The storm actually passed thirty to forty miles south of Key West, not making landfall on the Dry Tortugas until 10 September with winds of 150 miles per hour. The hurricane then traveled west through the Gulf of Mexico into Baffin Bay, Texas, on 14 September, dissipating two days later. Of the hurricane's 772 fatalities, 488 were lost on the Valbanera alone. It was one of ten ships sunk by the hurricane in the Florida straits. Although sources sometimes describe the storm's fatalities as

"Key West deaths," it is important to note that no one died on the island itself—all lost in the proximity of the Keys, rather, were lost at sea. That said, the city's docks and railroads incurred damages of some $2 million. Estimates throughout the entire Keys cite the cost of repairing storm damages at $28 million.

Hemingway's firsthand experience with a major Gulf hurricane would not occur for nearly three-and-a-half years after "After the Storm" was published. On 2 September 1935 an even more massive storm system than the 1919 disaster swept north of Key West, devastating the lower Matecumbe Keys around the city of Islamorada. Among the fatalities were 400+ Great War veterans working under the auspices of the Federal Emergency Relief Administration (FERA) to construct the final span of the Overseas Highway that had opened seven years earlier. The veterans' deaths led Hemingway to pen a fierce condemnation of the Roosevelt administration called "Who Murdered the Vets?" (1935), which accuses the federal government of manslaughter for failing to rescue the men.

283:20 **Mango Key:** No period map of the waters surrounding Key West identifies a land formation with this name. Nor do any period histories, Works Project Administration (WPA) guides, or boating periodicals refer to such a site. A 2 March 1905 *Miami News* article does mention a crew from Henry Flagler's projected Overseas Railroad surveying "from White streets across the harbor to Mango Key" ("Bloody Scrap" 1), suggesting a land mass off the northern harbor of the island not unlike nearby Tank Island—today known as Sunset Key—or Wisteria Island. The lack of any other reference to "Mango Key" in period reportage suggests this mention may be erroneous. Around the time Hemingway first moved to Key West, the most prominent mention of the name was in a serialized novel called *Devil-May-Care* by Arthur Somers Roche: the "Mango Key" reference appears in the 1 April 1928 edition of the *St. Petersburg Times* (among many other papers) (35).

In the near-century since then, "Mango Key" has become a fictional commonplace in Key West thrillers and mysteries, further suggesting it is an invention. It is tempting to suggest that Hemingway simply improvised this name to describe one of the many small keys that lie both north and south of the city. At the time most of these land formations would have been uninhabited and overgrown with mangroves, making them ideal hiding spots for a boat like the narrator's. Certainly, bootleggers availed themselves of such tiny islands; Hemingway dramatizes one in his 1936 sequel to "One Trip Across," "The Tradesman's Return," which later become part 2 of *To Have and Have Not*. That specific island was known as Sand Key, though, and sits southwest of Key West.

283:23 **Eastern Harbor:** The popular name in the 1930s for the inlet in the Marquesas Keys where Hemingway and his friends often moored to fish on their way to the Dry Tortugas. As early as 1928, only weeks after arriving in Key West, Hemingway wrote his father about this small circular chain of mangrove-thicketed islands some thirty-five miles west of the island: "You will have to come down next time and go on a trip to Marquesas," he told Clarence. Hemingway insisted that the Marquesas had "the best tarpon fishing and shooting—plover, cranes, curlew etc." (*Letters vol. 3*, 390). Despite Ernest's enthusiasm, the elder Hemingway, who had just passed through Key West and enjoyed a chance encounter with his son, never made it to the Marquesas: six months after his son's letter, he committed suicide.

The Marquesas lie roughly halfway between Key West and the Dry Tortugas. Hemingway returned there in both 1929 and 1930 with various members of "the Mob."

283:24 **Brother, that was some storm:** This odd address to the reader is the first instance of what became a narrative tic of Hemingway's throughout the 1930s. Subsequent to "After the Storm," it would appear in such *Esquire* essays as "Notes on the Next War: A Serious Topical Letter," where the address is nearly always combative ("But you will die, brother, if you go to [war] long enough" [*BL* 210]). Hemingway would employ it upward of eight times in *To Have and Have Not* in lines such as "The old marlin headed out to the nor'west like all the big ones go, and brother, did he hook up" (17). Both here and in 1920s and 1930s hard-boiled fiction where it is equally prevalent, the "brother" address conveys a tone of condescension and aggression. The term became even more popular thanks to the Depression anthem "Brother, Can You Spare a Dime?" (1930), written by Edgar "Yip" Harburg (1896–1981) and Jay Gorney (1894–1990).

283:25 **white as a lye barrel:** In rural areas, lye barrels were used to make homemade soap by combining ash and water. Typically, the barrel sat on bricks and had small holes bored into the bottom. As rainwater flowed over the remains of burned logs, it leeched lye from the ashes, which then filtered through pea gravel into a tub placed under the barrel. The chemical properties of the lye, strong enough to burn skin, usually stained the inside of the barrel white. Once collected in pans, the lye water was boiled with beef tallow and salt and then poured into flat pans to be cut into soap squares.

238:26 **Sou'west Key:** Not to be confused with Southwest Key, a land formation that sat near Loggerhead Key farther west past the Dry Tortugas until it disappeared underwater circa 1875 (and thus referred to afterward as a shoal). Rather, Sou'west Key was the colloquial name for one of the lower Marquesas. Hemingway refers to it in his correspondence with various Mob members, reporting to Waldo Peirce on 15 April 1932, for example, that, during a fishing expedition to the Tortugas with Archibald MacLeish and Mike Slater, the group's plan to fish for nurse sharks was interrupted by an intense storm that forced them to take refuge for three days in an inner channel. This is the same letter, not coincidentally, in which Hemingway, informing Peirce about the publication of "After the Storm," dismissed *Cosmopolitan* as a "stink" (*Letters vol. 5*, 98).

284:5 I seen a spar floating and I knew there must be a wreck: "Spar" is the general term for any mast, boom, or pole that holds up a sail on a boat. This wreck is not the liner the narrator will shortly come across; Hemingway builds anticipation by first having his hero discover a different ship—a "three-masted schooner" (see below)—that has sunk in waters too deep for him to search for cargo. The deep water is important as a contrast to the shallower waters where the liner is trapped; if the narrator cannot get near this ship, the other boat's near accessibility will ironically emphasize his powerlessness in nature.

At this point in the story, readers likely wonder what exactly the narrator's profession is. His insistence that "I didn't get anything off of" this "three-masted schooner" sunken just past the Marquesas with only "the stumps of her spars out of water" (284:6–8) makes him sound as if he is a professional salvager as much as a fisherman or charterboat captain. It is entirely likely that a man of the sea as the storyteller is would come from a long line of wreckers. If we imagine him having a background comparable to Bra Saunders, he would descend from white Bahamians who began working the Florida reefs as early as the mid-1700s. Shortly after Key West's official founding by John Whitehead and John Simonton in 1821, the Bahamians, distinguished by their Cockney-esque accents, began populating the city so they could lay legal claim to the goods they retrieved in the Gulf. (Americans living on the island instituted a law that only Key West residents had the right to salvage wrecks in the Gulf of Mexico.) Very quickly these immigrants became known as "Conchs," a nickname expanded in the twentieth century to include any native Key Wester (Reilly 26). Salvaging soon became the principal industry in Key West, worked both by Conchs and non-Bahamians. Initially, the enterprise was an opportunistic one, which contributed to the city's reputation for profiteering and roguery. Salvagers negotiated directly with ship owners over their percentage from sales of cargo they recovered, often leading to charges of graft and extortion: it was not uncommon for wreckers to claim 80 to 90 percent of auctioned goods.

In 1828, after numerous disputes, a federal court was established to license salvagers and impose arbitration standards on negotiations. The oversight not only legitimated the industry but helped expand it, and its influence on the island soon touched every sector of the economy. Despite the air of respectability wrecking garnered thanks to the federal court, the profession remained risky—though not mortally dangerous, as one might expect. According to Benjamin Reilly, "there is not a single known case of a wrecker killed while working a shipwreck, though history does record numerous injuries" (30).

By the 1850s, shipwrecks became less common with the advent of a lighthouse system throughout the Gulf of Mexico; improved mapping also lowered the frequency of foundered ships, as did the growing prevalence of steam-powered (as opposed to sail-powered) vessels.

The relative infrequency of wrecks by the early twentieth century had long driven most ships out of wrecking. In 1921, two years after the *Valbanera* sank, the District Court of the Southern District of Florida ceased even issuing wrecking licenses (Viele xiv). Nothing in "After the Storm" suggests the narrator possesses any such official license—Bra Saunders, by all accounts, did not—so it would be unlikely that he is a professional salvager. More likely, he is a fisherman who simply comes across the sunken boat and plans on plundering her for a black-market profit. His later comment about using a sponge-glass "like we use sponging" (284:29) suggests he is employed at least part time in the sponging industry (itself then in its twilight.)

284:6 **three-masted schooner:** A schooner is any sailing vessel with more than one mast, with the front one the shortest.

284:12 **way out toward the quicksands:** "The Quicksands" is the name of a sandy-bottomed area about twenty miles long that extends directly west of the Marquesas; Hemingway refers to the area's other nickname when two lines earlier the narrator describes leaving the three-masted schooner that's too deep for him to plunder and heading further west across the "sand-bars" (284:10). The water depth in this treacherous area ranges from five to eighteen feet, which is shallow enough to trap ships. A visitor today flying by seaplane to the Dry Tortugas can still see the remains of shipwrecks caught in the area.

According to Gerry Brenner, the sandbars that sink the liner also have literary parallels: in a footnote in his psychoanalytic analysis, *Concealments in Hemingway's Works* (1983), Brenner argues that the quicksand "erotically horrifies Hemingway's unconscious as the vortex in 'The Descent into the Maelstrom' does Poe's and the shivering sands in *The Moonstone* does Wilkie Collins's" (255n3).

284:13 **the Rebecca light:** This lighthouse is another landmark on the route between Key West and the Dry Tortugas. It sits roughly twenty-five miles west of the Marquesas and twelve miles east of Garden Key, the central Tortugas island. The light sits on Rebecca Shoals; construction on it was proposed as early as 1847, but design setbacks and financial difficulties prevented installation for eight years. Then twice in 1855, storms destroyed preliminary efforts to construct the beacon. After an 1858 effort to mark the shoals was likewise destroyed in a storm, the spot was marked by buoys instead of a light for the following twenty years. A beacon was finally installed in 1879, but not for another seven years would an actual lighthouse be constructed and manned by a crew. The crew's living quarters would have existed at the time "After the Storm" is set; the Coast Guard did not remove the house until 1953. The Rebecca Shoals remains the most dangerous of the reefs in the Key West–Dry

Tortugas chain. Hemingway mentions the Rebecca Light for historical accuracy: the *Valbanera* sank within sight of the shoals in 1919.

284:16 I could see something looked like a spar up out of the water: Here finally the narrator comes across the liner that would be the sunken *Valbanera*. Robert Paul Lamb cites the passage that follows this line to make a fascinating connection to a scene in Mark Twain's *Adventures of Huckleberry Finn* (1884) in which Twain's eponymous hero comes across a wreck he, too, intends to loot. Lamb thus claims Huck inspired the voice of "After the Storm":

> This sort of narration, in which an uneducated character speaks in his own idiom, is atypical for Hemingway, whose first-person narrators are usually either Nick Adams or other Hemingway persona. But here he uses methods similar to Twain's in *Huck Finn*. Note the unliterary vernacular discourse with its inelegant repetitions . . . the five uses of "water" in the second sentence; "as big as the whole world" and "the biggest boat I ever saw". . . . Also observe the attention Hemingway's narrator pays to function, to specific actions in a progressive sequence." (101–2)

All these elements, Lamb argues, are indicative of vernacular storytelling. Despite the colloquial similarities, however, he also notes "one glaring difference between these narrations": if Huck reports his feelings on discovering the wreck, "Hemingway's first-person narrator . . . tells us virtually *nothing* about his feelings. Even when he attempts to, it comes out vague and unrevealing" (102). Lamb does not connect the voice to Hammett and the tough-guy idiom of the 1920s and 1930s, which employs urban rather than rural or non-industrial vernacular. His interest is in the externality of Hemingway's style: "The key to Hemingway's style is his strict adherence to impressionism . . . and, concomitant to this, his making all forms of focalization as close to external focalization as possible" (102–3). This externality is especially important, he argues, when the narrator discovers the body of the dead woman and expresses no emotion, only concerned with whether he can salvage the jewelry still on her body (285:7).

284:20–22 there under water was a liner; just lying there all under water as big as the whole world: By using the word "liner," Hemingway makes the story's clearest connection to the *Valabanera*. As Beegel was the first to document, "with a few significant exceptions, Hemingway drew the events of 'After the Storm' from the facts of the actual sinking" (70) that occurred on 8–9 September 1919. The word "liner" clearly implies that the sunken vessel carried passengers; the narrator's imminent discovery of "a woman inside with her hair floating all out" (285:7) confirms that the ship is not merely shipping cargo or a military transport, intensifying the tragedy.

284:29 **a water glass like we use sponging:** A "water glass" is sometimes referred to in period literature as a "water telescope." It is simply a bucket or a box with a glass bottom that, when dipped into the ocean (though not fully submerged), allowed wreckers and spongers a clear view of what lay beneath the surface. A 1910 study of the sponging industry in Key West describes its use: "In the boat fishery from one to five men constitute the crew, the usual number being about three. A man working by himself must confine his operations to poling in shoal and smooth water, but two or more men, if occasion demands, may work together in rougher and deeper water by using the water glass" (Moore 457). The water glass was first used circa 1870 during the rise of the sponging era; some wealthier fishermen in Bra Saunders's later era owned glass-bottom boats, not unlike some of today's tourist charters.

284: 32 **things floating out all the time:** The image of the wreck's flotsam leaking out from the sunken ship has at least two important corollaries in Hemingway fiction. On the one hand, it echoes the moment in *Winner Take Nothing*'s "A Natural History of the Dead" in which a narrator comments similarly on the detritus surrounding the dead after a battle (337:33–41).

The idea that with an unnatural death comes the litter or pollution of human effluvia is reiterated with a more organic symbol in *To Have and Have Not*. Shortly after a shootout with Cuban revolutionaries, Harry Morgan lies dying in a borrowed boat. Thanks to bullet holes ripped into the boat's hull from the gun battle, the blood of the men Harry has shot dead leaks into the ocean, along with his own. Two schools of opportunistic fish circle the vessel's bottom, feeding off the "ropy, carmine clots and threads" (180).

The "things floating out" from the wreck in "After the Storm" effectively combines these images, serving as a transition from the earlier one to the later. All three are symbols of human integration in the environment, defining the borders between the body's borders and the world engulfing it: with the use of abstraction ("things") Hemingway creates a sense of mystery about what exactly this material is and whether it is inorganic, whether victims' possessions or parts of the ship, or whether it is composed of body parts.

284:39 **I could stand on the letters of her name on her bow:** As Beegel notes, one of the more intriguing departures Hemingway made from the historical record was to sink the unnamed ship in the story in shallow waters. The *Valbanera* was found one week after its disappearance "eight to nine fathoms (48 to 54 feet)" under the surface (72)—a depth closer to the three-masted schooner the narrator first comes across. Instead, this second fictional vessel is submerged only enough that he can still stand on the bow with his head above water, meaning the lives were lost in fifteen to twenty feet of water.

For Ben Stoltzfus, standing on the letters is a central image that dramatizes the narrator's unwillingness to grapple with the latent meaning of his story; the detail signals to the reader why a Lacanian analysis of the fisherman's narration is absolutely necessary. In Stoltzfus's view, the ship's name symbolizes "'the letter of the unconscious' . . . the name that embodies Lacan's system," which "gives us the tools with which to get at the latent meaning (and into the ship) that is embedded in quicksand" (55). That latent meaning, simply, is that the "storm that sank the ship, the fight, and the choking are metaphors for the primal scene" (52)—they reveal that the real conflict is the narrator's "anger and hostility directed at the Law," or, more specifically, what Lacan calls "the Symbolic," those seemingly intractable elements external to the self that limit its conceptions of its own power (as opposed to the "Imaginary," which is the font of self-actualization). In "After the Storm" then, the narrator's inability to pry his way into the ship "confirms the overriding Law of the Phallus. Failure is synonymous with castration and the perceived death of the self" (53). The narrator fails to acknowledge his powerlessness, though, in part because he will not confront his psychological crisis. The letters on the bow are signs to the reader of his essential alienation from the deeper import and the need that he cannot recognize to plumb the depths. In essence, the story depicts a man all too content to stick to the surface.

Stoltzfus's reading makes the important point that the story's realistically rendered external detail is the most significant and that what readers traditionally assume is the core conflict—man vs. nature—is only a metaphor for the interior struggle of man vs. his own self-awareness.

284:41 **the grains pole:** A "grains" is simply a long instrument with one or more barbed prongs for spearing or harpooning fish. In *To Have and Have Not*, Harry Morgan's first mate, Eddy Marshall, sounds the depths of a cove with a grains pole as Harry looks for a shallow place to unload the Chinese immigrants that Mr. Sing hired him to carry and sneak into Key West (*THHN* 56).

284: 46 **She must have had five million dollars worth in her:** As a passenger ship, the *Valbanera* would not have carried such a large sum of currency or goods. Hemingway emphasizes the value of the salvage to heighten the theme of "winner take nothing"—the essential paradox that, despite his bravery and stoicism, the narrator, had he been able to break into the sunken ship, would have been a thief stealing goods from the dead. By identifying a monetary value, Hemingway is likely inspired by legends of the lost treasure of the *Atocha* and the *Margarita*, which in the early 1930s were still fifty years away from being recovered by Mel Fisher.

285:4-5 **I took off my clothes . . . and dove over off the stern:** As Beegel notes, the narrator's dive to the porthole to try to break into the liner is a detail that did not appear in "After the Storm" until the second draft (80). Hemingway recognized that, in the original tale-within-a-tale version, his narrator "Bra" remained detached from the tragedy by staying above water and trying to break into the ship with his grains pole. In a short note on the manuscript, he instructed himself: "Have him dive down and see the woman" (*SS-HLE* 308). In effect, Hemingway needed his narrator to immerse himself in the moral profundity of the scenario in order to realize his theme. As Beegel puts it, "The central diving episode of 'After the Storm' epitomizes Hemingway's characteristic obsession with courage. . . . [T]he nameless narrator . . . displays raw courage in pursuit of a sordid end. He persistently subjects himself to pain, endures exhaustion, and risks death by drowning or shark attack in order to loot a sunken ship full of corpses, to commit a species of grave robbery." And in the narrator's eventual failure to earn a reward (however ethically dubious) from his courage and endurance, Hemingway introduces what will become the recurring motif of his third story collection, encapsulating the meaning of his title. In Beegel's words, "The diving episode provides the story's 'winner take nothing' element by emphasizing unaccommodated man's heroic but futile defiance of nature" (81).

285:7 **there was a woman inside with her hair floating all out:** By having his narrator spy a dead body through the ship's porthole, Hemingway integrates "After the Storm" into a long literary tradition of gazing upon the corpse of a drowned woman, as in Shakespeare's *Hamlet,* in which Queen Gertrude interrupts a conversation between the King and Laertes to announce that the latter's sister has slipped into a "weeping brook":

> Her clothes spread wide,
> And mermaid-like, awhile they bore her up;
> Which time she chanted snatches of old tunes,
> As one incapable of her own distress,
> Or like a creature native and endued
> Unto that element. But long it could not be
> Till that her garments, heavy with their drink,
> Pulled the poor wretch from her melodious lay
> To muddy death. (4.7.146–54)

Two centuries after these famous lines were penned, British painter John Everett Millais produced a striking image of the tragic figure on her back in the water, her hands outstretched in typical iconography of a martyred saint. Ophelia's face barely floats above the surface; as the young woman madly sings the "old lauds," she is oblivious to the fact she is sinking because of her imperviousness to mortality. While no evidence suggests the Millais painting inspired Hemingway, Ophelia's hair is "floating all out" just as the drowning victim's is in "After the Storm."

Both in this passage and in one at 285:15–16 ("Her hair was tied once close to her head and it floated all out in the water"), Hemingway lingers over the image of the victim's hair in a way that lightly eroticizes the figure, calling attention to her femininity. He may not describe the dead body as beautifully as countless tributes to "L'Inconnue de la Seine" ("The Drowned Woman of the Seine") have since the death mask of a young woman purportedly pulled from Paris's axial river became a veritable muse in the early twentieth century; nevertheless, the hair floating out inexorably links this casualty to other images of drowned women that more overtly exploit the Gothic entrancing power of a female corpse, effectively reminding readers of Poe's insistence in "The Philosophy of Composition" (1846) that "the death . . . of a beautiful woman" is "unquestionably the most poetical topic in the world" (19).

The drowned woman also appears in the first version of "After the Storm," even though the narrator only sees her from the surface; not until the second draft would Hemingway add the crucial element of the protagonist's repeated dives to the porthole to break it open by hand (*SS-HLE* 310–11). Whether Bra Saunders claimed he had spotted a dead body in the *Valbanera* when in 1929 he told the tale that the first version appears to transcribe is not known; the fact that, as Beegel writes, accounts of the ship's sinking in 1919 reported that emergency responders failed to find any bodies in the vicinity of the ship suggest that Hemingway's fishing guide either gilded the lily or Hemingway added the detail himself. If the latter, the image of the woman in the porthole offers the clearest indication that he wrote not merely as a reporter would, recording known facts, but that he drew from rich bodies of literary tradition to give plot elements an artistic resonance—in this case, the corpse adds a Gothic touch to a stark, existential story.

285:16 **I could see the rings on one of her hands:** In a 1976 reading of "After the Storm," Robert Walker focuses on the woman's rings to detect an allusion to the second book of Plato's *The Republic*. After a "great deluge," a Lydian shepherd named Gyges enters a chasm that opens the earth and discovers a corpse wearing a ring. Gyges confiscates the jewelry and discovers it makes him invisible, allowing him to seduce the king's wife, kill the king, and assume the throne. The moral of the story, voiced by Socrates's interlocutor, Glaucon, is that "no one is just [or moral] of his own will but only from constraint." In Walker's view, the allusion (which presumes Hemingway's familiarity with *The Republic*—a rather optimistic presumption) is meant to be ironic: "Just as Glaucon's argument in favor of moral relativity gives way eventually to Socrates's moral absolutism, so we are meant to see, indeed, that the narrator does not express Hemingway's last word, that the cold and ruthless scavenger's lack of an ethical system must give way to one which places a price other than salvage value on human life" (375–76). As with Anselm Atkins's earlier analysis of the story, Walker typifies the critical effort in the first two decades after the author's suicide to insist that Hemingway's laconic narrators are ironic. Beneath their flat affect and aversion to grappling with morality lies a humanist Hemingway.

285:18–19 **When I came up I thought I wouldn't make it to the top before I'd have to breathe:** In a 1968 essay that, before Beegel's historical/textual studies analysis twenty years later, was generally considered the most thorough close reading of "After the Storm," Anselm Atkins calls attention to the emphasis on the narrator's breathing in these diving passages: "The breathing of the sponger is opposed to the suffocation of the drowned woman; and her trapped, motionless floating stands out starkly against his constant diving up and down." His respiration and her drowning also harken back to the opening scene of choking during the fistfight. "But," as Atkins argues, "these contrasts are nullified by the even flow of the narrative" (191). In the end, the narration itself is choked by the hero's emotional suppression and the ironic parallels between the primary action (the narrator's quest to break into the ship) and the secondary actions (the sinking of the liner) that seem to minimize the latter in favor of "paltry frustration" of the former (190). These parallels in turn create suspense in the reader by emphasizing the narrator's repression of emotion while the description of the woman and the tally of lost lives force the reader to confront the horror of drowning in a storm. As Atkins concludes, "The words and movement of the story lead the reader one direction, while his unconscious feelings want to go the other. The maimed, subhuman viewpoint of the narrator-hero precludes the reader's experiencing the impact of the story until he has swallowed the whole dose of available stimulus. The story then bursts inside [the reader] like a little time bomb—a time bomb without a tick" (192).

285:31 **a sponge hook:** A sponge hook is a long pole with a three-pronged hook attached to it, developed during the evolution of the sponging industry alongside the "water glass" (see 284:29) for working in deeper waters. The Greeks who loot the liner at the end of "After the Storm" brought such equipment to sponge fishing.

285:35 **a grapple for an anchor:** A grapple or "grappling hook"—sometimes known, too, as a "grapnel"—is a weighted anchor with a quartet of sharp flukes or tines designed to snag objects along the sea floor to prevent drifting. For the narrator, the grapple has two functions: it will carry him down to the porthole, and its weight will allow him to break the glass because it is heavier than the wrench with which he previously attempts to access the ship. The anchor threatens to drag him into the quicksand, though: he cannot clutch the porthole while retaining a grip on the grapple, and he ends up going "down and down, sliding along the curved side of her [the ship]" (285:38). He is forced to release the anchor, underscoring the theme that man lacks the tools, both literal and figurative, to operate in nature. When the storyteller subsequently ties his wrench to the grains pole and attempts to hammer the glass from the surface, it comes loose and sinks into the sea bed: "I saw it in the glass, clear and sharp, go sliding down along [the ship's side] and then off and down to the quicksand and go in. Then I couldn't do a thing. The wrench was gone and I'd lost the grapple" (286: 4–7).

286:12–14 **They come out from town and told me the fellow I'd had to cut was all right except for his arm and I went back to town and they put me under five hundred dollar bond:** Hemingway resolves the issue of whether the narrator killed the man he cuts in the opening scene with a relatively understated legal conclusion that also reinforces the "winner take nothing" theme. Although he technically wins the fight, he loses the battle with society: he must put down cash while his opponent, the loser, presumably gets off leniently—he is only injured, not under bond.

286:16–17 **the Greeks had blown her open and cleaned her out:** Late in the story, Hemingway introduces the narrator's second human antagonist besides his opponent in the bar fight. "The Greeks" refers to the significant population of immigrants from the Mediterranean coast who briefly dominated the sponging industry—not the salvaging industry, it should be noted—between 1905 and 1920. Roughly 500 to 700 Greek fishermen first relocated to Tarpon Springs at the turn of the century, some arriving from New York, others traveling from Key West. (Tarpon Springs today still has the highest per capita Greek population in the United States). What lured them was the industry's ripeness for technological advance. At the time, sponges were harvested in a relatively primitive fashion: crews worked in shallow waters with hooked grains poles that won them the nickname "hookers" (not a double entendre to them). The Greeks imported advanced diving equipment that allowed them to access sponges in greater depths up to 180 feet. By 1905, some Greek crews migrated to Key West, instantly provoking the resentment of Conchs who imposed restrictions to try to limit their new rivals' penetration into the market.

As Beegel notes, Hemingway ended the first, Bra Saunders-narrated version of "After the Storm" with a reference to a violent clash between Conchs and Greeks (77). In 1911, angry Conchs raided a Greek vessel called the *Triton* moored in the harbor and burned it. Other clashes occurred over the next few years. A 1914 syndicated news account captures the flavor of the violence: "HIGH SEAS PIRACY JUST OFF THE PEACEFUL COAST OF KEY WEST! BUCCANEERING! THE TYPE THAT LOOTS AND ROBS AND BURNS AND KILLS!" As the account reports, angry Key West citizens boarded a schooner called the *Amelia* and threw Captain Harry Bell overboard, forcing him to swim for his life. A few days later in the Marquesas Keys another ship, the *Edna Louise,* was attacked and robbed, and Captain Henry Mitchell was forced to board a smaller boat set adrift. The harassment ended only with the arrival of a revenue cutter ordered to keep the peace ("Terrific War Rages on Florida Main" 5). Hemingway alludes to such violence when his original narrator, Bra, tells his charter clients, "Those damned Greeks. They got nobody knows how many millions off wrecking that steamer and then they come back here to go sponging and we set all their boats on fire. We burned them in the harbor. The sheriff gave them warning to get out" (*SS-HLE* 309).

Hemingway likely deleted this story from his original draft due to the dramatic action. Had he included it, the significance of the narrator's battle against nature would have been de-emphasized in favor of the action-adventure rivalry and the burning. Forty years later, a movie about the Greek/Conch sponging conflict called *Beneath the 12-Mile Reef* was filmed in Key West, including a reenactment of the ship burning, and it possesses none of the existential aura of "After the Storm." Aside from starring a very young Robert Wagner, the movie is only memorable for an anecdote about its Key West premier: such was the lingering resentment against the Greeks in the 1950s that, when a scene featuring Wagner's Greek protagonist wrestling an octopus flashed on the screen, the audience cheered on the creature.

286:20–36 **It was a hell of a thing all right. . . . I could have seen them on that clear white sand:** In this passage the narrator effectively draws a parallel between his fate and those of both the liner's captain and its lost passengers. In noting that the ship "only missed going through" the channel separating the Rebecca Light from the Tortugas "by about a hundred yards" (286:42–43), which would have allowed it to miss the quicksands that sunk her, the protagonist implicitly reminds readers of how close he was to breaking into the wreck. Just as the captain was only yards away from survival, the narrator was only one broken porthole away from claiming the ship's million-dollar loot.

Most of the speculative details in this penultimate paragraph about how the liner sank are present in the first, Bra-narrated draft. References to the captain's possibly opening the ballast tanks (286:27–28) and the boilers exploding (286:33–34) suggest Hemingway borrowed them from his charter captain and used them in his initial version of the story (*SS-HLE* 307–08). As Beegel notes, however, "Exactly what happened when the *Valbanera* ran aground on Rebecca Shoals remains a mystery." In her view, Hemingway could have just as easily invented the detail of the opened ballast tanks to "show his fiction captain [of the liner] exhibiting grace and seamanship under pressure, only to have the quicksands render his self-control futile" (73). Unfortunately, naval records by the searchers who discovered the *Valbanera*'s remains nearly a week after it disappeared have long been lost.

286:30 **There were four hundred and fifty passengers and the crew on board:** Hemingway is in the ballpark of the casualty figures; as previously noted (see entry for 283:17–19), the exact tally was 488. The actual loss could have been much higher. More than half the original 1,142 passengers booked to ride to Havana, Cuba, disembarked on 5 September at Santiago de Cuba. Hemingway is also correct to note that "she couldn't get in or the owners wouldn't let the captain chance coming in" (286:21–22) to Havana harbor on 8 September as the hurricane whipped the island; as Beegel notes, when the *Valbanera* radioed for a tug to pull it into the port that fateful day when land was within sight, an agent for its owners, the Pinillos Co., advised it to head back to sea because the storm had closed the harbor (70). For four days, the ship raced to stay ahead of the winds as it headed north, hoping to find port in the Gulf of Mexico. The last communication from the ship was recorded in Key West on 12 September. When authorities on the island answered a mere ten minutes later, there was no response. Evidence thus suggests that the ship went down around 1:15 p.m. that day. The ship was not discovered for six days until 19 September; as Beegel writes, "This delay left plenty of time for a fisherman like Bra Saunders or a fugitive like Hemingway's narrator to find and attempt to plunder the wreck before its presence was officially known" (70).

286:37 **jewfish:** The fish Hemingway describes as residing in the remains of the sunken liner is a type of grouper known for its large size, usually 400 pounds at maturity. The species is so plentiful along the Keys that a city in Monroe County has been named Jewfish for more than a century. (An effort to change the name in 2002 failed.) There is also a Jewfish Key off Sarasota farther north. The fish is known for its fearlessness but also for its tendency to settle in large groups. In terms of symbolism, the jewfish parallels the narrator in that both are opportunists, taking advantage of others' misfortunes, although, as befits the "nature-defeats-man" theme, only the fish is victorious. The name "jewfish," of course, carries an anti-Semitic ring to contemporary ears. According to one recent article,

> There are several theories for how the jewfish (Promicrops itaiara), an Atlantic saltwater grouper with fins and scales, got its name. It may derive from the Italian "giupesce," which means "bottom fish," or may have originally been named "jawfish" for its large mouth. A less flattering theory is that in the 1800s, jewfish were declared inferior and only fit for Jews. (Artsy)

At best, traditional explanations claim the name arose because Jamaican Jews considered the fish kosher food; at worst, the speculation is the fish's scaly skin, bulbous face, and voraciousness appealed to Jewish stereotypes when it was named in the seventeenth century. From the 1960s on, the name drew so many complaints that in 2001 the American Fisheries Society finally announced the species' name would be changed to the "goliath grouper" in recognition of its size. The new moniker has not stuck with most fishermen in the Keys, often shocking unprepared tourists. Although Hemingway participated in the anti-Semitic discourse of his day—as ample criticism on his treatment of *The Sun Also Rises*'s Robert Cohn suggests—it feels like overreading to intuit any racial inflection in the use of the jewfish here. The species simply demonstrates the opportunism of nature in availing itself of space in the environment to survive.

287:15 **They never found any bodies:** One of the eeriest facts of the *Valbanera*'s sinking is that none of the victims was ever recovered. Initially, the lack of corpses on the ship raised questions about whether the ship discovered was the correct liner and not another missing one. Once the Navy positively identified the ship, however, supernatural explanations began to creep into newspaper accounts. To this day, the wreck remains a popular diving site in the Keys, with the mystery of the corpses a popular appeal. "Where Are the Passengers?" asks the headline of a website advertising outings to the remains of the ship:

> The great mystery shrouding this ship accident is that no bodies or human bones were recovered, and no life boats were launched. Since the life boats were still present, where did the people go? How could they have disappeared without a trace? . . .
>
> The sinking of the *Valbanera* was a major maritime ship accident. The mystery surrounding her passengers also makes this perhaps the most intriguing ship disaster of them all. It's possible that some day, someone scuba diving Florida Keys will find the answer. Until then, the enigma lives on. ("Valbanera")

287:18–19 **First there was the birds, then me, then the Greeks, and even the birds got more out of her than I did:** The story's final sentence did not come to Hemingway until his third, final version. The first draft ended flatly, with the Bra character simply sighing, "That's the worst luck I ever had. . . . I never got a nickel off her" (*SS-HLE* 309). The second version ended with Bra commenting on the Greeks set to sea by Conchs taking revenge for their looting this ship. Learning that Bra's fellow Key Westers burned the Greeks' ship and set them in a dinghy sailing for Tampa, some 300 miles away, "Hem" asks the captain if the men survived: "I don't know," Bra replies. "That's the last I saw of them" (*SS-HLE* 313). But with this rhythmic line, he found a much more memorable encapsulation of his "winner take nothing" theme, one that almost rings with the power of a maxim or common wisdom. It is an appropriately poetic admission of defeat that captures humanity's limited prowess in nature.

1. O'Brien was the influential editor of the *Best American Short Stories of . . .* series from 1915 until his death in 1941; he gave Hemingway's career an invaluable boost in 1923 by selecting "My Old Man" for that year's edition after reading it in manuscript, breaking his own rule that only previously published stories would be honored in his anthologies.

2. These passages are identical, except that "bop, bop, bop" is in italics and there's a hyphen in "showcase" in *The Complete Short Stories*.

3. Part 2 of the novel, originally published in *Esquire* in February 1936 as "The Tradesman's Return," is presented in third-person limited omniscience, and only intermittent chapters in Part 3 are told in first (see Curnutt 214–19 for the novel's multifarious narratological techniques).

WORKS CITED

After the Storm. Directed by Guy Ferland, performance by Benjamin Bratt and Armand Assante, TriMark/LionsGate, 2001.

Aldridge, John. *After the Lost Generation: A Critical Study of the Writers of Two Wars.* McGraw-Hill, 1951.

Anderson, Eric Gary, and Melanie Benson Taylor. "The Landscape of Disaster: Hemingway, Porter, and the Soundings of Indigenous Silence." *Texas Studies in Literature and Language,* vol. 59, no. 3, 2017, pp. 319–52.

Artsy, Avishay. "How the Jewfish Got Its Name." Jewniverse, The Jewish Telegraphic Agency, 29 Dec. 2015, https://www.jta.org/jewniverse/2015/how-the-jewfish-got-its-name.

Atkins, Anselm. "Ironic Action in 'After the Storm.'" *Studies in Short Fiction,* vol. 5, no. 2, 1968, pp. 189–92.

Baker, Carlos. *Hemingway: A Life Story.* Scribner's, 1969.

———. *Hemingway: The Writer as Artist.* 4th ed. Princeton UP, 1972.

Beegel, Susan F. *Hemingway's Craft of Omission: Four Manuscript Examples.* UMI Research P, *1988.*

Beneath the 12-Mile Reef. Directed Robert D. Webb, performances by Robert Wagner, Terry Moore, and Gilbert Roland, 20th Century Fox, 1953.

Benson, Jackson J., editor. *New Critical Approaches to the Short Stories of Ernest Hemingway.* Duke UP, 1990.

"A Bloody Scrap in Island City." *Miami News,* 5 Sept. 1905, p. 1.

Brenner, Gerry. *Concealments in Hemingway's Works.* Ohio State UP, 1983.

Burnett. W. R. *Little Caesar.* Literary Guild of America, 1929.

Buttitta, Tony. *After the Good Gay Times: Asheville-Summer of '35—A Season with F. Scott Fitzgerald.* Viking, 1974.

Carver, Raymond. *What We Talk About When We Talk About Love.* Knopf, 1981.

Chamberlain, John. "Books of the Times." Review of *Winner Take Nothing. The New York Times,* 27 Oct. 1933, p. 17.

Connolly, Francis, editor. *The Types of Literature.* Harcourt, Brace, 1955.

Cooper, James Fenimore. *Works of J. Fenimore Cooper, Vol. 7: Wyandotte, The Monikins, and Jack Tier.* Greenwood Press, 1969.

Crowley, Michael. "Reexamining the Origins of 'After the Storm.'" *Key West Hemingway: A Reassessment,* edited by Kirk Curnutt and Gail D. Sinclair, U of Florida P, 2009, pp. 189–205.

Curnutt, Kirk. *Reading Hemingway's* To Have and Have Not: *Glossary and Commentary.* Kent State UP, 2017.

Eastman, Max. *Love and Revolution: My Journey Through an Epoch.* Random House, 1964.

Eliot, T. S. "Ulysses, Order, and Myth." *Selected Prose of T. S. Eliot,* edited by Frank Kermode, Faber and Faber, 1975, pp. 177–78.

Grayson, Charles, editor. *The Fourth Round: Stories for Men.* Holt, 1953.

Hammett, Dashiell. *The Dain Curse.* Knopf, 1929.

Hanneman, Audre. *Ernest Hemingway: A Comprehensive Bibliography.* Princeton UP, 1967.

Hemingway, Ernest. "After the Storm." *Cosmopolitan,* May 1932, pp. 38–41, 155.

———. *By-Line Ernest Hemingway: Selected Articles and Dispatches of Four Decades.* Edited by William White. Scribner's, 1967.

———. *The Complete Short Stories of Ernest Hemingway: The Finca Vigía Edition.* Scribner's, 1987.

———. *Death in the Afternoon.* 1932. Scribner's, 2003.

———. *The Letters of Ernest Hemingway: Volume 3 (1926–1929).* Edited by Rena Sanderson, Sandra Spanier, and Robert W. Trogdon. CUP, 2015.

———. *The Letters of Ernest Hemingway: Volume 5 (1932–1934).* Edited by Sandra Spanier and Miriam B. Mandel. CUP, 2020.

———. "One Trip Across." *Cosmopolitan,* Apr. 1934, pp. 20–23, 108–22.

———. *The Only Thing That Counts: The Ernest Hemingway–Maxwell Perkins Correspondence.* Edited by Matthew J. Bruccoli. U of South Carolina P, 1998.

———. *The Short Stories of Ernest Hemingway: The Hemingway Library Edition.* Edited by Seán Hemingway. Scribner's, 2017.

———. *The Sun Also Rises.* Scribner's, 1926.

———. *To Have and Have Not.* Scribner's, 1937.

———. "Who Murdered the Vets?" *New Masses,* 17 Sept. 1935, pp. 9–10.

Hotchner, A. E. *Papa Hemingway: A Personal Memoir.* Random House, 1966.

Hyman, Stanley Edgar. Review of *The Hemingway Reader.* Meyers, pp. 424–25.

Kronenberger, Louis. "Hemingway's New Stories." Stephens, pp. 142–44.

Lamb, Robert Paul. *Art Matters: Hemingway, Craft, and the Creation of the Modern Short Story.* LSU Press, 2010.

Lone Justice. "After the Flood." *Lone Justice,* Geffen Records, 1985.

McLendon, James. *Papa: Hemingway in Key West.* Seeman, 1972.

Meyers, Jeffrey, editor. *Hemingway: The Critical Heritage.* London: Routledge, 1982.

Miller, Arthur. *After the Fall: Complete Text of the New Play.* Curtis, 1964.

Moore, Henry Frank. *The Commercial Sponges and the Sponge Fisheries: From Bulletin of the Bureau of Fisheries,* vol. 28. Washington, DC: Government Printing Office, 1909.

Philbrick, Nathaniel. "A Window on the Prey: The Hunter Sees a Human Face in Hemingway's 'After the Storm' and Melville's 'The Grand Armada.'" *The Hemingway Review,* vol. 14, no. 1, 1994, pp. 25–35.

Plath, James. "'After the Denim' and 'After the Storm': Raymond Carver Comes to Terms with the Hemingway Influence." *The Hemingway Review,* vol. 13, no. 2, 1994, 37–51.

Poe, Edgar Allan. "The Philosophy of Composition." *Edgar Allan Poe: Essays and Reviews,* edited by G. R. Thompson, Library of America, 1984, pp. 13–25.

Reilly, Benjamin. *Tropical Surge: A History of Ambition and Disaster on the Florida Shore.* Pineapple P, 2005.

Reynolds, Michael. *Hemingway: The American Homecoming.* Blackwell, 1992.

Rhys, Jean. *After Leaving Mr. Mackenzie.* Knopf, 1931.

Roche, Arthur Somers. "Devil-May-Care." *St. Petersburg Times,* 1 Apr. 1928, p. 35.

Shakespeare, William. *The Norton Shakespeare,* 2nd ed. Edited by Stephen Greenblatt. Norton, 2008.

Smith, Paul. "A Partial Review: Critical Essays on the Short Stories, 1976–1989." Benson, pp. 375–94.

Stephens, Robert O., editor. *Hemingway: The Critical Reception.* Burt Franklin, 1977.

"Stiff Upper Lip." Stephens, p. 144.

Stoltzfus, Ben. "Hemingway's 'After the Storm': A Lacanian Reading." Benson, pp. 48–57.

Strabel, Thelma. *Reap the Wild Wind.* Triangle Books, 1941.

"Terrific War Rages on Florida Main." *Fort Wayne Sentinel,* 5 June 1914, p. 5.

Trail, Armitage. *Scarface.* Clode, 1930.

Trogdon, Robert W. *The Lousy Racket: Hemingway, Scribners and the Business of Literature.* Kent State UP, 2007.

"The Valbanera Is a Ship Disaster of Intense Intrigue," https://www.florida-keys-vacation.com/Valbanera.html.

Viele, John. *The Florida Keys, Vol. 3: The Wreckers.* Pineapple P, 1996.

Walker, Robert. "Irony and Allusion in Hemingway's 'After the Storm.'" *Studies in Short Fiction,* vol. 13, no. 3, 1976, pp. 374–76.

Watts, Mary Stanbery. *Van Cleve.* Macmillan, 1913.

Wilson, Edmund. "Hemingway: Gauge of Morale." Meyers, pp. 297–313.

———. Review of *Green Hills of Africa.* Meyers, pp. 216–21.

Wimsatt, W. K. *The Verbal Icon: Studies in the Meaning of Poetry.* U of Kentucky P, 1954.

Young, Neil. *After the Gold Rush,* Reprise Records, 1970.

Young, Philip. "To Have Not: Tough Luck." *American Fiction, American Myth: Essays by Philip Young,* edited by David Morrell and Sandra Spanier, Penn State UP, 2008, pp. 89–96.

A CLEAN, WELL-LIGHTED PLACE

Alberto Lena

Originally published in the March 1933 issue of *Scribner's Magazine,* the second story in *Winner Take Nothing* (1933) captures the existential despair appearing in other stories in the collection such as "A Natural History of the Dead." The characters appearing in "A Clean, Well-Lighted Place" are few, and the dialogue is minimal. This simple but complex story fascinated James Joyce who considered it "one of the best short stories ever written" (Power and Joyce 123).

The American readers of *Winner Take Nothing* were no longer those of *Men Without Women* who had enjoyed economic prosperity and the romantic possibilities of the Jazz Age. Many Americans were now living under the grim reality of an economy in shambles after the 1929 Wall Street crash. Although the story is set in a Spanish urban environment and takes place in a quiet café terrace, it mirrors the social and existential anxieties of many human beings struggling to find meaning in a constantly changing and confused reality. However, some early readers such as Maxwell Perkins, Hemingway's editor at Scribner's, found that the story was "dangerously depressing for 1933" (Monteiro 111).

During the early hours of the day, a solitary elderly man seeks spiritual refuge in a deserted café after having recently attempted suicide. Hemingway might have been imagining the story ever since he had read a newspaper article in Valencia during the summer of 1925 or 1926 describing the tragic death of a widower. The desperate eighty-year old widower, Valentín Magarza, had thrown himself off the Miguelete Tower in Valencia because he was growing old and considered himself a bother to his granddaughter. Hemingway mentioned this tragic episode in his poem "To a Tragic Poetess," his lampoon of Dorothy Parker. In this poem, Magarza's desperate gesture is aligned with those of other Hemingway's code heroes, bullfighters Manuel Garcia "Maera" (1896–1924) and Miguel Báez Quintero "El Litri" (1869–1932). They all stoically face horror and despair, whereas Parker, the American writer, is portrayed as a superficial New York snob indulging in literary posturing and utterly unable to grasp the meaning of Spanish tragic culture (Stanton 137).

Furthermore, if the suicide theme had always been present in Hemingway's mind and work, it became more prominent after the suicide of his father, Dr. Clarence Hemingway, on 6 December 1928. This issue was especially reflected in

Hemingway's *Death in the Afternoon* (1932) and "A Natural History of the Dead," illustrating his fascination with violent death. This fascination depicted in his writing could be considered as "his own peculiar way of overcoming the shock of his father's suicide" (Stanton 94).

"A Clean, Well-Lighted Place" is also an example of Hemingway's keen interest in Spanish café culture. Between 1923 and 1932, Hemingway had visited Spain several times and had had a drink on the terrace of its most famous cafés such as Café Iruña in Pamplona and Café Madrid in San Sebastián. As Mónica Vázquez Astorga states, from the late nineteenth century, Spanish cultural life was located in cafés, such as Els Quatro Gats in Barcelona frequented by Pablo Picasso and Madrid's Café and botilleria de Pompo ("La vida social"). The intellectual atmosphere of cafés such as that of de Pompo was encouraged by Ramón Gómez de la Serna, an avant-garde agitator who shook Madrid's society out of its deep cultural lethargy. It is no wonder that, during the 1920s, the Basque philosopher Miguel de Unamuno (1864–1936) passionately defended café culture as the real core of Spanish artistic and intellectual life.

When Hemingway returned to Spain in the 1950s, he could tell that many of the old cafés had gradually disappeared. During the General Franco regime, bars such as Madrid's Chicote tried to appropriate the intellectual memory of the old cafés by defending that this locale once had been a kind of intellectual center. One day when Hemingway stopped at the entrance of Chicote, he said to the Spanish writer José Luis Castillo-Puche, "I don't really want to go in there. . . . It brings back lots of bad memories. And when I hear talk of its being a favorite hangout of *intellectuals,* it makes me laugh. I don't think it very likely that de Unamuno would ever have written *The Tragic Sense of Life* [*Del sentimiento trágico de la vida,* 1912], at one of the tables in there" (qtd. in Castillo-Puche 216).

Implicitly, Hemingway's work paid homage to a whole Spanish generation of intellectuals who deeply participated in café culture, writing in such public places complex philosophical works such as those by de Unamuno. In Hemingway's "A Clean, Well-Lighted Place," he does not describe a crowded café like the Café des Amateurs in Paris or Pamplona's Iruña, but rather a deserted one at night. Hemingway's quiet and unnamed café represents, however, an existential battlefield for some of the characters. The story unearths the main themes of Unamuno's *Tragic Sense* and those of other existential writers: *nada,* despair leading to suicide, the dark night of the soul, and the search for spiritual and intellectual light. This short and powerful story challenged a whole generation of American readers trapped in the clutches of economic depression.

Title: Although the bulk of the story takes place in a café, Hemingway did not call it "A Clean, Well-Lighted Café." The word "place" is more abstract. It is the longed-for destination of two of the characters, the solitary gentleman and the older waiter, a neat, quiet, and illuminated environment where they can stay existentially alone, although in proximity to other human beings. The word "place" takes on more significance. It also symbolizes a sanctuary in which the main characters keep an apparent firm grip on transparent and ordered reality, although they are aware of the void and despair associated with human existence.

288:1–5 **It was late . . . felt the difference:** During the summer, café terraces tend to be crowded with people enjoying the beautiful weather. Hemingway pointed out that, in Spanish cities, like Madrid, people particularly enjoyed staying up most of the night in the summer "until that cool time that comes just before daylight" (*DIA* 48). Hemingway's story introduces, however, the solitary figure of an old man sitting in a Spanish café terrace in the late evening because "the dew settled the dust" (288:4). Although the solitary figure sitting on the terrace is exposed to the public eye, his identity is partially protected by the shadow made by the leaves of the trees against the electric light. His strategic position also affords him a privileged view of the street. Although the old gentleman is deaf, he can feel that the mad rushing of modern life has slowed down with the stillness of the night.

From the beginning, the narrative introduces some of main symbolic motifs of the story: an old, deaf gentleman, a quiet café in the late evening, and the shadow of a tree produced by artificial light. As Edward F. Stanton states, this initial scene furnishes the reader with a good example of the Spanish concern for *ambiente:* "the atmosphere or ambiance that makes a place livable or acceptable at a given time" (133).

A previous draft reveals that Hemingway originally specified that the story was set in Zaragoza, a city intimately related to these themes (*SS-HLE* 226). Before writing "A Clean, Well-Lighted Place," Hemingway had visited Zaragoza several times. Zaragoza, one of the most important pilgrimage places in Spain, is associated with the Marian apparition to the Apostle James when he was praying by the banks of the Ebro, and it has also become a pilgrimage site devoted to the Virgin of Pilar (Our Lady of Pilar), the patron saint of the city as well as of Spain. In early October 1926, joined by Archibald MacLeish, Hemingway stayed for almost a week coinciding with the traditional pilgrimage to the Virgin of Pilar. The name of the Virgin was of great importance for Hemingway. Carlos Baker mentions that Pauline Pfeiffer chose Pilar as a secret nickname when she first fell in love with Hemingway (*Life* 259). Pilar is the name of one of the most moving characters in *For Whom the Bell Tolls* and for Hemingway's large boat for deep-sea fishing.

The first lines of the story render a literary homage to Zaragoza's greatest local painter. Goya was born in Fuendetodos, a small town forty kilometers from Zaragoza. Hemingway stated in *Death in the Afternoon,* "Goya did not believe in costume but he did believe in blacks and in grays, in dust and in light" (205). As Emily Stipes Watts writes, by "blacks and grays" Hemingway refers to the painter's peculiar use of light and his preference for somber colors, whereas by "in dust and in light" he suggests Goya's use of chiaroscuro effects (25). Like Goya, using chiaroscuro effects, dust and light, Hemingway built the atmosphere of the well-illuminated night café with the shadows made by the leaves against the electric light when the dew settles the dust. Thus, in *Death in the Afternoon,* Hemingway emphasized that, as much as he appreciated the works of El Greco and Diego Velasquez, Goya was his favorite Spanish painter (163). Some of Goya's most famous paintings, such as *The Third of May 1808* (*El tres de mayo de 1808 en Madrid*), are housed in the Prado Museum in Madrid, which Hemingway first visited in 1923. Stanton draws parallels between Hemingway's life and that of Goya, in that they were both self-educated men. Both were born in the provinces and "gravitated to metropolitan centers of artistic activity" where they would become revolutionary artists who challenged their predecessors' conventions (118).

Moreover, like the lonely old man sitting on the café terrace in Hemingway's short story, Goya was deaf and was acutely disappointed by the course of Spanish politics during and after the French invasion. He started to paint the dark universe appearing in the series *Los desastres de la guerra* (*Disasters of War*). On traveling to Zaragoza in early October 1808, Goya witnessed the desolation and destruction stemming from the French siege. Many of the etchings of *Disasters of War* would portray the horror and destruction of a cruel war that Goya had witnessed during his stay in that city. Its shattering ruins stood as testimony to the courage and endurance of its habitants' desperate heroic resistance to Napoleon's army (Hughes 288–90).

In fact, like the old man, in his youth Goya sought a quiet place to observe the world from a certain distance and confront his inner world. He bought a farmhouse, La quinta del sordo (the Deaf Man's House). Goya's focus on his inner world is intimately related to the title of Hemingway's short story. The title suggests the notion of place as the inner sanctuary of a tormented consciousness. Goya transformed the farmhouse into a studio where he started to depict strange compositions that would be called *The Black Paintings.* They showed the anxiety and terror of the world and were located in the two main rooms of the farmhouse (Junquera 41–43).

288:5–8 **The two waiters . . . watch on him:** Although the beginning of the story emphasizes the quiet atmosphere of the lonely café, there seems to be a looming conflict between the two waiters and the old man. In fact, the two waiters are strategically sitting at a table at the entrance of the café where they can watch over the old man who is "a little drunk" (288:6). If the old man leaves without paying, the waiters will not be compensated for the cost of the drink. Moreover, they will not receive the client's tip. As Vázquez Astorga points out, in Spain during the 1920s and early '30s, waiters earned their living through their clients' tips (*Cafés de Zaragoza* 139). Moreover, the fact that, on that evening, the old man is, as usual, "a little drunk" could be extremely embarrassing for an old gentleman. In 1920's Spain, alcoholism was associated with madness and moral degeneration (Campos Marín et al. 155).

288:9–15 **Last week . . . plenty of money:** Hemingway does not name any of the waiters engaged in the initial conversation about the solitary man. The ambiguity of this dialogue has puzzled critics and scholars. Studies, such as that of Ken Ryan, stress the ambiguity of the text, the fact that Hemingway "may have liked the way the confusion clouds the identities of the two waiters, despite the difficulty it presents to the reader" (89). In fact, since the 1950s, this story has raised persistent interpretive questions on issues of textual evidence and authorial intention.

In the 1960s, critics such as F. P. Kroeger, William Colburn, and John Hagopian argue that a typographical error in the text should be corrected. The heart of the matter is a sentence in the third exchange between the two waiters: "I know. You said she cut him down" (*SS-HLE* 228). Hagopian suggests that, for the remark to make sense, the sentence should be moved up one line to append it to the preceding line. He argues that in the extended dialogue between the two waiters Hemingway confused their identity, losing track of who was speaking which lines (Smith 281). Following the critics' advice, in the 1965 edition of *The Short Stories* the sentence "You said she cut him down" (289:35) was moved up one line to join the preceding speech that starts with the sentence "His niece looks after him" (289:35). From then on, scholars such as Charles May, Scott MacDonald, and David Kerner have challenged Hagopian's revision, asserting that the dialogue's confusion was deliberate. The manuscript of the story at the John F. Kennedy Library in Boston proves that the original published version of the story is the correct one. For this reason, David Kerner and other critics have requested that the version Hemingway originally approved be restored (Smith 281–84).

Irrespective of its ambiguities in terms of the participants' identity, the initial dialogue between the unidentified waiters (288:9–15) brings out the theme of the old man's attempted suicide. Like the bullfighter Litri appearing in the poem "To a Tragic Poetess," the old man also seems to be a sort of "*desesperado*" (*Poems* 88). Yet he is unlike Litri, whose despair was due to a concrete cause, when he had realized that his leg had been amputated without his permission in a Malaga hospital.

One of the waiters interprets the suicide attempt as that of a man in despair about nothing. The waiter interprets this "nothing" to mean that the old man had attempted suicide for a banal reason. Because the old gentleman is rich, the waiter reasons, there is no legitimate reason for attempting suicide. The waiter can only think of life in terms of satisfying material needs. In this regard, Steven K. Hoffman holds that the waiter uses the term "nothing" "to convey a personal lack of a definable commodity (no thing)" and, therefore, ignores that the word "nothing" could have metaphysical meaning (173). As Carlos Baker states, it could be something "huge, terrible, overbearing, inevitable and omnipresent that once experienced, it can never be forgotten" (*Writer as Artist* 128).

The narrative introduces the notion of existential despair, a common topic in modern philosophy, which was especially explored by Søren Kierkegaard (1813–55),

Tristes presentimientos de lo que está por venir (*Sad forebodings of what is to come*) by Francisco Goya, 1810.

Martin Heidegger (1889–1976), and Miguel de Unamuno, among others. In *Tragic Sense of Life*, de Unamuno highlights the modern condition in these terms: "Our affirmation is despair, our negation is despair, and from despair we abstain from affirming and denying" (183). For de Unamuno, this condition is linked to the constant uncertainty of human life, and this state of uncertainty is also the basis of faith, similar to the idea of nothing put forth by the French philosopher Henri Bergson (1859–1941) in his work *Creative Evolution* (*L'Évolution creatice,* 1907). For Bergson, "nothing" does not constitute a void but rather the striving toward an absence (272–80).

Existential despair is also linked to the first plate of Goya's *Disasters of War,* titled *Tristes presentimientos* (*Sad Forebodings*). The etching shows the solitary figure of an emaciated man kneeling on the bare earth. In his downturned mouth, plaintive eyes, and arms extended in surrender, there is indeed an overwhelming despair. Like Hemingway's old man, Goya's figure is alone, shrouded by disquiet darkness. As Richard Hughes points out, "[H]is face, eyes rolled to the sky, bears an expression of strain and inconsolable despair. . . . there will be no relief, no lightening, either for him or for us" (273).

288:19–21 **A girl and a soldier . . . hurried beside him:** From the café entrance, both waiters comment on a girl and soldier passing by. Whereas the old gentleman fears to be seen as half-drunk and finds protection under the shadows of the leaves, the soldier boldly seeks immediate pleasure. He seems unaware of being exposed to street lighting. The narrative also places emphasis on the fact that the girl does not wear any hat covering, making her a representative of the Spanish new woman in the late 1920s, *la nueva Eva* (the new Eve), the Spanish version of the flapper: a rebellious symbol of a new age (Barrera López 221–30). In the early 1920s, women such as the painter Maruja Malló (1902–95) walked the streets of Madrid without any hat covering, a fact that challenged patriarchal authority in cultural conservative Spain (Ulacia Altolaguirre 43).

288:22–25 **The guard . . . five minutes ago:** The fact that the police are after the soldier suggests that the young girl is a prostitute and he risks curfew violation. Although adult prostitution in Spain was not prohibited during the 1920s and early 1930s, exploitation of minors as prostitutes was against the law. Spanish penal code, particularly the law issued on 13 September 1928, stated that an adult male could be severely punished for sexual abuse of a person below the age of eighteen years old, irrespective of the victim's consent. The soldier could have been sentenced to prison for two years ("Codigo Civil," Articulo 774, 1519).

In Hemingway's early version of the short story, one of the waiters passes the following comment regarding the possibility that the soldier could be caught by the guard after having had sexual intercourse with the girl: "What does it matter if he gets ~~his tail~~ what he's after?" (*SS-HLE* 227). The word "tail" is the Spanish translation of *rabo* an extremely vulgar use of the language for referring to the male sexual organ. The waiter sympathizes with the soldier's illicit and risky love affair irrespective of the severe legal consequences that might stem from that act. This scene anticipates metaphysical paintings such as Balthus's *La rue* (*The Street*, 1933) by rendering the urban landscape as an uncanny site of sexual perversion.

288:28–219:2 **What do you want? . . . went away:** When the young waiter responds to the summons, he addresses the old client in a straightforward, even brusque, manner. He asks the old man, "What do you want?" (288:28). The Spanish waiter's direct manners contrast with that of the polite Swiss waiter featured in "Homage to Switzerland," in which the waitress addresses her customers using polite expressions such as "Please" (322:15) and "what would you like, sir?" (323:2), and she does this mechanically, suggesting a professional but impersonal relationship with her clients. On the contrary, in "A Clean, Well-Lighted Place," the young waiter behaves unprofessionally, venting his irritation when he invades the private sphere of his client, saying, "You'll be drunk" (289:1).

289:3–7 **He'll stay . . . full of brandy:** The young waiter's disrespectful manners toward the old gentleman mirrors the former's anxiety about returning home and finding physical gratification with his wife, who waits for him in bed. The young man's desires are predicated on those of his old client. The waiter is not concerned about pleasing his client or even getting a generous tip for his professional service.

289:8–9 **"You should have . . . more," he said:** The young waiter can indulge himself in criticizing the deaf client because the café is now empty at night, apart from the old waiter's presence, thus avoiding any consequences stemming from his lack of professionalism and basic incivility.

289:9–13 **The waiter poured . . . his colleague again:** Subtly, the young man's clumsiness when pouring the brandy into a glass indicates his resentment toward a rich client, a member of the leisure class. As much as the young man could be tired, his behavior is somewhat unusual. He is, indeed, a professional waiter working in a traditional Spanish urban café (*café clásico*). His outlandish behavior epitomizes the social tensions lurking beneath Spanish society in the late 1920s and early 1930s. In her work *Cafés de Zaragoza*, Mónica Vázquez Astorga has placed special emphasis on how political and social tensions deeply affected the relationship between waiters and clients in Spanish cafes, especially after the Spanish Second Republic was proclaimed on 14 April 1931 (141–43).

289:14–27 **He's drunk now . . . he was eighty:** The conversation between both waiters emphasizes the impossibility of understanding the reasons behind the old man's suicide attempt. The dialogue starts with "He's drunk now" (289:14), to which the response is, "He's drunk every night" (289:15). As Paul Smith points out, in the manuscript, "Hemingway drew a run-on line between the end of the paragraph and the first remark, marking it as the younger waiter's line, a revision that has not been incorporated to this day" (277).

The old man's motives for attempting suicide represent a mystery for both waiters. However, their dialogue reveals that one of them knows a great deal about his client and that the old man is not completely alone. He seems to live with his niece who, by cutting the rope, saved the old man's soul. Thus, the dialogue introduces a character who believes in a transcendental dimension of reality in which there is punishment for misdeeds and rewards for good behavior. Such a dimension serves as a counterweight to that of the young waiter anchored to the solid surface reality of everyday life.

Moreover, by cutting the old man's rope, his niece, implicitly, saves the family's social reputation. The Catholic Church did not grant burial in consecrated ground to someone who had committed suicide because it was considered among the gravest of sins (Nistal 32–38). In 1920's Spain where, in municipalities, everyone knew each other, this issue would have shamed the Catholic members of the old man's family.

289:28–41 **I wish he would . . . who must work:** The young waiter's exasperation about the length of the old man's stay at the café reveals that he lives in a secure and predictable world with a wife waiting in bed for him after work. It is no wonder that he looks down at social superiors, such as the old man, for having "no regard for those who must work" (289:40–41) until the early hours like him. Furthermore, the young waiter insinuates that the old gentleman, engulfed by his inner conflicts, may no longer enjoy love. The hurried waiter says of his client that a wife "would be no good to him now" (289:33). However, the older waiter disagrees, believing instead that the old gentleman "might be better with a wife" (289:34). Irrespective of their different opinions about the role of a wife in the old gentleman's life, both waiters realize the importance of family relations in a modern urban environment. The old man is not completely alone. We know that his "niece looks after him" (289:35) and that she saved his life when "she cut him down" (289:35).

The conversation between both waiters, their concern for the old man's ties with the rest of his family, mirrors notions of suicide such as a classic study by the French sociologist Émile Durkheim (1858–1917). According to Durkheim in his work 1897 work *Le suicide* (*Suicide*), suicide rates increased from the early twentieth century in Western countries because urbanization had severed the bonds between the individual and the group. Above all, Durkheim stresses that urbanization had woken the ancestral basis of family relations, increasing egotism and the risk of suicide (27–38).

Both the young man's impetuous behavior and his lack of consideration for those belonging to the social hierarchy signal the social aspirations and vindications of a new generation that emerged in Spain during the early years of the Second Spanish Republic. In the early 1930s, Hemingway expressed disappointment regarding the Spanish Republican government, especially because of the anticlericalism of the 1931 Constitution (Castillo-Puche 374).

The young waiter sees the client as an obstacle that prevents his rest, but the old waiter appreciates his client. The old waiter highlights the client's dignity and notices the latter's good habits such as that of drinking "without spilling" (289:38). These habits reveal the old man's inner struggle to maintain individual equilibrium and to avoid being completely overwhelmed by despair.

290:1–10 **"Finished," he said . . . but with dignity:** The young waiter's lack of professionalism reaches its peak when he vents his anger and anxiety in public. He treats a good client as though he were a child by "speaking with that omission of syntax" (290:1). This is one of the rare moments that the narrator loses his objectivity and condemns the behavior of the young waiter. Then, the young waiter wipes "the edge of the table with a towel" (290:5), indicating that the old man has outstayed his welcome and the café will be closed soon. The young waiter shows arrogance and utter indifference to the economic consequences that his behavior could result in. It is possible that the old man could leave the cafe without tipping him. The young waiter's behavior could be compared to Jake Barnes's comments in *The Sun Also Rises* on the peculiarity of Spanish waiters' manners regarding those of French waiters: "You can never tell whether a Spanish waiter will thank you. Everything is on such a clear financial basis in France" (*SAR-HLE* 249). On the other hand, there was not a traditional closing time to Spanish cafés during the 1920s. It varied from place to place according to the local context. However, two in the morning was certainly a late hour for a Spanish café.

The old man responds to the emotional challenge very politely, revealing his true character. Although half-drunk, he retains his self-control; he stands up and calmly counts the saucers. Clearly, he struggles to be aware of the amount of brandies he has ordered before paying the bill. In many respects, the cup of brandy gives courage to the desperate man. Brandy was closely linked to the story of the siege of Zaragoza by the Napoleonic troops. Maria Agustín (1784–1831) became a symbol of national heroism in nineteenth-century Spain "for the jug of brandy she lugged around to give the troops courage" (Hughes 302).

Before leaving the café, the old gentleman lavishes the rude waiter with generosity by leaving "half a peseta tip" (290:8), in fact, a huge tip for Spain in the 1920s, bearing in mind that a cup of brandy could cost 0.95 pesetas. In Spain between the late 1920s and early 1930s, an American could live well for about eight pesetas a day (Stanton 132). Indeed, the average weekly salary for an unskilled worker was around 44 pesetas ($6.60 in 1929 dollars), and a bottle of Hemingway's favorite Domecq Brandy cost 6.70 pesetas. A brandy bottle cost almost one dollar when Hemingway visited Spain in the late 1920s, as advertised in contemporary Spanish newspapers, such as *La Vanguardia* (DS 27; Martínez Méndez 14; Germán Zubero 385; *La Vanguardia* 10).

In the same fashion as a Hemingway's character such as Manuel Garcia, the aging bullfighter of "The Undefeated," the old man still displays grace under pressure after numerous brushes with death. In watching the old man's unsteady walk, the young waiter cannot help but appreciate the former's dignity. As Hemingway would write in his short story "The Capital of the World," "decorum and dignity rank above courage as the virtues most highly prized in Spain" (CSS 29–30).

290:11–33 **Why didn't you . . . and lock up:** The young waiter feels comfortable after expelling the old man from the café. Despite this, he develops a certain amount of empathy toward the old client. The young man is aware that the classic café represents a sanctuary for his customer, and it would be difficult to find this communal environment while drinking alone at home. The waiter is still young, contemptuous, living in a world of small certainties. Yet, as Steven K. Hoffman points out, the young waiter's confidence dwells on the most transitory conditions: youth, present employment, sexual prowess, and the loyalty of his wife (177). He does not realize that this apparently solid reality is constantly sliding out from beneath his feet. This issue comes to the fore when the old waiter calls into question the assumed loyalty of the young waiter's wife. The young waiter then realizes he is facing something he cannot control. He suddenly feels utterly lost and vulnerable. On the contrary, the old waiter is aware of his own limitations: he has "never had confidence," and he is "not young" (290:32).

Internalizing the realities of old age is also a sign of wisdom for many Hemingway characters. Thus, in *The Sun Also Rises*, Jake Barnes notices how the bullfighter Juan Belmonte is aware of his limitations with old age, the fact that he can no longer enter the terrain of the bull because he might be in great danger. He does not risk his life in dangerous circumstances. Contrary to some of the San Fermín runners, he implicitly internalizes that a big horn wound is not just for fun (*SAR-HLE* 171–72).

290:34–45 I am of those . . . shadows of the leaves: The waiters seem to belong to two different worlds. The young one is only concerned with his own problems. As Stanton remarks, the hurried waiter epitomizes "many lesser men that 'live in the midst of nada, surrounded by it, without feeling its presence. . . . [T]hey are those who, in Heidegger's terms, forfeit their authentic being to the petty concerns of everyday existence" (136). The young waiter also falls into the categories elaborated by José Ortega y Gasset's 1930 work *La rebelión de las masas* (*The Revolt of the Masses*) for describing the concept of "mass man," a new social character produced by modern society. Like Ortega's mass man, the young waiter possesses no quality of excellence and violently demands more and more, as if it were his natural right (73).

The old waiter, on the contrary, is portrayed as humble and a generous human being aware of the wretched old man, absorbed with his own misery. As Matthew Nickel suggests, the older waiter feels "a special communion with the old man, a struggle to keep a light through the darkness" (352). The gentleman and the empathetic waiter are like the two solitary hermits that stand up before a black background appearing in one of Goya's *Black Paintings, Dos frailes/Dos viejos* (*Two Old Men*). Like Hemingway's old man, one of Goya's old men, the one walking with a stick, might be deaf because his other companion, an animal-like figure, seems to be shouting into his ear. They are alone in the dark world, but they continue on their pilgrimage through life. Moreover, the older waiter fears the dark like the soldiers and veterans that pervade Hemingway's work. Fear of the dark was his typical code for a war veteran. This inner suffering bridges the gap between two different generations.

Furthermore, the old waiter not only symbolizes "a light for the night" (290:36) but human warmth and sympathy for other human beings. In many respects, his actions epitomize Unamuno's comment on the last dying words uttered by the German poet Johann Wolfgang von Goethe (1749–1832): "Light! More Light!" However, de

Unamuno remarks, "[M]ore light does not make more warmth . . . for we die of cold and not darkness" (327).

291:1–6 **Good night . . . for these hours:** After finishing talking with the younger waiter, the older waiter keeps the "conversation with himself" (291:3). Unlike the former, who is eager to leave the café and forget the conversation, the latter turns over in his mind his colleague's words. Despite the differences in their respective approaches to life, the old waiter internalizes the young waiter's discourse as part of himself. The old waiter establishes a dialogic connection between himself and the other waiter based on the differences existing between them. He speaks, listens, and feels the obligation to respond although the other has gone away.

Moreover, by "[t]urning off the electric light" (291:2) while engaged in that imagined dialogue with his coworker, the old waiter moves one step further than Hemingway's other characters caught in the nightmarish universe of war trauma. Unlike Nick Adams and Jake Barnes, the old waiter embodies a kind of Hemingway character who does not seem to be afraid of the dark. This marks a progressive triumph over darkness by a Hemingway protagonist, thanks to the man's approach to others' problems. For, alone, in the dark, the waiter keeps thinking about the old gentleman. He realizes that desperate people like his good client need the "ambiente" of a clean and quiet café to face the encompassing darkness of the night. His thoughts mirror the late 1920s and early 1930s when traditional old cafés were gradually disappearing. They were replaced by noisy bodegas and by luxurious bars offering jazz music and foxtrot dance shows.

291:6–9 **What did he fear? . . . cleanness and order:** In the same fashion as Montoya, the proprietor of the Pamplona hotel in *The Sun Also Rises,* who deeply cares for his guests if they are bullfighting *aficionados* such as Jake Barnes, the relationship between the old waiter transcends that of being a mere commercial relationship. As Jake Barnes points out, in Spain, a waiter "makes things complicated by becoming your friend by any obscure reason" (*SAR-HLE* 188). In fact, in "A Clean, Well-Lighted Place," the old waiter considers the old gentleman not merely a good client but a vulnerable human being. He seeks to understand the client's despair and why the old man avoids noisy bars and dirty bodegas. More to the point, the old waiter is aware of how light, cleanliness, and order serve to mitigate the old man's night fears and the irrational forces of the world. He notices how the old man depends on these external sources to confront the existential void.

291:9–10 **Some lived in it . . .** *pues nada:* The word *nada* is intimately related to a Goya's etching 69 of the *Disasters of War,* titled *Nada. Ello dirá* (*Nothing or the Event Will Tell*). The etching, which forms part of the "Caprichos enfáticos" (Emphatic Caprices), shows a half-disinterred cadaver rotted down almost to a skeleton before an agitated mass of watchers, howling faces of people and animals. It also shows a dark figure holding the unbalanced scales of justice. The cadaver carries a sheet of paper on which is inscribed the word *Nada*. As Emily Stipes Watts points out, the specter's message could be interpreted as indicating "a nothingness beyond the grave, or as nada, the nothingness of life. . . . [It] might also indicate the *nada* of war." Whatever its ambiguous message, Watts continues, the etching conveys a desolate sense of despair (74).

The old waiter confronts nothingness, a mysterious and terrible reality encompassing everything like that appearing in Goya's *Nada* etching. He challenges the void lightly by using the Spanish terms *"nada y pues nada,"* which can be translated as "there is nothing, alright then." Yet, by being aware of the void, he implicitly faces his radical contingency as a human being because he internalizes that he lives in an existential universe. As Hoffman points out, that kind of universe is dominated by "ontological disorder that perpetually looms over man's tenuous personal sense of order. . . . [N]ada is always a dark presence which upsets individual equilibrium and threatens to overwhelm the self" (174–75).

As de Unamuno suggests in *The Tragic Sense of Life,* the Swiss philosopher Henri-Frédéric Amiel (1821–81) in his 1885 *Journal Intime (Journal)* started to make use of the Spanish word *nada* because he found "none more expressive in other language" (228). Moreover, Stanton points out that the Spanish word *nada* has a sound more forceful than its equivalent in other languages. In addition to its everyday use as pronoun and adverb for refusing or rejecting something, *nada* "has an abstract meaning of not being, or the absolute lack of all being" (135). Hemingway had previously considered the Spanish word for Frederic Henry's *nada* ending in *A Farewell to Arms* (FTA-HLE 303–04). Moreover, when composing his memoirs, Hemingway titled the last passages *Nada y Pues Nada*. As David Murad remarks, "[A]lthough the book was certainly about Paris, Spain kept creeping in" (326). The mysterious sound of the word *nada* might have captivated Hemingway's imagination to his last days.

291:10–14 **Our *nada* . . . is with thee:** Stanton observes that Hemingway managed to grasp the colloquial presence of the *nada* negation in the old waiter's parody of the Lord's Prayer and Hail Mary (135). This parodic use of the word *nada* is also connected to Tristan Tzara's *Dada Nihilism*. As Watts points out, some of Tzara's writings are remarkably close to some of the notions appearing in "A Clean, Well-Lighted Place," when Tzara wrote "that is something to cry about the nothing that calls itself nothing" (qtd. in Watts 74). For, like Tzara, the old waiter invests nothingness with substance and personality. Furthermore, like *el gracioso,* a kind of jester character who makes funny remarks and frequently appears in Spanish Golden Age theater, the old man's parody of the prayers stands as an ironic counterpart to the old client's silent despair.

291:14–26 **He smiled . . . went out:** After confronting nothingness with grace, the old waiter searches for certain neatness, order, and light, as though he were the old client. He visits a bar in which there is an espresso coffee machine. Spanish café bars started to have espresso coffee machines in the late 1920s; for a café, they symbolized incipient modernity. As Mónica Vázquez Astorga writes, the most popular espresso coffee machine was the Omega Express which could be found in attractively renewed cafés, such as Café Central in Madrid and Royalty in Zaragoza (*Cafés de Zaragoza* 131). Standing before a "shining steam pressure coffee machine" (291:15), the character searches for a relief, and it is not trapped by horror like the gloomy images of Goya's *Nada*. The symbol of the steam-pressure coffee machine can be seen as an objective correlative for the old waiter's inner self. A material object like a steam machine illuminates his yearning self and protects him from the spreading shades of *nada* like those appearing in Goya's etching. Like the old gentleman, the waiter has also become the last customer at a local bar and enjoys the pleasures of drinking a cup of coffee in company. He seems to be afraid of returning home to a lonely room and a long insomniac night.

The old waiter ironically embraces "nothingness" by using *nada* when answering the barman's request. Like the young waiter in the café, the barman seems to be extremely tired and cannot grasp the meaning of the old waiter's joke. He thinks that the old waiter is pulling his leg by answering that he doesn't want anything. The barman understands *nada* to be nothing, while the old waiter knows that *nada* is something. His use of language reveals a growing anger toward the client by using expressions such as "*Otro loco más*" (291:18), meaning "another madman." The Spanish expression *copita* means "little cup," a diminutive for the Spanish noun *copa* or "cup." The barman's use of the term suggests a certain sarcasm. It denotes an extreme familiarity with an unknown client for a professional barman working in a 1920's stylish bar. No wonder that, irrespective of the pleasant light, the old waiter finds that something is missing in the *ambiente* of the bar: it is unpolished. The barman does not feel like talking with him. Plainly, he does not sympathize with the old waiter: light is not enough because there is a lack of human warmth. This atmosphere does not make the place acceptable for the old waiter, and he decides to go out.

291:26–30 **He disliked bars. . . . must have it:** The old waiter's confronting the *nada* could be seen as a path of purgation in which the penitent reaches all of God after going through the dark night of the soul in the same fashion as Saint John of the Cross's *Ascent to Mount Carmel* (Nickel 353). His irony could also be interpreted as a method to combat the darkness by internalizing the existential "nothing" that underlies everything and to face the hostile external world and inner suffering with exemplary courage and dignity (Hoffman 187–89). Regardless of the final interpretation of the text, either religious or existential, the end of the story shows the old waiter capable of transcending his internal suffering. Unlike other Hemingway's characters such as Nick Adams, whose inner horror keeps him from falling asleep and who is unable to find any relief, after experiencing the sense of nada, the old waiter internalizes his own insomnia with a sort of stoic serenity. His attitude symbolizes a progressive triumph over the enveloping darkness of the universe.

WORKS CITED

Baker, Carlos. *Ernest Hemingway: A Life Story.* Scribner's, 1969.

———. *Ernest Hemingway: The Writer as Artist.* 4th ed. Princeton UP, 1972

Barrera López, Begoña. "Personificación e iconografía de la 'mujer moderna.' Sus protagonistas de principios del siglo XX en España." *Trocadero,* vol. 26, 2014, pp. 221–40.

Bergson, Henri. *Creative Evolution.* Translated by Arthur Mitchell. Dover, 2013.

Campos Marín, Ricardo, Rafael Huertas García-Alejo, and José Martínez Pérez. *Los ilegales de la naturaleza: Medicina y degeneracionismo en la España de la Restauración (1876–1923).* Consejo Superior de Investigaciones Científicas, 2000.

Castillo-Puche, José Luis. *Hemingway in Spain.* New English Library, 1975.

"Codigo Civil." *Gazeta de Madrid,* 13 Sept. 1928.

Colburn, William. "Confusion in 'A Clean, Well-Lighted Place.'" *College English,* vol. 20, 1959, pp. 241–42.

Durkheim, Émile. *Suicide: A Study in Psychology.* Translated by George Simpson. Free Press, 1979.

Flora, Joseph M. *Reading Hemingway's* Men Without Women: *Glossary and Commentary.* Kent State UP, 2008.

Germán Zubero, Luis. "Coste de la vida y poder adquisitivo de los trabajadores en Zaragoza durante el primer tercio del siglo XX." *Razones de historiador: Magisterio y presencia de Juan José Carreras.* Edited by C. Forcadell Álvarez. Zaragoza: IFC, 2009, pp. 373–90.

Hagopian, John V. "Tidying Up Hemingway's Clean, Well-Lighted Place." *Studies in Short Fiction,* vol. 1, 1964, pp. 140–46.

Hemingway, Ernest. "A Clean, Well-Lighted Place." *Scribner's Magazine,* March 1933, pp. 149–50.

———. *The Complete Short Stories of Ernest Hemingway: The Finca Vigía Edition.* Scribner's, 1987.

———. *The Dangerous Summer.* Scribner's, 1985.

———. *Death in the Afternoon.* 1932. Scribner, 1999.

———. *A Farewell to Arms.* 1929. The Hemingway Library Edition. Scribner, 2012.

———. *For Whom the Bell Tolls.* 1940. Scribner, 1996.

———. *The Short Stories of Ernest Hemingway: The Hemingway Library Edition.* Edited by Seán Hemingway. Scribner, 2017.

———. *The Sun Also Rises: The Hemingway Library Edition.* Edited by Seán Hemingway. Scribner, 2014.

———. "To a Tragic Poetess." 1926. *Complete Poems.* Edited by Nicholas Gerogiannis. Rev. ed, University of Nebraska Press, 1992, pp. 87–90.

Hoffman, Steven K. "Nada and the Clean, Well-Lighted Place: The Unity of Hemingway's Short Fiction." *New Critical Approaches to the Short Stories of Ernest Hemingway,* edited by Jackson J. Benson, Duke UP, 1990, pp. 172–91.

Hughes, Robert. *Goya*. London: Vintage, 2004.

Junquera, Juan José. *The Black Paintings of Goya*. Translated by Gilla Evans. Scala, 2003.

Kerner, David. "The Manuscripts Establishing Hemingway's Anti-Metronomic Dialogue." *American Literature*, vol. 54, 1982, pp. 385–96.

———. "The Thomson Alternative," *Hemingway Review*, vol. 4, 1984, pp. 37–39.

Kroeger, F. P. "The Dialogue in 'A Clean, Well-Lighted Place.'" *College English*, vol. 20, 1959, pp. 240–42.

MacDonald, Scott. "The Confusing Dialogue in Hemingway's 'A Clean, Well-Lighted Place': A Final Word?" *Studies in American Fiction*, vol. 1, 1973, pp. 93–101.

Martínez Méndez, P. *Nuevos datos sobre la evolución de la peseta entre 1900 y 1936*.Banco de España, Servicio de Estudios, D.L., 1990.

May, Charles E. "Is Hemingway's 'Well-Lighted Place' Really Clean Now?" *Studies in Short Fiction*, vol. 8, 1971, pp. 326–30.

Monteiro, George. "A Frost/Hemingway Roundtable Co-Sponsored by the Robert Frost Society and the Hemingway Society: 28 December 2007, *Modern Language Association*, Chicago, IL." *Hemingway Review*, vol. 30, no. 2, 2011, pp. 99–117.

Murad, David. *American Images of Spain, 1905–1936: Stein, Dos Passos, Hemingway*. Kent State UP, 2013.

Nickel, Matthew. "Religion." *Hemingway in Context*, edited by Debra A. Moddelmog and Suzanne del Gizzo, CUP, 2013, pp. 347–56.

Nistal, Mikel. "Legislación funeraria y cementerial española: una visión espacial." *Lurralde: Investigación y espacio*, vol. 19, 1996, pp. 29–53.

Ortega y Gasset, José. *The Revolt of the Masses*. Edited by Kenneth More. Translated by Anthony Kerrigan. U of Notre Dame P, 1985.

Power, Arthur, and James Joyce. *Conversations with James Joyce*. 1974. Lilliput Press, 1999.

Ryan, Ken. "The Contentious Emendation of Hemingway's 'A Clean, Well-Lighted Place.'" *Hemingway Review*, vol. 18, no. 1, 1998, pp. 78–91.

Smith, Paul. *A Reader's Guide to the Short Stories of Ernest Hemingway*. G. K. Hall, 1989.

Stanton, Edward F. *Hemingway and Spain: A Pursuit*. U of Washington P, 1989.

Ulacia Altolaguirre, Paloma. *Concha Méndez: Memorias habladas, memorias armadas*. Mondadori, 1990.

Unamuno, Miguel de. *Tragic Sense of Life*. Translated by J. E. Crawford Flitch. Macmillan, 1921.

La Vanguardia, 31 Dec. 1926, p. 10.

Vázquez Astorga, Mónica. *Cafés de Zaragoza: Su biografía, 1797–1939*. Institución "Fernando el Católico," 2015.

———. "La vida social y cultural en los cafés europeos en el último cuarto del siglo XIX." *Comunicación y Ciudad*, edited by Miguel Ángel Chaves Martín, Universidad Complutense de Madrid, 2015, pp. 23–37.

Watts, Emily Stipes. *Ernest Hemingway and the Arts*. U of Illinois P, 1971.

THE LIGHT OF THE WORLD

Bryan Giemza

When Jane Kendall Mason's Hemingway manuscripts were on the Christie's auction block in May 2000, "The Short Happy Life of Francis Macomber" commanded almost $220,000; "The Light of the World" fetched about half as much (Schontzler). The latter might have represented a better value, however. Hemingway once remarked to A. E. Hotchner that "'A Clean, Well-Lighted Place' may be my favorite story." But in the same breath he added: "That and 'The Light of the World,' which no one but me ever seemed to like" (qtd. in Hotchner 164). Michael Reynolds deems "The Light of the World" "an enigmatic story whose center lay just beyond definition" (*1930s* 97). Hemingway may have been trying to rescue the story from his critics when he identified it as one of his favorites. It was not likely to please the conservative Oak Park crowd; *Scribner's Magazine* had rejected "The Light of the World" for its graphic content. Yet Hemingway ultimately circumnavigated prudery through a series of deft allusions, acceding to editor Maxwell Perkins's insistence on replacing three "anglo-saxon phrases" (*1930s* 144) and other risque language with more acceptable phrasing.

Hemingway completed the story around his thirty-third birthday while visiting the idyllic L Bar T Ranch in Wyoming. His wife Pauline typed up the twenty-four-page manuscript (Reynolds, *1930s* 97). Although Nick's name is not mentioned in "The Light of the World," related in first-person, it is consistent with Nick's upper Michigan ramblings and would be included in the posthumous Nick Adams collection, where it is the only story in which Nick's sidekick is named Tom. Few things are left to accident in Hemingway's oeuvre, including the arrangement of stories to support plot, character development, and narrative arc, so it is worth considering how the story is bookended within the collection where it originally appeared. Hemingway wanted "The Light of the World" to be the first story in *Winner Take Nothing,* another mark of its importance, but Maxwell Perkins persuaded him to place it later in sequence. "A Clean, Well-Lighted Place" precedes it. Like "The Light of the World," "A Clean, Well-Lighted Place" is a Hemingway story that concerns light and dignity poured out into the consuming darkness of nihilism. "A Clean, Well-Lighted Place" illustrates the meaning of the aphorism "If youth knew, if age could." "The Light of the World" explores how and what youth might know and see.

The story has perplexed critics from the beginning, and some have found it "markedly inferior to the boyhood tales of *In Our Time*. Despite his stout insistence that the story was a favorite of his," writes Kenneth Lynn, "Hemingway was clearly coming to the bottom of the Michigan barrel" (409). Joseph Flora, on the other hand, believes that "The Light of the World" is "perhaps the most 'literary' of the Nick Adams stories" (*Nick Adams* 69). As Flora suggests, aside from its obvious and multivalent biblical allusions, Hemingway's story is grounded in French literature, including work by Guy de Maupassant, lesser-noticed sources in the works of Zola and Baudelaire, too, and perhaps even visual sources from French artists including Manet and Gervex (Giemza 84).

Hemingway pointed readers of "The Light of the World" to de Maupassant, writing to Arnold Gingrich on 7 June 1933 that his story was "as good or better a story about whores than La Maison Tellier" (*Letters vol. 5*, 402). According to Reynolds, Hemingway "may have read ["La Maison Tellier"] as early as HS [high school]," and a copy mentioned in a 1933 letter to Maxwell Perkins was among the several de Maupassant volumes in his Key West library (*Hemingway's Reading* 157). In fact, some critics have used de Maupassant's work as a kind of decoder ring for unlocking Hemingway's story. James Martine focuses on a crucial passage in de Maupassant's text: "all night long a little lamp burned . . . such as one still sees in some towns, at the foot of the shrine of some saint." Thus, Martine concludes that the "Light of the World" is "the archetypal light on the archetypal houses of the oldest profession in the world" (465–66). Parallels between "The Light of the World" and "La Maison Tellier" (translated as "Madame Tellier's Establishment") extend to such details as the identical number of prostitutes taking a rail trip, the story's festival atmosphere, and its maudlin sensibility (Martine 465–66).

The story has much to say about homosocial and homosexual conduct, sexually transmitted illnesses, and prostitution, and this preface will consider those topics in turn within the scope of Hemingway's stories. But first let us consider how "The Light of the World" is fitted within *Winner Take Nothing*. If this short story considers the importance of the authentic and changing insight to "truth" with respect to different stations in life and age, "God Rest You Merry, Gentlemen," the story that follows it, continues to explore the cost of sexual desire, Christian mores, the desire for purity, and whatever wisdom may come of innocence and experience. It reminds readers that the psychic cost of an unattainable sexual morality can become an unbearable and disfiguring burden. Along the same lines, "The Light of the World" pairs closely with "One Reader Writes," a story in which a "malady" (syphilis) returns with a veteran to despoil the home of his faultless wife, who recently gave birth. The stories are counterparts: one is told to redeem the disease-bearer and the other to give the perspective of the disease-victim. In both, women are "poxed" by the world. The consequences of sexual transgression are irreversible and permanent—is this fair, in either the human or cosmic state of affairs?

"A Clean, Well-Lighted Place," the story that precedes "The Light of the World," suggests that compassion and courage create spaces where dignity can be affirmed. Some read "The Light of the World" through a dark lens and, in counterpoint to "A Clean, Well-Lighted Place," see the light of the world—emphasis on the fallen *world* we inhabit—as offering no quarter to the castoff and the compromised. Such a light merely draws into sharper relief the soiled nature of the human condition. In my view, the weight of the evidence favors another reading. Notwithstanding its ribald, scatological content and its gritty, ill-lit setting, the story reminds readers that the light of the world can shine in unlikely seeming places and people—that Christ had friends in low places.

Not all critics see it this way. William J. Collins suggests that the light of the world in the story is indeed the light of the *world* in contrast to the divine light. As such, it is hardly the light of a clean, well-lighted place, but rather the light that falls when the barman turns on the light at the end of the night, revealing fully its sordid human ugliness: the light that reveals Peroxide's pathetic fantasy and that shines on Alice's unsparing self-awareness. Collins points out that Alice's chronology for Ketchel does not square with the facts of his life, which Hemingway would have known. In Collins's view, then, Alice is a liar, too, but something of a Hemingway hero, in that she meets difficult realities head-on, "without self-serving denial or cowardice" (231).

Collins's originalist reading gives final authority to biographical facts and pre-sumes that Hemingway was challenging readers to sort out the truth. Hemingway was in his early thirties when he composed the stories of *Winner Take Nothing,* and, on one level, it is perhaps easier for a youthful idealist to see the world as ir-redeemably fallen than for a mature writer to surrender to such a lopsided view. The Collins thesis, in my view, does not fully compass the writer's artful blending of fact and fiction to achieve larger effects. Was that really Hemingway's intention, or was he setting a kind of snare for the reader, whose preformed judgments will, as they did for Tom, color their perception of the story's characters? In "The Art of the Short Story," Hemingway advises those who would understand the short story to learn French. "What I do is what the French call *constater,*" he explains (*SS-HLE* 133). The French is derived from the Latin *constat* (it is certain) from *constare* (to stand firm); the best English approximation is perhaps to "recognize" or "report." The writer's artistic imagination requires that he stand firmly with his characters, recognize and report their humanity, and ultimately, validate them, as Hemingway does for Nick and Alice in turn.

Can Nick stand with Alice? A morbidly obese prostitute probably little resem-bled his fantasies of the type. Hemingway's story plainly concerns the construction of femininity, as Nick must reconcile the real with the ideal. Hemingway continues, in his "Art of the Short Story" piece, to apply this ethos specifically to women:

That is what you have to learn to do, and you ought to learn French anyway if you are going to understand short stories, and there is nothing rougher than to do it all the way. It is hardest to do about women and you must not worry when they say there are no such women as those you wrote about. That only means your women aren't like their women. You ever see any of their women, Jack? I have a couple of times and you would be appalled and I know you don't appall easy.

What I learned constructive about women, not just ethics like never blame them if they pox you because somebody poxed them and lots of times they don't even know they have It—that's in the first reader for squares—is, no matter *how* they get, always think of them the way they were on the best day they ever had in their lives. That's about all you can do about it and that is what I was trying for in the story. (*SS-HLE* 5–6)

Here, then, is how Hemingway spoke of "The Light of the World," also adding a sly reference to another of the *Winner Take Nothing* stories, "One Reader Writes," in which a perfidious husband contracts syphilis while at the Chinese Civil War front. Hemingway averts to the fact that American puritanical sensibilities regarding "respectable" women are not prepared to confront the realities of French women. There is a gentle barb in this, of course; "The Light of the World" should make plain that American women can equal the French in the many-splendored varieties of human endeavor and abasement.

More important is what Hemingway says next, which points to the fact that women, as in so many arenas, take the blame for sexual misconduct (as evidenced, for example, by widespread criminal statutes that punish prostitutes rather than their clients). Prostitution flourishes in societies with marked discrepancies in power along gender lines and in which women especially are "poxed" by the scourge of human trafficking. More often than not, in keeping with long tradition, the propagation of sexually transmitted illnesses is pinned on "loose" women and "temptresses," even as the consequences of male appetite redound on women, a fact that the reader of "One Reader Writes" knows too well as she contemplates the future dimensions of her married life.

It is better, Hemingway suggests, to recognize the original brightness of women's humanity even as they are scapegoated for the sins of the world. Consistent with his code of values—which no doubt fueled some measure of his dissatisfaction with himself—no act of self-prostitution can be covered up and must be recognized as an assault on the better possibilities of dignity and courage.

Hemingway interacted with prostitutes in the later stages of his life, even as he despaired of ever rectifying his sins against marriage and women. It might be said that he fell prey to simony periodically in his own life and damaged himself in that way, because, at the end of the day, it was the concealment of such conduct that he could not abide. Although it may be counterintuitive, per the Hemingway code, one might indeed work as a prostitute as long as one owns it and acknowledges any attendant injury to dignity/selfhood—which seems to be what Alice does. Prostitution of principles is what Hemingway loathed, even as he repeatedly abrogated his own.

Elsewhere in Hemingway's oeuvre, an idealized version of the prostitute surfaces in the unfinished Nick story "The Last Good Country," where Nick's sister, with a sentimental imagination perhaps akin to Peroxide's in "The Light of the World," imagines herself as both her brother's wife and a glamorous madam. In Littless's fairytale version of prostitution, madams are polite, glamorous, and queenly, and the matron of them all is "just a bird in a gilded cage" (*CSS* 532). In Nick's sister's fantasy, the Queen of the Whores instructs her (the Queen's handmaiden) to tell her brother that he should "stop by the Emporium anytime he is at Sheboygan" (532), something that he will indeed later attempt to do. Including "The Last Good Country" in the Adams cycle raises attendant controversies, but it certainly serves to enrich the reading of "The Light of the World," where, as if by prophecy, Nick at last meets the Queen of the Whores.

Finally, "The Light of the World" should be prominent within a growing body of critical scholarship that offers readings of Hemingway's work attuned to sexuality and gender. Such readings encompass novels, such as the gay presence in *The Sun Also Rises* (consider Jake's fleeting thoughts of Count Mippipopolous), as well as short stories, including the Nick Adams stories (consider the homosocial jealousy of "The Three-Day Blow"). The not-always-subtle gay subtexts of "The Light of the World" are essential to understanding it. It should be obvious that the cook of the story is gay; more interesting is the fascination between him and Tom. On one hand, the lumberjack culture of the upper peninsula seems an unlikely habitat for an openly gay character. On the other, a number of scholarly works have demonstrated that American homosexuality in the first half of the twentieth century might have been more broadly accepted than in the latter half (in an urban setting, George Chauncy's *Gay New York* makes a compelling case).

In the same vein but in a rural setting, Sherwood Anderson's "The Man Who Became a Woman" was published in *Horses and Men* (1923) and concerns fluidity of gender and sexual identity, even in hardscrabble rural bars frequented by miners, gamblers, and drifters. The story, riddled with anxiety about male rape, is very much of a piece with "The Light of the World" and its fears of being "punked" and treatment of androgyny. Although *Horses and Men* is not listed among the titles in Hemingway's library, it predates his parodic *The Torrents of Spring* by just three years and coincides roughly with the period of the two writers' most intense—and fraught—friend/mentorship, around the time when Gertrude Stein was pressing them to rethink gender. The subject matter of "The Man Who Became a Woman" would have been irresistible to Hemingway, and it is hard to imagine that he would not have read it. The narrator of the story, who will elsewhere protest, "I'm not any fairy" (500), is swept into a barfight shortly after a moment in which "the face I saw in the looking-glass back of that bar, when I looked up from my glass of whisky that evening, wasn't my own face at all but the face of a woman" (499). Some of the parallels in theme and setting are striking enough to make one wonder if "The Light of the World" furnishes another example of Hemingway in dialogue with Anderson's work.

Fundamentally, the story looks at another facet of an enduring concern in the Nick Adams stories: Can a woman be both promiscuous and "good"? Can a man? What is the cost of inhabiting preformed gender and sexual roles? And what is the cost to human dignity in the murky posturing of mature sexuality, both licit and illicit, that cannot be taken at face value?

Having given Hemingway the first word on the value of "The Light of the World," perhaps we should let him have the last: "'The Light of the World' is really, no matter what you hear, a love letter to a whore named Alice" (qtd. in Flora, *Ernest Hemingway* 203) Like the French writers he borrowed from, Hemingway delighted in a clincher that was steeped in irony. In this world of "clean" prostitutes and shifting visions, appearances are not to be trusted. A close reading reveals why Hemingway believed so deeply in this story and how he might justifiably regard "The Light of the World" as one of his successes in "leaving everything out."

Title: Hemingway seemed to deflect the possibility that the story's title was suggested by William Holman Hunt's *The Light of the World,* an immensely popular and widely reproduced depiction of Jesus knocking at the door as described in Revelation 3:20 ("Behold, I stand at the door, and knock: if any man hear my voice, and open the door, I will come in to him, and will sup with him, and he with me"). Hemingway explained in "The Art of the Short Story," "I could have called it 'Behold I Stand at the Door and Knock' or some other stained-glass window title, but I did not think of it and actually 'The Light of the World' is better" (*SS-HLE* 5). But here we might do better to trust the tale and not the teller, for Hemingway may have been covering his tracks. Carlos Baker and Robert Fleming both suggest the painting's importance in reading the allegory, and Michael Reynolds joins them in pointing out that this was the painting that Grace Hemingway gave to her church in memory of her father (Baker 606; Fleming 285; Reynolds, *Young Hemingway* 317–19). Some, like Kenneth Lynn, take it as an established fact that Hunt's painting furnished the title; in their reading, the seedy barroom door and the train station door (a door that Nick will pointedly be asked to close, suggesting that he stands on the threshold in indecision) render a "blasphemous literary version of this scene" (409). In Hemingway's light parody of the Western genre that frames the first part of the story, the sun has set on the boys in the bar, a sure sign of danger. They find little light there; it's quite possible that the only other light in town, at the "other" end of it, is what naturally draws them to the station. And just what is the quality of the light there? Is it the light of the tabernacle, or of another notorious district?

The Light of the World by William Holman Hunt, 1851.

292:1–3 **When he saw . . . free-lunch bowls:** The story is, at its core, an exploration of the notion that there is no such thing as a free lunch—an American common-place that finds its earliest printed use in the 1890s and that would be popularized by twentieth-century writers as diverse as economist Milton Friedman and science fiction writer Robert Heinlein. The phrase's origins go back to the late-nineteenth/early-twentieth century practice of offering bar patrons a "free" lunch with the purchase of a drink. It was, in contemporary economic parlance, a loss leader, designed to draw in customers who would keep drinking. The fare, of which pig's feet is one example, was dependably cheap and unsatisfactory. But the gimmick had reached its height at the time of nickel beer and was already waning by the 1920s, eventually subsumed by the popular happy hour. It endures, notably, in the so-called gentlemen's clubs of our time.

Guy de Maupassant's "Madame Tellier's" ends with the lusty Madame offering a sort of free lunch. Caught up in happiness on her return from Paris, Madame Tellier charges two married brothel visitors for nothing "except the champagne, and that cost only six francs a bottle, instead of ten, which was the usual price, and when they expressed their surprise at such generosity, Madame Tellier, who was beaming, said to them: 'We don't have a holiday every day'" (67). In a line regrettably cut from Hemingway's original draft of "The Light of the World," Alice offers Nick a freebie too, inviting him "to stay for nothing" (Smith 257).

The allure of the free lunch is a familiar part of the false enticements of one version of the American dream, in which something is promised for nothing. Prostitution often relies on a similar inducement—the company is free, but the sex isn't. As the lads will later discover, the sanitized *Pretty Woman* and *Fancy Ladies* versions of prostitution, peddled by popular culture, have little in common with the realities of the sex worker or the once-common ritual, widely remarked in American fiction, of the loss of virginity through a visit to a brothel. Everything has its costs, and they are rarely as advertised.

The bartender quickly and accurately sizes up Tom and the narrator, generally presumed to be Nick Adams. Nick and Tom might already be drunk, to gauge from their behavior; they are reaching up for their majority; and they are not likely to have much money to spend. In contrast to the old man of "A Clean, Well-Lighted Place," they are not seeking an oasis of dignity and good company, but something more like swaggering misadventure or a pub crawl.

292:9–10 **He drew that beer . . . and pushed the beer across to Tom:** In each instance, the bartender waits for payment before providing anything to the two young men. By contrast, the man who orders rye, presumably a local, comports himself with dignity and does not pay for his drink until he leaves.

292:21 **"You know where," said Tom:** This is the first of several euphemisms in the story, and it requires little imagination to surmise what Tom is suggesting the bartender can do with the pig's foot. Indeed, the manuscript originally gave, "Up your ass." The bartender's refrain—What's yours?—goes well with *up yours*. Given Tom's apparent homophobia, there's some irony in his suggestion.

292:22–23 The bartender reached a hand: The implication is that the bartender is going to brandish a weapon and see them swiftly to the door. But the narrator has already discerned the importance of the transaction, so he buys his way out of a dilemma. The fifty cents he puts on the bar—enough to buy ten beers—considerably placates the bartender. It is a sum finally worthy of a "free" lunch.

292:29 You stink yourself . . . all you punks stink: Unlike the barman of "A Clean, Well-Lighted Place," this bartender has limited forbearance for youth. Appropriate to the topic of the story, the earliest usage of "punk" was as a term for a prostitute going back to the sixteenth century. That meaning yielded to "a man who is made use of as a sexual partner by another man" (*OED*) and, by the twentieth century, in American usage, was understood as "a young male companion of a tramp, esp. one who is kept for sexual purposes" (recall "The Battler" from *In Our Time*). More generically, the term can also be understood to apply to "a young person, or a person regarded as inexperienced or raw," a coward, or a juvenile delinquent.

Male dominance, and the threatening subtexts of homoeroticism, can be inferred from the etymology, but, regardless of which register one reads it in, the insult is fitting in multiple ways. The narrator's weak attempt to save face by claiming that leaving was his idea makes it clear that he has, in a sense, been punked. So does Tom's attempt to push his friend into the fray by noting the insult—"He says we're punks"—which also impugns his honor. Tom will hide behind his friend's honor once again with his hollow retort: "Tell him how wrong he is" (293:7). But the bartender isn't wrong. Their dignity been affronted, and they must back down. The bluff has already been called, and the bartender's saying they will not return is not so much a prediction as a warning. The bartender has called them out, a phrase that references dueling and being called out to settle a score.

The only other short story in the Hemingway oeuvre to use the term "punk" (setting aside the insult in the nonfiction *Green Hills of Africa* [189] and novel *Islands in the Stream* [58, 68]) is "Mother of a Queen," another entry in *Winner Take Nothing*. In that case, one line of speculation is that the narrator, Roger, is covering up (in the way of "A Simple Enquiry") and that he and the bullfighter have been lovers. Hemingway deploys both the ambiguity of the term and the relationship to heighten the intrigue. Those who fault the writer for hypermasculinity might be surprised to see his repeated acknowledgment in fiction that hypermasculinity is intrinsically linked to homosexuality. As the story unfolds, a double-standard does too. If the young men are threatened by same-sex sexual domination, they fail to grasp the humiliation implicit in the domination for hire that comes from consorting heterosexually with prostitutes.

This scene should be remembered in the concluding line of the story ("The other way from you," Tom told him [297:14]), a rebuff to the homosexual cook, at once pointing to masculine insecurity and implying that the young men's sexual orientation is another direction. From beginning to end, "The Light of the World" investigates what it means to be punked.

293:9 **Outside it was good and dark:** The statement begs the question, where is the light of the world? The phrase "the light of the world" is applied both to the followers of Jesus (Matthew 5:14) and to Jesus himself: "Then spake Jesus again unto them, saying, I am the light of the world: he that followeth me shall not walk in darkness, but shall have the light of life" (John 8:12).[1] The good of the outdoors is a respite from the man-made darkness and evil brewing in the tavern. Viewed one way, there is plenty of comic relief in the opening of the story; the proverbial music stops from the moment the lads pass through the swinging doors in extended scene-setting that sends up certain conventions of the Western. The sheriff (bartender) has unceremoniously ejected them from a sundown town. Yet there is a real subtext of danger, too, and the road to hell seems near. Tom says in an ingénue's voice, "What the hell kind of place is this?" (293:10) (In the next story, Doc Fischer will say, in response to "The hell with you" (301:11) that he has had only a brief look into [hell]—the story of the sexually tormented young man would seem to suffice.) The darkness is unlikely to cover shame, however. Their efforts to affect a more experienced masculinity are transparently contrived and unconvincing and will soon be tested again.

293:12 **We'd come in that town at one end . . . out the other:** Consider the scatological nature of this line, which implies that the town has eaten them alive, reducing them, like the trees and animal hides (and pigs' feet, the cheapest byproduct that could be put on the menu) to excreta. They are being digested by a commodity town, where people, too, may be commodified.

293:16–17 **five whores . . . six white men and four Indians:** If one pays attention to the number of people in the station, it seems that some disappear (the count goes from four Indians to two in two pages). Scholarship has shown that this is not a case of "vanishing" Indians but simply an error introduced during the story's revision process—a moment when Homer nods, perhaps. However, there are other cases of disappearing Native Americans in Hemingway's work, such as "Ten Indians." The people are catalogued by race and station. There is an aroma of hellfire and sense of enclosure in the station.

293:20 **Shut the door, can't you?:** The homosexual cook phrases the question formally, and the implication is that the two not-from-heres at the door have some uncertainty about entering or are too drunk to mind their manners. Kenneth Lynn assumes that Holman Hunt's painting of Christ knocking at the door furnished Hemingway's title; in his reading, the barroom door and the train station door render a "blasphemous literary version of this scene" (409). A Christ who knocks at the doors in this Michigan town will find plenty of sinners to visit.

Crossing a threshold, or standing athwart one, is generally an important signifier in Hemingway's work. Several clues can be inferred here, particularly with reference to "A Simple Enquiry," a story from *Men Without Women* that introduces homosexuality as a threatening subtext. "A Simple Enquiry" presents a parallel situation: nineteen-year-old Pinin knocks "on the half-opened door," and the presumably gay major instructs him to come in "and shut the door" (*CSS* 251). His not-innocent question to the young man—"you are not corrupt?" (251)—employs an implicature similar to the substitution of "bugger" for "interference" in "The Light of the World." When Pinin is finally dismissed, "He was really relieved: life in the army was too complicated." The Major instructs him, "[D]on't be superior and be careful some one else doesn't come along and take you" (251). Again, strong parallels exist between the stories: in both, there is a sounding out of complicated sexuality resulting in adolescent embarrassment and confusion, a youthful presumption of superiority, and the fear of being taken as a punk. In both stories, the youths will be relieved to exit a space that is psychologically and physically too warm and restricted.

In "The Light of the World," just a few lines later, the cook will succeed in getting the narrator to do his bidding, notwithstanding his reflexive homophobia.

293:23–24 **his face was white and his hands were white and thin:** At first blush, the cook's face and hands aren't weather-beaten or hardened in the way that might be expected of a lumberjack, details taken in by the observant narrator. Like painters before him, Hemingway seems to play on a verbal iconography of difference, employing synecdoche here—but to what end? Is it to play on the stereotype of homosexuals as preening and refined? In *The Sun Also Rises,* Brett's homosexual entourage is described in this way: "As they went in, under the light I saw white hands, wavy hair, white faces, grimacing, gesturing, talking" (28).

The cook is identified as a white man, so why does he bleach his skin? In Hemingway's time, skin-bleaching beauty products were widely available. One possibility is that Hemingway presents a sort of "passing" in which a character can pass across lines of race or sexuality that the young men find threatening. Throughout the story, white is beautiful: a little later, the whiteness of the "most beautiful man that ever lived" (295:27–28), Steve Ketchel, will be affirmed three times. Hemingway sets up a subtle contrast here. The cook may be visibly white; but, within the social hierarchy, his sexuality is his most salient feature, and from the moment the young men cross the threshold, he is devalued in turn.

293:28 Ever interfere with a cook?: The original manuscript gave "bugger" as the verb. Like "punk," "interfere with" is another sexual euphemism, most often applied to a minor, defined in this register in the *Oxford English Dictionary*: "to molest or assault sexually." The phrase, of a piece with legal euphemisms such as "criminal conversation" and "contributing to the delinquency of a minor," persists today as a criminal charge in some jurisdictions and remains more common in British than American usage. Once again, there is a flustering subcurrent of homosexuality that the young men seem ill-prepared for, and once again, appearances are shown to be less than trustworthy. Underpinning this anxiety about sexual norms in "The Light of the World" is the notion that the young men could be perceived as punks, desired by a punk, or be punked themselves. In a room with "five whores," they naïvely expect to be projecting male desire, not receiving it.

In this scene the notion of doing unto others is a strong subcurrent. Whether or not they are cognizant of it, Tom and the narrator have the tables turned on them: they are now the ones to be subjected to desire, the judgments of others, or even objectification. In this unsettled subjectivity, they have a small inkling of what it might be to stand in the place of a prostitute, or to be prostituted.

293:34–41 One of the whores . . . peroxide blondes: Those who read "Madame Tellier's Establishment" will notice de Maupassant describes the good Madame in terms very similar to Alice: "All the frequenters of the establishment made much of her; but people said that, personally, she was quite virtuous, and even the girls in the house could not discover anything against her. She was tall, stout and affable." Moreover, "[s]he was always smiling and cheerful, and was fond of a joke" but set off from the other prostitutes, since "she very frequently used to say that 'she and they were not made of the same stuff'" (55).

Like de Maupassant's Madame, Hemingway's Alice is brilliant, luminous, friendly, and corpulent. Her voice is distinctive and pleasant, and it is interesting that Alexandre-Jean-Baptiste Parent-Duchâtelet, the leading researcher on French prostitution in the nineteenth century, failed to discern a distinctive physiology for prostitutes and could only reduce shared characteristics to "plumpness and harsh voices" (Clayson 43).

A possible model for Peroxide (294:44, later distinguished from the lowercase peroxides introduced in this passage) also stands out in de Maupassant. Madame Tellier employs a staff of four "types" to appeal to all customers, including a fat, lazy "country girl" with "almost colorless, tow-like hair" (56). For his part, Hemingway refuses to elaborate on his story's "ordinary looking whores" beyond describing their size and hair color. Alice is the "biggest whore . . . and the biggest woman" (293:34–35); three of the prostitutes weigh in at over two hundred and fifty pounds (294:5). (Maupassant mentions that Fernande is "rather fat" and Rosa has "a little roll of fat"). A less historicist reading might take de Maupassant's plump Madame and Hemingway's fat Alice as the incarnation of the Madonna/Whore complex, their corpulence itself a fertility fetish.

293:44–45 **big disgusting mountain of flesh:** Note the peculiar turn of phrase, "mountain of flesh." It is reprised later in the story as "big mountain of pus" (296:42).

294:2 **Oh, my Christ:** One of the many blasphemies in the story—or is it in the nature of invocation and prayer on Alice's lips? Christ, after all, is the light of the world. Tommy swears "to Christ" a few lines later (294:15), in an ingenue's voice, that he has never before been to such a place. "Christ" is as much a trope of *Winner Take Nothing* as "nothing" and appears in the sort of prayer of "One Reader Writes," in which a woman's veteran husband returns with syphilis.

294:13 **Must be like getting on top of a hay mow:** The narrator shares in the shame here, as he will repeat the aspersion to Tommy. It might be significant, in the way that Hemingway's stories speak to each another, that some part of Nick's sexual education takes place during a wagon ride with the Garners in "Ten Indians." In that story, the Garners' earthy expression of sexual desire for one another contrasts with Nick's buttoned-up and mannered parents. Like "The Light of the World," "Ten Indians" also tacks between guilt and pleasure, while Nick's Indian girlfriend presents challenging questions about disparities of class and caste and how a white American of Nick's class and station should sow his wild oats and lose his virginity.

294:18 **I'm ninety-six and he's sixty-nine:** Credit the French for introducing *soixante-neuf* to American idiom; it had made its way into print by the late nineteenth century. Tommy's double entendre shows his eagerness to prove that he can be ribald too. Alice's solitary laughter—"Ho! Ho! Ho!" (294:19)—plays on *whore,* and, imponderably, Santa Claus, a jolly symbol of the Christian season marking the entry of light into the world. "God Rest You Merry, Gentlemen," the story that follows, is indeed set "on the day, the very anniversary, of our Saviour's birth" (300:44–45).

294:22 **"We're seventeen and nineteen," I said:** The narrator's honesty has little place in this world of adult doublespeak and alias, and it is not well received by Tommy. The cook is not deceived by the boys and serves as a peacemaker in the story. Far from having designs of "interference," he will plead for decency at 294:21 and to "speak decently" (295:10–11). Like Peroxide, though, he seems to cherish some romantic notions about the life that might be versus the life that he actually inhabits.

294:25 **You can call me Alice:** The ensuing banter is ambiguously shaded. It's not clear that the cook knows Alice well enough to know her real name, but the possibility is left open that it's not just the sort of name she'd have—it could be her real name. "Hazel" and "Ethel," common contemporaneous names she bequeaths to the others, could be the aliases of working girls. The impossibility of discerning the honest and the true in the world of the experienced is underscored again. With a view to the presence of the divine in the story, it might be noted that fear of exposure before judgment—whether human or final—can lead to the strange distortions of maturity and the desire for cover. Most of the characters in the story mask their sexual histories in various ways, with the notable exception of Alice.

294:34–35 **They weren't very bright:** The contrast is drawn both to Alice's inner luminosity and her wit.

294:40 **"What's yours?" I asked:** The bartender's question comes from the narrator's mouth now. Note that "what's yours?" is the bartender's question in "A Clean, Well-Lighted Place," too (291:16), and the preface to the exposure of various maladies and malaise. The other prostitutes are not interested in the teenagers' clumsy conversation and flirtation.

294:44 **Not with you:** Are the boys old enough to play on this field? Tommy will invoke a version of Peroxide's rejection—his words are "The other way from you" (297:14) at the end of the story. In Hemingway, there is pleasure in repetition, and this story shows how entire dialogues can be spun out of simple, repeated phrases.

294:45 **She's just a spitfire:** The reader can surmise that spitfire is likely a substitution for "bitch" here.

295:2 **"Goddamned mossbacks," she said:** "Mossback" sometimes referred to those, especially from the South, who avoided being conscripted during the Civil War by hiding out for its duration. But it can also refer to an old fish or turtle, or a very conservative or rustic person. This last seems the most likely register. The prostitutes might reclaim some measure of power by matching their clientele, insult for insult.

295:4 **There's nothing funny:** This is the only line of the story where the word *nothing* appears, in contrast to the stories that flank it. "Nothing" becomes a modernist mantra in *Winner Take Nothing*, a way of indicating the nihilism and absence of divine intervention that underwrites human experience. In the stories that bookend "The Light of the World," a kind of Lord's Prayer to nothingness is offered in "A Clean, Well-Lighted Place"—the old man is "in despair" about "Nothing" (288:11, 288:13)—and a sixteen-year-old tormented by lust is told, "There's "nothing wrong with you" (299:43–44) in "God Rest You Merry, Gentlemen."

The cook's pleas for dignity are not likely to find much traction with the crowd in the station. In de Maupassant's "Madame Tellier's," we learn that the Madame's "serious conversation was a change from the ceaseless chatter of the three women; it was a rest from the obscene jokes of those stout individuals who every evening indulged in the commonplace debauchery of drinking a glass of liqueur in company with common women" (55).

295:7 **I want to go to Cadillac:** Cadillac is a town in Michigan, about a two-hour drive from Petoskey, Hemingway's childhood summer haunts.

295:9–13 **He's a sister himself . . . the shy man said:** As mentioned earlier, "sister" (and the familiar "sissy") is a derogatory term for a gay man. The lame joke does not accord the cook the dignity he seeks. By implication, the shy man, one of the two lumberjacks who "listened, interested but bashful" (294:8), might be involved with the cook, as he tries to provide some conversational cover from homophobia here.

295:14–30 **Steve Ketchel . . . only man I ever loved:** In invoking Steve Ketchel as "the finest and most beautiful man that ever lived" (295:20–21), sacrificed by his father, and loved "like you love God" (295:26–27), the peroxide blonde calls up the Christian metanarrative at multiple levels in this dialogue. But Peroxide is hazy on the details, beginning with the man's name, and the implication is that her own fantasy and wishes are animating her vision.

In fact, Stanisław Kiecal (1886–1910), who went by Stanley Ketchel, was a real-life boxer known as "The Michigan Assassin." At the time when the teenaged Hemingway roamed Upper Michigan, Ketchel was a well-known figure in popular culture, having held the World Middleweight title before being murdered at twenty-four. Ketchel lived fast and died young after being shot and robbed by a vengeful ranch hand, Walter Dipley (1887–1956), who went by the alias Walter Kurtz. His accomplice, a woman named Goldie Smith who falsely claimed to be his wife, helped lure Ketchel into the ambush but ultimately served only seventeen months for the murder. Some sources suggest that the boxer was paying too much attention to Goldie. It is difficult to know how far to take these parallels, but Peroxide and Goldie would seem to be connected by name and ill repute.

Peroxide says that she "knew" Ketchel—playing perhaps on the biblical connotation of the word—before he moved to the West Coast in 1907. Given Ketchel's documented proclivity for prostitutes, her story is at least plausible—until the others pick it apart. "Wasn't his name Stanley Ketchel?" (295:18), the cook asks. Whether he catches out Peroxide has been a matter of contention for a number of Hemingway scholars; several have surfaced sources that suggest that Stanley was known as Steve to his friends.

295:40 **It was a trick. . . . That big dinge took him by surprise:** *Dinge* is a derogatory term for a black person. "Trick" refers to a prostitute's client or an act of prostitution. Here again, Peroxide's account is grounded in history. Ketchel's highly touted 1909 fight with Jack Johnson, an African American, was a sort of original "Great White Hope" matchup that placed white supremacy on the line. It played out more or less as described here, with Ketchel's knockdown of Johnson followed by a knockout of Ketchel.

In a letter to Howell Jenkins (20 March 1922), Hemingway used similarly derogatory language to describe the fight: "he was a swell battler but too small for that damned smoke" (*Letters vol. 1*, 334). It is widely assumed that the fight was fixed, with some contending that Ketchel's knockdown of Johnson was unscripted and a swaggering gesture.

Moreover, the carousing Johnson and Ketchel were no strangers to brothels. And if Peroxide was unwilling to take a black man as a client, one way to read between the lines in Hemingway's sly scene is that she might not have been above taking Ketchel for her trick.

295:31–33 Every one was very respectful. . . . I felt it sitting by her: Everyone was respectful—except for Alice, who recognizes that Peroxide's soliloquy is sentimental and vapid and more than likely an overblown figment of her imagination. Somewhat unusually for Hemingway, the text provides editorial interpretation for the action, tipping the balance by telling the reader that the recollection is delivered in a "high stagey way" (295:32).

295:44 He turned to smile at me: The consummation of Peroxide's story is the fabulist assertion that his affection for her was his downfall. Regardless of Peroxide's version of events, historical film footage of the fight does not show Ketchel flirting with anyone in the moment before his short-lived rebound.

295:45 I thought you said: For Ketchel to shine his favor on Peroxide at the match would have required her to be present in Colma, California, just south of San Francisco.

296:5 I hope to God he was: Peroxide invokes the name of God twice more in the ensuing dialogue (296:14, 296:21) and a reference to "Jesus" (296:32). "I hope to God" might be a euphemistic substitution for "swear to God." In any case, Ketchel is transfigured in these lines, as "like a god" (296:6), and even, in an animist way, for the second time, as "like a tiger or like lightning" (296:7)—as a force of nature in a moment when, without explanation, the Indians absent themselves from the scene. Peroxide insists on dualism of body and soul, perhaps a self-serving division given the prostitution of her body. Similarly, she sees marriage as validated only by God, and we might recall Matthew 22:30 here: "For in the resurrection they neither marry, nor are given in marriage, but are as the angels of God in heaven." The drumbeat of religious language is in keeping with the story's title and theme. Is Peroxide representing a false marriage, as Goldie did with Walter Dipley? Is she holding herself out as Mary Magdalene to Ketchel's Jesus?

Whatever the answer may be, it is clear that she's caught up in the momentum of her own story, and the evocation of Steve Ketchel initially lands powerfully on her audience, as they are "all very moved" (296:8–9). By contrast, the speech moves Alice because of its apparent inauthenticity: "I looked and saw she was crying" (296:9–10). It could be that she resists Peroxide's self-vindicating narrative; according to Hemingway's fair-play code, next-day regrets cannot reset virginity any more than self-pardon restores purity. One lives with the consequences.

296:15 Everybody felt terribly. It was sad and embarrassing. Finally, it seems that Peroxide goes too far in saying her soul belongs to Ketchel, laying bare an unseemly measure of self-prostration. Her worshipful attitude has the paradoxical effect of cheapening Peroxide and the memory of Steve Ketchel. Dissembling, false idols, pride, self-aggrandizement, self-deception: all are part of Peroxide's tale, leading ultimately to the denigration of her dignity and susceptibility to venality.

296:16 You're a dirty liar: Alice, who claims perhaps more plausibly to have known Ketchel, calls out Peroxide for her cheap sentimentalism and her pride in using Ketchel to elevate herself. Recall that Peroxide began her tale by calling Stanley Ketchel, "Steve" (295:14). Now the word that is repeated, and in contention, is "true" (296:19).

296:20 Mancelona: a small village in northern Michigan, about forty-five minutes south of Petoskey. In "The Battler," the freight train heads toward Mancelona after the brakeman throws Nick Adams off the side (*CSS* 98).

296:28 You're a lovely piece, Alice.: Peroxide will claim that this wasn't the way Ketchel talked. And yet its unvarnished directness and objectification have the ring of plausibility; after all, it is good-natured and indeed lovely Alice who acknowledges that Ketchel treated her like a prostitute.

In *The Sun Also Rises,* Mike Campbell compliments Brett Ashley similarly, by saying, "I say, Brett, you are a lovely piece" (85).

296:40–41 I *was* a lovely piece . . . you dried up old hot-water bottle: Alice asserts that she was (past tense) indeed lovely when she encountered Ketchel. We might see in this, more accurately, her desire to be loveable and loved. Hemingway has written the story to award this round of the fight to Alice. Her conviction and the change in her demeanor signal that she is telling the truth.

Calling Peroxide a "dried up old hot-water bottle" is a jab in several respects. The image is vaginal, but it is also a comment both on her disease-induced sterility and on the "cures" she may be taking. Alice will, a few lines later, assert that she is "clean" (297:1).

296:42 **You big mountain of pus.** Even after *Scribner's Magazine* rejected "The Light of the World" in part for its bad language, the potentially offensive phrase "mountain of pus" remained in *Winner Take Nothing*, whereas "bugger" and "up your ass" were replaced with euphemisms. The peculiar swipe that Peroxide takes at Alice when she calls her a "big mountain of pus" might point to another source. First, the obvious: *pus* connotes venereal disease, as does Alice's rejoinder suggesting that Peroxide's only "real memory" was of taking a cure for gonorrhea.

Similar language occurs in a possible literary precursor, Émile Zola's novel *Nana*, with another type-defining fleshy prostitute in the title role. Hemingway kept a 1941 paperback edition of Zola's 1880 classic in his Cuban library (Brasch and Sigman 414) but was familiar with Zola at least as early as 1932. In a 9 August 1932 letter to Paul Romaine, Hemingway opined, "Zola and Hugo were both lousy writers" (*Letters vol. 5*, 187). Paul Smith believes that Hemingway probably completed a first draft of "The Light of the World" in May or June 1932 (257), so his comment to Romaine may have followed on the heels of the story's completion.

The insult trading of Peroxide and Alice echoes a heated exchange between Nana and Count Muffat in Zola's novel. Nana explains how prostitutes do not steal men from "honest women," protesting, "they aren't even clean, your honest women aren't!" (trans. Davidow 195) "The Light of the World" echoes this passage insofar as Alice counts herself among the honest: "I never lie" (297:2).

If Hemingway used Nana as a source, he might have been most interested in the punitive death by smallpox that Zola concocted for her. Zola's description is notoriously stomach-turning, describing her syphilis-ridden body as "a heap of pus and blood, a shovelful of putrid flesh" (trans. Holden 470). "Mountain of pus" is an insult that seems to be unique to Hemingway in the American lexicon. It was not, and is not, a common expression. Regardless, comparisons with *Nana* can go only so far: the femme fatale that Nana represents is demonstrably different from the prostitute Nick finds so captivating.

296:45 **having your tubes out and when you started C. and M.:** Reader Milija Rubezanin had written to Hemingway asking him what C and M stand for, and, in his 17 May 1934 reply, he explained, "The reference in that story is to Cocaine and Morphine" (*Letters vol. 5*, 606). In "A Train Trip," when Jimmy asks if the two murder suspects on the train are "dope fiends," his father, in a voice reminiscent of Hemingway's father, says, "Many people use [dope]. But using cocaine or morphine or heroin doesn't make people talk the way they talked" (*CSS* 566). Class, education, morality, and addiction form a puzzling complex of issues to be parsed in a boy's mind and stand as an unsettling presence to middle-class respectability. In "The Light of the World," too, the protagonist peers more deeply into the way that euphemism, coarse language, and drug abuse are regimented by class and social station. Then, as now, opioids and stimulants might be counted as tools of both the medical and oldest profession. Perhaps the two often-prescribed and highly addictive painkillers were given in the wake of Peroxide's surgery; perhaps dependency followed in their wake. Regardless, it is a pointed insult. With her tubes "out," Peroxide is presumably infertile, whereas everything about Alice seems life-affirming.

297:4 Leave me with my memories . . . With my true, wonderful memories: Peroxide's hand-to-forehead melodrama reaches a high pitch here, and this line might offer readers some comic relief.

297:6–7 her face lost that hurt look and she smiled and she had about the prettiest face I ever saw: The story closes with Alice regaining her composure after suffering an attack, as she perceives it, on the sanctity of her soul. The transformation is not lost on Nick in this moment, and neither is Alice's inner beauty.

297:10–11 Tom saw me looking at her . . . "Good-bye," said Alice: Recall the aforementioned generosity of de Maupassant's Madame Tellier, who says to some of her clients, "We don't have a holiday every day" (67). Variants of the whore-with-a-heart-of-gold, neither de Maupassant's Madame nor Hemingway's Alice profane the day. Alice closes the story with a benison, saying "Good-bye" (297:11) to the narrator, an expression that means "God be with you." Having been ejected from the bar, Nick has had a holy day of his own with the revelation of the illustrious Alice. The lesson she bears, like her body, is almost too big for him to grasp.

297:14 "The other way from you," Tom told him: The closing line of the story is rich in irony and raises the question of whether merely asserting sexual orientation suffices or whether it must be satisfactorily "proven." It reminds us of an allegorical source for Tom's name, as well; as a doubting Thomas, Tom does not perceive what is in front of him. Tom seems to balk at the thought of Nick's pursuing Alice, perhaps leaving him alone with the others, including the cook. Going with one of the prostitutes would have been the avowedly heterosexual thing to do, and which way one "goes" could be a pointed question, coming from a homosexual. Moreover, Tom refuses once again to see that the light of the world could shine in such company. In the gospel of John, Jesus says, "Then spake Jesus again unto them, saying, I am the light of the world: he that followeth me shall not walk in darkness, but shall have the light of life" (8:12). Tom is determined to walk instead into the darkness of the cold Michigan night.

Jesus's "light of the world" phrase falls just after his refusal to pass judgment on a woman caught in adultery and his admonition to let those without sin cast the first stone. It is followed by his remonstrance to the Pharisees: "Ye judge by the flesh; I judge no man" (John 8:15).

The phrase "the light of the world" is held in unique balance in the gospels since it appears in a different way in Matthew via the Sermon on the Mount. Following the beatitudes and Jesus's reminder that "Blessed are ye, when men shall revile you, and persecute you, and shall say all manner of evil against you falsely, for my sake," he speaks of salt and light. Alice, to be sure, is the salt of the earth, and more, as Jesus says: "Ye are the light of the world. A city that is set on an hill cannot be hid. Neither do men light a candle, and put it under a bushel, but on a candlestick; and it giveth light unto all that are in the house. Let your light so shine before men, that they may see your good works, and glorify your Father which is in heaven" (Matthew 5:14–16).

Perhaps the most obvious reading of the story, then, is that Alice is in some sense the light of the world. Seeing the good in others, however "fallen" in the eyes of society, and suspending judgment are part of the Christian call. Notwithstanding her trade, Alice retains an unsullied purity of spirit, a cleanliness in a dirty world, and an adherence to the truth. She refuses to hide her light. The swaggering young men are unmanned by this luminous woman in a defiantly countercultural and deeply empathetic story about the worth and dignity of the socially "undesirable."

NOTES

The author wishes to express his gratitude to his readers, including Philip J. Kowalski, who provided important insights into queer readings of Hemingway; Verna Kale, who, through great persistence, sourced "C. and M." and helped document Hemingway's enduring concern with Ketchel; and Joseph Flora. Selected elements of this chapter were reproduced or condensed from my article "The French Connection," originally published in *The Hemingway Review* and sourced below.

1. Here and throughout, Bible quotations are from the King James Version on which Hemingway was raised.

WORKS CITED

Anderson, Sherwood. "The Man Who Became a Woman." *The Portable Sherwood Anderson*, edited by Horace Gregory, Viking, 1949, pp. 478–51.

Baker, Carlos. *Ernest Hemingway: A Life Story*. Scribner's, 1969.

The Bible. Authorized King James Version. OUP, 1998.

Brasch, James Daniel, and Joseph Sigman. *Hemingway's Library: A Composite Record*. Garland, 1981.

Clayson, Hollis. *Painted Love: Prostitution in French Art of the Impressionist Era*. Yale UP, 1991.

Collins, William J. "Taking on the Champion: Alice as Liar in 'The Light of the World.'" *Studies in American Fiction*, vol. 14, no. 2, 1986, pp. 225–32.

Dow, William. "*A Farewell to Arms* and Hemingway's Protest Stance: 'To Tell the Truth Without Screaming.'" *The Hemingway Review*, vol. 15, no.1, 1995, pp. 72–86.

Fleming, Robert E. "Myth or Reality: 'The Light of the World' as Initiation Story." *Hemingway's Neglected Short Fiction: New Perspectives*, edited by Susan F. Beegel, U of Alabama P, 1992, pp. 283–90.

Flora, Joseph M. *Ernest Hemingway: A Study of the Short Fiction.* Twayne, 1989.

———. *Hemingway's Nick Adams.* LSU Press, 1982.

Giemza, Bryan. "The French Connection: Some Visual and Literary Sources for the French Connection in Hemingway's 'The Light of the World.'" *The Hemingway Review,* no. 30, no. 1, 2010, pp. 82–102.

Hemingway, Ernest. *The Complete Short Stories of Ernest Hemingway: The Finca Vigía Edition.* Scribner's, 1987.

———. *Islands in the Stream.* Scribner's, 1997.

———. *The Letters of Ernest Hemingway: Volume 1 (1907–1922).* Edited by Sandra Spanier and Robert W. Trogdon. CUP, 2011.

———. *The Letters of Ernest Hemingway: Volume 5 (1932–1934).* Edited by Sandra Spanier and Miriam B. Mandel. CUP, 2020.

———. *The Short Stories of Ernest Hemingway: The Hemingway Library Edition.* Edited by Seán Hemingway. Scribner's, 2017.

———. *The Sun Also Rises.* 1926. Scribner's, 2003.

Hotchner, A. E. *Papa Hemingway: A Personal Memoir.* Random House, 1966.

Lynn, Kenneth. *Hemingway.* Simon and Schuster, 1987.

Martine, James J. "A Little Light on Hemingway's 'The Light of the World.'" *Studies in Short Fiction,* vol. 7, 1970, pp. 465–67.

Maupassant, Guy de. *The Best Short Stories.* Wordsworth Editions Ltd, 1997.

O'Toole, Garson. "There Ain't No Such Thing as a Free Lunch." *Quote Investigator,* Blog. 27 Aug. 2016. https://quoteinvestigator.com/2016/08/27/free-lunch/.

"punk, n.1 and adj.2." *OED Online,* OUP, September 2020.

Reynolds, Michael S. *Hemingway: The 1930s.* W. W. Norton, 1998.

———. *Hemingway's Reading, 1910–1940: An Inventory.* Princeton UP, 1981.

———. "Holman Hunt and 'The Light of the World.'" *Studies in Short Fiction,* vol. 20, no. 4, 1983, pp. 317–19.

Ross, Lillian. *Portrait of Hemingway.* 1961. Avon, 1965.

Schontzler, Gail. "Hunting for Hemingway in Yellowstone." *Great Falls Tribune,* 16 Aug. 2015, p. 1.

Smith, Paul. *A Reader's Guide to the Short Stories of Ernest Hemingway.* G. K. Hall, 1989.

Zola, Émile. *Nana.* 1880. Edited by Roger Ripoll. Garnier-Flammarion, 1968.

———. *Nana.* 1880. Translated by Leonard S. Davidow. Consolidated Book Publishers, 1937.

———. *Nana.* 1880. Translated by George Holden. Penguin, 1972.

GOD REST YOU MERRY, GENTLEMEN

Suzanne del Gizzo

There is no other way to say it: "God Rest You Merry, Gentlemen" is a weird, disturbing story. Two doctors, who don't like—or respect—each other very much, discuss with the narrator—whose real name may or may not be Horace—the story of a young boy, who has mutilated himself on Christmas Day. In addition to the bizarre central event of the story, the settings—a wasteland version of Kansas City in winter and an overheated hospital emergency room smelling strongly of cigarettes and carbolic acid—and the characters—an incompetent doctor, a disgraced but compassionate doctor, a confused young man, and a thinly described narrator—all border on the surreal. In this uncomfortable environment, the reader is asked to grapple with racial and ethnic stereotypes, problems with professionalism, and strong religious beliefs that contort individuals. It is, perhaps, not surprising, then, that most Hemingway readers and critics pass through this story rather quickly, but "God Rest You Merry, Gentlemen" rewards a closer look; in the end, the complex story invites readers into confusing misreadings/misunderstandings and inverted stereotypes that powerfully present the sinister side of accepted, normative beliefs.

First published as a stand-alone, limited-edition print run of 300 copies by Louis Henry Cohn's bookstore, House of Books, in April 1933 (the title of this edition, incidentally, did not include the comma), the story ultimately appeared as the fourth of fourteen stories in the short story collection *Winner Take Nothing*, published by Scribner's on 27 October 1933. Although a bizarre story, "God Rest You" fits comfortably in the collection; other stories include characters such as a "lesbian wife [in a heterosexual marriage]" and a "homosexual bullfighter," and themes such as "divorce, suicide, and death by water" (Reynolds, *1930s* 88). *Winner Take Nothing*, as the title indicates, is dark and full of loneliness and disconnection. The stories, however, also seem intent on challenging puritanical American beliefs about sex and intimacy; they show how normative beliefs can distort individuals and their relationships into grotesques, and they seem to cry out for importance of empathy in human relationships. In these raw stories, according to Michael Reynolds, Hemingway not only cemented his break away from the "genteel tradition" of literature, but he also "opened new possibilities in American fiction, a part of the landscape which his reading audience was not quite ready to explore" (*1930s* 88).

The stand-alone version of the story sold out, and *Winner Take Nothing* sold at a healthy rate, but "God Rest You" did not impress critics at the time and has not impressed scholars much since then. There are very few (roughly six, by my count) full-length articles about the story and only scant mention of it in other, longer works of Hemingway criticism. The current critical neglect is surprising: the story is brilliantly and hauntingly executed, and it addresses some of Hemingway's most enduring themes such as the quandaries of sexual desire, the importance of competence, the lures and dangers of exclusivity (morally, racially, religiously, among others), and the profound longing for love and connection in a hostile world. Critical response to the story, however, has ignored these broader themes and connections. Rather, critics have tended to approach the story as an oddity and focused on specific curiosities of the text, such as its title, the odd comparison between Kansas City and Constantinople in the opening paragraph, and the portrayal of the Jewish Doctor Fischer.

Shannon Whitlock Levitzke and Nicole Camastra explore the significance of the unusual comparison between Constantinople and Kansas City at the start of the story. Levitzke studies revisions to the story's manuscript to demonstrate that Hemingway's connection between the two cities was intended to evoke a sense of dirtiness and neglect, which creates a haunting "emotional climate" for the personal tragedy at the story's center (23). Camastra starts with George Monteiro's observation that the Christmas carol referenced in the story's title derives from a scriptural source that warns about Satan's power over the flesh in order to track the significance of Constantinople through the tradition of hymns and church music. She identifies the Hemingway family's connection to church music (Ernest's great-great-great-grandfather, Dr. Edward Miller, and his son William Edward Miller were prominent church musicians and composers in England) and discusses the role of castrati in religious music (castrati are strongly connected to the Byzantine Empire). Robert Paul Lamb and Horst Kruse address the portrayal of the Jewish Dr. Fischer and agree that, in this sympathetic portrayal, Hemingway may have wished to atone for his previous anti-Semitic characters such as Robert Cohn in *The Sun Also Rises* (1926). George Monteiro and Peter L. Hays highlight the conundrum over sexual desire, and Hays connects "God Rest You" to *The Sun Also Rises* through the motifs of the wasteland and the Fisher King (whose name, of course, is echoed in Dr. Fischer).

Important and perceptive as these critical interpretations are, they tend to miss the story's connection to other Hemingway works and themes. The specific concern with desire and genital mutilation recalls Jake Barnes's crisis in *The Sun Also Rises*. Whatever reluctance Hemingway had about describing Jake's wound, though, has disappeared. In this story, he confronts directly the loss of the penis; the story makes it clear that the boy did not know what it meant to "castrate" himself" and that he amputates his penis, rather than performing a orchiectomy. Unlike Jake's war wound, this act is intentionally performed because the boy wishes to stop feeling sexual urges, believing they are impure. The irony is heightened because if he lives, he will experience desire without the means to satisfy it. This dynamic allows the story to function as a powerful critique not only of extreme religious belief that causes self-loathing for a natural impulse but also of people's ignorance about their bodies and desires due to taboos concerning sex. In this way, the story resonates with another story in the collection, "Fathers and Sons," where an older Nick Adams recalls his father's prudish sexual advice: "His father had summed up the whole matter by stating that masturbation produced blindness, insanity, and death, while a man who went with prostitutes would contract hideous venereal diseases and that the thing to do was to keep your hands off of people" (371:23–26).

There is also the significance of the medical setting, which raises themes of competence and empathy that preoccupied Hemingway in a variety of ways throughout his career, but which are strongly reminiscent of "Indian Camp," in particular. In the earlier story, a young Nick Adams watches his father, a doctor, perform an emergency Caesarian section without anesthesia. The doctor proclaims that he does not hear his patient's screams because "they are not important" (*CSS* 68). Moreover, the brutality of the operation may be the cause of the husband's suicide in the bunk above as he had to witness this treatment of his wife. The doctor is presented as competent but callous and boastful, and even though the husband's suicide indicts this behavior, a young Nick seems to miss that point. In "God Rest You," Hemingway is fully prepared to reject the idea of callousness in medical treatment by associating it with the incompetent Doctor Wilcox.

In addition to these connections, "God Rest You" has a stylistic and linguistic complexity that few critics have appreciated. Lamb is the exception here. He has addressed the semiotic confusion and misreadings that inform the discombobulated, off-kilter world of the story. Still more important, as part of the dark *Winner Take Nothing*, this story captures a moment in Hemingway's career when he risked his popular success and presented some of the key themes in his writing in a particularly raw and powerful way.

Title: The title comes from one of the oldest extant English Christmas carols, dating from the sixteenth century, possibly earlier. The earliest known printed version of this carol, which is sometimes also called "Tidings of Comfort and Joy," is in a broadsheet dated to around 1760.

The transitive use of the verb "rest" is archaic and means "to remain" or "to stay," which was a common usage in sixteenth- and seventeenth-century English. The comma is placed after "merry," so the "gentlemen" addressed are encouraged to "rest merry" or to "remain merry."

The scriptural source for the Christmas carol is likely "the physician Luke's account of Satan's power over the flesh and the Savior's role in keeping men safe from that power" (Monteiro, "Christmas Carol" 208). The carol exhorts listeners to remain merry or at peace/happy and not to be dismayed because Jesus Christ, the savior, has been born, and he will save all "men" from evil and "Satan's power." The song, thus, brings "tidings" or news of "comfort and joy" since all "men" will be forgiven even if they go "astray."

The positive message of the carol conflicts with the bleak events of the story in which a boy of about sixteen attempts to castrate himself because he believes his burgeoning feelings of sexual desire are sinful; he reports that he "pray[s] all night about it" but "nothing helps" (299:37). Rather than finding "comfort and joy" through his belief in the Christian religion, the young boy finds shame for, fear of, and alienation from his body. In this way, the story appears critical of the way religion can be used to make people feel embarrassed about or ashamed of their bodies and their desires.

298:1–3 **In those days . . . Constantinople:** The opening lines of the story make a puzzling comparison between Kansas City and Constantinople. They do clearly indicate, however, that the story is narrated at some temporal distance from the events and that the location is Kansas City.

Hemingway was familiar with Kansas City from his time as a cub reporter with the *Kansas City Star* from October 1917 until April 1918. As a young reporter, he covered a beat that included the 15th Street police station, the Union Station, and the General Hospital. He wrote about crime, accidents, and the transience of people passing through the train station. As a result, many critics, such as Levitzke and Steve Paul have observed that Kansas City figures in his fiction as a site of morally questionable behavior.

Hemingway returned to or traveled through the city periodically throughout his adult life, most notably for the births of his sons Patrick in 1928 and Gregory in 1931. During his 1931 sojourn, he befriended Dr. Logan Clendening, a syndicated medical columnist. Carlos Baker speculates that "God Rest You" is based on a letter Clendening received "from a youth in West Englewood, New Jersey, who had spent many years worrying about the problem of sexual desire" (227). Another story in *Winner Take Nothing*—"One Reader Writes"—also draws inspiration from Hemingway's relationship with Clendening and his interest in the doctor's correspondence.

Constantinople was the capital city of the Roman Empire (330–95), the Byzantine Empire (395–1204 and again 1261–1453), the brief Latin empire of Constantinople (1204–1261), and the later Ottoman Empire (1453–1923). The ancient Byzantium became the new capital of the Roman Empire; it was renamed Constantinople in honor of the Roman emperor Constantine the Great and dedicated in 330.

Hemingway probably recognized that readers would find Constantinople exotic; however, he had visited the city while covering the Greco-Turkish War as a correspondent for the *Toronto Star* in 1922 and had found it dirty and dusty. He wrote several articles, including "Constantinople, Dirty White, Not Glistening and

Sinister," which challenges the romantic idea of the city most people have from the movies or paintings.

The comparison of Kansas City to Constantinople is puzzling, as the narrator acknowledges, "No one believes this; but it is true" (298:4). The comparison hinges on a shared image of "dirt [blowing] off the hills" (298:2). The result is an opening scene that presents a somber picture of Kansas City in the "early dark" (298:5), snow, and dirt; it creates a landscape that feels deserted and lonely, a place where men eat free turkey dinners with strangers on Christmas.

This bleak, wasteland-like setting prompted Peter L. Hays to suggest that the story is a retelling of the Fisher King myth, but "the roles in the tale of a fisher king wounded in the genitals, and healed by a young, pure knight, have been divided and reassigned: it is the young innocent who is wounded, and it is the fis(c)her who is the healer" (227).

Nicole Camastra argues that the comparison between Kansas City and Constantinople makes more sense in light of the story's concern with castration and Christianity, since "the use of castrated boys in church choirs and the subsequent tradition of employing them in Italian opera had their inception in fifth-century Byzantium" (51).

298:6 **Dans Argent:** The narrator "believed" these French words on a car he admires to mean "silver dance or the silver dancer" (298:7–8), but the phrase actually means "in silver." This mistranslation introduces the theme of "misreading" in the story. It also introduces the theme of smugness even when misreading, as the narrator recalls that he is "pleased by [his] knowledge of a foreign language" (298:9).

298:7 **I:** The "I" abruptly introduces of the narrator; his name, it is later revealed through conversation, is most likely Horace. The narrator is curious, a thin, undeveloped character. It is also unclear why he is visiting the hospital since he does not appear to work there. Some critics, such as Levitzke, suggest he is a reporter, probably because Hemingway served as a reporter in Kansas City and because Horace was the name of a well-known Roman poet, but there is no textual evidence to support this assumption.

298:10 **Woolf Brothers' saloon:** Hemingway here is likely referring to Wolf's saloon. According to a footnote (68n1) to a letter that references Wolf's in volume 1 of *The Letters of Ernest Hemingway (1907–1922)*, a 1917 directory listed Wolf's Famous Place at 117 W. Ninth St. and Wolf's Famous New Place at 1327 Grand Ave., about four blocks north of the *Kansas City Star*. Hemingway also refers to it in a letter to his family on 30 November 1917: "Yesterday was Thanksgiving but I worked all day. We all went to Woolf's famous place where they served a 5c pig and turkey dinner at noon. All the reporters went up" (*Letters vol. 1*, 67–68).

However, the misspelling ties the saloon to the then prominent Woolf brothers,

Alfred and Samuel, who came to Kansas from New York after the Civil War and founded a store that made and sold fine men's shirts in Leavenworth; they and the store relocated to Kansas City in 1879. Alfred's son, Herbert Morris Woolf, worked his way up in the business and became president of the company in 1915. Under his leadership, the store expanded and became one of the finest luxury department store chains in the Midwest. The Woolfs were Jewish, and Herbert was a cousin of Leonard Woolf, a British political theorist and husband of novelist Virginia Woolf. There is, in reality, no relation between the Wolf Saloon and the Woolf Brothers, but the decision to call it the Woolf Brothers Saloon does introduce the theme of Jewishness, a theme that is intensified because Doc Fischer is Jewish. Since the story takes place on Christmas Day, a Christian holiday, the Jewish character and references highlight the feeling of alienation and marginalization in the story. It is also notable that this story features, according to Jeremy Kaye, arguably the "most sympathetic" Jewish character Hemingway ever created (344). Robert Paul Lamb suggests this "may have been Hemingway's attempt to apologize for his treatment of Harold Loeb [in *The Sun Also Rises*]" (32).

298:12 **city hospital:** Probably based on the General Hospital with which Hemingway would have been familiar from his time as a reporter. According to Steve Paul, the story is set in General Hospital No. 1 (the white folks' hospital), which stood at 23rd and Locust, roughly the site now occupied by Children's Mercy Hospital, which is part of the larger Hospital Hill complex.

298:14 **ambulance surgeons:** Ambulance surgeons are today known as emergency room surgeons. The concept of the "ambulance surgeon" appears to have originated with Red Cross surgeons who operated on battlefields and in ambulances.

298:14–15 **Doc Fischer and Doctor Wilcox:** This first reference to the doctors reveals the narrator's affection for and connection to Fischer through the use of the informal "Doc," whereas Wilcox remains "Doctor." Fischer's name (which is alternately spelled Fischer and Fisher in the only extant version of the story found in *The Complete Short Stories of Ernest Hemingway*) marks him as Jewish. The name Wilcox may be a pun given the story's focus on the amputation of a willful penis. A draft of the story in folder #428 in the Hemingway Collection at the John F. Kennedy Library in Boston confirms Hemingway's intentionality with the names. The original names were "Fisher" and "Cox" and a note at the top says "correct names to Fischer and Wilcox" with a circle around the two surnames.

The physical descriptions of the doctors also create a sense of confusion and inversion. Fischer, who is Jewish, is presented as "sand-blond" (298:16), and the gentile Wilcox is described as "short" and "dark" and carrying a book (298:17–18), thus reversing physical stereotypes.

298:17 **gambler's hands:** This description refers to Doc Fischer's hands. At this point in the story, the meaning of this reference is unclear; however, later it becomes apparent that he took risks that remain unspecified as a doctor when practicing on the East Coast (see entry at 301:6–11). The reference also points to "The Gambler, the Nun, and the Radio," a story that tackles issues of religion, vice, and empathy and that was also included in *Winner Take Nothing.*

298:18 *The Young Doctor's Friend and Guide:* I cannot find evidence of the existence of this book, but Doctor Wilcox, the gentile doctor who is presented as incompetent and unempathetic, carries this book with him. In fact, the reader is told Dr. Wilcox was advised by one of his professors: "you have no business being a physician and I have done everything in my power to prevent you from being certified as one. Since you are now a member of this learned profession I advise you, in the name of humanity, to obtain a copy of *The Young Doctor's Friend and Guide,* and use it, Doctor Wilcox. Learn to use it" (298:27–299:2).

Readers are also told that Dr. Wilcox "was sensitive about this book but could not get along without it" (298:24–25). The book indexes symptoms and treatments on a variety of subjects, and it is "also cross-indexed so that being consulted on symptoms it gave diagnoses" (298:19–20). Moreover, Doc Fischer highlights Doctor Wilcox's inability by joking that "future editions should be further cross-indexed so that if consulted as to the treatments being given, it would reveal ailments and symptoms" (298:21–23). The introduction of the book and Fischer's jokes about it establish the dynamic between the two doctors: the capable, kind, sympathetic Fischer and the incompetent, serious, and surly Wilcox.

Moreover, the book is described as being "bound in limp leather" (298:25). The word "limp" further suggests not only the subject of the story—a decidedly unlimp penis that distresses the young boy—but also Dr. Wilcox's impotence in helping the young man.

299:5 **Horace:** The name Doc Fischer uses to greet the narrator. It may or may not be the narrator's actual name since later on Doc Fischer asks him "you don't mind me calling you Horace, do you?" (299:22–23). The name associates the narrator with a well-known classical author; "Horace" is addressed for the first time by Doc Fischer, and their other exchanges suggest they have a warm friendship not shared by Dr. Wilcox.

299:6 **cigarettes, iodoform, carbolic and an overheated radiator:** Iodoform is a pale-yellow crystalline substance with a distinctive odor (sometimes referred to as the smell of hospitals). It is occasionally used as a disinfectant and was commonly used as an antiseptic for wounds and sores. Carbolic is a mildly antiseptic soap made of carbolic acid or cresylic acid. This sentence creates the distinctive atmosphere of the hospital, which is both clean (iodoform and carbolic) and dirty (cigarettes) and hot and intense with the overheated radiator. It captures the tense, conflicted atmosphere of the boy's story and his interactions with the hospital staff.

299:8 **What news along the rialto?:** This line from William Shakespeare's *The Merchant of Venice* (1.3.33, 3.1.1), which Hemingway also uses in *Across the River and into the Trees,* is spoken by Shylock, a Jewish moneylender and the antagonist of the play. In this way, it references Jewishness and anti-Semitic portrayals of characters. The line also plays with location of the story as did the earlier reference to Constantinople, this time by referencing an area of Venice, Italy; the Rialto is the financial and commercial heart of Venice. The reference illustrates Doc Fischer's knowledge of the world and playfulness with the narrator, as well as introducing a reference to anti-Semitism, which becomes more pronounced later in the story. The line's reference to a vital and bustling part of Venice also contrasts sharply with the deserted wasteland of the opening lines.

299:10 **The free turkey at Woolf's:** This second reference to the Woolf Brothers' saloon (see 298:10) emphasizes the irony of a saloon owned by Jewish brothers providing a "free" Christmas dinner, continuing the play between Judaism and Christianity seen throughout the story. The subsequent dialogue suggests a lonely Christmas, spent drinking with strangers in a saloon, rather than with family, a detail that reinforces the somber, dark atmosphere of the story—and indeed the entire collection—in which people seem alienated from each other and themselves.

299:13 **Many of the confrères present?:** "Confrères" is a French word for colleagues or fellow members of a profession. The narrator's profession is not clear, but the context suggests that Doc Fischer is using this term playfully to mean other people who enjoy drink. Doc Fischer euphemistically asks, "You partook?" (299:11) to which "Horace" responds, "Copiously" (299:12) at the Christmas dinner at Woolf's. However, the narrator's next line suggests, in contrast to the reference to the confrères present, the saloon was nearly empty; he says, "All of them. The whole staff" (299:14). These details add to the sense of a sad, lonely atmosphere of the Christmas holiday in the story, since the doctors are working as is the staff in the saloon, and "Horace" is drinking with strangers at a saloon, and Doctor Wilcox is drinking at work.

In addition, Doc Fischer's use of words like "confrères," "partook," and "Yuletide" (299:13, 299:11, 299:15) indicate his intelligence as well as his playfulness with the narrator, traits that contrast sharply with Wilcox's incompetence and dourness.

299:15 **Much Yuletide cheer?:** "Yule" is an archaic term for Christmas. The "cheer" here seems to move away from the references to drink and refer to "happiness" or "joy" because, although "Horace" admits to partaking "copiously" above, here he says there was "[n]ot much" (299:16) Yuletide cheer.

299:17 **Doctor Wilcox here has partaken slightly:** An allusion to the fact the Doctor Wilcox has been drinking, one of the first signs that he is in distress over something that has happened.

299:29 **eunuch-hood:** A eunuch is a man who has been castrated, or—and this meaning points to Doctor Wilcox—an ineffectual person. Wilcox and the young boy are connected in several ways, both are eunuchs—albeit, in different ways—and the name Wilcox appears to pun the boy's willful penis and his willful decision to cut it off, as well as Wilcox's own willful decision to become a doctor in the face of advice that he should not.

299:30–31 **He was a boy about sixteen:** The boy's age strongly indicates that he is in the midst of puberty and thus experiencing strong sexual urges due to increased levels of testosterone.

299:32–33 **He was curly haired and well built and his lips were prominent.** This description presents the boy physically with emphasis on his "curly" hair, muscular build, and large lips. The sensuality of the description suggests the boy's body is both desirous and desiring, that his body is preparing for sexual activity. Also, due to common stereotypical depictions at the time, Hemingway presents the possibility of an ethnic or racial othering in these lines due to the prominent lips and curly hair. Although there is not enough information to conclude with complete confidence that the boy is ethnically or racially "other," the possibility is intriguing given the association between racial and ethnic others and sexual potency that provided a troubling rationale for white supremacist behavior, especially in the beginning of the twentieth century.

299:35 **I want to be castrated:** This line introduces the main drama of the story; this young boy wants the doctors to castrate him because he feels what he calls "[t]hat awful lust" (299:39). He also tells the doctors that he prays "all night about it" (299:41) and that he has "prayed" and "done everything and nothing helps" (299:37). These lines indicate that his religious views lead him to believe that his body's development and his subsequent sexual thoughts are morally wrong or sinful. Doc Fischer singles himself out again as the compassionate, capable doctor when he asks the boy about what happens. Once the boy explains, Doc assures him, "There's nothing wrong with you. That's the way you're supposed to be. There's nothing wrong with that" (299:43–45).

300:1–2 **It's a sin against purity. It's a sin against our Lord and Saviour:** The boy repeats his conviction that his sexual feelings and desires are immoral, and Doc Fischer again assures the boy that his experiences are natural and that someday he will think he is "very fortunate" (300:4). These lines anticipate the boy's later remark: "It is a sin, a constant sin against purity" (300:18).

This exchange continues for quite some time as Doc tells the boy "certain things" (300:6). These things are left unsaid, but they are presumably guidance about sex and the benefits and pleasures of sexual desire and the sex act. Doc Fischer even tries to comfort the boy using religion; he says, "If you are religious remember that what you complain of is no sinful state but the means of consummating a sacrament" (300:15–16). It is notable that it is the Jewish Dr. Fischer who reminds the boy that sexual desire is the way one consummates that sacrament of marriage. In the Christian church, sacraments are regarded as outward and visible signs of inward and spiritual divine grace. It is also notable that matrimony is a sacrament in the Roman Catholic and Orthodox churches and not the Protestant church (the only sacraments for Protestants are Baptism and the Eucharist). Hemingway was raised Protestant but converted to Catholicism, although he called himself a bad Catholic. In a letter to Ernest Walsh in 1926, Hemingway claimed, "If I am anything I am a Catholic." He continued, referencing his wounding on the Italian Front in 1918, "Had extreme unction administered to me as such in July 1918 and recovered" (*Letters vol. 3*, 7). Reynolds observes that Hemingway's rediscovery of his Catholicism was likely helped along by his relationship with Pauline Pfeiffer, a devout Catholic (*Paris Years* 346).

300:9 **"You're just a goddamned fool," Doctor Wilcox said to the boy:** During the long, compassionate exchange between Fischer and the boy, Wilcox's interjection reveals that he is frustrated with the youth; he even belittles him, calling him a "fool" rather than attempting to console the boy and explain his situation to him.

300:19 **"Oh, go and——" Doctor Wilcox said:** Doctor Wilcox again demonstrates his frustration with the boy as well as his lack of empathy as a doctor throughout this piece of dialogue. In the version printed by Scribner's, the first line of this dialogue appears with a dash; however, the smaller run printed by House of Books includes the words "jack off" in place of the dash. Wilcox dismisses the boy again, casually and crassly offering masturbation as a remedy to the boy's distress. This suggestion evidently further offends his religious sensibilities, as is indicated by the boy's rejection: "When you talk like that I don't hear you" (300:20). After appealing to Doc Fischer to perform the operation one last time, which Fischer refuses politely to do, Doctor Wilcox impatiently says, "Get him out of here" (300:23).

300:27–33 **So at one o'clock this morning . . . we receive the youth self-mutilated with a razor. . . . Loss of blood:** The tragic consequences of the story are revealed in these lines. The young boy comes back to the emergency room after attempting to castrate himself with a razor. However, when the narrator asks if the boy was

"Castrated?" (300:29), Doc Fischer explains, "No. . . . He didn't know what castrate meant" (300:30). In his ignorance, the boy cut off his penis rather than his testicles, a reading further supported when Doc Fischer explains to the narrator, "It was an amputation the young man performed" (300:40–41). Unwittingly, the boy has preserved the male sex organs that cause sexual desire and drive (the testicles), while removing the penis, which is the organ through which sexual desire is expressed and released. Unfortunately, the boy, if he lives, will still experience the "awful lust" (299:39) he was trying to eradicate. However, as Doc Fischer explains to the narrator, the boy "may die" (300:31) due to "[l]oss of blood" (300:33). This misunderstanding of castration recalls the narrator's earlier mistranslation of "Dans Argent" and the fact that misreadings are central to the story.

300:35 **he was unable to find this emergency listed in his book:** Doc Fischer suggests the Doctor Wilcox's incompetence may have caused this tragic event because the "emergency" was not listed in *The Young Doctor's Friend and Guide,* on which readers have been told Doctor Wilcox relies. However, the exact nature of the incompetence is left unclear—was it incompetence when the boy returned by not treating him quickly enough? Or was it, as Doc Fischer's dialogue indicates, that Doctor Wilcox's lacked empathy and gentleness in dealing with the boy earlier in the evening because his guidebook addresses only physical symptoms and not how to interact with patients compassionately?

300:38–39 **his hands that had, with his willingness to oblige and his lack of respect for Federal statutes, made him his trouble:** This line hearkens back to the line about Doc Fischer's "gambler's hands" (298:17) earlier in the story and, coupled with the later reference that he had been "[t]oo damned smart on the coast" (301:7–8), implies a back story for Doctor Fischer. The "lack of respect for Federal statutes" (300:39) suggests that Doc Fischer performed abortions when on the coast and that this "gamble" led to professional marginalization, resulting in his presence in Kansas City. Robert Paul Lamb observes that abortion, however, would have fallen under state not federal statues, but he believes "it is quite possible that Hemingway was simply unaware of this." In addition, as Lamb explains, the self-mutilation caused when women attempted a self-induced abortion, which may have compelled Doc to help them, connects to the theme of self-mutilation in the story. Lamb also points out that the only other possible meaning for these lines is that Doc Fischer performed euthanasia, but he dismisses this reading: "it is difficult to believe that [Fischer] would have avoided jail and/or the loss of his medical license" (29).

300:42–301:5 **Well, I wish you wouldn't ride me about it . . . and the ride for Palm Sunday:** The word "ride" evolves in this passage from the playful meaning of "tease" or "cajole" to a reference to the fact that Jesus rode a donkey (or an ass) on

Palm Sunday, indirectly associating Doctor Wilcox with the ass. The evolution of meaning pivots on Doc Fischer's allusion to "the very anniversary, of our Saviour's birth" (300:44–45). Doctor Wilcox asks, "*Our* Saviour? Ain't you a Jew?" (301:1). Wilcox's blunt questions, however, are not important to Doc Fischer, who does not seem to be particularly religious and who claims to have "never given it [religion] its proper importance" (301:2–3).

301:6–11 **You're too damned smart. . . . The hell with you:** As Lamb notes, Doctor Wilcox's "two trademark responses ("The hell with you" [300:36, 301:11] and "You're too damned smart" [301:6, 301:25]), each uttered twice in the story, have particular import for Fischer as expressions of cultural hostility to his ethnicity. The former implies that, as a Jew, he has been damned to hell by the mainstream religious culture. The latter appeals to the stereotype of the "smart Jew" (31). In addition, as a Jew, Doc Fischer presumably doesn't believe in hell. Lamb also observes that, for Doc Fischer, hell "happens on earth," and the boy's experience was a hell on earth in response to his fear of being banished to hell for his lust; thus, Fischer's comments about hell suggest the "communal responsibility for the boy's tragedy" beyond Wilcox's obvious incompetence (32).

301:18–24 **On Christmas Day, too. . . . the doctor pursues his advantage:** Doctor Wilcox laments that the boy mutilated himself on Christmas, a traditionally happy or "merry" holiday, but Doc Fischer's retort, "The significance of the particular day is not important" (301:19), allows the boy's suffering and pain to transcend a particular faith. Wilcox, according to Lamb, "can only express a distorted and bigoted version of Christianity that defines itself through exclusivity" and not transcendent love (32). The piece ends with Wilcox irredeemably exclusive and unwilling to appreciate the scope of the tragedy that has occurred or the communal responsibility for it.

WORKS CITED

Baker, Carlos. *Ernest Hemingway: A Life Story.* Scribner's, 1969.

Camastra, Nicole J. "Hemingway's Modern Hymn: Music and the Church as Background Sources for 'God Rest You Merry, Gentlemen.'" *The Hemingway Review,* vol. 28, no.1, 2008, pp. 51–67.

Hays, Peter L. "Hemingway and the Fisher King." *The University Review,* vol. 32, no. 3, 1966, pp. 225–28.

Hemingway, Ernest. *The Complete Short Stories of Ernest Hemingway: The Finca Vigía Edition.* Scribner's, 1987.

———. *The Letters of Ernest Hemingway: Volume 1 (1907–1922).* Edited by Sandra Spanier and Robert W. Trogdon. CUP, 2011.

———. *The Letters of Ernest Hemingway: Volume 3 (1926–1929).* Edited by Rena Sanderson, Sandra Spanier, and Robert W. Trogdon. CUP, 2015.

Kaye, Jeremy. "Race and Ethnicity: Jews." *Hemingway in Context,* edited by Debra A. Moddelmog and Suzanne del Gizzo, CUP, 2012, pp. 339–46.

Kruse, Horst H. "Allusions to *The Merchant of Venice* and the New Testament in 'God Rest You Merry, Gentlemen': Hemingway's Anti-Semitism Reconsidered." *The Hemingway Review,* vol. 25, no. 2, 2006, pp. 61–75.

Lamb, Robert Paul. "Hemingway's Critique of Anti-Semitism: Semiotic Confusion in 'God Rest You Merry, Gentlemen.'" *Studies in Short Fiction,* vol. 33, no. 1, 1996, pp. 25–35.

Levitzke, Shannon Whitlock. "'In Those Days the Distances Were All Very Different': Alienation in Ernest Hemingway's 'God Rest You Merry, Gentlemen.'" *The Hemingway Review,* vol. 30, no. 1, 2010, pp. 18–30.

Monteiro, George. "Hemingway's Christmas Carol." *The Fitzgerald/Hemingway Annual,* 1972, pp. 207–13.

———. *The Hemingway Short Story: A Critical Appreciation.* McFarland, 2017.

Paul, Steve. *Hemingway at Eighteen: The Pivotal Year That Launched an American Legend.* Chicago Review P, 2018.

Reynolds, Michael. *Hemingway: The Paris Years.* Norton, 1998.

———. *Hemingway: The 1930s.* Norton, 1998.

Shakespeare, William. *The Norton Shakespeare.* 2nd ed. Norton, 2008.

THE SEA CHANGE

Carl Eby

Since the posthumous publication of Hemingway's unfinished novel *The Garden of Eden* in 1986, "The Sea Change"—until then a comparatively neglected story—has emerged as an important work in the Hemingway canon. In some ways an almost capsule version of the novel Hemingway would begin to write more than fifteen years later, "The Sea Change" packs into a very tight space a hint of the plot and many of the erotic symbols and obsessions that preoccupy Hemingway in his late novel: love triangles, lesbian affairs, sun-bleached closely cropped hair, deep suntans, erotic throat swelling, twin-like lovers, the experience of dissociation in front of mirrors, and mysterious "sea changes." And if we consider "The Sea Change" manuscript, to this constellation we can add sibling romance and anxiety about male homosexuality.

But as much as it prefigures, and is retroactively illuminated by, Hemingway's later work, "The Sea Change"—the story of a young woman leaving her male partner to have a lesbian affair and of the transformation produced by this in the man—fits smoothly into the thematic flow of *Winner Take Nothing*. The collection is unified by what Hemingway's contemporaries might have regarded as a *Waste Land*-ish strand of psychological and sexual malaise: "A Clean, Well-Lighted Place" (depression); "The Light of the World" (prostitution); "God Rest You Merry, Gentlemen" (sexual self-mutilation); "A Way You'll Never Be" (PTSD—and male homosexuality trimmed out of the manuscript); "The Mother of a Queen" (male homosexuality); "One Reader Writes" (syphilis); "Homage to Switzerland" (misogyny concealing male homosexuality or sexual fear); and "The Sea Change" (lesbianism and male attraction to it). The theme culminates in the volume's final story, "Fathers and Sons," where the lovemaking of Nick and Trudy in the Edenic forest seems to code young Nick, by contrast with so many of the collection's other characters, as heteronormative and "natural." However, the older Nick's recognition that his father's sexual advice had been both "cruel" (370:24) and "unsound" (370:31)—Dr. Adams confuses homosexuality and bestiality and seems to consider any "nonnormative" sexuality "one of the most heinous of crimes" (371:17)—not to mention young Nick's desire to do something nonnormative himself someday ("mashing," as he misunderstands it), suggests that the older Nick has a broader, better-informed, and less cruel appreciation for the complexity and range of human sexuality. Since Nick is a well-established persona and stand-in for Hemingway, he may even be regarded, much as he has been for *In Our Time* (Moddelmog), as the implied author of *Winner Take Nothing*, so that his broader view of human sexuality functions as a judgment informing the rest of the book. The stories of *Winner Take Nothing*, through a layer of dispassionate presentation, an unsentimental compassion for those commonly coded as nonnormative, and the contrast between younger and older Nick—with the older Nick fleshed out by the entire content of *Winner Take Nothing*—may relegate the notion of normativity to a mythic Eden that is always already lost. "The Sea Change" contributes importantly to establishing this broader view of human sexuality. When Phil tries to dismiss his partner's lesbian desire as "perversion" (304:10), insisting "That's the name for it" (304:24), she rejects the term and responds, "You don't have to put any name to it. . . . We're all made up of all sorts of things. You've known that. You've used it well enough" (304:23, 25–26). And this *does* help Phil to understand.

The four different stories Hemingway told about the origins of "The Sea Change" should collectively serve as a cautionary tale for readers inclined to take Hemingway's origin stories for his fiction at face value. In a 17 November 1933 letter to Maxwell Perkins, Hemingway claimed he wrote some stories "absolutely as they happen," while "others [he] invent[ed] completely." "The Sea Change," he assures Perkins, is one of the latter (*Letters vol. 5,* 542). In a 1952 letter to Edmund Wilson, Hemingway claimed—in a ridiculous yarn—that the story was enabled, if not inspired, by a conversation with Gertrude Stein:

> She talked to me once for three hours telling me why she was a lesbian, the mechanics of it, why the act did not disgust those who performed it (she was at this time against male homosexuality but changed later out of patriotism) and why it was not degrading to either participant. Three hours is a long time with Gertrude crowding you and I was so sold on her theory that I went out that night and fucked a lesbian with magnificent results; i.e. we slept well afterwards. It was this knowledge, gained from G.S., that enabled me to write A Sea Change, which is a good story, with authority. (*SL* 795)

Hemingway's supposed prowess at seducing lesbians aside, if "The Sea Change" relies on an awareness of the "mechanics" of lesbian sexuality, such iceberg content remains deeply submerged. Hemingway did, however, hold up the story as an exemplar of his iceberg theory.[1] In "The Art of the Short Story"—an abandoned 1959 introduction for a projected student edition of his stories (written when he was working on *The Garden of Eden*)—Hemingway tells a quite different origin story for "The Sea Change"—one that he repeated with a slight variation to A. E. Hotchner:

If you leave out important things or events that you know about, the story is strengthened. If you leave or skip something because you do not know it, the story will be worthless. The test of any story is how very good the stuff is that you, not your editors, omit. . . . In a story called 'The Sea Change,' everything is left out. I had seen the couple in the Bar Basque in St. Jean-de-Luz and I knew the story too too well, which is the squared root of well. . . . So I left the story out. But it is all there. It is not visible but it is there. ("Art of Short Story" 88)

For Hotchner, Hemingway identified the male of this couple as the novelist and journalist Charles Wertenbaker and called the woman "the most beautiful girl I ever laid eyes on," adding as a postscript that he later saw "Charley's girl walking along the beach with the girl she had gone to," who was not "a typical bull-dyke" but was "as pretty as Charley's girl" (128).

Whatever we think of these incompatible origin stories, they collectively suggest that Hemingway felt both a need to account for the origins of "The Sea Change" and a desire to mask those origins. This may be because, within *Winner Take Nothing*'s exploration of the varieties of sexual experience, "The Sea Change" comes closest to Hemingway's own desires, later explored at such length in *The Garden of Eden*. (See Eby's *Hemingway's Fetishism*.) A letter of 29 October 1930 suggests Hemingway may have begun the story as early as the autumn of 1929 (*Letters vol. 4*, 394), a few months after Pauline Pfeiffer first dyed her hair blonde as a surprise for him during their seaside stay at Hendaye (Kert 219; Reynolds 17). In the letter, Hemingway told Ray Long, editor at *Cosmopolitan,* that he had three stories finished but he'd be "afraid to even send them through the mail let alone ask you to publish them." With the memory of how *A Farewell to Arms* had been banned in Boston still fresh in his mind, Hemingway told Long that he'd have to print these stories in a "special asbestos edition" (*Letters vol. 4,* 394)—yet "The Sea Change" and the sexual content of *Winner Take Nothing* also seem to have been a provocative riposte to precisely such censorship. Hemingway played with the idea of sending "The Sea Change" as one of "Three Love Stories" to bait Henry G. Leach, who, as editor of *The Forum*, had solicited stories using a form letter with conservative un-Hemingwayesque advice about the formal properties of fiction (Smith 223). Instead, Hemingway sent the story to Edward W. Titus, who published it in the December 1931 issue of *This Quarter.*

Criticism of the story has been quick to note its resemblance to *The Garden of Eden,* with critics like Warren Bennett using their readings of *Eden* to inform their readings of "The Sea Change." Earlier criticism frequently notes the story's formal similarity to "Hills Like White Elephants" and tends to focus on the title's allusion to Shakespeare and Phil's attempt to quote Pope's *An Essay on Man,* generally in an attempt to describe the transformation experienced by Phil at the moment when he tells his partner to go. In one of the most important and compelling readings of the story, Robert Fleming discovers in Phil a writer whose "own vice" is his "perverse willingness to use others for the sake of his art" (50). The resemblances between "The Sea Change" and *The Garden of Eden* ensure that this short story will continue to receive attention in coming years.

Title: The title of the story comes from Ariel's song to Ferdinand in Shakespeare's *The Tempest*:

> Full fathom five thy father lies.
>> Of his bones are coral made;
> Those are pearls that were his eyes;
>> Nothing of him that doth fade
> But doth suffer a sea-change
> Into something rich and strange,
> Sea-nymphs hourly ring his knell:
>> Ding dong.
> Hark, now I hear them
>> Ding-dong bell. (1.2.400–08)

Robert Fleming has suggested that the process of decay poeticized in these lines serves as a metaphor for the decay of Phil as he gives way to "vice," and Warren Bennett has suggested that the allusion to Shakespeare is refracted through Phlebas the Phoenician in T. S. Eliot's *The Waste Land* and "Dans le Restaurant," pointing to themes of sexual malaise (Fleming 51; Bennett 226). J. Gerald Kennedy has called attention to the sea change the couple, presumably American, would have experienced by their transposition to Europe and especially Paris, the city famous for sexual liberation and its thriving lesbian community (122). Most criticism has stressed the change experienced by Phil near the end of the story, after he tells his female companion to leave. No doubt, this change is the central one in the action of story, but, as the ironic final line of the story makes clear, the title also carries a broader resonance within Hemingway's work, suggesting that another crucial sea change has happened during the summer months before the couple arrives at this bar in Paris. This change precipitates the secondary change we witness in the bar.

As I have argued in *Hemingway's Fetishism*, hair dyeing, hair cutting, and deep suntans all carried a special erotic charge for Hemingway—functioning as components in a series of fetishistic associations and obsessions in his fiction and private life that grew more pronounced as he aged. Hemingway's fondness for the Shakespearean expression "sea change" was apparently rooted in the sun's and sea's ability to naturally bleach hair, a recurrent motif in *To Have and Have Not* (19), *For Whom the Bell Tolls* (3), *Islands in the Stream* (18), and *The Garden of Eden* (6). The phrase may memorialize Pauline Pfeiffer's 1929 experiment at Hendaye beach in Spain where she dyed her hair blonde shortly before Hemingway began this story. The couple in the story are "both tanned, so that they looked out of place in Paris" (302:12–13), and the title implies that they've spent the summer by the sea—a surmise made explicit in the manuscript. Here Hemingway breaks the "fly-on-the-wall" external focalization that structures the story before the girl's departure to convey precisely this point. We're told that "the sun had varied the color" of the girl's hair, that "[t]he man was very browned by the sun at the seashore," and that his hair was "streaked by the sun a little too" ("Sea Change" ms., item 679 1)—observations a "fly-on-the-wall observer" presumably wouldn't be able to make.

Since the publication of *The Garden of Eden,* it has become difficult to imagine the changes that presumably precede and lay the groundwork for the action of "The Sea Change" without retroactive reference to the changes experienced by David and Catherine Bourne in Hemingway's posthumous novel. In fact, Hemingway considered reusing the phrase "The Sea Change" as a subtitle for one of the three books of *The Garden of Eden (MF* ms.),[2] and he uses the phrase in the *Eden* manuscript to describe transformations strikingly similar to those of Phil and his partner in this short story. Debating with himself about the metamorphoses he is undergoing through his gender-swapping experiments with Catherine—experiments that include short haircuts and suntans so deep that the characters look like "a special dark race of [their] own"—David struggles with the word "corruption," much like Phil and his partner in "The Sea Change" struggle with the words "vice" and "perversion." "She enjoys corrupting me and I enjoy being corrupted," David thinks; but he reconsiders: "She's not corrupt and who says it is corruption? I withdraw the word." More significantly, this metamorphosis is a *sea change:* "It can only be made . . . in the strong sun against the reflection of the sand and the sea. So we must have the sun to make *this sea change. The sea change* was made in the night and it grows in the night and the darkness that she wants and needs now grows in the sun" (my emphasis, *GOE* ms. 1.4.4.).[3]

302:1–2 **All right. . . . What about it?:** The abrupt *in medias res* introduction, the reliance on dialogue with minimal narration, and the external "fly-on-the-wall" focalization throw the reader immediately into the action of the story. As many critics have noted, the style—at least until the girl's departure—recalls that of "Hills Like White Elephants," and the interpretive demands placed on the reader are similar. One important difference, however, is that we quickly learn what the argument is about. That Philip's partner wants to go off, at least for a time, with another woman is no mystery to be solved. But the subtext that we need to interpret, or at least guess at, isn't so different: what does their conversation imply about their relationship? What happened during the summer to bring them to this moment? What is the nature of, and what is at stake in, the girl's desire? And what is the nature of, and what is at stake in, Phil's "sea change" when he tells her to go?

302:3 **the girl:** The woman in the story remains unnamed and is consistently referred to as "the girl." This calls attention to a patriarchal power dynamic that she is challenging by leaving Phil, however temporarily, to pursue a lesbian experience.

302:3–4 **can't . . . won't:** The distinction between desire and need is fundamental and immediately begins to shape our sympathies. Phil insists that his partner's actions, as yet unclear, are motivated by *choice;* what she needs, according to Phil, is mere self-control. She insists that she *has* no choice; it is beyond her power and is not a matter of measured selection from among a given set of options. The issues at stake are deep and go to the core of sexuality. Is it a matter of casual choice, or is it rooted in something deeper, beyond choice?

The resemblances between "The Sea Change" and *The Garden of Eden,* however, suggest that what's at stake might not be simply the familiar distinction between sexuality misunderstood as a matter of "choice" and sexuality understood as a mode of being, hard-wired into identity. *The Garden of Eden* is deeply interested in a sort of compulsive sexuality that is experienced as oppositional to at least part of a divided self. When Catherine Bourne becomes a "boy" in Madrid, she at first presents it as a choice but later corrects herself: "I lied when I said I didn't have to" (*GOE* 56). And describing her attraction to Catherine and her own desire for fetishistic haircuts, Barbara Sheldon, a character from the *Eden* manuscript deleted in the Scribner's edition, puts the matter in starker terms: "I didn't know things took possession of you. Then's when you've gone wrong of course. . . . Now it owns me or did and will again" (*GOE* ms 3.5.8bis). In "The Sea Change," as the story progresses, there are hints of this sort of conflictual desire in the behavior of both Phil and his partner.

302:9 **You did for a long time:** As Lisa Tyler has noted, this line informs us that "this couple has had an unequal relationship for a long time." The woman is empowered by her new ability to walk away from Phil, and he, until then "the dominant partner," experiences this as a personal disempowerment, as if power in the relationship were "a zero-sum game" (75). Tyler suggests that, like Phil, critics have refused "to see the 'girl' as the separate human being she is," and she reads the story as being about the girl's successful effort to "break away" from Phil and get him "to recognize her emotional independence" (80). Tyler's reading is compelling, but it underestimates the woman's need for Phil's permission (303:42) and her immense relief when Phil grants it (304:39). It also minimizes the importance of the transformation Phil experiences at this moment, which structures both the crisis and denouement of the story.

302:10 **café . . . barman:** Deleted lines from the manuscript tell us that the café is on the rue Delambre, and this suggests that Hemingway was thinking of the Dingo, the famous "American bar" (what the French called a bar that serves cocktails) at 10 rue Delambre. Hemingway first met F. Scott Fitzgerald in 1925 at the Dingo, and Hemingway mentions it several times in *The Sun Also Rises*. He later wrote the introduction to *This Must Be the Place* (1934), the memoirs of the Dingo's most famous barman, Jimmie Charters. It is noteworthy, then, that the barman in "The Sea Change" is named "James" (304:11).

302:11–14 end of the summer and they were both tanned . . . tweed suit . . . blonde hair was cut short: These details of the couple's physical appearance are retroactively colored by the ironic final line of the story: "You look very well, sir. . . . You must have had a very good summer" (305:22–23). Something happened during the summer which is coded as "unhealthy," and the physical features the barman takes for signs of health are, in fact, fetishistic markers of the "sea change" that so disturbs and (later) excites Phil. What is merely hinted at here is, again, stated baldly in *The Garden of Eden* manuscript, where we can see that haircuts and suntans are interrelated markers of the couple's sexual transformation. When David Bourne asks Catherine why she "want[s] to be so dark," she replies, "I don't know. Why do you want anything? . . . I don't know why I want it so much. It's like I wanted to have my hair cut. . . . ~~It's to be a different person I guess.~~ ^another me Maybe that's part of it. It's like growing something.^ But it makes me excited too. Just good excited all the time." She asks David if it excites him, too, and he replies: "~~Of course~~ ^Uh-huh.^ I love it" (*GOE* ms 1.4.2). In other words, suntans are somehow like haircuts, and "wearing them" gives expression to "another me," the split-off other-sex half of the ego that is central to the structure of fetishism. It should be noted that women's "tweed suits" were coded as a "masculine" style during the 1920s, so this is a subtle indicator of the summer sea change experienced by "the girl."[4] (See entry for 303:8.)

The manuscript of "The Sea Change" makes clear that Phil's hair, like the girl's, is "streaked by the sun," so both partners carry the same markers of Hemingway's hair fetishism (item 679 5). As Tyler observes, this establishes a twin-like, or mirror-image, relation between the two that is important to understanding what Phil sees in the mirror at the end of the story (77). It also harkens back to the pseudo-twin relationship between Ernest and his sister Marcelline that played such an important role in the etiology of his fetishism. Although Marcelline was eighteen months older than Ernest, their mother twinned them for several years, cutting their hair and dressing them alike, sometimes in a "boyish" and sometimes in a "girlish" manner, so that, when Ernest was three-and-a-half, he was afraid Santa Claus wouldn't know if he was a boy or a girl. Some lines on the verso of the first page of "The Sea Change" manuscript point in this direction: "They were a brother and sister who lived together and loved each other very much. This was considered admirable in the old days" (item 679).

302:26–27 **Poor old Phil:** It is perhaps significant that, for the first forty pages of *The Garden of Eden* manuscript, Hemingway used the name "Phil" for his protagonist before rechristening him David Bourne. This suggests a possible continuity in Hemingway's thinking between these two stories. In *The Face in the Mirror: Hemingway's Writers*, Robert Fleming has also linked this Phil to the protagonists of *The Fifth Column*, "Get a Seeing-Eyed Dog," and the posthumously published "Philip Haines Was a Writer"—all writers named "Phil." Fleming suggests that "for Hemingway, Philip (or Phillip) was a writer's name," and this Philip, too, is a writer (146). There is important evidence for this in the story.

303:8 **I understand. That's the trouble. I understand:** It is worth pondering exactly what Phil "understands." Surely, he's implying that he understands something more than the mere fact that his partner wants to go off to have a lesbian experience. And Phil's partner agrees that he *does* understand (303:9). The fact that Phil "know[s] about it," she thinks, should help Phil to forgive her, though Phil doesn't agree (304:1–2). We might think that what Phil understands is simply the profound power of erotic and emotional desire or compulsion. (See entry for 302:3–4.) But his partner's next question sends us deeper: "You don't think *things we've had and done* should make any difference in understanding?" (my emphasis, 304:3–4). In other words, something about their own sexual practices should help Phil understand his partner's desire to be with another woman. This should make us wonder about the sea change that happened during the summer before this story begins.

Again, *The Garden of Eden* might help us understand what is happening here. The day before Catherine Bourne meets Marita and begins her lesbian affair, she and David, both deeply tanned from their time by the sea, get their hair cut identically and dyed as light as "the bark of a young white birch tree" (81). The two look "the same" (*GOE* ms. 3.18.5). Whereas at the beginning of the novel, in le Grau du Roi, such tonsorial games allow Catherine to become a "boy" while David becomes her "girl," this transformation on the Côte d'Azur allows David to be Catherine's "Danish girl," while Catherine *doesn't change:* "'I'm still a girl,' Catherine said. 'I never changed at all. That's why it's so complicated" (*GOE* ms. 3.18.19). In other words, Catherine and David have shared a sort of lesbian experience—with both of them playing "girls" in bed. It's no coincidence that this directly precedes Catherine's affair with Marita.

As I explain at much greater length in *Hemingway's Fetishism*, the dynamics of fetishism are structured around a disavowal of sexual difference and a bisexual splitting of the ego most visible in moments of fetishistic cross-dressing, or transvestism—that is, when the fetishist "wears" the fetish to facilitate a cross-gender identification. Thus, with his hair specially cut and dyed, David Bourne can literally adopt another name, "Catherine"—the same alter-ego Hemingway adopted in his own fetishistic practices (Eby, *Fetishism* 176–80, 199–207). At such moments, in heterosexual intercourse, the split-off female half of the male fetishist's ego can think of itself in lesbian terms. Trying to explain transvestism to large audiences, the brilliant transvestite comedian Eddie Izzard has chosen to describe himself precisely as "a male lesbian."[5]

When Phil's partner suggests that the "things we've had and done" should help Phil understand, this is probably what she has in mind. And this was probably an essential part of the change they experienced at the seashore along with their deep suntans and sun-bleached hair.

303:14 **If it was a man—:** One of the essential clues about what is happening in the story, this fragment also implies that Phil is at a loss. Conventional codes exist for what a man should do when his partner is "stolen" by another man, but here we are beyond traditional social conventions.

303:15–16 **Don't say that. It wouldn't be a man. You know that. Don't you trust me?:** Phil experiences this "Don't you trust me?" as sadly comic, but we should consider the immediacy and sincerity of the girl's outburst. She does love Phil, and she wouldn't leave him for another man. He isn't being coded as sexually and romantically inadequate as a male lover; what she needs is something a man cannot provide. On some level, she is insisting on her fidelity to Phil at precisely the moment she is apologizing for breaching that fidelity.

303:21 **I'll come back if you want me:** This line implies that the girl is seeking a temporary lesbian experience, not a new long-term partner. This is reemphasized when she repeats her promise to Phil: "But I'll come back. . . . I'll come back right away" (304:30–31). In other words, her desires are bisexual, not exclusively lesbian. She imagines that, once she has had this experience, she can return to Phil, though she acknowledges the high stakes of the moment and the risk she takes of losing him. This again sounds like Catherine's experience with Marita in *The Garden of Eden*.

303:42 **Couldn't you just . . . let me go?:** It's important to note that while the "girl" is stating her needs, she also seems to need Phil's permission, and Phil's reply—"What do you think I'm going to do?" (303:43)—implies that he feels entitled to give or withhold it. By the same token, when Phil *does* grant his permission (304:38), the girl's happy response, "Really?" (304:39), conveys genuine excitement and relief. This is the language of a woman seeking an experience, and not seeking to leave Phil permanently. It may also suggest that somehow this experience can form part of their shared sexual relationship.

304:3 **You don't think things we've had and done . . . ?:** See entry for 303:8.

304:5 **Vice is a monster of such fearful mien:** Much criticism of the story has hinged on Phil's imperfect attempt to remember these lines from Alexander Pope's *An Essay on Man:*

Vice is a Monster of so frightful mien,
As, to be hated, needs but to be seen;
Yet seen too oft, familiar with her Face,
We first endure, then pity, then embrace. (II.217–20)

Phil replaces "frightful" with "fearful," replaces "hated" with "something or other" (304:6), and then forgets most of the second couplet, in the process confusing an embrace of *vice* with *the couple's* embrace: "we something, something, then embrace" (304:6–7). Phil seems to forget the very lines that explain why these couplets came to mind in the first place. He apparently intends to accuse his partner of having become so familiar with what he prudishly calls "vice," something he thinks he has been complicit with too long, that she has now fully embraced it in her lesbian desire. The irony that drives the denouement of the story—and that may explain why Phil stumbles over the second couplet—is that Phil immediately realizes that these lines better describe his own circumstances and desires.

Bennett has published the most thorough and interesting consideration of this allusion to Pope. He contrasts what he calls the neoclassical logic of Phil's belief that sexuality can be chosen (see entry for 302:3–4) and judged, with the naturalistic logic of the girl's assertion that human sexuality is beyond choice and simply not something that can be "labeled good or bad, virtue or vice." To Bennett, Phil's suppression of the word *hate* implies that "vice in the contemporary naturalistic world is much less objectionable" than in the neoclassical era of Pope. "Vice is neither hated nor temporarily endured," Bennett writes, "and the process of initial revulsion, familiarity, toleration, and sympathy before it is finally accepted is no longer applicable. Vice is now simply seen and tried, and, although 'something or other' also takes place, if it is found pleasurable it is accepted" (399). Bennett suggests, however, that Phil has forgotten other important lines from Pope's epistle that argue that men are so incapable of distinguishing for long between good and bad that they quickly "into the notion fall / That Vice and Virtue there is none at all." This, Bennett argues, is the position taken by the girl when she suggests that "[y]ou don't have to put any name to it. . . . We're made up of all sorts of things" (304:23–25), and Phil's acceptance of this, as Bennett sees it, represents his own fall into this position.

Throughout his work, Hemingway uses the word "vice" to refer not only to sexuality but to things as various as writing, gambling, eating, drinking, religion, patriotism, and reading his own press clippings and (after his two 1954 plane crashes) obituaries. The common underlying principle in his usage seems to be a sort of obsessive compulsion. "Vice" is a minor theme in *The Garden of Eden* manuscript, with Catherine suggesting early in the novel that "we need some good vices" (1.1.3) and Barbara Sheldon telling David, "Don't you try to tell me when pleasure, good lovely pleasure, turns into vice because I know" (3.5.8bis). The quotation from Pope certainly inflects Hemingway's interest in "vice" here, but that interest extends well beyond Pope and his sense of the word. When it comes to so-called nonnormative sexuality, Hemingway's characters struggle with "vice," "corruption," "perversion," and "sin." They seem to oscillate between two contrary positions—acquiescence and resistance—in a way that is structured by the rift in the ego central to the structure of fetishism (Eby, "Gardens" 73–76).

304:10 **Perversion:** Fleming reads Phil's accusation as ironic, since, as a writer, Phil perversely uses other people to create his art. What's more, Fleming claims, Phil's "perversion is more degrading" than the girl's, something we see in his parasitic desire for the girl to "come back and tell him 'all about' her sexual experiences" (49). This reading is suggestive, but it overlooks the obvious erotic nature of the excitement Phil experiences when he tells the girl to go and return with tales of the experience. I would suggest that the bitterness of Phil's accusation is colored by his awareness that it is a self-accusation. Following on the lines from Pope, Phil realizes that his critique applies to himself as much as it does to the girl.

304:11 **James . . . clients:** In naming his barman, Hemingway may have been inspired by the famous barman of the Dingo, Jimmie Charters (see entry for 302:10). Warren Bennett asserts that the two clients in the bar are gay, but what little evidence he offers to support this is unconvincing.

304:23–25 **You don't have to put any name to it. . . . We're made up all sorts of things:** This affirmation of the range and rich complexity of human desire has implications for the entirety of *Winner Take Nothing,* with its thematic interest in what is coded as nonnormative human sexuality. In rejecting our vocabulary for describing sexuality as impoverished and coercively diagnostic, the girl echoes the wisdom of Robert Jordan in *For Whom the Bell Tolls,* who asserts, "We know nothing about what happens to us in the nights" (175), and of Catherine Bourne in *The Garden of Eden* manuscript, who asks, "Who's normal? What's normal? I never went to normal school to be a teacher and teach normal. You don't want me to go to normal school and get a certificate do you?" (*GOE* ms. 3.24.34). At the risk of using this same impoverished diagnostic vocabulary (what escape is there?)—this critique is particularly relevant in the case of fetishism, dependent as it is on a bisexual splitting of the self and the partner and resistant as it is to the straitjacket of the culturally dominant gay/straight dichotomy (Eby, *Hemingway's Fetishism* 161–80).

Making room for the range of human sexuality was a career-long concern for Hemingway, although, as is revealed by his frequent expressions of homophobia, he was far from consistent about it. Or, rather, he was consistently divided about it—at odds with himself—and this division was structured by the rift in his ego (Eby, "Gardens" 73–76). He did, however, become more expansive in his embrace of sexual variety as he grew older. We see this in the manuscript of *Islands in the Stream* when Hudson doesn't care if his desires are "perverse" because he is "a long way past any thought of what were perversions and what were not" (83). Similarly, in *The Garden of Eden* manuscript, Catherine *is* initially afraid that her desires are "abnormal," but she decides that this doesn't matter; it's "just people being brave enough to do what they wanted" (3.1.7). This moment in "The Sea Change" is Hemingway's first expression of that important theme.

304:26 **You've used it well enough:** How has Phil "used" this knowledge? Robert Fleming has offered the most compelling answer: Phil is a writer, and his understanding of human complexity has allowed him to see more deeply into the people and situations he portrays.

304:27 **You don't have to say that again:** Something in the girl's suggestion that Phil has *used* his knowledge of human complexity stings. Fleming's reading of the story as a critique of the "writer's perverse willingness to use others for the sake of his art" offers the most persuasive interpretation of this (50).

304:30–31 **But I'll come back. . . . I'll come back right away:** See entry for 303:21.

304:40–305:1 **"Go on. . . . And when you come back tell me all about it." His voice sounded very strange. He did not recognize it:** As is indicated by a shift in focalization, this is the pivotal moment in the text. Until now—with the exception of a brief moment when we glimpse the thoughts of the bartender (303:37–41) and when the narrator uses the word "comfortable" to describe the glance of the other customers (304:19)—the story has been structured by external "fly-on-the-wall" focalization; from this moment forward, the story is focalized through Phil, and we now have access to his sensations and thoughts.

Some critics have doubted Phil's sincerity at this moment, but the story turns precisely on the depth—and origin—of his sincerity. Newly aware of the nature of his own desires, Phil is suddenly turned on by the idea of the girl's affair and wants to participate vicariously, both through the granting of permission and through her account of it. This point makes more sense when we understand the pseudo-lesbian aspects of his own sexual relationship with the girl. (See entry for 303:8.) The sure sign of his arousal is what happens to his voice—a recurrent sign of erotic desire in Hemingway's work, occurring in *A Farewell to Arms*, *For Whom the Bell Tolls*, *To Have and Have Not*, *Islands in the Stream*, *Across the River and into the Trees*, and *The Garden of Eden* (Eby, *Hemingway's Fetishism* 41–42). But we see something more than a thickening of the voice; Phil doesn't even *recognize* his own voice. This failure to recognize the self is a corollary of what Phil will soon experience in the mirror; it is a sign of psychological dissociation. (See entry for 305:14.)

305:1–2 **He was settled into something:** The girl recognizes that what has happened is not the mere granting of permission. Something else is going on.

305:4–5 **Right away. . . . Now:** These are not the words of a man granting *permission*. These are words of *desire*. Phil is erotically excited by the idea of his partner's lesbian affair, which makes him, in effect, a vicarious participant in it.

305:13 **Vice . . . is a very strange thing:** In a manuscript fragment among "The Sea Change" papers, Phil asks the barman at this point in the story what "punks" drink: "What can you recommend to a recent convert? . . . Take a look at me and mix whatever you like" (item 681). Hemingway seems to use "punk" here in its slang sense as a word for a passive male homosexual, a usage suggested as well in his stories "The Light of the World" and "A Lack of Passion." This has sometimes been held up as evidence for an argument made by several critics that Phil, like the girl, will now have his own homosexual affair.[6] As Tyler notes, however, such an affair is hardly likely. What seems more likely is that Phil's self-castigation, as Comley and Scholes suggest, reflects a homophobic attempt to distance himself from his own anxieties. In some pages discarded from *The Garden of Eden* manuscript, Nick Sheldon expresses these same anxieties about his fetishistic gender-swapping games with Barbara, fearing that his long hair makes him look like a "bloody sodomite" (item 422.2 39.5). In a world where, as Phil's partner notes, the language for the complexities of human sexuality is impoverished and where so much is reduced to the gay/straight dichotomy, Phil may well struggle to understand the nature of his own desires. His homophobia may well be rooted in a fear of losing his gender identity. (See entry for 305:14.)

305:14–15 **As he looked in the glass, he saw he was really quite a different-looking man:** What are we to do with the text's thrice-repeated insistence that Phil is now not only a "different man" but a "different-*looking* man"? The sea change in Phil's physical appearance is presented to us as something that is not merely in his head. The *narrator* tells us, "He was not the same-looking man as he had been before he had told her to go" (305:7–8). The fact that we are told this in the narrator's voice, *before* Phil goes over to the bar and confirms the transformation in the mirror, seems to give his metamorphosis an external reality. The reader is left with a choice: either the difference is merely the expression on Phil's face, or something quasi-supernatural has happened. Given the paucity of the supernatural in Hemingway's work, the obvious choice would be the former, yet there is good reason to believe that something quasi-supernatural has, indeed, occurred.

Such quasi-supernatural physical transformations are a minor motif in *The Garden of Eden*. Catherine Bourne's sexual transformations alter her facial features. When Catherine's fetishized haircuts allow her to become "a new girl" for David, he sees that "her mouth was changed too" and she is not simply pouting or contorting her lips (*GOE* 47). In the manuscript version of this same passage, after Catherine and David have made love and Catherine becomes "a girl again"—implying that she's temporarily been a boy during their lovemaking—Catherine asks David if he notices that her "mouth is changed too." David tells her that her new haircut has just "brought it out more," but she knows better. She tells him that her mouth has "been changing ever since [she] thought of changing back" to the way she was at le Grau du Roi. "That's imagination," David tells her, but she insists on the difference and makes David feel it, which he does (*GOE* ms. 3.6.4). A chapter later in the manuscript, Catherine tells David that he *made* her "mouth change." It started to change the first time they made love in Paris, she tells him, but then "changed back at le Grau du Roi." Even more tellingly, as they make love—with Catherine becoming a boy and David becoming her girl—David can *feel* her mouth "changing" as she is transformed (*GOE* ms. 3.12.13) Elsewhere, David tries to dismiss such physical transformations as "crazy" (*GOE* ms. 3.21.11); yet, when they make love, he experiences them too, and, when he becomes Catherine's "girl" in bed, he *feels* "the change so that it hurt him all through" (*GOE* ms. 1.1.23).

It's no coincidence that these physical transformations occur at moments of cross-gender identification—when Catherine becomes a "boy" or David a "girl"—nor is it a coincidence that Phil, in "The Sea Change," witnesses his metamorphosis in a mirror. As I have explained at more length elsewhere, it is precisely while wearing the fetish in front of the mirror that the fetishist becomes the fetishistic cross-dresser (or transvestite) and experiences an identification with the split-off other-sex half of his ego (*Hemingway's Fetishism* 208–16). As Tyler notes, with his dark tan and (in the "Sea Change" manuscript) sun-streaked hair, Phil is, at least fetishistically, the mirror image of his departed "girl." Bennett is right to suggest that Phil "now has an image of himself as [his] girl's 'first girl,'" but this is less, as Bennett suggests, because the girl "has won the contest," thereby emasculating him (236), than it is because Phil has been forced to acknowledge the fetishistic and transvestic aspects of his own desire, and along with this, the split-off other-sex half of his ego. Phil's alienation from his own image in the mirror—something Hemingway protagonists frequently experience—reveals a degree of dissociation that is a hallmark of such moments, because the split-off other-sex half of the ego is "other"—other enough to warrant its own name and personality (Eby, *Hemingway's Fetishism* 209). (Thus, Catherine Bourne becomes "Peter," David becomes "Catherine," much as Mary Welsh Hemingway became "Peter," and Ernest became "Catherine" [Eby, *Hemingway's Fetishism* 172–80; 199–207].) Phil's physical transformation in "The Sea Change," like Catherine's changing mouth in *Eden,* is an example of what I have elsewhere described as a brief "psychotic flash," or hallucination, such as are experienced by several Hemingway characters at the moment when the split-off other-sex half of the self "takes over"—usually during the act of sex (Eby, "He Felt the Change").

305:22–23 **You must have had a very good summer:** The deep irony of James's remark forces readers to wonder what happened during the summer to lay the groundwork for this moment. See entry for 302:12.

NOTES

1. For a fine essay devoted to silences and what remains unsaid in the story, see Erik Nakjavani's "The Rest Is Silence: A Psychoanalytic Study of Hemingway's Theory of Omission and Its Application to 'The Sea Change.'"

2. Written on the verso of a page from the *Moveable Feast* manuscript, the passage contains a list of titles and subtitles for *The Garden of Eden* written at a time when Hemingway was considering using the name "Catherine" for *both* Catherine Bourne *and* Barbara Sheldon. Beneath the title, *The Two Catherines,* Hemingway lists the following subtitles: (1) "The Sand Castle"; (2) "The Huntress"; and (3) "The Sea Change."

3. When citing *The Garden of Eden* manuscript, I use book, chapter, and page number. So, 3.4.5 would mean book three, chapter four, page five. Unless otherwise noted, all citations from the *Eden* manuscript are from item 422.1.

4. Hemingway was a particular fan of O'Rossen suits, recommending them to his sister in 1928 (*Letters vol. 3,* 395) and dressing Catherine Bourne in them in *The Garden of Eden* manuscript (3.19.14). A 1931 advertisement proclaimed that the Parisian couturier made "the most marvelously tailored suits in all the world. He himself is actually a man's tailor who is now making women's clothes" (*Boston* 578). The O'Rossen suit was considered a "boyish ensemble" that "out flappers the flapper" (Finamore 155).

5. See Izzard's hilarious "Dress to Kill" show. Warren Bennett comes close to realizing that Phil has played the role of a male lesbian, but he misses the psychological depth of the experience and reduces it to the practice of cunnilingus (232).

6. The two critics who most clearly take this position, Wycherly and Kobler, do so without reference to this manuscript fragment or the word "punk."

WORKS CITED

Bennett, Warren. "'That's Not Very Polite': Sexual Identity in Hemingway's 'The Sea Change.'" *Hemingway's Neglected Short Fiction: New Perspectives,* U of Alabama P, 1989, pp. 225–45.

Boston Symphony Orchestra Concert Programs, 1931–1932. Boston Symphony Orchestra, 1931.

Comley, Nancy R., and Robert Scholes. *Hemingway's Genders: Rereading the Hemingway Text.* Yale UP, 1994.

DeFalco, Joseph. *The Hero in Hemingway's Short Stories.* U of Pittsburgh P, 1963.

Eby, Carl. "Gardens of *Eden* and *Earthly Delights*: Hemingway, Bosch, and the Divided Self." *The Hemingway Review,* vol. 37, no. 2, 2018, pp. 65–79.

———. "'He Felt the Change So that It Hurt Him All Through': Sodomy and Transvestic Hallucination in Hemingway." *The Hemingway Review,* vol. 25, no. 1, 2005, pp. 77–95.

———. *Hemingway's Fetishism: Psychoanalysis and the Mirror of Manhood.* SUNY P, 1999.

Finamore, Michelle Tolini. *Hollywood before Glamour: Fashion in American Silent Film.* Palgrave, 2013.

Fleming, Robert. *The Face in the Mirror: Hemingway's Writers.* U of Alabama P, 1994.

Hemingway, Ernest. "The Art of the Short Story." *The Paris Review,* vol. 79, Spring 1981, pp. 85–102.

———. *Ernest Hemingway: Selected Letters, 1917–1961.* Edited by Carlos Baker. Scribner's, 1981.

———. *For Whom the Bell Tolls.* Scribner's, 1940.

———. *The Garden of Eden.* Scribner's, 1986.

———. *The Garden of Eden* manuscript, items 422.1 and 422.2, Ernest Hemingway Collection, John F. Kennedy Library, Boston.

———. *Islands in the Stream.* Scribner's, 1970.

———. *Islands in the Stream* manuscript, item 112, Ernest Hemingway Collection, John F. Kennedy Library, Boston.

———. *The Letters of Ernest Hemingway: Volume 4 (1929–1931).* Edited by Sandra Spanier and Miriam B. Mandel. CUP, 2017.

———. *The Letters of Ernest Hemingway: Volume 5 (1932–1934).* Edited by Sandra Spanier and Miriam B. Mandel. CUP, 2020.

———. *A Moveable Feast* manuscript, item 123, Ernest Hemingway Collection, John F. Kennedy Library, Boston.

———. "The Sea Change" manuscript, items 679, 680, and 681, Ernest Hemingway Collection, John F. Kennedy Library, Boston.

———. *To Have and Have Not.* Scribner's, 1937.

Hotchner, A. E. *Papa Hemingway: A Personal Memoir.* Random House, 1966.

Kennedy, J. Gerald. *Imagining Paris: Exile, Writing, and American Identity.* Yale UP, 1993.

Kert, Bernice. *The Hemingway Women: Those Who Loved Him, the Wives and Others.* W. W. Norton, 1986.

Kobler, J. A. "Hemingway's 'The Sea Change': A Sympathetic View of Homosexuality." *Arizona Quarterly,* vol. 26, Winter 1970, pp. 318–24.

Moddelmog, Debra A. "The Unifying Consciousness of a Divided Conscience: Nick Adams as Author of *In Our Time.*" *American Literature,* vol. 60, no. 4, 1988, pp. 591–610.

Nakjavani, Erik. "The Rest Is Silence: A Psychoanalytic Study of Hemingway's Theory of Omission and Its Application to 'The Sea Change.'" *The North Dakota Quarterly,* vol. 65, no. 3, 1998, pp. 145–73.

Pope, Alexander. *An Essay on Man. Eighteenth-Century English Literature,* Harcourt, Brace, and World, 1969, pp. 635–51.

Reynolds, Michael. *Hemingway: The 1930s.* Norton, 1997.

Shakespeare, William. *The Norton Shakespeare.* 2nd ed. Edited by Stephen Greenblatt. Norton, 2008.

Smith, Paul. *A Reader's Guide to the Short Stories of Ernest Hemingway.* G. K. Hall, 1989.

Tyler, Lisa. "'I'd Rather Not Hear': Women and Men in Conversation in 'Cat in the Rain' and 'The Sea Change.'" *Hemingway and Women: Female Critics and the Female Voice,* edited by Lawrence Broer and Gloria Holland, U of Alabama P, 2002, pp. 70–80.

Wycherley, H. Alan. "Hemingway's 'The Sea Change.'" *American Notes and Queries,* vol. 7, 1969, pp. 67–68.

A WAY YOU'LL NEVER BE

Mark Cirino

The central unifying element of Hemingway's three volumes of short stories—*In Our Time* (1925), *Men Without Women* (1927), and *Winner Take Nothing* (1933)—is the trilogy of masterful stories chronicling Nick Adams at war and then struggling with its effects, both physical and psychological. As an examination of Nick Adams's war experience, "Big Two-Hearted River," "Now I Lay Me," and "A Way You'll Never Be" are three of Hemingway's most enduring and forceful probes into the psyche of a veteran. In "Big Two-Hearted River," Nick struggles against the current of trauma, memory, and fear. He fishes in his familiar Michigan woods in an act of solitary rehabilitation, a psychic retreat, a return to nature to mitigate the damage done. "Now I Lay Me" portrays the gnawing panic as it manifests itself through a dreadful bout of insomnia and a fear of the dark. "A Way You'll Never Be" dramatizes Nick's losing battle with his own psychic state, his mind unraveling and out of control. It is surely the most harrowing depiction of shellshock Hemingway ever wrote, a moment where he stared unflinchingly into his own war experiences as projected through his most common fictional alter ego.

Although "A Way You'll Never Be" was published last of the three stories, it takes place earliest, when the corpses from the Battle of the Piave in summer 1918 are just beginning to decay on the Italian countryside. Like the decade in between *A Farewell to Arms* (1929) and the autobiographical events that inspired it, this short story took several years to write. In Hemingway's snide essay "The Art of the Short Story," he remembers that the story was "written at Key West, Florida, some fifteen years after the damage it depicts, both to a man, a village, and a countryside, had occurred" (*SS-HLE* 11). Likewise, Hemingway told his friend A. E. Hotchner that following several attempts of writing the story, "one day" in Key West, "fifteen years after those things happened to me in a trench dugout outside Fornaci, it suddenly came out focused and complete" (qtd. in Scafella 181).

As Lillian Ross reports Hemingway saying in 1948, "'I can remember feeling so awful about the first war that I couldn't write about it for ten years,' he said, suddenly very angry. 'The wound combat makes in you, as a writer, is a very slow-healing one. I wrote three stories about it in the old days—"In Another Country," "A Way You'll Never Be," and "Now I Lay Me"'" (48). Of course, Hemingway wrote more than those three, but it is instructive that these stories are the ones he recalls most prominently.

"A Way You'll Never Be" is one of the great beneficiaries of the Hemingway Library Edition of *The Short Stories of Ernest Hemingway* (2017). In addition to the story itself being reprinted, this new edition includes glimpses at the manuscript, to reveal how Hemingway arrived at such a meticulous version of a story that has all the appearance of being chaotic and rambling. Hemingway initially attempted the story from a first-person perspective, writing, "I had seen no one since I left Fornaci" (*SS-HLE* 206), before shifting it into a third-person investigation into the tortured mind of Nick Adams. The development from conception to publication demonstrates that Hemingway's story took an inward turn, from a narrative about the battlefield to a devastating account of Nick's struggle to maintain control over his mind and memories. An earlier version of the story depicts Captain Paravicini dismissing as a "nasty trick" two Italian soldiers copulating in the barracks (*SS-HLE* 210–11). While this episode did not survive the drafting stages, the various manuscript efforts show Hemingway's calculating efforts to represent the Italian front and also the psyche of his protagonist.

In his *Reader's Guide* (271), Paul Smith usefully breaks down the structure of the story into seven parts, to which I will add the page and line numbers from the *Complete Short Stories:*

1. Return to battlefield and meeting with the officer   306:1–308:25
2. First conversation with Paravicini   308:25–310:10
3. First "dream"   310:11–311:20
4. Nick's lecture   311:21–313:25
5. Second conversation with Paravicini   313:26–314:19
6. Second "dream"   314:20–314:24
7. Departure   314:24–315:4

Smith, the most authoritative scholar on Hemingway's short fiction, believes the story "deserves a place among Hemingway's major stories" as one of his "most original, even daring fictions" (*Reader's Guide* 275). In his review for *The New Statesman and Nation,* David Garnett refers to the story as "the finest picture of shell-shock that I've read" (192).

As important as the story is in the Hemingway canon and in our consideration of Nick Adams as a character, it also emphasizes some of the most crucial themes in *Winner Take Nothing.* "A Way You'll Never Be" joins "A Clean, Well-Lighted Place" in its exploration of sanity and the post-traumatic effects of warfare. "A Natural History of the Dead" emerges as a companion piece, as in both narratives Hemingway captures the battlefield carnage he remembered from the aftermath of the Battle of the Piave in Fossalta di Piave in Summer 1918.

Title: A story that began with a first-person narration and settled on a third-person narration instead contains a second-person address in its title. The "you" of the title refers specifically to the actress Jane Mason (1909–81), Hemingway's friend and possible paramour in the early 1930s. Mason was prone to mental illness, and Hemingway's title is at once a gesture of assurance—"things could be worse"—and condescension—"you haven't been through what I have." Biographer Carlos Baker gives the following explanation for Hemingway's title: "He [Hemingway] later explained his enigmatic title by saying that the heat of Havana had reminded him of the way it was on the lower Piave in the summer of 1918. At the same time, said he, he was watching a hell of a nice girl going crazy from day to day. He gave his story its title in order to cheer her up on the grounds that the 'citizen' in the story, Nick Adams, had been 'much nuttier' than this girl was ever going to be" (228). The title can be comforting, but also a Hemingwayesque performance of one-upsmanship, assuring the person that no one has known the troubles he had.

306:1 **The attack:** Although it is unspecified, the historical event depicted in the story is World War I, the aftermath of the Battle of the Piave in northeast Italy, which pitted the Italian army against the Austro-Hungarians. The battle lasted from 15–23 June 1918. Another Hemingway protagonist—Colonel Cantwell from *Across the River and into the Trees*—is also wounded during this battle. The action of this story is unstated, but according to the manuscript, the action takes place in July: "July was a bad month for him" (JFK #813). If we accept that, it would mean that the bodies had been in a state of putrefaction in the Italian summer for a significant period of time, perhaps weeks. The Austro-Hungarian offensive was countered by Italian, French, British, and even American troops, led by Italian General Armando Diaz (1861–1928). As Hemingway's story indicates, poison gas was freely used as part of the Austro-Hungarian arsenal.

306:3 **the town:** The town in question is Fossalta di Piave in the Veneto, the site of Hemingway's own wounding on 8 July 1918 on the banks of the Piave River. Fossalta is a small town approximately twenty miles northeast of Mestre, which is on the mainland off the lagoon. Fossalta rests roughly midway between two other towns mentioned later in the story, Zenson di Piave and San Donà di Piave.

306:6 **Nicholas Adams:** This character is Hemingway's fictional alter ego, the protagonist he would return to most frequently in his short stories. In 1972, Hemingway scholar Philip Young collected all of the Nick Adams fiction in an excellent compendium, *The Nick Adams Stories,* chronologizing the stories by the action it describes in Nick's life, rather than by date of composition or publication. Here, Nick is called Nicholas for one of the few times—also in "Fathers and Sons" (another *Winner Take Nothing* story) and "Summer People" (written in 1924). In this story, he is called

"Nicholas" once and the Italian version—"Nicolo"—six times. He soon becomes the more familiar "Nick Adams" (307:19).

306:7–9 They lay alone . . . the scattered papers: This thirty-seven-word paragraph is isolated in Roger Cohen's recent *New York Times* column on the recurrence through history of the brutal reality of young lives ended on battlefields. Cohen refers to Hemingway as "a reporter with an unerring eye," and considers this short paragraph one of "telegraphic description" (A26). Particularly striking is the use of "clumps" to refer to corpses, rather than debris or clods of land.

See *Winner Take Nothing*'s "A Natural History of the Dead" (337:20–338:24) for a parallel scene of the aftermath of this same battle.

306:13 stick bombs: A small bomb attached to a handheld stick for use as a projectile. In *A Farewell to Arms,* too, Frederic sees a German bicycle troop and notes: "Stick bombs hung handle down from their belts" (*FTA* 211). The fifth and final flashback of "The Snows of Kilimanjaro" contains just one memory, of "Williamson, the bombing officer" who is "*hit by a stick bomb some one in a German patrol had thrown as he was coming in through the wire that night*" (*CSS* 53, emphasis in original). See also *Across the River and into the Trees,* when Cantwell remembers killing the enemy, who were wearing stick bombs (38).

306:14–15 stick bombs, helmets, rifles: As if to emphasize the lack of order and the profusion of material scattered about the terrain, Hemingway eerily repeats "stick bombs, helmets, rifles" just one line after the same sequence was introduced (306:13). Hemingway also repeats "photographic . . . photographs . . . photographers" in just a two-line span (307:1–2).

For further consideration of Hemingway's technique of repetition, consider his insistence on the word "dead" as a devastating noun:

PHRASE	PAGE/LINE #
1. "the position of the dead"	306:6
2. "much paper about the dead"	307:3–4
3. "These were new dead"	307:5
4. "Our own dead"	307:6
5. "our own dead"	307:6
6. "Why don't they bury the dead?"	314:10–11

See also the title of another short story from *Winner Take Nothing*, "A Natural History of the Dead."

306:15 star-shell pistols: A "star shell" is filled with material that emits a bright light as the shell explodes, used for illumination. In Hemingway's extraordinary 21 July 1918 letter, written on his nineteenth birthday to his parents following his war wounding, he concludes by describing the Austrian paraphernalia he collects for souvenirs, including "star shell pistols" (*Letters vol. 1,* 118).

306:18 **breech block:** The device that closes the breech (the back) of the weapon at the moment of discharge.

306:22–23 **as in a football picture for a college annual:** Hemingway frequently compared war to football, often to show the irony of his own former innocence or even fecklessness. In *A Farewell to Arms,* after Frederic has deserted the army, he observes that the "war seemed as far away as the football games of some one else's college" (*FTA* 291). In *Across the River and into the Trees,* Cantwell describes an attack by comparing it to a broken-field play when "you are Minnesota and the others are Beloit, Wisconsin" (214), an arcane allusion that baffles his Italian girlfriend. In a 1942 letter to Maxwell Perkins, he wrote, "I was an awful dope when I went to the last war," he said. "I can remember just thinking that we were the home team and the Austrians were the visiting team" (qtd. in Baker 38).

Paul Smith reports that one of the earliest pieces of fiction Hemingway wrote about the war was called—evoking this same sports comparison—"The Visiting Team" ("Trying-out" 32).

306:24 **propaganda postcards:** Postcards intended to exhort citizens to support the government or to dehumanize the soldiers and citizens of the opponent's country were common during World War I. Whether Hemingway is alluding to this specific postcard or not, here is a reasonable approximation of the image he describes:

Museo Francesco Baracca, Lugo, Italy, photo made by Istituto Beni Culturali della Regione Emilia-Romagna. The text reads: "Do you hear the cries and wails of women from the other side? It is the barbarian who rapes Italian women. ITALIAN SOLDIER, PROTECT THEM; if you surrender, your woman will also suffer the outrage."

306:28–29 **inciting . . . offensive:** "offensive" is used both in the military sense and punning on "inciting."

307:1 **scattered with the smutty postcards:** In a story where the focus is on Nick desperately trying to control his psyche and his thoughts scattered from the effects of post-traumatic stress disorder (PTSD), we might note the proliferation of this word: the papers of the dead are "scattered" around the corpses (306:9); there is "much material" that is "scattered over the road" (306:10–11); the shells of the pistols are "scattered about" (306:16); the balls of shrapnel are "scattered in the rubble" (307:18). The recurrence of "scattered" appears early in the story, which allows Hemingway to set the external scene of war's aftermath and the theme of Nick's internal disorder.

Hemingway also uses the word "scatter" to emphasize the disorder of the scene in "A Natural History of the Dead": "the amount of paper that is scattered about the dead . . . the two hip pockets pulled out and, scattered around them . . . the amount of paper scattered" (337:33–34, 337:38, 337:40–41), three instances used within a sequence of only nine lines.

307:3 **letters, letters, letters:** Reminiscent of Hamlet's dismissive "words, words, words" (2.2.192) to Polonius, Hemingway's formulation is at once more specific—letters of the alphabet are components of a word—and broader, since words are components of letters, as in correspondence.

307:5–6 **but their pockets:** This scene mirrors a description in "A Natural History of the Dead," which focuses on the proliferation of paper and the inside out pockets of the uniform of the corpse. In that story, Hemingway writes, "The heat, the flies, the indicative positions of the bodies in the grass, and the amount of paper scattered are the impressions one retains" (337:39–41). .

See entry at 307:1 for a discussion of the word "scattered."

307:9 **hot weather . . . swollen:** The action of the scene is most likely July 1918. In the manuscript, Hemingway had drafted that the sun had swollen all the bodies indiscriminately, regardless of nationality or "whether they were the winners or losers" (*SS-HLE* 205).

In "A Natural History of the Dead," Hemingway describes the remains of the same battlefield: "The dead grow larger each day until sometimes they become quite too big for their uniforms, filling these until they seem blown tight enough to burst. The individual members may increase in girth to an unbelievable extent and faces fill as taut and globular as balloons" (337:29–32).

307:11 **had evidently been defended:** Indeed, the massive Austro-Hungarian offensive that began the Battle of the Piave on 15 June 1918 was repelled over the next few weeks, salvaging the war for the Italians.

307:19 **Fornaci:** In late June 1918, Hemingway was relocated from Schio to the Italian front, to a position near Fornaci and Fossalta on the Piave River. From Fornaci to Fossalta di Piave would be less than five miles, traveling east toward the river. Fornaci is also mentioned two other times (308:36, 315:4), including the last word of the story.

Given the heat, the setting is apt; Fornaci is the Italian word for *furnaces*.

307:21 **mulberry leaves:** Mulberry leaves should invite the reader following Nick Adams's development to recall "Now I Lay Me," from *Men Without Women,* which begins with an insomniac Nick listening to silkworms munching inexorably on mulberry leaves (*CSS* 276). These same mulberry trees are referenced as being "in full leaf" in "A Natural History of the Dead" (338:6).

307:25–26 **the placid reach of the river:** This serene image belies the tragedy that this setting had witnessed just weeks earlier. The writer is accentuating the incongruous irony of this natural setting being "over-foliaged" (307:20), "very lush" (307:27–28), and "over-green" (307:28) despite serving as an ossuary.

307:28 **becoming historical:** This phrase suggests a reading of "become hysterical"— also "historical" in the sense of war history but also personal memory. The manuscript had "history" before the improvement was made (*SS-HLE* 206).

307:30 **battalion:** A battalion typically consists of a few hundred soldiers.

307:30–31 **series of holes in the top of the bank:** This image anticipates Nick's anxiety that he should have been trepanned and also Paravicini's assurance that Nick is in "top-hole shape" (see entries at 310:1 and 310:4).

307:35 **red-rimmed, very blood-shot eyes:** Hemingway is clearly intending to convey that this man has withstood Austro-Hungarian gas attacks. In a draft of this story, this phrase is repeated, except "very blood-shot" is replaced with the more explicit and clunkier adjective "gas-injured" (*SS-HLE* 217). In "A Natural History of the Dead," Hemingway describes a doctor with eyes "red and the lids swollen, almost shut from tear gas" (339:36).

307:36 **pointed a pistol:** In an extraordinary moment of storytelling, we move from Nick scanning the battlefield littered with the dead to an almost seamless examination of soldiers who are sleeping (307:33) to those who simply do not challenge his presence (307:33), until finally—suddenly—Nick encounters the second lieutenant who points a gun at him.

In the manuscript of "A Way You'll Never Be," Paravicini reveals that this gun-wielding soldier is "quite mad . . . quite gone off his head" (*SS-HLE* 209).

307:40 **tessera:** Italian for "card," it was used in older English to mean "token" or "ticket."

307:41 **third army:** During the disastrous Italian defeat at the Battle of Caporetto in October–November 1917 and the subsequent retreat, the Second Army was annihilated, while the Third Army stayed together under the leadership of the Duke of Aosta (1869–1931). He too was forced to lead a retreat as the Second Army was being routed in the north by the Austrians. As Lewis and Roos observe, "The Third Army survived the retreat virtually intact and helped the Italians stop the Austrian advance at the Piave River. Thus, the Third Army was regarded as undefeated during the war" (77).

307:43 **Nick said:** Another conspicuous decision Hemingway makes throughout the story is that his dialogue attribution is persistently understated, either omitted, or presented with the most unobtrusive verbs. In the fifty-nine instances of dialogue attribution in the story, Hemingway uses "said" fifty-five times, "told" once, "asked" twice, and "called" once. Despite the dispute here with a man who has pointed a gun at him or, later, when Nick has lost control of his mind and his emotional restraint, Hemingway never overplays his hand by loading dialogue attribution with dramatic verbs and/or adverbs.

308:3 **cheerfully:** This unexpected adverb picks up the "ranked and ruddy cheerfulness" (306:22) of the machine gun unit pictured in the postcards.

308:3–4 **company commander:** This officer is in charge of a company, which is generally about one hundred troops.

308:6 **All right.:** The phrase "all right" becomes resonant when Nick is happy that Paravicini "was all right" (308:13) and also when he tells Paravicini that he is, at first, "perfectly all right" (309:42) and then later, merely "all right" (309:44). For a similar usage, see the beginning of Hemingway's early story "The Battler" when, after being thrown from a train for trying to sneak on, Nick gets up and is unconvincingly described as "all right" (*CSS* 97), more trying to assure himself than us of that fact.

308:6 **Captain Paravicini:** Hemingway's biography has no obvious link to the name Paravicini, which is not a particularly common Italian surname. The great Italian

Hemingway scholar Giovanni Cecchin mentions that Paravicini was the name of the commander of the 153rd Infantry of the Novara brigade, the sector just south of Ancona. "Hemingway," Cecchin explains, "could have met him in front of the Fornaci-Osteria roadway of Fossalta, just beyond the trenches of [Red] Cross sections, in his tour of distributing 'general comforts' to the soldiers" (197, my translation).

308:7 **architect:** This information about Paravicini's profession recalls a similar detail from *A Farewell to Arms,* in which Frederic Henry is in Italy because he "wanted to be an architect" (*FTA* 242).

308:11 **The second:** The reference is to the Second Company, which Paravicini had previously commanded before his promotion.

308:13 **Para:** This nickname is an indication both of Nick's familiarity with the Captain and of his fondness of him. He is referred to with the diminutive "Para" thirteen times in the story, and by his full name eight times, both by Nick and by the narrator.

308:19 **His pistol made Nick nervous:** It is fascinating to observe Hemingway's description of Nick's attitude toward an object that expands to a description of his consideration of the second lieutenant as a person: here, it is his "pistol" that makes Nick "nervous." Then, the description is varied to indicate that it is the "officer" that makes Nick "very nervous" (308:23–24).

308:28 **I didn't know you:** The unusual instance of "know" assumes a heavy burden in this scene. Earlier, Nick asks the second lieutenant if he "knows" (308:6) Paravicini, and the second lieutenant responds, "You know him?" (308:8). Here, the verb "know" may be unexpected, in place of a word like "recognize."

308:32 **How was the show?:** The word "show" also is repeated conspicuously. In the common term for warfare, like "theater of war," Paravicini then uses "show" in the more common meaning, which would be "to demonstrate" (308:33, 308:35), when he illustrates the events of the attack by using a map. See also 309:24.

308:36 **Fornaci:** See entry at 307:19.

308:41 **How odd:** Hemingway has enough confidence as a writer not to give Paravicini any dialogue attribution or to offer a heavy-handed verb and adverb to signal to us how he is saying those two words. If he did, it would tell us explicitly that Paravicini is being sarcastic. However, a careful reading shows that he and Nick are on the same page with the dubious orders he has received. Nick refers to what he is "supposed to" do three times, to "move around" (308:40), to have them believe that more Americans are on their way (308:42–43), and to distribute chocolate and other treats (309:8).

308:42–43 **make them believe others are coming:** After decrying Italian anti-Austrian propaganda postcards, Nick discusses the form of propaganda in which he is participating, the disingenuous boosting of morale by assuring Italian soldiers that American help is on the way. In fact, the 332nd Infantry Regiment out of Ohio was known as the "propaganda regiment." After the disaster of Caporetto, the Italians requested an American battalion to make its presence known in Italy. The request was not made for military strategy, but for the purposes of morale. The Italian government wanted to display "tangible proof of the co-operation of the American nation" (Dalessandro and Dalessandro 47) and received an entire regiment (roughly three battalions) rather than merely one battalion.

309:3 **Like a bloody politician:** Anticipating the "homburg hat" (309:6), Nick is anachronistically referring to British politician and future prime minister Anthony Eden (1897–1977), who was the British foreign affairs minister at the time of this story's composition but had been an officer that served on the Italian front during World War I. In the early 1930s, Eden became associated with the homburg hat to the extent that it is referred to in Britain as the Anthony Eden hat. In Hemingway's 1935 *Esquire* piece, "Notes on the Next War: A Serious Topical Letter," he mentions Anthony Eden as representing British commercial designs on a water project in the Sudan (*BL* 208).

The adjective "bloody" also emerges as an unmistakable British-ism, even though here it is the American Nick who adopts the parlance. Given the carnage of the war scene, "bloody" is also grimly appropriate. This formulation continues with "bloody balls" (310:18, 310:25), the haunting image of a "bloody American uniform" (311:9), and also "bloody sick" (314:13).

In the manuscript, this sarcastic remark is even more pointed, as both Paravicini and Nick agree that the whole charade is "fairly disgusting" (*SS-HLE* 208).

309:7 **fedora:** Like the Homburg hat, the fedora is a felt hat with a curled brim and a length-wise indentation. See later, when Nick's helmet is "cloth-covered" (313:20).

309:8 **pockets full:** Nick's description of his "pockets" echoes the similar image of the pockets of the dead, told in excruciating detail as the story began (see entry at 307:5–6).

309:9 **musette:** a small haversack.

309:9 **chocolate:** Hemingway distributed small gifts of these kinds during his brief stay on the front in late June and early July 1918. He was in the act of handing out "chocolate and cigarettes" when he was wounded by an Austrian mortar strike on 8 July 1918 (Reynolds, *Young Hemingway* 18). In his citation for the Silver Medal of Valor, Hemingway was commended for distributing "sundries (articles of comfort)" to the combat troops (qtd. in Lewis, "Making it Up" 224).

309:13 **appearance:** Paravicini's gentle teasing continues, with the double meaning of appearance: Nick's *presence* will be welcome, but the concern also regards the way he *looks,* which might very well evidence his fatigue, any physical injuries, and even betray his lack of mental stability. When Paravicini says, "I'm sure" (309:13), we can be sure that Paravicini is anything but sure. In fact, when Nick responds by saying, "I wish you wouldn't" (309:14), he is telling him to lay off the friendly ribbing.

309:18 **No, thank you,":** This line should have a beginning quotation mark, which it does in the first edition. Other editions do not contain this typographical error.

309:19 **ether:** When a young Hemingway met the Arditi—the highly esteemed shock troops of the Italian Army, they told him they drank "rum and ether . . . usually with a chaser of opium" before they conducted their assault (Griffin 92). In a 1917 letter, John Dos Passos also claimed that World War I soldiers were given rum and ether before an attack: "No human being can stand the performance without constant stimulants" (qtd. in Landsberg 2).

309:20 **I can taste that still:** Just as the composition of this story might have been inspired by the kind of associative memory of the senses—the cauldron of a Cuban or Key West summer—depending on when Hemingway was telling the story— bringing back the memory of summer 1918 in Italy—here Nick asserts that not only can he remember the taste, but that the taste was so powerful it still remains. This characterization might be compared with "A Natural History of the Dead," when the narrator claims that "one cannot recall" the way a battlefield smells; it is "gone as completely as when you have been in love. . . . the sensation cannot be recalled" (337:42, 338:1–2), a distinction between the memory of a sensation and the recurrence of that same sensation.

This moment is a macabre update to Proust's classic madeleine episode in *Swann's Way,* in which Marcel's memory is triggered by a cake dipped in tea. Marcel's memory is so powerful that he is convinced the memory reveals his essence, an element that was within him all along. In Proust's case, the involuntary associative memory is "an all-powerful joy" (60), while in Hemingway, the taste of grappa and ether perpetuating itself calls to mind a memory that is rueful, traumatic, a gruesome scene of death.

309:28 **I know how I am**: In a story where identity serves as a major theme, Nick is under no pretensions that he is a true warrior. He knows he is brave and making a noble sacrifice; he is on the front voluntarily and helping the soldiers, but he also knows his own limitations. "In Another Country" takes place in a military hospital during World War I, and the American protagonist—perhaps an unnamed Nick Adams—says that the other soldiers "were like hunting-hawks; and I was not a hawk, although I might seem a hawk to those who had never hunted" (*CSS* 208).

Soon after Nick tells Paravicini, "Let's not talk about how I am . . . It's a subject I know too much about to want to think about it any more" (309:35–36).

309:31 **Mestre:** A borough in the mainland of Venice. Hemingway stayed in Mestre in June 1918 the night before he was transferred to the front. During Frederic Henry's escape in *A Farewell to Arms,* he hides in a gun car until his train makes it to Mestre, from where he can continue to Milan. In "A Veteran Visits the Old Front" Hemingway refers to Mestre as "one of the great railheads for the Piave" (*DLT* 178).

Chapter VII of *In Our Time* references the Villa Rossa, a whorehouse in Mestre. Similarly, Hemingway's early poem "Riparto d'Assalto" depicts lieutenants who "thought of a Mestre whore" (*CP* 46).

309:31 **Portogrande**: Hemingway here intends to write Portegrandi, or Porte Grandi. A Portogrande does exist in Italy, but it is in the South and was not part of the war front. Hemingway mentions this town in his 1922 essay "A Veteran Visits the Old Front," as he returned to the terrain he knew from the war. "Near Porto Grande," he writes, "in the part of the lower Piave delta where Austrians and Italians attacked and counterattacked waist-deep in the swamp water" (178).

Also mentioned on 311:2.

309:43 **No. I mean really:** Paravicini's line is the most touching in the entire story. It is the question (a follow-up question) of a friend exhibiting true concern for a man who is clearly struggling with the effects of the war. It would have been quite easy for Paravicini to move along after Nick brushes him off with the empty assurance, "I'm fine" (309:42), but he probes deeper, wanting to know the true state of Nick's psyche. See entry at 308:6.

This exchange recalls the end of "Hills Like White Elephants," when Jig tells her manipulative, condescending boyfriend or husband: "I feel fine. . . . There's nothing wrong with me. I feel fine" (*CSS* 214). If her companion were as caring and authentic as Captain Paravicini, perhaps he also would have said, "No. I mean really."

309:44 **without a light:** The fear of the dark is a constant motif for the veterans Hemingway chronicled, including Jake Barnes of *The Sun Also Rises* and Nick Adams. In "Now I Lay Me," Nick explains that, because he was "blown up at night" (*CSS*

276), he fears that his soul will leave his body during the night, hence the ominous connotations of the prayer referenced in the title. After Nick's various schemes to pass the sleepless night, he tells us, "finally it would be light, and then you could go to sleep, if you were where you could sleep in the daylight" (277). As Nick tells Paravicini in this story of his fear, somewhat optimistically, "That's all I have now" (309:44–45).

In "A Clean, Well-Lighted Place"—in addition to the suggestion in the title—the same insomnia due to battle trauma is implied: the story concludes by stating, "with daylight, he would go to sleep" (291:29), characterizing the old waiter's condition as one shared by many of his generation.

One of Hemingway's great meditations about the fear of the dark can be found in the manuscript of *A Farewell to Arms,* in which Frederic states that "Death comes in the dark" (*FTA-HLE* 300), and actually tries to figure out the point at which the night became frightening for him.

310:1 **trepanned**: In other words, Paravicini believes the doctor should have operated on his skull by "trepanning," or by making a hole to reduce cranial pressure.

In the manuscript of *The Garden of Eden,* there is a strong implication that the protagonist David Bourne was also trepanned during World War I. As David tells his wife, "It's just like being circumcised. . . . Only it's the head." (JFK #422).

310:3 **I don't seem crazy to you:** This line proves that Nick is again concerned with "appearances": not simply being bodily present on the military front but being an individual for Paravicini and the others to trust and even admire. Nick has already declared that he knows too much about his own condition to want to dwell on it, but he doesn't necessarily want the others to know the truth, particularly those he respects. As the narrative continues, Nick is "very disappointed" that he is in a disturbed state of mind (310:11), but "more disappointed" (310:12) that Paravicini knows it.

310:4 **You seem in top-hole shape:** C. Harold Hurley points out that "top-hole" constitutes a subtle pun, one that ostensibly compliments Nick for being in fine or "top notch" condition but actually backs up the notion that a trepan, that is, drilling a hole in Nick's skull, would have been the better option (109–10). Charles Coleman also observes that Paravicini "is using the expression here to suggest that Nick has recovered just as well as if he had been trepanned" (11).

310:11 **Nick lay on the bunk:** Until 311:20, Hemingway engages in an extended, tortured flashback that simultaneously reveals the "scattered" nature of Nick's mind, but also explains the substance of his trauma and his shellshock. Here he lies down; at the end of the flashback, he will sit up. This 786-word journey through Nick's psyche and memory is in many ways the heart of "A Way You'll Never Be" and its most memorable sequence.

The phrase recalls "Nick sat against the wall" from Chapter VI of *In Our Time,* moments after his wounding (*CSS* 105). Hemingway's first effort at fictionalizing his war experiences—immediately after they occurred—begins, "Nick lay in bed in the hospital" (*SS-HLE* 19), the opening line of the posthumously named "Untitled Milan Story."

310:13 **not as large a dugout as:** This phrase of comparison indicates that Nick is weighing his current surroundings with the recent past, the dugout he shared with his fellow soldiers and their panicked behavior.

310:13–14 **the class of 1899:** The so-called class of 1899 is a legendary in Italian military history. This phrase refers to Italian males who were born in 1899 and, because of their draftable age, bore the greatest burden of fighting during 1918, following the catastrophic defeat at Caporetto in fall of the previous year. It is estimated that 260,000 Italian teenagers from this birthyear were called into the Italian army after receiving only minimal training.

Among them was Randolfo Pacciardi, born 1 January 1899, who would become a member of the Bersaglieri troops and ultimately the Italian minister of defense in 1948. He is gently lampooned in *Across the River and into the Trees* as "the Honorable Pacciardi" (44). Hemingway himself was also born in 1899. At the site of Hemingway's wounding in Fossalta di Piave, there is a monument erected in honor of the "Ragazzi del '99." Perhaps the most famous such monument is the Monumento Nazionale Ai Ragazzi del 99 in Bassano del Grappa, the site of an impressive World War I museum.

310:18 **it was all a bloody balls:** The phrasing recalls another *Winner Take Nothing* story, "A Clean, Well-Lighted Place": "It was all a nothing" (291:7–8). For a discussion of "bloody," see the entry at 309:3.

310:19–20 **I'd shoot one but it's too late now:** This horrifying aside—told in the present tense—actually seems to refer to Nick's mindset during the attack, where Italian officials would decimate troops by killing their own, in order to "inspire" them to bravery, as well as to punish them for perceived cowardice. During the Battle of Caporetto, many Italian troops deserted and refused to fight, leading to the killing of every tenth man, or the decimation of some troops. In *A Farewell to Arms,* such a decimation is dramatized. In his magisterial history of the Italian front during World War I, Mark Thompson refers to 1917 as "the year of decimation" (263).

310:20–21 **They've put it back to five-twenty:** Part of the urgency of this confused flashback is that Nick is recalling a moment right before an attack, when he and his troops were the most frightened. Here, he recalls the delay of the attack and, inherently, the extension of the fear he was experiencing.

310:27 **Savoia:** This is an abbreviated form of "Avanti Savoia!"—"Go Savoia!"—which was a war cry that predated World War I. As Lewis and Roos explain, "It was used to exhort soldiers in the Italian army into battle in support of the King and the Royal Family, which was known as the House of Savoy (94). Thompson's history of the Italian front beautifully sets the scene of an attack:

> The countdown was excruciating; after fixing bayonets and draining the double tot of grappa, the men had to get through endless minutes before their officer shouted '*Avanti Savoia!*' and led them into the smoking din. . . . The men knew an attack was imminent when the military police mounted their machine guns behind the trench, ready to shoot at soldiers who lingered when the cry of "Savoy!" went up. (226–27)

Frederic describes the Italian major saying "Savoia" as the bombardment begins (*FTA* 52).

310:27 **no time to get it:** By "Making *it* cold" (310:27, emphasis added), Hemingway uses "it" in a highly suggestive manner (see entry at 311:4). Nick makes the order "Savoia" cold and simultaneously makes his mindset "cold," both contributing to his ability to avoid getting "it," that is, to avoid a panic attack. Nick couldn't find "his own" (310:28), directly referencing the watch that he consulted before the attack, but the phrase is ambiguous enough to include the understanding that he could not find his own platoon formation and even the center of his own psyche. Likewise, the description that "one whole end had caved in" (310:28) might refer to the dugout, to the platoon, and even possibly to Nick's head. In the manuscript of *A Farewell to Arms,* the protagonist first describes his injury similarly: "I'm wounded. . . . In the feet, legs, and hands and my head's been caved in" (*FTA-HLE* 288).

310:30 *teleferica:* Italian for *cableway.*

310:33 **Gaby Delys:** Gaby Deslys (1881–1920) was a notorious French actress, whose surname Hemingway misspells. In 1915, she starred in *Her Triumph* with Harry Pilcer, who was also her boyfriend. According to Michael Reynolds, Hemingway never saw her perform (*The 1930s* 331n24). The definitive examination in Hemingway studies on this obscure reference was written by E. R. Hagemann, who offers speculation on how Deslys might have entered Hemingway's consciousness, even if their paths never crossed. According to Hagemann, Hemingway is appropriating Nick Adams's timeline, which would have allowed him to see Deslys "most likely in 1917" (27).

Deslys is also mentioned in F. Scott Fitzgerald's "Porcelain in Pink," a story from *Tales of the Jazz Age* (1922).

310:34–35 **you called me baby doll a year ago:** This lyric refers to the Al Jolson 1916 hit "A Broken Doll," a simple song about a broken love affair. "You called me baby doll a year ago / You told me I was very nice to know." This song was transposed into the satire of a war song, "One of England's Broken Dolls." A T. S. Eliot scholar finds echoes of this same lyric early in *The Waste Land*: "You gave me hyacinths first a year ago" (Smith 31). This song was also mentioned as a soldier's favorite in Malcolm Cowley's Lost Generation classic, *Exile's Return* (49), which focuses on Hemingway and other expatriates.

310:35 **the great Gaby:** An obvious pun on F. Scott Fitzgerald's *The Great Gatsby* (1925), just as "the far side of the taxis" (310:36) suggests Fitzgerald's first novel, *This Side of Paradise* (1920).

310:36 **Harry Pilcer:** Pilcer (1885–1961) was an American entertainer and the boyfriend and frequent stage collaborator of Gaby Deslys (see entry at 310:33). He died six months before Hemingway.

310:38 **Sacré Coeur:** This basilica in the Montmartre section of Paris had only been erected in 1914.

310:42 **a low house painted yellow:** The traumatic recollection of the attack is sublimated through objects, specifically this house and the bend in the river (also 311:15–16 and 314:23–24). While most descriptions of such a house might be "yellow house," Nick is specific to recall a "house painted yellow," as if distinguishing between the essence of the house, its interior and organic form, and its appearance to the viewer. The house becomes of preeminent importance to Nick, and every night it appears in his dreams.

310:42 **willows all around it:** The haunting image of these willows (also mentioned on 311:1) recalls *Hamlet,* in which Gertrude's speech describes her discovery of Ophelia's suicide: "There is a willow grows aslant a brook" (4.7.137)—where the branches are referred to as "dead men's fingers" (4.7.142), all leading "To muddy death" (4.7.154).

310:44–45 **it frightened him:** This explicit statement recalls T. S. Eliot's "The Love Song of J. Alfred Prufrock (1915): "And in short, I was afraid" (l. 86).
This phrase is repeated (310:46).

311:3 **come wallowing:** We usually associate "wallow" either with an animal in the mud or a person basking excessively in a certain emotion, usually sadness or self-pity. See also "Big Two-Hearted River" for the same striking vocabulary, when Nick "wallowed down the stream" and knew that to go upstream, one had to "wallow against the current" (*CSS* 176, 178).

"Wallow" also quickly follows the mention of the "willow" that Nick associates with the site of his near-death experience.

311:4 **Who ordered that one?:** This familiar sentiment of a soldier criticizing the ignorant orders from a military superior is identified as Colonel Cantwell's main sadness in *Across the River and into the Trees*: "Other people's orders" (194).

311:4–5 **If it didn't get so damned mixed up:** No writer used the word "it" as evocatively and carefully as Hemingway. Here, Hemingway writes, "If *it* didn't get so damned mixed up he could follow *it* all right" (emphasis added), but there's no certainty that "it" means the same thing in both instances. It could be: "If Nick's brain didn't get so mixed up, he could follow the orders." Or, "If Nick's confused memory didn't get so mixed up, he could trace it successfully." Or, "If the orders didn't get so confusing, Nick could follow the commands." The ambiguity makes the sequence more powerful. But "it"—the sentence—is confused (311:7) so that memory and the present time are indistinguishable. The confusion is such that it is quite possible that Nick is acting out the scene from the past, attracting horrified attention from the Italian troops.

This progression of the use of "it" leads to a later moment during Nick's conversation with the adjutant, when he "felt it coming on now" (311:41) and "[h]e felt it coming on again" (313:46), clearly meaning the rush of some intense anxiety or traumatic recall. He is familiar enough with this sensation to know that quieting down may temper it. The crescendo of the story occurs during Nick's attempt to govern this inner attack: "He was trying to hold it in" (314:2), then "He knew he could not stop it now" (314:4), and then "Here it came" (314:6). In the way he reports the attack to Paravicini, he states, "I had one then but it was easy. They're getting much better. I can tell when I'm going to have one because I talk so much" (314:32–33), referring to these psychic attacks with the vague designations "one," "it," and "they."

For more on Hemingway's technique regarding the pronoun "it" and the way he implements the strategy in "The Snows of Kilimanjaro," see Cirino, *Thought in Action* (118).

311:5 **damned mixed up:** This language is presented as Nick's, through free indirect discourse. The word "damned" in this narration (311:5) prefigures the way Nick uses it freely in dialogue: the helmets are "a damned nuisance" (313:28) and "no damned good" (313:32); Nick tells Paravicini he has a "damned small battalion" (314:9); and, in the penultimate sentence of the story, Nick refers to his "damned bicycle" (315:3).

311:11–13 **The Paris part . . . she had gone off . . . take the same driver twice:** In this associative part of Nick's memory, the implication is that his fear is based on his embarrassment if a driver knew that he had been humiliated by this unnamed woman. In repose, Nick's stream of consciousness is chaotic and illogical.

311:13 **That was what frightened about that:** Without "him" or "Nick" as a direct object, his identity is eliminated from this sentence and becomes ghostly.

311:21 **they stiffened:** In addition to his head injury, Nick has incurred the same injury as Hemingway himself, a leg injury that required him to relearn how to walk and left him on crutches for several months. Joseph Flora asks an interesting practical question: with such a recent leg injury, how can Nick negotiate this war-torn terrain on a bicycle (124)?

311:27–28 **In that army an adjutant is not a commissioned officer:** A rare moment of exposition in which Hemingway inserts information he was evidently anxious to share with the reader. In the United States military, a commissioned officer receives a commission from a military academy, while noncommissioned officers are recruited.

311:30 **There will be several millions of Americans here shortly:** With this statement—and by his very presence—Nick has become part of the propaganda machine, a benign personification of the gruesome postcards the story mentions. Although America officially entered the war in April 1917, most of its four million soldiers were committed to the Western Front, particularly France.

If he is making this statement in late June or early July 1918 as it appears, he is correct, as the 332nd Infantry Regiment out of Ohio would come to bolster the Italian military effort and to act as as "propaganda troops," serving both a vital military purpose and a symbolic one for purposes of morale. Americans would be arriving on the Italian front soon but not the "untold millions" (312:16) that he promises; the vast majority of Americans would go to the Western Front.

See entry at 308:42.

311:38 **Spagnolini made it:** Fratelli Spagnolini was a clothier based in Milan, which was famous for providing military outfits for the Italian army. Hemingway elected to purchase a Spagnolini for himself in September 1918, aligning himself with the military dress he found more impressive than the American Red Cross uniform. Richard Owen points out that the Spagnolini shop was adjacent to the Red Cross headquarters in Milan on Via Manzoni (39), home to many fashionable clothing stores.

Also mentioned on 312:32.

311:45 **Italian medals:** In November 1921, Hemingway received the *Medaglia Argento al Valore Militare* (the Silver Medal for Military Valor) and the *Croce al Merito di Guerra* (the War Cross of Merit). In a 1927 letter, Hemingway confessed that these medals were not for any special bravery, but "simply because I was an American attached to the Italian army" (*Letters vol. 3*, 212), the same arbitrary system reflected in "In Another Country." Later, referring to himself in the third person, he would state that these two decorations "are the only ones that he respects" ("Hemingway Is Bitter About Nobody" 110).

312:5 **Eritrea:** In the late nineteenth century, Italy colonized Eritrea—a small country in northeast Africa that neighbors Ethiopia on its southern border, Sudan on its western border, and the Red Sea on its east.

312:6 **Tripoli:** The capital city of Libya. Libya is on the opposite side of the Sudan from Eritrea. Italy, which claimed possession of Tripoli, launched a military incursion against the Ottoman Empire in 1911.

312:9 **Carso:** The Carso is a rocky plateau southeast of Gorizia that was the site of incredible carnage between Italy and the Austrian army from 1915 to 1917. In *Across the River and into the Trees*, Cantwell refers to the "stupid butchery" on the Carso (62), a historically accurate assessment of extended, inconclusive actions to wage war over this land. *A Farewell to Arms* begins in 1915 with a dry assertion: "the whole thing going well on the Carso" (6), a devastatingly ironic remark. And in his powerful introduction to the collection of war writing that he edited in 1942, *Men at War*, Hemingway includes an assessment of fighting on the Carso: "The last war, during the years 1915, 1916, 1917, was the most colossal, murderous, mismanaged butchery that has ever taken place on earth. Any writer who said otherwise lied" (xiii). Hemingway is referring to the twelve Battles of the Isonzo, whose casualties exceeded one million soldiers.

Hemingway's 1922 piece "A Veteran Visits the Old Front" contains a sequence of elegiac beauty, reflecting on the action at the Carso:

> Their best men were dead on the rocky Carso, in the fighting around Goritzia, on Mount San Gabrielle, on Grappa and in all the places where men died that nobody ever heard about. In 1918 they didn't march with the ardor that they did in 1916, some of the troops strung out so badly that, after the battalion was just a dust cloud way up the road, you would see poor old boys hoofing it along the side of the road to ease their bad feet, sweating along under their packs and rifles and the deadly Italian sun in a long, horrible, never-ending stagger after the battalion. (*DT* 178).

The Italian Third Army served on the Carso.

312:11–12 **now I am reformed out of the war:** In Chapter VI of *In Our Time,* Nick declared a "separate peace" to Rinaldi (*CSS* 105), his fellow soldier, after being seriously wounded, later to be echoed more famously in *A Farewell to Arms.* This phrase is a more oblique reference to his lack of passion for the cause or for any kind of fighting. He has a new attitude about the war and his enthusiasm has been eliminated, whether from knowledge, experience, or the wound.

Charles Coleman points out that the word "reform" also signals the re-forming, the physical rehabilitation that Nick has undergone (27).

312:16–17 **grasshopper:** As the introduction to this chapter mentions, each of Hemingway's three volumes of short stories has a story that continues this coherent narrative in Nick's life, essentially forming a through-line to all of Hemingway's short fiction. *In Our Time* (1925) has Hemingway's masterpiece, "Big Two-Hearted River," which shows Nick as a veteran by himself in the Michigan woods, trying to rehabilitate himself from his war wound with a solitary fishing and camping trip. "Now I Lay Me" from *Men Without Women* (1927) dramatizes Nick's insomnia from the same war wound and reveals his state of mind through his late-night conversation with his friend John. "A Way You'll Never Be" continues this dramatic strain in Nick's life, although it actually precedes the other two stories in the chronology of Nick's life, although Hemingway wrote and published it last among the three.

In "Big Two-Hearted River," Nick sees grasshoppers who have "all turned black from living in the burned-over land" (*CSS* 165). In the second part of the story, Nick gathers grasshoppers for bait, finding "plenty of good grasshoppers" (173), and choosing about fifty of the "medium-sized brown ones" (173). Grasshoppers are also Nick's favorite mode of imaginary fishing in "Now I Lay Me," and he describes using them for bait and for throwing into the stream for the trout to eat.

The comparison of the grasshopper to a locust recalls the eighth plague of ancient Egypt (Exodus 10:1–20). In an earlier version of the story, shrapnel balls littered on the ground are compared to unmelted hailstones, the seventh plague.

Nick's simile precipitates this lengthy discourse about grasshoppers (although interrupted, it spans 312:16–22 and then 312:26–29 and then again from 312–35 to 313:11).

312:20–21 **at the moment I cannot recall:** This rupture in memory should be juxtaposed to the enduring memory of the taste of ether in 309:19–20.

312:24 **I can see you have been wounded:** Because Nick does not have any visible wounds that we know of, the adjutant can "see" Nick's injury by his behavior, by his rambling discourse. The obviousness of this injury recalls Nick's awareness that Paravicini can also see that Nick is unwell.

312:41 **blowsy**: That is, unkempt. A "blowze" refers to the female companion of a beggar.

312:45–46 **hit them with a bat**: The first edition reads "hit them with a hat" (*WTN* 79), which makes more sense. This change gives it a more irrationally violent effect. Although most subsequent editions use "bat," Philip Young, editor of *The Nick Adams Stories,* has left it as "hat" (164).

313:15 **Sir Henry Wilson**: Field Marshal Henry Hughes Wilson (1864–1922) was a highly decorated senior official and principal British military advisor. During World War I, Wilson was the general officer in command on the Eastern Front from 1917 to 1918 and the chief of the imperial general staff from 1918 to 1922. As Hemingway indicates in the story, Wilson visited Italy in late June 1918.

In *The Sun Also Rises,* Mike Campbell refers to "the night they'd shot Henry Wilson" (140), which was 22 June 1922.

313:15–16 **either you must govern or you must be governed**: It is unsurprising given his state of mind that Nick has botched this geopolitical aphorism. In fact, the phrase emerges from a disagreement about British options in governing Mesopotamia after World War I. In August 1919, a year following the action of the story, John Shuckburgh (1877–1953), secretary of the political department, quipped "We must either govern Mesopotamia or not" (qtd. in Paris 89). However, this rejoinder had nothing to do with Sir Henry Wilson, but was instead Shuckburgh's answer to Sir Andrew Talbot Wilson (1884–1940), the British civil commissioner in Baghdad during World War I.

This quote has resonance with respect to Nick's determination to govern his own memories, his psyche, his emotions. Certainly, if he cannot govern himself, or get control of himself, they will control him.

Nick repeats this maxim on 313:18–19.

313:35 **I think you should go back**: Paravicini concludes, ironically, that Nick would depress, rather than raise, the morale of his troops. Given Nick's behavior, his rambling speech, and his scattered mind, Paravicini would prefer to keep Nick away from them. Although Hemingway does not convey this information explicitly, we can conclude that Paravicini is gently guiding Nick away and is not being unkind. Even with this rather direct "I won't have it" (313:38–39), Paravicini protects Nick's dignity by inventing excuses (Nick can come back once he gets his supplies; Paravicini doesn't want to bunch up the soldiers to create a target for the enemy).

When the scene concludes with Paravicini saying, "I won't have you circulating around to no purpose" (313:44), his dialogue is attributed not to Para (as in

313:30) or even Paravicini (as in 313:26), but "Captain Paravicini," indicating that his military role has now superseded his role as a friend. He does have his men to protect. Nevertheless, Paravicini's empathy is always present. In one of the story's few instances of adverbs in dialogue attribution, he speaks to Nick "gently" (314:8) during Nick's psychic attack.

313:42 **Zenzon:** Zenson di Piave is a small municipality northeast of Venice. Zenson borders Fossalta and was the site of action during the Battle of the Piave, where on 19 June 1918 an Italian cavalry troop repelled an Austro-Hungarian charge (Raab 77).

313:42 **San Dona:** About seven miles east of Zenson, San Donà di Piave is a commune northeast of Venice that incurred great damage during World War I. In *Across the River and into the Trees,* San Donà is "a cheerful town" that had been rebuilt in the three decades since it was destroyed during the First World War (25).

313:43 **the bridge:** Nick is referring to the iconic landmark in San Donà, the Ponte della Vittoria, which was built in the late nineteenth century, destroyed during the First World War, but rebuilt in 1922.

314:10–11 **Why don't they bury the dead?:** This question suggests Matthew 8:22 and Luke 9:60: "leave the dead to bury their own dead."

314:20 **in place:** Although Freud focuses on childhood memories, this same concept of a traumatic incident being replaced by a more benign object is at the heart of his notion of screen memories, or "concealing memories." Instead of the emotionally terrifying image of the man shooting at him, that memory is displaced by a representative object, the yellow house. As Freud describes it, instead of the actual object in question being faithfully represented, "something else comes as a substitute" (34). Hemingway reproduces this phenomenon portraying war trauma instead of childhood trauma.

314:22 **choking:** Throughout his career, Hemingway returned to this word at moments of peak intensity. In "Big Two-Hearted River," Nick is disturbed by his thoughts of the war, but he "knew he could choke it" (*CSS* 169), having exhausted himself through an unnecessarily long hike. In the manuscript of *A Farewell to Arms,* Hemingway describes the "chemical choking" of the operation and then the moment of Frederic emerging from general anesthesia similarly: "my legs hurt so that I tried to get back into the choked place I had come from but I could not get back in there" (*FTA-HLE* 299).

314:24 **Christ**: Of all the epithets to use, this one has particularly potency, given the figure of the bearded man shooting at him in the culminating flashback.

314:35 **I know the way:** Nick means, literally, that he can return to his post in Fornaci without being accompanied by a runner that Paravicini might assign. However, given the title of the story, the "way" also signifies that Nick is assuring his friend that he is aware of his own psychological state, his needs, his limitations, and his capabilities. This phrase sets up the last line of the story, where he is determined not to "lose the way to Fornaci" (315:4).

However, between Nick's statement of assuredness and the last line comes a fracture in his stability. His immediate surroundings force a momentary flashback to another wartime scene, this time seeing the Terza Savoia cavalry (314:45), recalling the Italians war cry "Savoia." See entry at 310:27.

314:40–41 *ciao . . . Ciao:* In the manuscript draft of this story, Hemingway misspells this Italian word for hello and goodbye *"ciaou"* as Nick explains of Paravicini, "He was the first who had taught me to say it many months before when I had embarrassed him by my ungrammatical formalities. It is a vulgar the colloquial form of saying goodbye used between people who are fond of each other on terms of the same position who are on terms of good friendship" (*SS-HLE* 218). A second exchange of "ciaou" [sic] between Nick and Paravicini ends the story in the manuscript version (*SS-HLE* 219).

Hemingway often addresses his American characters' difficulties with the Italian language. In *A Farewell to Arms,* Frederic Henry speaks with an accent that reveals him as a foreigner and prevents him from advancing in the military ranks. In "In Another Country," the American protagonist is exhorted to "Speak grammatically!" (*CSS* 209).

WORKS CITED

Baker, Carlos. *Ernest Hemingway: A Life Story.* Scribner's, 1969.

Cecchin, Giovanni. *La Grande Guerra: Cronache Particolari.* Bassano del Grappa: Collezione Princeton, 1998.

Cirino, Mark. *Ernest Hemingway: Thought in Action.* U of Wisconsin P, 2012.

———. *Reading Hemingway's* Across the River and into the Trees. Kent State UP, 2016.

Cohen, Roger. "Young Lives Interrupted." *New York Times,* 30 Nov. 2015, p. A26.

Coleman, Charles A., Jr. *PTSD and Hemingway's "A Way You'll Never Be": The Mark of Confidence.* PTSD Press, 2014.

Cowley, Malcolm. *Exile's Return: A Literary Odyssey of the 1920s.* Viking, 1956.

Dalessandro, Robert J., and Rebecca S. Dalessandro. *American Lions: The 332nd Infantry Regiment in Italy in World War I.* Schiffer Military History, 2010.

Eliot, T. S. *The Complete Poems and Plays, 1909–1950.* Harcourt, Brace & World, 1971.

Flora, Joseph M. *Hemingway's Nick Adams.* LSU Press, 1982.

Freud, Sigmund. *Psychopathology of Everyday Life.* Translated by A. A. Brill. Dover, 2003.

Garnett, David. "Books in General." Review of *Winner Take Nothing*. *The New Statesman and Nation*, 10 Feb. 1934, p. 192.

Griffin, Peter. *Along with Youth: Hemingway, The Early Years*. OUP, 1985.

Hagemann, E. R. "The Feather Dancer in 'A Way You'll Never Be.'" *Hemingway Notes*, vol. 6, no. 2, 1981, pp. 25–27.

Hemingway, Ernest. *Across the River and into the Trees*. 1950. Scribner's, 1996.

———. *Complete Poems*. Edited by Nicholas Gerogiannis. U of Nebraska P, 1992.

———. *The Complete Short Stories of Ernest Hemingway: The Finca Vigía Edition*. Scribner's, 1987.

———. *A Farewell to Arms*. 1929. Scribner's, 2003.

———. *A Farewell to Arms: The Hemingway Library Edition*. Edited by Seán Hemingway. Scribner's, 2012.

———. *The Garden of Eden* manuscript, item 422, Ernest Hemingway Collection, John F. Kennedy Library, Boston.

———. "Introduction." *Men at War*. Edited by Ernest Hemingway. Bramhall House, 1979. xi–xxvii.

———. *The Letters of Ernest Hemingway: Volume 1 (1907–1922)*. Edited by Sandra Spanier and Robert W. Trogdon. CUP, 2011.

———. *The Letters of Ernest Hemingway: Volume 3 (1926–1929)*. Edited by Rena Sanderson, Sandra Spanier, and Robert W. Trogdon. CUP, 2015.

———. *The Nick Adams Stories*. Edited by Philip Young. Scribner's, 2003.

———. "Notes on the Next War: A Serious Topical Letter." *By-Line Ernest Hemingway: Selected Articles and Dispatches of Four Decades*. Edited by William White. Scribner's 1967, pp. 205–12.

———. *The Short Stories of Ernest Hemingway: The Hemingway Library Edition*. Scribner's, 2018.

———. *The Sun Also Rises*. 1926. Scribner's, 2003.

———. "A Veteran Visits the Old Front." *Dateline: Toronto: The Complete* Toronto Star *Dispatches, 1920–1924*, edited by William White, Scribner, 1985, pp. 176–80.

———. "A Way You'll Never Be" manuscript, item 813, Ernest Hemingway Collection, John F. Kennedy Library, Boston.

———. *Winner Take Nothing*. Scribner's, 1933.

"Hemingway Is Bitter about Nobody—But His Colonel Is." *Time*, 11 Sept. 1950, p. 110.

Hurley, C. Harold. "'Top-hole' in Hemingway's 'A Way You'll Never Be.'" *Explicator*, vol. 69, no. 1, 2011, pp. 109–12.

Landsberg, Melvin. "Obscuring Hull House—Highlighting Male Predominance in *U.S.A.*" *John Dos Passos Newsletter*, vol. 10, 2002, pp. 1–4.

Lewis, Robert W. "Making It Up." *Journal of Modern Literature*, vol. 9, no. 2, 1982, pp. 209–36.

Lewis, Robert W., and Michael Kim Roos. *Reading Hemingway's* A Farewell to Arms. Kent State UP, 2019.

The New Oxford Annotated Bible: Rev. Standard Version. OUP, 1973.

Owen, Richard. *Hemingway in Italy*. Armchair Traveller, 2017.

Paris, Timothy J. *Britain, the Hashemites and Arab Rule, 1920–1925: The Sherifian Solution*. Cass, 2003.

Proust, Marcel. *In Search of Lost Time: Vol. 1: Swann's Way*. 1913. Translated by C. K. Scott Moncrieff and Terence Kilmartin. Revised by D. J. Enright. Modern Library, 2003.

Raab, David. *Battle of the Piave: Death of the Austro-Hungarian Empire, 1918.* Dorrance, 2003.

Reynolds, Michael. *Hemingway: The 1930s.* Norton, 1998.

———. *The Young Hemingway.* Norton, 1998.

Ross, Lillian. *Portrait of Hemingway.* Avon, 1961.

Scafella, Frank. "The Way It Never Was on the Piave." *Hemingway in Italy and Other Essays,* edited by Robert W. Lewis, Praeger, 1990, pp. 181–88.

Shakespeare, William. *The Norton Shakespeare.* 2nd ed. Edited by Stephen Greenblatt. Norton, 2008.

Smith, Grover Cleveland. *T. S. Eliot and the Use of Memory.* Bucknell UP, 1996.

Smith, Paul. *A Reader's Guide to the Short Stories of Ernest Hemingway.* G. K. Hall, 1989.

———. "The Trying-out of *A Farewell to Arms.*" *New Essays on* A Farewell to Arms, edited by Scott Donaldson, CUP, 1990, pp. 27–52.

Thompson, Mark. *The White War: Life and Death on the Italian Front, 1915–1919.* Basic Books, 2010.

THE MOTHER OF A QUEEN

Krista Quesenberry

"The Mother of a Queen" represents gossip as both a central theme and possible source. It is widely believed to have been one of the stories Hemingway was referring to when he wrote in the glossary of *Death in the Afternoon* that among bullfighters, "There are many very, very funny Spanish fairy stories" (418). As he was finishing up the *Winner Take Nothing* stories in the summer of 1933, Hemingway wrote in a 7 June letter to Arnold Gingrich that "The Mother of a Queen" is "about Ortiz the bullfighter" (*Letters vol. 5,* 402), and Miriam B. Mandel has identified Mexican bullfighter José Ortiz Puga (Pepe Ortiz) as "recognizably the historical prototype" for Paco (*vol. 5,* 154). Carlos Baker further conjectures that Hemingway likely "learned the story from Sidney Franklin" (606). Hemingway also regarded "The Mother of a Queen" as one of a handful of *Winner Take Nothing* stories that he had written "absolutely as they happen," which he noted in a letter to Maxwell Perkins of 17 November 1933 (*Letters vol. 5,* 541).

Perhaps because it is a dramatic monologue, "The Mother of a Queen" simply *sounds* like a story told many times over. The narrator is Roger, who is telling an unidentified listener (a stand-in for the reader) about the end of his years-long intimate—though unspecified—relationship with Paco, a supposedly gay bullfighter and the "queen" of the title. Roger and Paco once shared nearly everything, including a home, but, after an ugly falling out, they have become, by the time of Roger's narration, nearly strangers with very different memories of their past. As Roger aims to convince his listener that Paco is stingy, irresponsible, heartless, promiscuous (both sexually and financially), illiterate, and unsuccessful, Roger also reveals himself to be nagging, boastful, begrudging, obstinate, and, of course, a gossip. As Charles J. Nolan describes it, the heart of the story is "the process of asking and then answering a number of questions that Hemingway inherently poses as he creates two very complicated and perhaps not very likeable characters" (90–91).

Composed sometime between the late summers of 1931 and 1932, "The Mother of a Queen" was, according to Paul Smith, a story Hemingway described as "done for a book," meaning that Hemingway understood the story "could not gain entry to the more conservative magazines but, in the company of his more reserved stories, would be allowed into a collection" (264–65). In 1991, Susan F. Beegel identified "The

Mother of a Queen" as among the Hemingway stories generally ignored by critics "because they do not fit the heroic paradigms" (10) and perhaps "because of their grotesque subject matter" (14). Then in 1998, Carl P. Eby wrote that the story has been "marginalized" alongside other queer-themed stories, "which are now recognized as being an integral part of Hemingway's work," even if making "these stories *central* to his work would perhaps be as misguided as ignoring them, since they are generally not his best work" (5). Otherwise, scholars have reduced the story to a biographical vindication, such as Kenneth Lynn's reading of the story as simply reflecting Hemingway's tension with his mother "by dealing symbolically with their current financial relationship" (408), and Nancy R. Comley and Robert Scholes's description of the story's "odd mixture of maternity and economics" as the author's way of "bury[ing] the mother problem by telling a story in which a mother remains unburied" (32). However, in August of 1932, Hemingway offered Maxwell Perkins a group buy for *Scribner's Magazine* of three "excellent stories," including "The Mother of a Queen" (*Letters vol. 5*, 190) and after *Winner Take Nothing* was published, Hemingway wrote to Arnold Gingrich that "Mother of a Queen and Day's Wait are better stories than you think they are" (531). Along with Hemingway, one of the story's few champions is Gerry Brenner, who described it in 1990 as a "long-neglected masterpiece" (165).

Considering "The Mother of a Queen" in relation to Hemingway's other queer-themed stories, such as "The Sea Change" and "A Simple Enquiry," this story differs most significantly in that social stigma is acknowledged and weaponized. Unlike the narrators in these other stories, Roger *names* Paco's sexuality and places it at the center of the narrative, rather than treating sexuality as an unspoken horror or even a mystery to be uncovered. And more like "God Rest You Merry, Gentlemen" and "One Reader Writes," "The Mother of a Queen" centers on the conflict of how characters—and even readers—react to socially stigmatized sexual identities that are expressed in the open. Queerness is a substantive factor of plot and characterization in this story. Roger's resentment of Paco may be rooted in the loss of their relationship, but it is expressed through homophobic language because homosexuality carries a stigma that Hemingway's vindictive narrator can mobilize.

Title: For a writer who regularly gestured in his titles toward his male protagonists— as in "Fathers and Sons," "My Old Man," or *The Old Man and the Sea*—this story's title stands out as doubly feminized, highlighting not only a *mother* but also a *queen*. As early as 1982, Charles Stetler and Gerald Locklin argued that homosexuality did not "appear to be the primary target in this story" (69) and that readers should focus more on the "mother" than the "queen" because Hemingway couldn't resist a story about "Mothers and bitchy women" (69).

At the start of the story, the "mother" of the title presumably refers to Paco's mother, whose burial instigates the characters' initial argument. Roger is understandably identified by many scholars as Paco's business associate who "manages his affairs" or as "someone in the matador's cuadrilla" (Comley and Scholes 33, 137). However, as Brenner and Nolan have each argued, Roger also "resembles some angry and domineering mother" (Brenner 166). Indeed, the character flaws that Roger reveals about himself (such as nagging and gossiping) are culturally associated with women, and Hemingway withholds Roger's name until twelve lines before the story's end: the story's big reveal, then, is not that Paco is "a queen" but that his "mother" figure in the story is Roger, a man.

This understanding of Roger as a stand-in "mother" for Paco also categorizes the characters' relationship not along romantic or professional lines but as a *queer family* or *chosen family*. Such arrangements often develop (even today) out of the financial and emotional vulnerabilities that occur when families cast out LGBTQ+ members because of their identities. In a study of such extrafamilial connections throughout Hemingway's fiction, Debra A. Moddelmog defines "queer families" as "characters who support each other emotionally and sometimes materially" and whose bonds are "sealed with some form of queer desire" ("Queer Families" 188). For Moddelmog, these relationships are "queer not simply because they are chosen rather than inherited but also by virtue of their transience and the ways they blur the boundaries between non-erotic and erotic, sanctioned and taboo bonds" to the point that "they reconfigure the bonds of belonging" and "challenge the traditional family to do the same" ("Queer Families" 175). Roger and Paco's relationship is a perfect demonstration of such an arrangement. By blurring the distinction between traditional and "queer" mothering, this story offers a challenge to these "bonds of belonging" that extends from the queer family to the traditional family structure.

Another function of the title is to invoke translation, as many *Winner Take Nothing* stories do. The syntax "The Mother of a Queen" resembles the Spanish possessive form, in contrast to a more familiar possessive form in English, such as "The Queen's Mother." In addition to placing more emphasis on the word "queen," this title establishes not only the awkwardness but also the formality and distance that can come from translation, particularly rough translation that insufficiently accounts for syntax. Roger and Paco seem to experience some level of miscommunication and emotional distance, even if mistranslations are not the *cause* of their disagreements. Translation also emphasizes the situation of the dramatic monologue because the past interactions in the story were presumably conducted in Paco's native language, Spanish, while Roger's narration is in his native language, English, for the benefit of his English-speaking listener/reader. All Paco's words and intentions, then, have been translated both literally and emotionally by Roger.

316:1–3 **When his father died . . . he would have the plot permanently:** Family and financial matters are intertwined from the story's very first sentence, when Roger reveals that Paco was young when his father died and that Paco's manager at the time decided how to handle and pay for the father's burial. This sentence, too, carries forward the awkwardness of translation established in the title, with Roger's clarification for the listener that "perpetually" means "permanently," as well as with the pronoun-antecedent confusion over which "he" is being "buried" by the former manager—Paco or Paco's father. Perhaps one is buried metaphorically and the other literally. Roger's articulation of the former manager's consummate control represents Paco as passive and disinterested when it comes to both his family and his finances.

316:3–4 **But when his mother died . . . might not always be so hot on each other:** Hemingway plays another pronoun trick here, as the sentence starts out focused on Paco and his mother then quickly turns toward Paco and the former manager, creating pronoun-antecedent confusion over which "they" are the ones who "might not always be so hot on each other." The suggestion is that Paco may have had a contentious relationship with his mother, with his manager, or with both, thereby emphasizing the indeterminate boundaries of Paco's professional and familial relationships.

Two details already cast doubt on Roger's perspective. First, if Paco was young when his father died, then he and his manager would presumably *not* have been in a romantic relationship at the time, so that can be ruled out as the manager's motivation for the first burial decision. Roger could be misinterpreting or misrepresenting the previous manager's reasons for treating Paco's parents' burials differently, as perhaps those decisions had nothing to do with their romantic relationship. Second, Roger's story largely focuses on the moral limitations of the bullfighter, but this significant decision—the temporary burial of the mother—is credited as exclusively the choice of the former manager, possibly without Paco's input. These awkward opening lines provide sufficient evidence that the story is being filtered, shaped, and even exaggerated according to Roger's current feelings about Paco.

316:4–5 **They were sweethearts; sure he's a queen:** Casually introducing the fact of Paco's sexuality in the third sentence, Roger first identifies Paco and his manager as "sweethearts" and then uses this fact to demean Paco with the epithet "queen." The choice of "queen" is interesting, as even in the *Death in the Afternoon* glossary Hemingway provides a range of possible translations for the Spanish slur *maricón*—namely, "a sodomite, nance, queen, fairy, fag, etc." (417). Any of these terms would have conveyed the same basic meaning, but "queen" both feminizes Paco and suggests a measure of untouchability, which is one of Paco's characteristics that Roger most harshly criticizes. Roger's descriptions of Paco do not represent him as especially effeminate or flamboyant, but Paco conveys stereotypical "queen"-ness by not concerning himself with trivial matters, like squaring his finances, and by always expecting to get his way.

316:5 **didn't you know that, of course he is:** With the introduction of "you," Roger's position as narrator of this dramatic monologue comes into focus. The "you" listener is never revealed or named in the story, but, from this moment, it is clear that the listener shares the reader's point of view. Any bias or confusion in the sentences above can now be fully attributed to Roger's first-person limited viewpoint, just as the reliability of his narrative can now be fully questioned. With his spiteful, dismissive tone, Roger makes his negative attitude toward Paco quite clear. At the same time, Roger's careful use of pronouns here—"of course *he* is," rather than "he was," or "*they* are," or even "*we* are"—creates some distance between himself and Paco, such that Paco appears (in Roger's telling) to be the only "queen" in the story.

Even more significantly, Roger's casual treatment of Paco's sexuality here presents it as old information, hardly worth noting. With the phrasing "of course he is," Roger eliminates any sense of secrecy or impropriety that might otherwise attend the moment at which Paco's sexuality is revealed to the listener/reader for the first time, and Roger indicates that Paco's sexuality is something the listener/reader should regard as unremarkable. Unlike other Hemingway stories—perhaps most notably "The Sea Change" and "A Simple Enquiry"—Roger is unconcerned with softening or hiding his meaning, and he appears to take no issue with outing Paco. That being said, this revelation is offered in the same breath as the situation of the dramatic monologue is revealed, so that Roger both boldly states and at once undermines the notion that Paco's homosexuality is common knowledge: it appears the listener/reader was unaware until Roger flung open the closet door. Paco being a "a queen" cannot be both common knowledge and something that Roger must reveal explicitly—yet he does in the most casual terms, without even a hint of scandal.

316:5–6 **So he just buried her for five years:** The opening conjunction "So" here draws a verbal connection between Paco's sexuality and what Roger perceives as Paco's unjust treatment of his mother: Roger represents the decision about the burial to be a *result* of this failing relationship between Paco and his manager and, thus, a result of Paco's sexuality.

In these first five sentences, we receive all the basic details about the inciting conflict of Roger's story; however, aside from Roger's weak notion of causality, it is unclear what Paco's sexuality has to do with the burial of his parents or with his lack of fiscal responsibility. Even so, because Roger has now conceptually and narratively linked Paco's disrespect of his mother to his being "a queen," Roger is able to pile insults on Paco that are unrelated to his sexuality and that seem to carry much more negative weight for Roger than the simple fact that Paco is "a queen."

316:9–10 **It was only twenty dollars for perpetual:** Roger provides the price in dollars, suggesting that he and his listener/reader are more familiar with dollars than pesos. Twenty dollars would have been equivalent to about seventy-one pesos at the time, with the US buying power of about $395 today (MeasuringWorth Foundation).

316:10–16 I had the cash box then and I said let me attend to it, Paco. But he said no . . . "It's right here in the cash box.": At this point, Roger enters the story (as yet unnamed), revealing not only that the opening events occurred several years in the past but also that his narrative up to this point has not been his own firsthand experience. Roger has heard about Paco's relationship with the previous manager and the decisions about burying Paco's parents either from Paco himself or through gossip; regardless of the source, this further calls into question Roger's accuracy, fairness, and attributions of motive for the background of his story.

Additionally, although Roger may "have the cash box," he is clearly not at liberty to draw from it, suggesting that his primary role in Paco's life is not to manage business affairs. In fact, Roger and Paco's relationship is intimate enough that Roger feels he can offer unsolicited advice about Paco's financial and family matters, just as Paco's previous manager had; but, unlike the previous manager, Roger cannot independently decide how Paco's money will be spent. While Roger's focus is on Paco's irresponsibility, Roger reveals to the listener/reader that he is subservient to Paco—seeking Paco's permission and not acting without it. As Stetler and Locklin point out, "Usually the roles are reversed, with the manager controlling the purse strings" (68). Over this disagreement, the tension between the characters builds: Roger appears overbearing, while Paco appears stubborn.

316:17 No, he said. Nobody could tell him what to do: Here Roger may be paraphrasing Paco, which would suggest Paco's growing independence from and resentment of Roger. Otherwise, Roger may be himself observing that "Nobody could tell him what to do," which lays the groundwork for what will become one of Roger's major complaints about Paco—his untouchability.

316:18–19 What's the sense in spending money sooner than necessary?: Roger quotes Paco directly for the first time, though likely as both a recollection and translation of Paco's original Spanish statement. In Roger's telling, Paco appears unfazed by the warnings of what will happen to his mother's remains, and he is equally breezy about his expenses. Roger suggests that Paco's vague and simple explanation for not handling this business verifies his overall lack of responsibility, but Paco's uncaring tone may indicate nothing more than a lack of interest in burial traditions or expenses—the two represent different value systems, not unlike the older and younger waiters in "A Clean, Well-Lighted Place."

316:20–23 "All right," I said, "but see you look after it." . . . He was just tight, that's all: As George Monteiro points out, Roger switches back and forth between pesos and dollars here (117), though it is unclear whether this is a purposeful exaggeration of Paco's income or a simple matter of translation and confusion. Roger's math is, in any case, a bit rough: he claims Paco was contracted for "six fights at four thousand pesos a fight" (316:21), which would equate to approximately $1,124 per fight and a six-fight total of less than $7,000 in 1933 (MeasuringWorth Foundation); this would mean Paco's "benefit fight" (316:21–22) would have more than doubled his income to "over fifteen thousand dollars there in the capital alone" (316:22). By using both dollars and pesos to describe Paco's finances, Roger not only creates confusion for the listener/reader but also introduces further uncertainty about his role in Paco's business. It seems Roger may not have the full picture. Regardless, Roger represents Paco as uncaring, stingy, and irresponsible, without seeming to recognize how this telling also represents himself as demanding, unrelenting, and judgmental—a nagging mother who does not respect Paco's autonomy.

316:24–28 **The third notice came . . . that afternoon when he went to town:** Roger's growing frustration is indicated by his increasingly crass language—particularly Roger's description of Paco's mother's body being "dumped on the common boneheap" (316:26–27). Even as Roger implies that Paco is acting heartless and inconsiderate by delaying the matter, Roger also shares those qualities as he badgers Paco and repeatedly chooses this unkind language.

317:1–2 **"Keep out of my business," he said. "It's my business and I'm going to do it.":** Paco rejects Roger's nagging, and Paco's request for Roger to "keep out of [his] business" would be nonsensical if their relationship were primarily professional.

317:5–8 **He got the money out of the cash box . . . so of course I thought he had attended to it:** Roger again pays close attention to Paco's money, while Paco flaunts it. If Paco "always carried a hundred or more pesos with him all the time" (317:5–6), as Roger claims, then Paco must be making a flagrant show of his attention to Roger's request by drawing the money from the cash box instead of his pocket. This appears to satisfy Roger's expectations, even if Paco seems to be behaving spitefully instead of genuinely. Roger, already duped many times over by Paco's empty promises, appears naïve.

317:10–11 **so his mother's body had been dumped on the boneheap; on the public boneheap:** Roger has now repeated the grotesque word "boneheap" four times (316:26–27, 317:10, 317:11, 317:14), continuing to demonstrate his own disrespect and insensitivity. Beyond that, Roger's phrasing suggests that his outrage is much more about Paco's irresponsibility and failure to follow through on promises than about respecting the memory of Paco's mother.

317:18–20 **What kind of blood is it in a man that will let that be done to his mother? You don't deserve to have a mother:** Roger transitions his critique of Paco from behavioral to biological with this rhetorical question, suggesting that

Paco's moral corruption goes as deep as blood. The irony is that whatever "kind of blood" Paco has would have been inherited directly from his biological mother.

Blood took on important symbolic meaning in queer communities during the late twentieth century because of the HIV/AIDS crisis, but, at the time of Hemingway's writing this story, the most relevant and popular conceptions of queer identities would have come from of sexology. Sexologists, for the most part, explained homosexuality through psychological inversion, aberration, or perversion, rather than biological causes (though physical arguments were not entirely unheard of). Moddelmog has thoroughly traced Hemingway's reading of and investment in the work of sexologists, especially Havelock Ellis ("Sex, Sexuality, and Marriage"). In this story, Roger views Paco's sexuality as the common cause of his character flaws, so Roger is able to leap quickly from critiquing Paco's actions (not paying for his mother's perpetual burial) to critiquing Paco's biology ("what kind of blood"), which makes Roger's complaint more literal and more permanent—psychotherapy has no hope of changing the "kind of blood" Paco has. In this way, Roger's understanding of sexuality is somewhat out of step with the sexologists of the time; it is more rooted in vague stereotypes and Roger's desire to thoroughly ruin Paco's reputation.

317:21–24 **"It is my mother," he said. "Now she is so much dearer to me. . . . Now she will always be with me."** Roger's quoting of Paco here reveals a looser, more spiritual value system than Roger's traditional, patrilineal one. While it must be considered that Roger could be exaggerating Paco's comments to represent him as flighty, unserious, and even silly—more characteristics of the distant, dispassionate "queen"—at the same time, Roger seems not to notice that Paco's placid, more naturalistic conception of his mother's burial could appear to the listener/reader as enlightened and mature. Roger is disturbed by the lack of a standard, private, long-term burial for Paco's mother, while Paco demonstrates a peaceful acceptance of his mother's death. It is *Paco's* mother, after all, and Roger never met her, so perhaps Paco's perspective should be taken more seriously than Roger's.

317:25–26 **"Jesus Christ," I said, "what kind of blood have you anyway? I don't want you to even speak to me.":** Roger's exasperation with Paco is apparent in his dismissive rejection ("I don't want you to even speak to me"), which sounds more like a fight among intimates than business partners.

317:28–31 **At that time he was spending all kinds of money around women. . . . He owed me over six hundred pesos and he wouldn't pay me:** Here Roger again links finances with sexuality, adding to his list of insults that Paco is a debtor and a hypocrite. Several interpretations are possible for Roger's accusation that Paco is practicing conspicuous heterosexuality—spending money extravagantly to do so. The first (but least likely) is that Roger may be entirely inventing Paco's homosexuality; perhaps

Paco's interactions with women are in earnest and not, as Roger charges, "trying to make himself seem a man and fool people" (317:28–29). In that case, Roger's reframing of Paco's sexual promiscuity as hypocrisy would reemphasize Roger's accusation that Paco is "a queen" and dissuade the listener/reader from considering Paco's public behavior to be counter-evidence. A second reading is that Roger's anger here is not over Paco's generally wanton behavior but over his refusal to direct that sexual energy *toward Roger*. As Brenner argues, "The durability of [Roger's] grudge against Paco and the heat with which he tells it to his listener indicate the feelings of a rejected would-be lover who still winces from memory of his failure to win the affection of a desired object" (166). A third (and most likely) reading, based on Roger's previous nonchalance about Paco's sexuality, is that Roger does not believe being "a queen" is shameful but that falsely representing oneself as heterosexual *is* an offense worth public criticism. In fact, Roger's framing of Paco's behavior suggests that he believes the listener/reader will be more upset by Paco's hypocrisy than by his homosexuality.

Regardless of why Roger's feelings are hurt, this attack reveals unequivocally that Roger's *primary* frustration is the fact that Paco has not repaid this long-standing debt. Six hundred pesos at the time would have converted to slightly less than $170, equivalent to more than $3,300 today (MeasuringWorth Foundation).

317:31–39 **"Why do you want it now?" he'd say. "Don't you trust me? Aren't we friends?" . . . "You don't know all the needs I have for money.":** In addition to the difference of opinion on finances and burials, Roger and Paco also disagree on time; Roger urges Paco to be pragmatic and immediate with his financial responsibilities, while Paco views financial matters as weightless concerns that can be handled when it is convenient. Again, Roger depicts Paco as empty-headed and unreliable, while Paco appears to value friendship and trust more than settling debts. When faced with opposing value systems, Paco attempts to reason with Roger, but Roger gives no consideration to Paco's views.

Also noteworthy in this passage is that Paco downgrades the intimacy of the relationship by referring to it as a friendship ("Aren't we friends?" 317:32). While "friend" can certainly serve as coded language for a same-sex romantic partner, Paco's plea may be a genuine appeal to their friendship and a gesture toward a queer-familial connection that supersedes biological or legal family responsibilities. Otherwise, the use of "friend" here may signal a purposeful mistranslation or misrepresentation by Roger, intended to cover up their more intimate relationship. Regardless, Roger's narration suggests that Paco may perceive his relationship with Roger as more casual than Roger understands (or desires) it to be.

317:40–43 **I stayed here all the time you were in Spain . . . and now I need it and you can pay me:** While Roger and Paco's relationship has been leaning toward intimacy, here it leans toward business, when the listener/reader learns that Paco has previously "authorized" Roger to handle his financial affairs (317:40), much like Paco's previous manager and presumed romantic partner. With this revelation, Roger becomes associated with a more domestic (or motherly) role, within which Roger nags Paco about money, just as he nagged Paco about the burial plot. Roger claims to need this repayment urgently, which may have to do with his trying to escape the relationship. Any romantic or interpersonal sources of tension at this point begin to appear secondary to this significant financial conflict.

318:2 **Why don't you pay me some on account?:** In the face of Paco's obstinacy, Roger represents himself as willing to negotiate by accepting partial payment. Roger also seems not to have learned from Paco's earlier repeated failures to fulfill promises, as Roger continues to ask for and respect Paco's word.

318:4 **He had only fought twice in Spain, they couldn't stand him there:** According to Mandel, "In Hemingway's day, Mexican *alternativas* (q.v.: promotions to the rank of *matador de toros*) were not valid in Spain, and Mexican bullfighters often had difficulty obtaining contracts in the jealous, competitive world of the Spanish bullfight" (278). As such, Roger here emphasizes an insult to Paco's ranking in his profession, even as Roger comes across as jealous, aiming to assassinate not only Paco's character but also his career. Roger has strayed far from his initial complaints about Paco's treatment of his mother and financial irresponsibility.

318:5–8 **he had seven new fighting suits made . . . and he couldn't even wear them:** The *trajes de luces* (suits of lights) worn in the bullring are extravagant, highly adorned, symbolic costumes. For Paco to invest in this attire but fail to protect his investment demonstrates carelessness akin to the lack of respect Roger believes Paco has shown his mother. The emphasis on fashion and decorum may constitute veiled references to Paco's sexuality, but they mainly serve Roger's larger critique of Paco's financial negligence—apparently much more offensive to Roger than Paco's sexuality.

318:13–24 **Why don't you pay me the money you owe me so I can leave? . . . "No, you won't," I said:** This portion of the argument further muddies the relationship between the men; their power dynamics seem fixed but are not predictably clear. Roger suggests he is trapped in the relationship by Paco's debt, but Paco expresses a desire for Roger not to leave, suggesting that Roger may hold more power over Paco than has previously been apparent. When Paco threatens to take control of the cash box, Roger rejects his threat but ultimately does not leave, suggesting that Paco remains the decision-maker. Roger's representation of this argument casts himself as less dependent on Paco than he previously seemed, but at the same time it demonstrates Roger to be fairly helpless, trapped, and not at liberty to act according to his own desires or best interests.

318:25 That very afternoon he came to me with a punk: The *Oxford English Dictionary* pins the earliest nominative uses of "punk" to references to prostitutes in the late 1500s, and a century later the term had expanded to include "a boy or young man kept by an older man as a (typically passive) sexual partner, a catamite" ("punk, n.1"). By the late nineteenth century, US slang had picked up the term to mean "[a] person of no account; a despicable or contemptible person," and the *OED* actually provides Hemingway's "The Mother of a Queen" as a reference for this usage. Other meanings, such as "amateur" and "petty criminal," also circulated at the time; however, given Roger's vicious tone and the story's central treatment of sexuality, it seems more likely that Roger intended the word "punk" here to serve as another attack on Paco's sexuality and character, following the *OED* definition: "A young male companion of a tramp, *esp.* one who is kept for sexual purposes" ("punk, n.1"). Among the many anti-gay slurs Roger might have chosen here, "punk" also has the function of tying together sexuality and financial precarity.

Hemingway's personal usage of the term "punk" was inconsistent though not infrequent. In his letters, he regularly disparaged his own correspondence by apologizing for writing a "punk letter," with no apparent nod toward the queer-inflected meaning. Elsewhere in *Winner Take Nothing*, Hemingway uses "punks" as an insult with possibly queer implications in "The Light of the World" (292:29, 293:1, 3).

318:26–27 Here is a *paisano* who needs money to go home because his mother is very sick: Paco's description of this person as a "*paisano*" (fellow countryman or peasant) is free of the antagonism of Roger's term, "punk," and highlights Paco's desire to help this person. Roger seems, again, unaware of the irony in wanting Paco to appear careless, financially irresponsible, and easily duped, while Roger himself demonstrates Paco to be caring, generous, and sympathetic about the sick mother of this *paisano* (yet another mother in the story). Roger also seems oblivious to the possibility that Paco views repaying Roger as less important than supporting the *paisano* because Roger's need is not as urgent as this *paisano*'s, and Paco seems to want nothing in return from the *paisano*, which draws a sharp contrast with Roger's strong sense that money loaned must be repaid in full and as promptly as possible.

318:27–30 This fellow was just a punk, you understand, a nobody he'd never seen before . . . and he wanted to be the big, generous matador with a fellow townsman: To the list of Paco's offenses Roger here adds conspicuous *generosity*, as he again offers the least charitable description of Paco's behavior that he can. Roger is unable to understand Paco's compassion for the *paisano* as anything other than self-aggrandizement, just as Roger could not understand or respect Paco's feeling of peace about the outcome of his mother's burial. Roger's critique of Paco's financial thoughtlessness is curbed somewhat by Roger's disapproval of Paco's interest in charitable giving. If Roger's goal is to demonstrate Paco's moral bankruptcy, this particular complaint undermines that effort.

318:31: **"Give him fifty pesos from the cash box,"** he told me: Roles reverse a bit here, as Paco asserts dominance by asking the narrator to draw the money for the *paisano* from the cash box. If Paco kept cash on hand as the narrator described earlier (317:5–6), he would have had plenty of money to give to the *paisano* without involving Roger at all. By Roger's account, this entire episode seems designed for Paco to antagonize Roger.

318:35: **"You bitch,"** I said: Like "queen," the insult Roger chooses here feminizes Paco. Stetler and Locklin argue that this retort makes Roger "sound like the stereotype" of a gay man (68), but this line more importantly betrays that Roger feels insulted by Paco's generosity with the *paisano* and hurt that Paco's generosity does not, apparently, extend to repaying Roger.

Otherwise, Roger's anger may suggest that the *paisano* is not simply a down-and-out fellow countryman but, in fact, a prostitute, according to some other definitions of "punk." In that case, Paco seems to be parading the "punk" in front of Roger, asking Roger to deliver Paco's payment for sexual services. While that reading would justify the narrator's anger—whether over Paco's sexual infidelity or financial extravagance—it does not square with the narrator's previous candidness about Paco's sexual orientation. Roger is quite willing to identify Paco as "a queen" and a hypocrite, so it seems unlikely he would be vague about Paco's use of prostitutes.

What is more likely is that Roger views Paco as "a bitch" because of Paco's desire to support a *paisano* and to give freely of his money while not repaying his debt to Roger. The fifty pesos Paco offers the *paisano* (about $14 at the time) is significantly less than the nearly $170 Paco owes to Roger (MeasuringWorth Foundation), but Roger nonetheless derides Paco for his willingness to share this amount with the *paisano*.

318:38–40 **It was his car but he knew I drove it better than he did. . . . He couldn't even read and write:** The narrator adds Paco's driving and alleged illiteracy to his mounting list of insults, though this short and petty snipe has the opposite effect—it makes Roger, rather than Paco, look worse. Roger's boasting comes across as empty, egotistical, and mean.

318:41–43 **He came out and said, "I'm coming with you and I'm going to pay you. We are good friends. There is no need to quarrel.":** Roger continues to take both this argument and their relationship much more seriously than Paco does, while Paco seems to think a promise of repayment is all that Roger needs. Paco's tranquil formality may be a result of Roger's translation of Paco's Spanish, or it may be that

Roger remembers this exchange more for the way it cut his pride than for Paco's actual words. Either way, in this exchange as throughout the story, Paco's dialogue consistently contradicts the deep emotional intensity that Roger appears to feel.

318:45 **he pulled out twenty pesos:** At less than $6 in 1933 currency, Paco offers Roger a pittance—less than half what Paco has just offered to the *paisano* and only 3 percent of the debt he owes Roger.

319:2–5 **"You motherless bitch . . . I wouldn't take a nickel from you. You know what you can do with it.":** With crude language and a great deal of anger, Roger demonstrates himself to be quick-tempered and insulting—which Paco never is. Roger's vicious lashing out at Paco shows the deep hurt he feels over this disagreement.

319:6–7 **I got out of the car without a peso in my pocket and I didn't know where I was going to sleep that night:** Roger is explicit about the fact that Paco's income was also his own livelihood, and Paco's home was his home. Roger's insistence that Paco repay the debt of six hundred pesos seems less justified, given Paco's ongoing material support of Roger. Although this fact does not clarify their relationship, it does settle the point that Roger was Paco's dependent and likely not a business partner or manager.

319:8–10 **I met him walking with three friends in the evening on the way to the Callao cinema in the Gran Via in Madrid:** A boulevard at the center of Madrid, the Gran Via is famous for shopping, entertainment, and ornate architecture, and the Callao theater was built in 1926 near the Spanish Capitol Building. Hemingway's novel *The Sun Also Rises* ends with Jake Barnes and Brett Ashley riding in a taxi down the Gran Via. After the Spanish Civil War (1936–1939), Madrid's best-known LGBTQ-friendly neighborhood, La Chueca, emerged near the southeastern end of the Gran Via.

319:11 **"Hello Roger, old friend," he said to me:** This is the first instance of the narrator's name being mentioned, nearly at the end of the story. By keeping Roger's name unspoken until this point, Hemingway has left open the possibility for readers to interpret the narrator as a woman, rather than a man, and this reveal also coincides with Roger's mention of himself walking the Gran Via.

319:11–12 **People say you are talking against me. That you say all sorts of unjust things about me:** Roger reveals that this dramatic monologue is a story he has told before and will likely tell again. Despite his detached tone, Paco comes across as an even-tempered, forgiving, and generous person, while Roger appears to be vindictive, hurtful, and—as is now confirmed—a gossip.

319:13–14: "All I say is you never had a mother," I said to him. That's the worst thing you can say to insult a man in Spanish: Hemingway is generally correct about this bit of Mexican slang. According to Francisco J. Santamaría's *Diccionario de Mejicanismos,* the phrase *"no tener uno madre"* or *"ni madre"* is vulgar slang (*"baja y soez"*) used to criticize someone for shamelessness (*"al que carece de vergüenza,"* 678). Primarily used in Mexico, the description of some*thing* as "without a mother" can be positive—a party that does not have a mother is a great party. But in reference to some*one,* the phrase is unmistakably negative, suggesting not only socially inappropriate behavior but also a certain shameless about it.

319:15–16 My poor mother died when I was so young it seems as though I never had a mother. It's very sad: Just as Paco has explained away the outcome of his mother's burial and the role of the *paisano* in earlier parts of Roger's narrative, in this moment Paco explains away Roger's sharpest insult. This is an act of mistranslation—possibly purposeful mistranslation—in which Paco turns the idiomatic phrase into a literal comment on his childhood and uses it to exaggerate the age at which he lost his mother (assuming Roger's timeline is even roughly accurate). Like Roger, Paco turns himself into the victim. In the same move, Paco makes Roger's attempted insult appear to be, at best, incorrect or, at worst, mean-spirited and insensitive. Whether by a strategic move or a translation error, Paco seems to win the exchange by being unaffected.

319:17 There's a queen for you: Roger's frequent insinuation that Paco's sexuality is the root of his poor character—encompassing social, financial, moral, and professional failings—is confirmed with this comment. After Roger's "never had a mother" (319:13) insult falls flat, he defaults to his original characterization of Paco as a "queen," though this late mention of sexuality lacks the casual and unconcerned tone of Roger's first use of "queen" (316: 5). Here, at the end of the story, Roger clearly means "queen" (319:17) to be the ultimate insult. This is a calculated accusation, whether it is intended to make the assassination of Paco's character complete or to make the listener/reader less likely to view *Roger* as another "queen," based on his use of derogatory terms like "queen" and "punk." Even so, through this and all Roger's other complaints about Paco, Roger appears to feel a persistent desire to be both distanced from and connected to the titular "queen."

319:17–19 You can't touch them . . . they never pay: Roger's primary concern with Paco is, as always, financial; however, by the end of the story, his complaint has become personal in a new way. Roger seems upset by Paco's calm in the face of this criticism, his ability to coolly take these insults in stride. Perhaps expecting Paco to be distressed by the insults, Roger categorizes Paco's lack of outrage as yet another symptom of his sexuality ("you can't touch *them,*" 319:17, emphasis added), when, in fact, Paco may be unfazed simply because the accusations do not affect him. To be outraged and distressed by such an accusation would indicate that Paco had something to lose, but, as long as his sexuality is common knowledge ("didn't you know that, of course he is," 316:5), it is reasonable for Paco to be as unaffected by the rumors as he would be by the truth. Of course, you "can't touch them" when everyone already knows who they are.

319:21–22 What kind of blood is it that makes a man like that?: Whereas initially Roger does not treat "queen" as an insult, he ultimately offers this socially stigmatized identity as an explanation for any number of unrelated negative traits—that Paco didn't respect his mother, that he is both stingy and financially careless, that he is an unsuccessful bullfighter, that he is a liar and a hypocrite, that he is unskilled at driving and unable to read, that he is unflappable. Roger *wants* to find a link for these disparate criticisms of Paco. He doubles down on the suggestion that all gay men share such negative attributes by casting these characteristics as deeper than sexual orientation, as the "kind of blood" a person has.

Thanks to Roger's unreliability as narrator, there is no way of knowing if Roger's claims about Paco's sexuality are true or wild accusations intended only to hurt Paco's reputation: readers will never know the unbiased truth as to whether Paco is gay, closeted, or straight, let alone the nature of Paco's relationship with Roger. Instead, Hemingway's story emphasizes the complex psychological gymnastics Roger is willing to practice as the speaker of this dramatic monologue. This, of course, reveals more about Roger's character than about Paco's. Hemingway demonstrates, too, that this same-sex relationship—whatever its nature—is constituted by the same emotional depths, financial complexities, interpersonal conflicts, and social pressures as any traditional family relationship, thereby highlighting some of the complicated entanglements (especially when relations turn sour) that a "queer family" entails, even when it lacks legal, biological, and other formal connections.

The story, furthermore, demonstrates one significant function of social stigma: namely, that identity may serve as a repository for wide-ranging and unrelated negative characterizations. What begins for Roger as a basic, insignificant fact about Paco turns into a harsh affront and the common cause for all of Paco's shortcomings, as soon as Roger lands on the idea that he can relate those idiosyncratic character flaws (whether true or not) back to Paco's identity as a "queen" with a flawed "kind of blood." With Roger's singular focus on Paco's sexuality, the story also showcases Hemingway's early interest in the stigmas that surround nonnormative sexualities. "The Mother of a Queen" demonstrates the impact of such stigmas, which will become more overt in Hemingway's later works and which are here explored not by implication and suggestion (as in other short stories) but as a central point of interest—and insult.

NOTE

Special thanks to Miriam B. Mandel, Jessica Geva, Marcia Lisker, and Enric Sullà for their assistance with research into Hemingway's use of Spanish-language and Mexican slang.

WORKS CITED

Baker, Carlos. *Ernest Hemingway: A Life Story.* Scribner's, 1969.

Beegel, Susan. "Introduction." *Hemingway's Neglected Short Fiction,* edited by Susan F. Beegel, U of Alabama P, 1989, pp. 1–18.

Brenner, Gerry. "From 'Sepi Jingan' to 'The Mother of a Queen': Hemingway's Three Epistemologic Formulas for Short Fiction." *New Critical Approaches to the Short Stories of Ernest Hemingway,* edited by Jackson J. Benson, Duke UP, 1990, pp. 156–71.

Comley, Nancy R., and Robert Scholes. *Hemingway's Genders: Rereading the Hemingway Text.* Yale UP, 1994.

Eby, Carl P. *Hemingway's Fetishism: Psychoanalysis and the Mirror of Manhood.* SUNY P, 1999.

Hemingway, Ernest. *The Complete Short Stories of Ernest Hemingway: The Finca Vigía Edition.* Scribner's, 1987.

———. *Death in the Afternoon.* Scribner's, 1932.

———. *The Letters of Ernest Hemingway: Volume 5 (1932–1934).* Edited by Sandra Spanier and Miriam B. Mandel, CUP, 2020.

Lynn, Kenneth. *Hemingway.* Harvard University Press, 1987.

Mandel, Miriam B. *Hemingway's* Death in the Afternoon: *The Complete Annotations.* Scarecrow P, 2002.

MeasuringWorth Foundation. *MeasuringWorth.com.* http://www.measuringworth.com.

Moddelmog, Debra A. "Queer Families in Hemingway's Fiction." *Hemingway and Women: Female Critics and the Female Voice,* edited by Lawrence R. Broer and Gloria Holland, U of Alabama P, 2002, pp. 173–89.

———. "Sex, Sexuality, and Marriage." *Ernest Hemingway in Context,* edited by Debra A. Moddelmog and Suzanne del Gizzo, CUP, 2013, pp. 357–66.

Monteiro, George. *The Hemingway Short Story: A Critical Appreciation.* McFarland, 2017.

Nolan, Charles J. "Essential Questions: Keys to Meaning in Hemingway's 'The Mother of a Queen.'" *South Atlantic Review,* vol. 68, no. 4, 2003, pp. 85–94.

"punk, n.1 and adj.2." *OED Online,* OUP, September 2020.

Santamaría, Francisco J. *Diccionario de Mejicanismos.* 1st ed. Editorial Porrua, 1959.

Smith, Paul. *A Reader's Guide to the Short Stories of Ernest Hemingway.* G. K. Hall, 1989.

Stetler, Charles, and Gerald Locklin. "Beneath the Tip of the Iceberg in Hemingway's 'The Mother of a Queen.'" *The Hemingway Review,* vol. 2, no. 1, 1982, pp. 68–69.

ONE READER WRITES

Robert W. Trogdon

"One Reader Writes" has the dubious distinction of being one of Hemingway's most critically neglected short stories (Smith 299). There have been no academic articles in English focused exclusively on the story since Paul Smith published his study of Hemingway's stories in 1989. And in his overview, Smith summarizes only four critics who wrote anything on the story. Smith attributes most of this critical neglect to the unusual composition of "One Reader Writes." As outlined by Carlos Baker in his 1969 biography, Dr. Logan Clendening sent six letters he received from readers of his medical advice column to Hemingway. One letter was "from a woman in Harrisburg, Pennsylvania, whose husband had contracted syphilis while serving in the United States Marines in Shanghai. . . . Ernest edited the letter slightly, changing the date and place-names, and adding a short introduction and conclusion. The result was 'One Reader Writes'—probably the easiest story he ever devised" (Baker 227). Smith opines that "it is likely that some critics have been offended by Hemingway's opportunism" (299). The manuscript bears the initial title of "The Syndicated Column" (JFK/EH #635). Although unusual for the writer, "One Reader Writes" was not the first epistolary story Hemingway wrote; it harkens back to one he composed in 1921, "A Portrait of the Idealist in Love," first published in Peter Griffin's *Along with Youth* (161–64).

While scholars have dismissed the story through their silence, at least a few of the first readers of *Winner Take Nothing* singled out "One Reader Writes" for special praise. In her review of the volume for New York's *Sunday News,* Alicia Patterson noted that Hemingway's "use of repetition is a supreme achievement. In 'One Reader Writes' . . . he turns it to especial advantage" (67). The *Minneapolis Star's* John H. Harvey singled it out as one of the stories that showed Hemingway's special handling of tragedy: "Tragedy to Hemingway is but a reflection of hope, reversed in the mirror of life. He embellishes it, toys with it, and then succeeds in making you enjoy his picture of that tragedy. Time and time again he does that: in "One Reader Writes," "The Mother of a Queen," Wine of Wyoming," and "The Light of the World" in the present volume" (17).

Whether Patterson and Harvey would have been as complimentary if they had known of the composition history of the story is doubtful. But these reviews do suggest that "One Reader Writes" might have more to offer us if we could get past our need for Hemingway to create wholly original works.

320:8 **Dear Doctor:** Logan Clendening (1884–1945) received his medical degree from the University of Kansas in 1907. At the urging of H. L. Mencken, who admired his first book *Modern Methods of Treatment* (1924), Clendening wrote *The Human Body* (1927), a book on anatomy for lay people that was issued by Mencken's publisher, Alfred A. Knopf. Its success led to Clendening's retirement from private practice and to his syndicated medical column. At the time of his death, his column appeared in 383 daily newspapers. In addition to his medical work, Clendening was an avid book collector, especially of material relating to Charles Dickens and Sir Arthur Conan Doyle (Major 257–58).

Baker reports that Hemingway met Clendening, a lifelong resident of Kansas City, around the time of Gregory Hemingway's birth, 12 November 1931 (237). But evidence suggests that the two men met earlier, perhaps in the summer of 1928 when Ernest and Pauline were in Kansas City for the birth of Patrick Hemingway. "One Reader Writes" was not the first time the relationship had proven inspirational for one of them. Before Hemingway included Clendening's letter in his story, Clendening included the following anecdote about Hemingway in the chapter on alcohol in his *The Care and Feeding of Adults* (published in October 1931):

> Mr. Ernest Hemingway, who has certainly done yeoman service in making drinking popular since the war, told me the pathetic story that on blue days in Paris he used to bring his little boy down [to the Société Antialcoolisme on the Boulevard Saint-Germain] and the two of them would stand gazing in admiration at the colossal object lesson [clay models of cirrhotic livers], while the father discoursed in learned terms of the physical dangers of the demon chemical, C_2H_5OH. A moving and delightful picture and one which shows the fascination such models have for all first-rate minds. (96)

(Hemingway's account of visiting what he called the Ligue Nationale Contre Alcoolisme ran in the 8 April 1922 issue of the *Toronto Star* and was reprinted in *Dateline: Toronto* [124–25].)

In a 1938 profile of the doctor in the *Kansas City Star,* Clendening reported that he met the author when Hemingway was writing *Death in the Afternoon* and owned a copy inscribed "to Ingeborg [Clendening's maid] (and Logan) Clendening, in memory of many happy prescriptions" (Van Brunt 1). The inscription hints that Clendening may have prescribed alcohol to Hemingway during Prohibition. Hemingway had a copy of *The Care and Feeding of Adults* at Finca Vigía, and Clendening owned an autographed copy of *Men Without Women*.

Although some of Clendening's columns featured questions from readers—some of which dealt with venereal diseases—there is no evidence that he ever answered the letter used in this story.

320:13–14 **U.S service in 1929 . . . China, Shanghai:** Hemingway revised the original letter to obscure the husband's enlistment in the United States Marine Corps (Baker 229). In early 1927, France, Great Britain, and the United States sent troops to Shanghai (controlled by the warlord Chang Tsung-cháng) to protect Western nationals and business interests in the city's International Settlement from the advancing forces of Chiang Kai-shek (Condit and Turnbladh 126). Following the capture of the city by Chiang in mid-April 1927, the Marine force was reduced to the 4th Regiment, which—along with French and British troops—remained in the city to protect the International Settlement from 1927 to 1941. As noted by Condit and Turnbladh, "Shanghai was one of the worst places on earth to maintain a regiment in fighting trim. Temptations were plentiful and cheap, and were close at hand with the regiment quartered in the narrow confines of the International Settlement" (145). With increasing tension between the United States and Japan, the force was fully withdrawn on 28 November 1941 (Condit and Turnbladh 193).

In "Che Ti Dice La Patria?" Hemingway's narrator says that he "read the account of the Shanghai fighting aloud to Guy" during one of their stops (*CSS* 228).

320:17 **course of injections:** The correspondent's husband is probably being treated with the arsenic compound salvarsan (sometimes called arsphenamine), the "magic bullet" discovered by Dr. Paul Ehrlich in 1910 (Clendening, *Human Body* 393).

320:19 **"sifilus"** The *Annual Report of the Surgeon General, U.S. Navy* for 1932 notes that the rates of venereal diseases for sailors and marines in China were high due to the "hours of liberty, the presence of a large number of easily obtainable prostitutes, and freedom from restraint of prohibition" (56). According to the report, 479 of the 1,298 marines in China in 1931 were treated for some type of venereal disease, the highest rate of any US Navy ship or shore installation for that year (63).

In his books and newspaper columns, Clendening seems to have had a fairly open-minded attitude about venereal disease, advocating for direct talk about prevention and treatment. In *The Human Body,* he notes that prevention was possible but that

Public prevention can never be accomplished until prostitution, especially irregular prostitution, is abolished, which I suppose everyone admits is an unattainable ideal. But regulation and supervision of prostitutes by public health authorities would go a long way towards prevention. It would mean, of course, Government licensing of prostitution, and that has always been prevented by the false sanctimony of public opinion. Prudes, religious bigots, in the pulpit or out, would always prefer to have boys diseased, women ruined and made barren, and babies blinded than admit that the strongest human instinct after hunger should be allowed a legitimate manner of satisfaction. (391)

320:24 **became:** A compositor's error. In the 1933 *Winner Take Nothing*, the father's line is "once they become a victim of that malady" (100). The compositor for *The Fifth Column and the First Forty-Nine Stories* (1938) mistakenly made it "once they became a victim of that malady." The first version's use of "become" gives a greater sense of tragedy as, unlike the preterite "became," "become" functions in the past, present, and future tense, indicating the possible hopelessness of the husband's case.

321:1–11 **Maybe he can tell me . . . I don't know why he had to get a malady:** The conclusion's use of stream of consciousness is reminiscent of Chapter VII of *In Our Time* and Frederic Henry's narration before Catherine Barkley's death in the last chapter of *A Farewell to Arms*. While Hemingway did not use this type of narration often, he would employ it more frequently in the 1930s and 1940s, most notably in Marie Morgan's narration in the last chapter of *To Have and Have Not* and in *For Whom the Bell Tolls*.

WORKS CITED

Annual Report of the Surgeon General, U.S. Navy Chief of the Bureau of Medicine and Surgery to the Secretary of the Navy for the Fiscal Year 1932. Government Printing Office, 1932.
Baker, Carlos. *Ernest Hemingway: A Life Story.* Scribner's, 1969.
Clendening, Logan. *The Care and Feeding of Adults.* Knopf, 1931.
———. *The Human Body.* Knopf, 1927.
Condit, Kenneth W., and Edwin T. Turnbladh. *Hold High the Torch: A History of the 4th Marines.* Historical Branch, G-3 Division, US Marine Corps, 1960.
Griffin, Peter. *Along with Youth.* OUP, 1985.
Harvey, John H. "Hemingway's Tales Brutal in Humor, Forcefully Told." Rev. of *Winner Take Nothing,* by Ernest Hemingway, *Minneapolis Star,* 30 Dec. 1933, p. 17.
Hemingway, Ernest. *The Complete Short Stories of Ernest Hemingway: The Finca Vigía Edition.* Scribner's, 1987.
———. *Dateline: Toronto.* Edited by William White. Scribner's, 1985.
———. *A Farewell to Arms.* 1929. Scribner's, 2014.
———. *For Whom the Bell Tolls.* 1940. Scribner's, 2003.
———. *The Letters of Ernest Hemingway: Volume 4 (1929–1931).* Edited by Sandra Spanier and Miriam B. Mandel. CUP, 2017.
———. "One Reader Writes" manuscript, item 635, Ernest Hemingway Collection John F. Kennedy Library, Boston.
———. *To Have and Have Not.* 1937. Scribner's, 1996.
———. *Winner Take Nothing.* 1933. Scribner's, 1933.

Major, Ralph H., M. D. "Obituary Logan Clendening 1884–1945." *Bulletin of the Medical Library Association,* vol. 33, no. 2, April 1945, pp. 257–59.

Patterson, Alicia. "One Brutal, One Funny, Both Great." Rev. of *Winner Take Nothing,* by Ernest Hemingway, and *After Such Pleasures,* by Dorothy Parker." *Sunday News,* 29 Oct. 1933, p. 67.

Smith, Paul. *A Reader's Guide to the Short Stories of Ernest Hemingway.* G. K. Hall, 1989.

Van Brunt, Henry. "Layman's Diagnosis of a Doctor." *Kansas City Star,* 6 Mar. 1938, Society section, pp. 1, 3.

HOMAGE TO SWITZERLAND

Boris Vejdovsky

If "Homage to Switzerland" is one of the most puzzling and least commented on stories in Hemingway's canon, it is because it does not seem to have the expedient efficacy and ostensible symbolic simplicity of stories such as "Hills Like White Elephants," the fictional transfiguration of autobiography of the Nick Adams stories, or the metaphysical overtones of "A Clean, Well-Lighted Place." Yet, like the location of the story itself, "Homage to Switzerland" occupies a strategic point in Hemingway's writing production from a personal, geographical, and stylistic point of view.

The story presents itself as a "curious triptych" (Baker 145), and each section of this tripartite narration begins a little like a "game of seven mistakes"; each part has an almost identical central character, an American expatriate on his way to Paris, presumably returning from Italy, and each begins and unfolds in a similar manner in an environment where only small details change. This creates an impression of déjà-vu and circularity that questions the notions of time and space in the story and makes us think that the three men may really be avatars of the same character, like a modernist version of Herman Melville's Confidence Man.

As Julian Barnes has it, "Homage to Switzerland" may appear to be "a quiet story" that does not take place in one of the flamboyant locales of Papa's life (n.p.). It is neither bohemian and nostalgic Paris nor eroticized Spain or Africa nor masculinity-infused Key West or Cuba. As a result of its setting, the story assumes from its inception a tone of ironic desperation quite typical for the high modernist piece of writing it turns out to be.

Switzerland in the heart of Europe and the Alps owes its early inception at the beginning of the thirteenth century to the control over communication routes between the north and south of Europe and between the West and the Middle and Far East. "Homage to Switzerland" takes place in three different train stations on the Simplon railway line; this is one of the major routes that, from the Punic Wars to the War of Gaul to the Italian Wars and to the two World Wars, has been a strategic crossroad. The story thus establishes a tension between the apparent placidity of Switzerland and the fact that, as with the life or lives of the protagonist(s) of the story or stories, the country is situated at a determining crossroad.

Title: When George Orwell would write two years after "Homage to Switzerland" his own *Homage to Catalonia,* the heroic intent would be clear: Catalonia was the proud underdog fighting the forces of fascism—but Switzerland? For what should Switzerland receive an "homage," a word that resounds with medieval chivalric privileges and honors? Even the rather rare Latinate word "homage" and its pronunciation, which can be English or French, has ironic overtones. Indeed, the French pronunciation of Latinate words has carried, at least since Shakespeare's *Henry V,* the idea of something odd or even effeminate, a breach in the heteronormative apprehension of the world. An /o m a: j/ to Switzerland, then, becomes evocative of Jake Barnes's quip, "Isn't it pretty to think so?" at the end of *The Sun Also Rises* or J. Alfred Prufrock's impotent hesitations, to name just two fragile masculine figures of that period.

The location of the story is primordial. Today, Switzerland is still a small, neat, and discreet country of some eight million inhabitants (roughly twice the number than at the time of the story); it is known internationally for its diplomatic and financial discretion and reliability and for its pastoral sceneries. At the time the story was written, like today, few people knew anything about Switzerland beyond a few clichés. The "Homage" paid to Switzerland—notwithstanding its ironic overtones—is a moment of self-observation for the characters of the story who are in an environment that does not distract them from themselves but forces them to confront their fears and insecurities.

322:1 **Part I:** By examining the early manuscripts of the story, Paul Smith determined that, in its earliest version, the three characters were called Mr. Wheeler (252). The division of the story indicates that this is either a story in three parts or three stories subsumed under one title. In either case, the Roman numerals present a series, a linear development or a geometric arrangement. As a tripartite story, "Homage to Switzerland" also suggests it may be a three-act play with a presentation, a development, and a denouement. The three parts similarly evoke a simplified version of the articulations of Ciceronian rhetoric in which we might expect the third part of the speech or the story—Cicero's *peroratio*—to finish with what the narrator of *Death in the Afternoon* refers to as a "wow" (182). We may also be tempted to refer to the story, as Carlos Baker does, as a triptych, in which case we need to consider the central part (about Mr. Johnson) as the centerpiece for which the first and third parts would function as narrative side panels. In fact, "Homage" both uses and questions all these possibilities, and it is difficult to privilege one without forcing that possibility to become an interpretive model.

The division of the story, the repetitions, and their sequencing all pose the question of time and space, which is, in effect, the question of history and the question of the characters' life stories. "Homage to Switzerland" is about geographic and existential crossroads, about where the characters come from and where they are going on this train line but also with their lives. In that respect, it is quite in line with a number of Hemingway "marriage tales" (Smith 254) such as "A Canary for One" or "Hills Like White Elephants" "which begi[n] and en[d] on a station platform" (Smith 254) and in which trains serve both as décor and as a metaphor for life journeys and decisions. Trains and train stations are also tied to loss within these stories, a thematic association Hemingway experienced personally when his first wife Hadley lost his manuscripts in the train station as she prepared for the trip from Paris to Lausanne in 1922 (see 331:2). Thus, despite its apparent oddity, "Homage to Switzerland" is a typical Hemingway story where observable details are limited by perspective and focalization and where the details are markers of omission and loss.

322:2 **PORTRAIT OF MR. WHEELER IN MONTREUX:** The names of the three protagonists seem to be puns participating in the linguistic play of the story. Wheeler, the first, evokes a spinning wheel and the circularity of the story; the second, Johnson and his finnicky word plays (see 324:20, 325:8), evokes Samuel Johnson of the eponymous dictionary as well as a sexual innuendo (see 325:1); the third, Harris, points to a father–son relationship (Harris meaning "son of Harry") and sounds like "harass," indicating that Mr. Harris is more bothered than he pretends to be. The first title is typically modernist and reminiscent of James Joyce's *A Portrait of the Artist as Young Man* (1916). Joyce started *Portrait* (initially titled *Stephen Hero*) as an autobiographical novel, and we can see Mr. Wheeler as a "portrait" of Hemingway as a young artist. It is impossible to reduce the characters to some referential origin, but all three are versions of a modernist male lost in time and space, hesitant about his value and place in the world. For them, time and space are "out of joint"; the story seems to be spinning on itself and to be going nowhere.

322:2 **Montreux:** All three train stations of "Homage to Switzerland" are on the Simplon line and on the shores of Lake Léman, but they are not arranged in the story in a linear manner: coming from Italy, the train first goes through Territet,[1] then Montreux, and then Vevey. Hemingway knew the area well, and, as a thorough editor of his own work, he could have placed the stories in linear order. All three places are less than an hour away from the cantonal capital and main town in the area, Lausanne, where in 1923 he had covered the peace treaty after the Greco-Turkish war. Montreux was evocative for Hemingway of happy times of skiing with Hadley in Les Avants, a village perched above Montreux and near Caux where they rented a small house near the train station. It is also the place of the pastoral idyll between Frederic and Catherine in *A Farewell to Arms*:

> The snow lay over all the country, down almost to Montreux. The mountains on the other side of the lake were all white and the plain of the Rhone Valley was covered. We took long walks on the other side of the mountain to the Bains de l'Alliaz. . . .

There was an inn in the trees at the Bains de l'Alliaz where the woodcutters stopped to drink, and we sat inside warmed by the stove and drank hot red wine with spices and lemon in it. (*FTA* 302)

In their sensuousness, the details are typical of Hemingway's depiction of happiness; Montreux is associated in the novel with a moment of paradisal bliss that precedes the brutal expulsion from it with Catherine's death in childbirth in Lausanne (see 331:2).

322:3 **Inside the station café:** Since the nineteenth century, many writers had used the train as latter-day symbol of human destiny: the Romantics denounced the spoiling of the natural scenery, while their heirs such as Henry David Thoreau or Henry Adams saw in technology the new theoteleology of humanity.[2] Hemingway himself was no stranger to the metaphor, and stories such as "Hills Like White Elephants" or "A Canary for One," in particular, but also the distant echoes of freight trains in *The Sun Also Rises* play with the associations between the railroad and the war that thunders through men's lives with all its might and indifference. In "Homage to Switzerland," instead of having a train that goes in a straight line toward inevitable destiny, we have episodes that seem to repeat each other in a sequence and the relations among these episodes are not linear or chronological. Instead, as Michael Reynolds points out, they are reminiscent of Albert Einstein's then recent theory of relativity, which Hemingway would have been aware of it, for, as Smith notes, "the *New York Times* carried 172 stories about Einstein . . . and almost 100 articles appeared in English and American periodicals" (qtd. in Smith 255). As a 1923 educational movie stated, "relativity" means "the relationship of" or "the dependency on."[3] "Homage to Switzerland" explores the relationships of the characters to the world and the dependency of one part of the story on the other; in that, it is a typically fragmented modernist work and a story emblematic of Hemingway's oeuvre where small details only make sense in relation to others, though they never close the hermeneutic circle.

For a man born in the nineteenth century, the train was state of the art technology.[4] Einstein's theory of relativity "contributed a new imagery: mechanical objects moving at high speeds in literature share some of their meanings they had for science" (Berman 47). The story centrally features trains and clocks, the two technological devices that gave twentieth-century people their understanding of time and space and of their place and meaning in history. One of the central ideas of Einstein's theory was the relativity of motion; he revolutionized the notion that time and space had but one direction, a notion on which fictional narrative and ideas such as beginning, middle, and end or life and death are predicated. The first thing relativity does to us—and that is why it was such a revolution—is to alter our sense of where we are in time and space; therefore, it alters what and how things are.[5] Without seeking to draw on the philosophical dimension of the theory, "Homage to Switzerland" makes time the fourth dimension of the existence of the three characters.

322:3–4 **Inside the station café it was warm and light:** The opening of the story is reminiscent of some of Hemingway's favorite locales, such as a clean, well-lighted café or of the "good café" on Place Saint-Michel in *A Moveable Feast*. The narrator tells us it is "warm and light," and this impression of coziness is reinforced by the chairs that have "comfortable" seats though their backs are "carved" (322:5–6). Hemingway's meticulous attention to details—another feature of modernist writers and his stylistic signature—turns the ordinary into the exotic and even the sensuous. Thus, the "baskets of pretzels" in their simplicity evoke plentiful and generous food sharing (322:4–5), even the "glazed paper sacks" (322:5) evoke the sense of sight and the way the fading light of this snowy afternoon in the story plays on that material—so much depends on details in Hemingway, just as in William Carlos Williams's red wheelbarrow "glazed with rain / water / beside the white / chickens" (ll. 5–8). Hemingway thrives in this ambiance where the public and private meet and can only be appreciated in relation to each other. While the café is a protective space, the pretzels and their wrappings are also an ambivalent detail that must have registered with Hemingway. In a scene that forms a precedent to "Homage to Switzerland," he has Frederic Henry in *A Farewell to Arms* muse on dark forebodings in front of that snack: "I sat back in the corner with a heavy mug of dark beer and an opened glazed-paper package of pretzels and ate the pretzels for the salty flavor and the good way they made the beer taste and read about disaster" (292).

322:6 **a carved wooden clock:** Carved wooden clocks are a trademark product of Switzerland; Hemingway plays with the cliché as the presence of the clock, the cleanliness and warmth of the place, makes it both stereotypical and welcoming. Time is thus emphasized for the first time in the story. The repetition of "carved"— now in a different sense—and "clock" singles out the timepiece and reminds us that looking at the clock and waiting for time to pass are what one does in a waiting room or a station café, as suggested also by Mr. Wheeler's repetitive actions such as looking out the window at the falling snow and at the clock (322:18–19, 322:26).

322:7 **it was snowing:** Hemingway's characteristic use of mono- and disyllabic words accentuates the impression of time that passes without passing; the simplicity of the words and their repetition make the progress of time and narration moot. The phrase is reminiscent of the same register of repetition in "Cat in the Rain": "It was made of bronze and glistened in the rain. It was raining. The rain dripped from the palm trees" (*CSS* 129), and the continuous form of the verb contrasts with the staccato of the short words.

322:8 **new wine:** The area where the story takes place is renowned for its wines; new wine indicates that this is November or early December—close to what Robert Frost refers to as the "darkest evening of the year" (l. 8). Time is not only data given by the clock, but it is also the emotional change brought by the seasons and the time of the everyday human work. The characters of "Homage to Switzerland" too have promises to keep and miles to go before they sleep in an atmosphere that reminds them that their time is running out.

322:9 **the Simplon-Orient Express:** The Orient Express was a luxury train launched in 1883 by the French Compagnie des Wagons-Lits. The northern line of the company first connected Paris to Vienna and Venice; from 1919, it ran all the way to Constantinople (renamed Istanbul in 1923). Between the two World Wars, the Orient Express had its golden age and opened new lines including the Simplon-Orient Express line after the construction of the Simplon Tunnel through the Alps in 1906. The train was the symbol of a traveling intelligentsia, the equivalent of what the "jet set" would be after World War II.

322:12 **The Express is an hour late:** Switzerland is known for its punctuality. The precision of time is relative in this story, and, for Wheeler and the other two American protagonists, the time is out of joint. As the porter announces the delay of the train, we are reminded of the expatriate situation of Mr. Wheeler. Dialogue in Hemingway often reminds us that the story takes place in another country. Thus, the waitress repeats the same sentence (322:12), the second time presumably in English, for the benefit of Mr. Wheeler whom she has identified as an American.

322:14-15 **"If you think it won't keep me awake." "Please?":** The waitress replies somewhat awkwardly to Mr. Wheeler's flirtatious tease. The remark comes as a subtle reminder that, although the conversation and the narration take place in idiomatic English, it is not her mother tongue, and her reply translates the *Bitte?* that a German speaker would use instinctively. Her reply also enables us to hear what we cannot hear, presumably Mr. Wheeler's American (Midwestern, like Hemingway's?) accent, and the other accents: the waitress must have a Germanic accent, while the porters presumably speak with a French-sounding accent.

322:21 **I speak German and French and the dialects:** The waitress again displays her idiomatic English and the complex linguistic situation of Switzerland; the country had three national languages in 1933 when *Winner Take Nothing* was published, and it has had four national languages since 1938.[6] Montreux, like the other two locations of the story, is in the French-speaking part of Switzerland, but the waitress appears to be Swiss German and to have come from the northern part of the country to work in a café on the Swiss Riviera. Mr. Wheeler pulls her leg and later makes inappropriate advances to her, but her reply shows that she is not just the toy of his macho game; not only does she have moral fortitude, but also, unlike monolingual and culturally estranged Mr. Wheeler, she speaks at least four languages.

323:1 **Fräulein:** In the dialogue that follows, Mr. Wheeler sexually harasses the young woman with increasing boldness. "Fräulein" (323:1) and "Mademoiselle" (323:18, 33, 34, 42) are the honorific terms for unmarried women in German and French. They suggest that Wheeler is aware of the sexual availability and vulnerability of the young woman and of the power game he is playing, a game in which his age (he is clearly older than the waitress), his status (he is the client and she must defer to him, as her hypercorrect answers suggest), and his financial means (he purports to offer 300 Swiss francs for intercourse) give him a decisive advantage. It is a cowardly game—a "very inexpensive sport" (324:11) in which, like all macho cowards in Hemingway's fiction, he "never took chances" (324:17–18).

323:4 **You must not joke me like that:** The archaic use of the verb with a direct object points to the formal linguistic training of the waitress; the slight oddity of her language emphasizes her helplessness but also her decided stance.

323:12–15 **I want you . . . Why don't you go away, then?:** Mr. Wheeler's peremptory tone and the syllogistic games he plays contribute to the power structure of the narrative.

323:26–27 **She was losing her English:** The waitress is destabilized by the harassment, and this shift is reflected in her language. The narrator comment is reminiscent of the narrator in *Alice in Wonderland:* after Alice says that things around her are "curiouser and curiouser," the narrator comments, "she was so much surprised, that for the moment she quite forgot how to speak good English" (Carroll 15).

323:36 **three hundred francs:** *Winner Take Nothing* was published in the crisis that followed the Black Tuesday of 1929 when major stock exchanges crashed. Hemingway, an affluent and successful writer at the time, has often been accused of being insensitive to the plight of the hundreds of thousands of people impoverished by the crisis, not only in the United States but also around the world. Although "Homage to Switzerland" cannot be called a political story, it certainly echoes nationalistic, capitalist, and sexual politics. Hemingway makes no explicit statement about it, but in 1930 the exchange rate between the French franc and the US dollar was about 25 to 1. Mr. Wheeler is acutely aware of that: his inner thoughts, ironically reported by the narrator, "Seventy-five centimes [for the tip] would have been better" (324:13), and "One franc Swiss is five francs French" (324:14–15), reveal the petty power game he is playing. The 300 Swiss francs he purports to be offering for sex corresponds to

1,500 French francs, but only to some 75 dollars—a "very inexpensive sport," indeed, since Mr. Wheeler has no intention to give up that money.[7] At the time, the average wage in France was about 3.3 francs per hour, that is, some 35 francs per day. In Switzerland, wages would have been slightly higher, but what Mr. Wheeler is offering the young woman is roughly a month's pay.[8] Mr. Wheeler's name suggests a "wheeler-dealer," and his status and economic power make the sadistic game he is playing with the waitress a mode of exploitation reminiscent of sexual tourism in the third world. Not only were workers such as the waitress or the porters harshly hit by the 1930s' crisis, but also her status as a single woman working in a culturally different and possibly hostile environment makes her particularly vulnerable.[9]

324:3–8 He's ugly, . . . ugly and hateful. . . . What people those Americans: As is often the case in Hemingway's fiction, the narrator seems to adopt the male protagonist's point of view; we realize that the focalization of the description of the café that comes from an ostensibly neutral and omniscient narrator is really seen from Mr. Wheeler's point of view. The conclusion of Part I, however, shifts the narrative point of view to the young woman's internal monologue, and she receives the readers' empathy as they realize that the whole story must be read from the ironic point of view that concludes Part I. However, after he has tilted the moral balance toward the waitress, Hemingway also shows the limits of the power women can have in his narratives. The heroic resistance of the waitress and the moral high ground she holds are questioned by her concluding thoughts where she admits to herself that she had "done that," done "a thing that is nothing to do" "for nothing" (324:4–5). Of course, the passage highlights Mr. Wheeler's sadistic harassment but also confines the waitress and women in a blocked position where they need either to resist and be frustrated or submit to patriarchal authority and violence and get and say "nothing."[10]

324:15–16 He was very careful about money and did not care for women: Part I ends with an indictment of men without women. An early version of the story portrayed Mr. Wheeler as homosexual; Smith notes that Hemingway deleted an ending of Part I that made that clear (253). It is not even necessary to consider, as Smith does, that this deletion "italicizes Wheeler's homosexuality," for he simply *does not care* for women like many of Hemingway's male characters who may win at the petty games at which they "never [take] chances" (324:17–18) and, as a result, take nothing.[11] The indictment is also of an arrogant American capitalist culture that appropriates the world in every possible way. In *Death in the Afternoon*, published one year before *Winner Take Nothing*, Hemingway wrote, "We [Americans], in games, are not fascinated by death, its nearness and its avoidance. We are fascinated by victory and we replace the avoidance of death by the avoidance of defeat" (22). Mr. Wheeler holds his victory, and with the last words of the waitress reported by the narrator, "What people those Americans" (324:7–8), we start to understand why this may be an "homage" to Switzerland.

324:20 **MR. JOHNSON TALKS ABOUT IT AT VEVEY:** On the Simplon line, if one were traveling from Italy, Vevey comes after Montreux, which signals the first disruption of the linearity of the story. Vevey and Montreux are places Hemingway sojourned, and they live in the imagination of Anglo-American readers. The Castle of Chillon, near Montreux, was a favorite of the English Romantics, and Lord Byron composed his poem "The Prisoner of Chillon" at the Hôtel d'Angleterre in Lausanne, the nearby regional capital that appears in Part III of "Homage." Jean-Jacques Rousseau and Fyodor Dostoyevsky, among others, resided in Vevey, which was part of the Grand Tour that revealed Switzerland to the world. Theodore "Laurie" Laurence was educated there before moving next door to the March family in *Little Women* (1868), and it is also one of the settings of Henry James's *Daisy Miller* (1879).

Hemingway is also being suggestive about the word "it" in the title of this section. For a fuller discussion of how Hemingway exploits the ambiguity of "it," see also 328:10–12.

324:21 **Inside the station café it was warm and light:** A close comparison of the opening paragraphs of Parts I, II, and III reveals that they start in *almost* the same way. The first clauses of Part I and II are identical (though in Part I it stands alone as a complete sentence), creating an eerie impression of déjà-vu. The same thing happens with the "seats" (322:5) that become "wood seats" (324:25) in Part II and "wooden seats" (328:19) in Part III: the description is of the same thing, yet it is different and implies a difference of perception. We are thus reminded that any statement—in fiction or in expository prose—is only meaningful in relationship to or in its dependency on other statements. As the conversation develops between Mr. Johnson and the waitress, the impression of déjà-vu becomes more uncomfortable. Why would the writer who had written the year before about the beauty and the dignity of the iceberg, the necessity of severe editing, and the art of elision say (almost) the same thing three times? When Hemingway unsuccessfully proposed the story to *Cosmopolitan* editor William Charles Lengel in 1932, he insisted on the circular nature of his story: "The fact that the three parts all open the same way or practically the same is intentional and is supposed to represent Switzerland metaphysically— where it all opens in the same way always. . . . But possibly, Mr. Lengel, you have been in Switzerland yourself—Anybody will have been there when they read the Homage" (*Letters vol. 5*, 164).[12]

325:1 **Have a cigar:** Like Mr. Wheeler, Mr. Johnson starts an inappropriate flirtatious conversation with the waitress; he too offers her a cigar. Even if she were not working in the café, it would be socially inappropriate for a young woman to smoke a cigar in public, but the phallic symbol of the cigar (see also 322:24, 325:1, 328:40) and its Freudian overtones that recur in Part III makes the sexual advance even more crass. In all three instances, the waitress, who is the only and isolated female presence in the story, is the unwilling participant in the men's game; contemporary readers cannot but be shocked by the ease with which these men get away with attitudes that amount—especially because of their insistence—to sexual harassment. Thus, Mr. Johnson's flirting game resonates with the somewhat dated phallic euphemism "Johnson" coined in 1863 (Kipfer and Chapman 318). The pun becomes even clearer when Mr. Johnson asks the waitress if she wants to "play" with him (325:10); this is a linguistic game in which seemingly disconnected things acquire new relative positions.

325:8 **Signorina:** Mr. Johnson's economic advantage over the wage workers at the station appears in the loose way he deals with language. He calls the waitress "Signorina" and "Fräulein" (325:42), "Miss" in Italian and German, respectively, but also the generic term once used to call female café aides. "Miss" signals the absence of marital bind and therefore sexual availability; the fact that the term was—and sometimes still is—used so commonly suggests that economic and sexual dependency is equated with menial jobs—waitresses, secretaries, flight and shop attendants—in which women were (often still are) systematically employed but which also *signified* for men real or fantasized sexual availability. Johnson's ignorance of or indifference to the linguistic and cultural place he is in also signals his disinterest for the people around him. "Signorina" also suggests that Mr. Johnson is coming from Italy, and, like many (American) tourists, he might consider that one foreign word is just as good as any other to hail an aide.

325:13 **I don't mean anything violent:** In "Negation" (*Die Verneinung*) of 1925, Sigmund Freud proposes, "the content of a repressed image or idea can make its way into consciousness, on condition that it is negated. Negation is a way of taking cognizance of what is repressed; indeed, it is already a lifting of the repression, though not, of course, an acceptance of what is repressed" (*Standard Edition* 235). Mr. Johnson's strange declaration points to the repressed violence of the story that appears in the self-deprecation of the male characters, their need to dominate others, in particular women. The sentence thus means exactly the opposite of what it purports to say.

325:17 **the Civil War:** Johnson's next remark also seems to come out of the blue and hints at the violence the story contains. His suggestion that the waitress get a substitute to cover for her while she goes to a party with him in Vevey the way "[t]hey used to do that in the Civil War" is an ironic quip that echoes Hemingway's preoccupation with honor and valor. Hemingway's maternal grandfather had been a Civil War veteran, and *For Whom the Bell Tolls* and other novels refer to that war as a test of manhood.

The Civil War is also the first anticipation of the theme of the suicide of the father that closes Part III; "that other one that misused the gun" (*FWBT* 338) is Jordan's father who commits suicide in *For Whom the Bell Tolls,* just like Hemingway's father who shot himself with his own father's Civil War pistol (see Meyers 2).

325:18–20 **myself in the person. . . . At the Berlitz school:** Berlitz is a language school established in 1878 in Providence, Rhode Island. It has become one of the symbols of language learning around the world and of American cultural expansion; again, we are reminded that, although we are in Europe, in a trilingual country, the conversation is carried out mostly in English and from an American point of view. Johnson makes the waitress nervous, and her desire to maintain a distance from the client who harasses her makes her "[lose] her English," as had been the case with the waitress in Part I (323:26–27). Her insecurity makes her fall into hypercorrectness, and she mixes three phrases—"myself," "in person," and "in the flesh" (325:18).

325:23 **Scott Fitzgerald:** By the time of the publication of the story, Hemingway had known Fitzgerald for eight years. As Scott Donaldsonhas definitively established, Hemingway always admired Fitzgerald yet asserted that the latter had never lived up to his talent as a writer. It is impossible to discuss this aspect here fully, but the close association of the Civil War with Fitzgerald brings in the idea of "substitutes": those, like Henry James, who managed to dodge the war and those like Fitzgerald who dodge their responsibility as writers and prefer frivolous "necking and petting" with "smoothies" (325:22–23).

325:35 **They were old men:** Mr. Johnson is thirty-five, the traditional middle of life. In Dante's *Divine Comedy,* the pilgrim speaks of "nel mezzo del cammin di nostra vita"—age thirty-five. Francis Macomber, another man at the mercy of a woman, is thirty-five at the end of his short happy life, and Hemingway was thirty-four at the time of publication of the story. The themes of time, waiting and wasting, are obsessive in the story. The focalization of the dialogue through Mr. Johnson shows he is reflecting on the time he still has, maybe before becoming an old man himself, maybe before dying, maybe before taking his own life.

325:36–45 **Wollen Sie trinken? . . . Laquelle est le best?:** Johnson's informality in calling to the porters in German signals his class and cultural callousness: "*Wollen Sie trinken?*" ("Do you want to drink?"). One of the porters replies in French, "*Oui, monsieur*" (325:37, 325:39).[13] Johnson seems to be surprised that they respond in French, and the few words he exchanges with them are riddled with mistakes. Thus, "*Connais-vous des champagnes?*" ("Do you know Champagne wines?") (325:40) is grammatically and syntactically wrong, though understandable intradiegetically for the porters and recognizable extradiegetically as "French" for an American reader; the same kind of mistake occurs in the next sentence, "*Faut les connaître*" (literally, "gotta know them") (325:42).[14] As we progress in Part II, we realize that these are not just acceptable mistakes for a nonnative speaker of French, but that these mistakes are really Mr. Johnson's "clowning with the language" (326:25) because he is capable, when he wishes, to speak "good French" (326:25). When he asks, "*Laquelle est le best?*" (325:45), he plays with the porters, just as he would like to "play" with the waitress.[15] In his reply, the first porter to speak—presumably, the most confident linguistically—implicitly corrects Mr. Johnson when he asks "*Le meilleur?*" (326:1). Sexual and linguistic games are always closely connected in "Homage to Switzerland."

326:14 **Put yourself here, please:** The porter means "Please, have a seat" or "Sit here, please," but, in his desire to ingratiate the "gentleman" who is paying for expensive wine, he too uses hypercorrect English and translates literally from the typically Swiss French phrase, *mettez-vous là, je vous en prie*. This detail signals the importance of language for Mr. Johnson (who is the focal point of the dialogue) and, of course, for Hemingway himself.

326:17–18 **It's not a fête. My wife has decided to divorce me:** In January 1927, Hemingway divorced Hadley Richardson, his first wife; the divorce was finalized in April, and he married Pauline Pfeiffer that May. As his biographers have pointed out, Hemingway remained haunted by his first divorce, and it would reappear throughout his fiction. The flirtation with the waitresses in the first two variations of the story now acquires more somber overtones. The image of separation and divorce is often associated with train travel in Hemingway's stories, as for instance in "A Canary for One," "Hills Like White Elephants," or the ending of *A Moveable Feast* where the character Hemingway is supposed to travel to rejoin his wife, but he does not "take the first train, or the second or the third" (210). The dialogue that ensues from Johnson's confession that his wife wants to divorce him inverts the power roles at the beginning of Part II: now the joke is on him as the opening statement—"It's not a fête" (this is no party)—suggests. He is evidently powerless in the divorce request of his wife, and he becomes the object of observation and of the ironically empathetic comments from the porters.

326:32 **I myself am somewhat in retard:** Another pun on time and mortality: M. Johnson uses the British formal phrase suggesting that he is behind in terms of development or progress—something that applies to many Hemingway's male characters. He also mixes the French phrase *en retard* (late) with calling himself self-deprecatingly and offensively "a retard." As is often the case, the violence directed at others by male characters can rapidly turn against themselves.

326:27–28 **They don't divorce much here:** Cultural differences are emphasized when one of the porters remarks about the rarity of divorce in Switzerland, to which Johnson replies, "With us [Americans] . . . it's different. Practically every one is divorced" (326:29–30). When Johnson says that he is thirty-five and that this is his first divorce, the porter replies *"Mais vous êtes encore jeune"* [But you are still young] (326:34), which seems to suggest that Johnson still has the time to remarry or, cruelly, to get divorced again, as Hemingway's life would illustrate. Through the three avatars, the story clearly explores some of Hemingway's haunting themes: self-worth as a man and a writer, sexual union, marriage and divorce, and finally suicide. These themes are arranged in a nonlinear manner and echo one another.

327:10 **Is it a system always to respond in a different language in Switzerland?:** The multilingual conversation places Johnson at the margin of it and presents him (and the other two avatars of the story) as emotionally crippled and unable to establish a meaningful verbal or emotional relation to others. Johnson's isolation (like Wheeler's or Harris's) is linguistic as well as social and emotional. He tells the porters "You're not interested in my troubles" (327:30–31), and when he tries to change the conversation to bond with his interlocutors, his obsessions—that is, his wife who is walking out on him and writing—resurface.

327:39 **I am a writer:** Almost all Hemingway protagonists are writers or else artists whose craft, like the work of the bullfighter or the painter, is comparable to that of the writer. "Homage to Switzerland" thus appears as one of the many reflections on the art of fiction for which *Death in the Afternoon* is the clearest manifesto in Hemingway's oeuvre. One is hard-pressed to find stories or novels where writing or the figure of the writer does not play a central role, and, in most cases, writing is the ultimate test of self-worth and courage. It is also, however, that which sets the writers apart from society and turns them into men without women. Writing is neither an "amusement" (327:38) nor something "interesting" (327:43), as Johnson sardonically remarks; it can bring, in Henry James's words "honours and emoluments" (379), but it condemns the male writer to a fruitless life of waiting and solitude, as the story suggests.

328:10–12 **Inside the café . . . it had only made him feel nasty:** Mr. Johnson's failure to connect with the porters who offer only polite conventional conversation is emphasized by his leaving the table "three-quarters of an hour" (327:45) before the arrival of the train and by the fact that, after finishing the wine from the first bottle bought by Johnson, the waitress returns the second bottle behind the counter; Johnson imagines they are just going to split the price of the bottle among them. To them, he is an affluent American but nothing more. Johnson, like Wheeler and Harris, cannot let down his social and cultural guard: Wheeler "never [takes] chances"

(324:17–18), Johnson mentions his divorce in passing, and Harris reveals the suicide of his father in a grimly sarcastic quip. The obsessive repetitions of almost the same story suggest that the real subject of these narrations—self-worth as a writer, love and marriage, death and suicide—belongs to a melancholiac circle from which the characters (and presumably Hemingway himself) cannot escape.

The theme of the train and its telos in a snow-ridden Swiss town reappears like a doleful rumination with hallucinatory details characteristic of a bad dream: the chairs, the light, the pretzels, but also the clock and the train schedule that count and materialize the time that leads to "it." In conversation, Wheeler, Johnson, and Harris are self-absorbed, continuing the inner monologue about "it"; even the champagne brand "Sportsman" (326:6) is reminiscent of the "inexpensive sport" (324:11) that pointless flirtation is for Wheeler. We are reminded of the sentence from the beginning of *Death in the Afternoon*—"We, in games, are not fascinated by death, its nearness and its avoidance. We are fascinated by victory and we replace the avoidance of death by the avoidance of defeat" (22)—and we are reminded of the title of this collection of stories, which emphasizes this theme. Conversation is good sport, as is drinking champagne, or engaging in a cheap flirtation; but this game of appearances cannot conceal the existential angst about "it" that keeps cropping up.

Hemingway liked small words both from the point of view of semantics and spelling. "It" is certainly one of the most remarkable. By the time we reach the end of Part II, its title becomes clearer: "Mr. Johnson talks about it at Vevey " (324:20). The word is crucial in many places in Hemingway's writing, but most notably in *The Sun Also Rises* where Jake Barnes's emasculation is never mentioned explicitly and referred to as "it"; or in "Hills Like White Elephants" where Jig's abortion appears only in the form of the pronoun. The "it" at the end of Part II reminds the readers that Hemingway's fiction is always about that "it" that only "serious" writing can attain and express, while social contacts and conversation only make it sound like a joke—"I suppose it was funny" (38), Jake Barnes sardonically comments. Writing is about taking risks, as Hemingway insists in *Death in the Afternoon*; socially awkward Wheeler, Johnson, or Harris cannot take that kind of risk and hide behind their money, their clowning, or their dark humor. This is also why the links between the three avatars and Ernest Hemingway are both unavoidable and insufficient: all three are doppelgängers of sorts that melancholically repeat that which Hemingway seeks to avoid. He needs to get at "it," and, while it is unattainable for his characters, it might become partly visible for Hemingway's readers.

As the multilingual situation of "Homage to Switzerland" suggests, the characters are in another country and seem to speak at cross-purposes and not even to share a common language with their interlocutors. "In Another Country" is another story that centrally features the question of language, and Mark Cirino has shown the importance of "Hemingway's method of conveying foreignness" through "his literal translation of everyday Italian words and phrases into their English counterparts" (49). The "foreignness" highlighted by Cirino is central to the experience of the characters of "Homage" and indeed to so many Hemingway's characters—and one might presume to Hemingway himself. The technical prowess comes out only on close examination of the writing. But these effects are only available extradiegetically to the serious reader, just as they can only be produced by the serious writer. Intradiegetically, they are of no use for the character(s) of the story, which is why the last word of Johnson's internal monologue is "nasty" (328:12).

328:14 **THE SON OF A FELLOW MEMBER AT TERRITET:** The title of Part III increases the unconventionality of the three titles. Part I proposed rather classically a "portrait" of Mr. Wheeler, though, as we have seen, it is rather a portraiture of the character's failings and lack of qualities; Part II shows that all three parts are really about an "it" that the character(s) cannot cope with and can only rehash in a melancholiac manner; though grammatically correct, the title of Part III seems to propose more questions than offer actual information and leaves moot the relation among the words: a member of what? What is the syntactic relation between "member" and "fellow"? The word "son" and its resonance with the word "father" (and the father's suicide) opens further questions. The relative position of the words in the title and the relative value of the titles themselves reinforce the impression of circularity.

328:14 **Territet:** The small town is composed of three smaller municipalities, Territet itself (on the lake shore) and Collonge and La Veraye on the heights above Lake Geneva. Today, the small town has become part of the larger municipality of Montreux, but, in the 1930s, Territet renowned for its vistas and luxurious international hotels. Over the years, Territet hosted a number of famous people including Franz Joseph I of Austria in 1893 and his wife Empress Elisabeth of Austria (Empress Sissi). Hemingway uses the aura of the place in a way reminiscent of what Henry James does with Vevey in *Daisy Miller*. A train coming from Italy would stop at Territet first, then in Montreux, and then Vevey. The geographic oddity of the placement of the last stop of "Homage to Switzerland" reinforces its obsessive and circular character.

328:15 **In the station café at Territet it was a little too warm:** Part III slightly modifies the opening sentence of the first two parts: the café said to be "warm and light" (322:3–4, 324:21) is now "a little too warm." These variations suggest repetition and difference: the theme of Part III is an escalation of the repressed pain felt by the characters from Mr. Wheeler's cheap flirtation to Mr. Johnson's divorce and now to the suicide of Mr. Harris's father.

328:17 **cardboard pads for beer glasses:** As in the other two parts, the details come from the external narrator, but the focalization is that of the protagonist. His eyes wander from one detail to the next during this time of waiting (hence, the clock again) and also to keep his mind off "it."

328:22 **A porter:** Whereas, in the previous parts, it is "another" porter who comes in to say that the train is late, here the closest narrative antecedent is "an old man drinking coffee . . . under the clock and reading the evening paper" (328:21–22). This confirms the focalization through Harris.

328:33 **Do you speak other languages besides English?:** This is one of the sentences that is repeated verbatim three times in the story (also 322:20 and 324:39), thus participating in its formal unity. The waitress's idiomatic English reinforces the importance of linguistic performance in the text.

328:40 **You wouldn't take a cigar?:** Cigars are offered by the men—and refused by the women—in all three parts of the story with slight variation on the crass informality of the proposal (see 322:25 and 325:1). The theme of sexual pursuit thus recurs, but this time with a more phallic and possibly Freudian symbol because of the ending of the story. Cigars as a sign of masculinity and domination appear regularly in Hemingway's fiction; one may think of the racially charged moment in "Indian Camp" when Uncle George hands out cigars to the "Indians" who have just ferried him, Nick, and his father across a lake. The Freudian dimension is present in the name of Harris's interlocutor, the old man under the clock, called Dr. Sigismund Wyer. Sigismund and Schlomo were Freud's given names. In the 1930s, his popularity was immense; the iconic 1921 photo of Freud with a cigar remains an indelible representation of him.

328:42 **Neither do I:** Like Wheeler who proposes intercourse to a woman knowing it is not going to happen, Harris, who does not smoke, offers the waitress a cigar. This is again and easy and somewhat cruel sport, but it also reinforces the sexual innuendo of the cigar.

328:42 **David Belasco:** Belasco (1853–1931) was an American theatrical producer and playwright who made his reputation with important innovations in the techniques and standards of staging and design. However, the latter contrasted with the quality of the plays he produced. This comment—which the waitress, of course, cannot understand and which suggests that Harris is really talking to himself—also reflects on the relation between performance and the intrinsic quality of a play. The name expands the (ironic?) reference to Scott Fitzgerald, as it resonates with the play on appearances and substance. In *The Great Gatsby,* a drunken character famously says of Gatsby, "This fella's a regular Belasco" (45). In "Homage to Switzerland," the character(s) seek to put on a good show for social appearances, but they know (and so does the reader) that it is a Belasco show: sports and clowning with no real substance to back it up.

329:2–3 **his collar on backwards:** In many pictures, Belasco wears a sort of white al-most priest-like dog-collar, which makes him (like Freud's cigar) immediately recog-nizable and iconic. Clearly, "Homage to Switzerland" is playing with cultural clichés to tease out the deep thoughts of the protagonist.

329:3–4 **Then, too, he's dead now:** Belasco died in 1931, so this would be factually correct if we assume the narrative time of the story to be around the time of its publi-cation. However, the arresting detail here is "too," which comes as a surprise because there has been no mention of anyone dead. The reference must be to the father and confirms that the show put on by Harris has little to do with his actual obsession with the suicide of his father.

329:10 **I beg your pardon if I intrude:** The emphasis on language continues in Part III, but here the language is formal to the point of becoming theatrical, another possible allusion to Belasco. The waitress's impeccable English anticipates the gen-tleman's obsequious introduction. From then on, the story continues in the tone of a somewhat stuffy comedy of manners.

329:11–12 **the National Geographic Society:** For no apparent reason, Dr. Wyer as-sumes that Harris might be a member of the society. Does he assume that all Amer-icans are? Familiarity with Hemingway's work suggests rather that Wyer is a lonely man (as his sitting alone under the clock suggests) who is looking for some chance to speak to someone. The National Geographic Society was established in 1888 and had been publishing a monthly magazine since that date. The magazine was known then, as it is now, for its wide variety of geographic, historical, and cultural subjects and for its dramatic use of photographs. In the 1930s, before television and the internet, the magazine was the only access for many people to foreign and exotic places. The magazine is also known for its rectangular format with a wide yellow frame. It was the magazine of world discovery par excellence, associated with gen-trified coffee tables and doctors' waiting rooms. Until 2015, the magazine circulated only in English, so its title and the English language in which it was printed also defined what was "exotic" for an American readership. Thus, the magazine also reinforces the importance of locality and space of the story.

329:16 **kirsch:** Kirsch is the abbreviation of *Kirschwasser*, "cherry water," a colorless brandy made from the double distillation of cherries. It can be served either as an aperitif or as a digestif; it is still popular in Switzerland where it is associated with cheese fondue and certain pastries. Hemingway would remember the brandy in a moving passage from "There Is Never Any End to Paris" in *A Moveable Feast* that evokes precisely the years of composition of "Homage to Switzerland," recalling his nickname was "the Black-Kirsch-drinking Christ" (206).

329:18 **old gentleman:** He had been referred to before twice as the "old man" (328:21, 329:7) and twice as "the gentleman" (329:13, 329:15); the change in the designation, as do other small changes in the descriptive opening parts of the story, suggests subtle differences in perspective and focalization.

329:22 **That is my certificate of membership:** In Hemingway's writing (and in modernist aesthetics in general), the most banal is the most extraordinary. Though it may be "puzzling," it is unfair to call this dialogue "gratuitous," as Erik Nakjavani does in his otherwise precise reading of the story (279). As in "A Clean, Well-Lighted Place," the dialogue in "Homage to Switzerland" reveals the profound existential solitude of the "old man" and the desperate way in which he seeks to uphold his dignity. Harris is just a little too eager to respond to the man's platitudes, which the latter has probably repeated many times in conversations for which his certificate of membership serves as a prop. As Nakjavani further points out, "his 'certificate of membership' . . . provides him with a sanctioned mode of entry into this world where everyone is someone in general and no one is anyone in particular" (280).

329:22–23 **Frederick J. Roussel:** The old man's question is comical, for he assumes that, as an American, Harris should know Frederick Roussel, a "very prominent" (329:25) fellow American.

329:30 **Aren't you sure?:** The humor of the dialogue is reinforced when the man seems to doubt Mr. Harris's really being an American because he does not know with certainty where the headquarters of the society is. The trivial details show how the man seeks to make sense of the world in which he lives; the *National Geographic* thus becomes a mode of identity and a map to read the world.

329:33 **No. But my father is:** It is possible that the old man already reminded Mr. Harris of his father, which may also explain why the focalization changes from "old man" to the more empathetic "old gentleman." But the conversation obsessively returns to "it," that is, to the suicide of the father and to the fascination with and fear of suicide. The use of the present tense may be a slip of the tongue on Mr. Harris's part, but it is more likely to be a repression of the father's death. (See also 331:13–14.)

329:38 **I am sorry you are not a member:** The National Geographic Society from this moment onward remains the only point of contact between the two men, with the Swiss man walled up in the prison of old age and repeatedly mentioning one thing after another about the society and its magazine and the American increasingly absorbed in his morbid thoughts.

330:1 **Yes. I have it in Paris:** Hemingway lived in Paris between 1921 and 1927, which he evoked in *A Moveable Feast*. For "Homage to Switzerland," these are the years of his marriage to (1921) and divorce from Hadley (1927) and the suicide of his father (1928). The conversation with the old man thus turns out to be not merely comic but also tragic, for it reopens all the wounds Mr. Harris (alias Hemingway) is seeking to heal.

330:4–5 **George Shiras three:** George Shiras III (1859–1942) was a US representative of Pennsylvania. During and after his time in Congress (1903–5), he was a passionate nature photographer who developed a technique for taking pictures of animals at night. *National Geographic* dubbed him the "father of wildlife photography" (Wender). Hemingway may have enjoyed also the way his photography "captured" the animals and turned them into (image) trophies very much like Hemingway did throughout his life with actual trophies.

330:6 **They were damned fine:** Mr. Harris's impatience appears as he quips at the old man's senile recitation of all the photographs and names he can remember; again, the dark thoughts come to crack the thin varnish of sociability. When the man is surprised by this outburst, Harris mends his ways and corrects his answer to "They were excellent" (330:8) and to appease the old man he even offers that he and Shiras are "old friends" (330:10).

330:11 **interesting:** Banal conversation is always the visible part of the iceberg in Hemingway: the six repetitions of "interesting" in nine lines deprive the word of any concrete meaning. We are reminded of the narrator's admonition in *Death in the Afternoon,* "all our words from loose using have lost their edge" (71).

330:21 **The Sahara Desert:** The issue of *National Geographic* the two men discuss came out in April 1911, and the magazine captioned the photo (a foldout) "The most extraordinary desert scene ever published" (qtd. in Reynolds 259).

330:21 **That was nearly fifteen years ago:** In her poem "In the Waiting Room," Elizabeth Bishop uses *National Geographic* of February 1918 to situate herself in time and space; the magazine confirms to her that she is a war child and a woman: "you are an I, / you are an *Elizabeth,* / you are one of *them*" (ll. 60–62), the child-narrator of the poem says on contemplating pictures of the "awful hanging breasts" of African women (l. 81). Hemingway's use of *National Geographic* is so close to Bishop's that it may be an antecedent for her use of it. Hemingway's reference to the magazine further emphasizes the centrality of time and space in the story. The contrast to Bishop's poem also shows how the scenes evoked by the two men are infused with a typically masculine sense of grandeur, magisterial gaze, or military bravery, as suggested by the mention of Colonel Lawrence (see also 330:30).

"Arab man sitting atop a sand dune in the Sahara Desert" by A. Bougault (Courtesy of the National Geographic Image Collection)

As Michael Reynolds has demonstrated, the section about *National Geographic* further emphasizes the relativity of time in the story. On the one hand, it seems to give us a specific date: 1911 plus fifteen years would place the story in 1926; but, as Reynolds also notes, Hemingway was familiar with T. E. Lawrence's book *Revolt in the Desert,* published in 1927, which Hemingway bought that September (*Letters vol. 3,* 224). This time sequence echoes Mr. Harris's mentioning his father's suicide; Hemingway's father took his own life in December 1928, which would place the story in 1929, but the mention that "[Belasco] too is "dead now" (329:3–4) puts the composition of the story in or after 1931.[16] Hemingway revisited key moments of his own life in his fiction—most importantly those featured in "Homage to Switzerland"—and though they can all be retraced to an ascertainable historical moment, they kept acquiring for him new relative significance throughout his life. From that point of view, "Homage" is the laboratory of what Hemingway's oeuvre would become. One may, for instance, revisit all the Nick Adams stories (and Nick's less-explicit avatars in the rest of the works) not only by referring the stories to a supposed original moment that generated them but also to the relative and possibly moving positions they occupy with respect to one another.

330:22 **That was one of my father's favorites:** The somewhat shallow conversation spills like a layer of oil over the submerged or repressed current of cold water that carries the image of death and suicide connected to the father. The repression is again expressed in the temporal confusion that appears in the tenses. Harris says it *"was* [his] father's favorite," but, when the Swiss man asks if Harris's father *does* not prefer more recent issues of *National Geographic,* Harris replies, "He probably *does* . . . But he *was* very fond of the Sahara panorama" (330:24; emphasis added). The use of the tenses renders relative the temporality of the story, just as the dating or the placement of the parts in Vevey, Montreux, and Territet undermine not only the linearity of the narration but also the linearity of our experience of time. Writers like Proust, Joyce, Borges, and Beckett have alerted us to the relativity of our experience of time. William Faulkner would famously rephrase it in *Requiem for a Nun:* "The past is never dead. It's not even past" (535). "Homage to Switzerland," like much of Hemingway's fiction, is about a past that does not pass.

330:28 **Mecca:** Mecca and Medina in Saudi Arabia are the two holiest sites of Islam. Mecca is known as the birthplace of the Prophet Muhammad and home of the Kaaba in the direction of which Muslims pray. This last aspect is clearly the source of the confusion between Mr. Harris and Wyer. It is also typically the sort of feature that *National Geographic* would bring with its blend of historically ascertainable facts, dramatic sceneries, and heroic masculinity.

330:30–31 **Colonel Lawrence's book:** Colonel T. E. Lawrence (1888–1935), known as Lawrence of Arabia, was an archeologist, a British soldier, and liaison officer during the Arab revolt against the Ottoman, 1916–18. Lawrence was a military strategist who sought to coordinate the Arab forces. In 1919, he unsuccessfully defended Arab independence at the Paris Peace Conference that established a settlement after World War I. Lawrence became an epic and romantic figure, especially after the publication of his autobiographical memoir *The Seven Pillars of Wisdom* (1926). "Homage to Switzerland" seems to be referring to an abridged version of Lawrence's 300,000-word memoir *Revolt in the Desert* that Hemingway bought that year.

In 1921, Lawrence was recalled as an adviser on Arab affairs to the colonial minister, then Winston Churchill. After the Cairo political settlements, which kept but few of the idealistic wartime promises Lawrence had made, he turned down offers to work for the British government. Instead, he enlisted under an assumed name (John Hume Ross) in the Royal Air Force in 1922. The press revealed the story, and the RAF released Lawrence. After reinstatement in the RAF proved impossible, Lawrence enlisted as a private in the Royal Tank Corps in 1923 before being transferred again to the RAF through the intervention of powerful friends, including George Bernard Shaw and Prime Minister Stanley Baldwin.

331:2 **Lausanne:** Lausanne is the capital of the Canton de Vaud, one of the cantons of the Suisse romande (see 327:12–13), that is, French-speaking Switzerland. Hemingway first visited Lausanne in 1922 as a correspondent for the *Toronto Star* to cover the International Peace Conference after the Greco-Turkish War. After the conference, Hemingway cabled Hadley telling her to pack sweaters so they might go skiing at their nearby chalet in Caux, above Montreux. Hadley decided to surprise her husband by bringing him all his Parisian manuscripts, but they were all lost after the valise that contained them was stolen. As is constantly the case in "Homage to Switzerland," apparently trivial details bring back traumatic memories: Lausanne resonates with the stolen manuscripts and also with the ending of *A Farewell to Arms* in which Catherine dies in childbirth and Frederic wanders off in the rain through the streets of the town.

331:5 **I come here for coffee after dinner:** Not only does this line point to the old man's loneliness but also to the proverbial clockwork regularity of Switzerland. Americans like Wheeler, Johnson, and Harris come through, but the Swiss stay: you can enter that café after dinner time in Territet ten times, and you will find Dr. Wyer, just as you can enter into ten Swiss railway stations and find the (almost) same wooden chair, the clock, and the pretzels in the glazed paper.

331:6 **University:** The University of Lausanne was established in 1537 as a school of theology; it became a university in 1890.

331:8–9 I'm just waiting for the train. . . . for the States: The trip evoked by Harris is reminiscent of those taken by Hemingway when he travelled from Europe back to the United States. Harris, like the other two characters of the story, is on the move. After Mr. Harris has moved on, after Mr. Johnson has divorced, and after Mr. Wheeler has more "inexpensive sport" elsewhere (324:11), the Swiss remain: one American passes, and another comes, but Switzerland abides forever; this is also possibly why it deserves this homage.

331:10 I have never been to America: In the economically depressed Europe of the 1930s, traveling to the United States was a difficult endeavor. "Homage to Switzerland" portrays the dollar riding high and the constancy of Switzerland.

331:11–12 I would be very happy to meet your father: Insistently, the image of the father and his suicide returns. Like the inevitable arrival of the train, the story tracks back to its obsessive theme. The man says that he *would* like to meet Mr. Harris's father because the latter has until then maintained a tense confusion suggesting that his father is still alive (see 330:22). Here, as Harris finally reveals what has been on his mind all the time, the tense changes to the past conditional, thus expressing an impossible hypothesis: "he would have liked to meet you" (331:13; see also 330:24–25). The repressed suicide of the father prepares us for the final Freudian image that concludes the story.

331:13–14 Shot himself, oddly enough: Hemingway's father, Clarence Edmonds Hemingway, committed suicide on 6 December 1928. Hemingway states in *Death in the Afternoon* that he was "much interested in suicides" (20), and the reappearance of that "interest" in his fiction is pervasive. Significantly for "Homage to Switzerland," Hemingway was waiting for a train to Florida with his first son when he received the cable telling him of his father's death. Ernest's often-quoted reaction to the news— "I'll probably go the same way" (Miller 115)—cast a long shadow on Hemingway's life and was tragically confirmed by his own suicide on 2 July 1961. Not only suicide, but most of all men who "quite deliberately" (Reynolds 16) shoot themselves would be an object of morbid fascination in Hemingway's prose and life. The suicide of Harris's father echoes with Hemingway's but also with the father in "Indian Camp" because he "couldn't stand things" (*CSS* 69) and even more with Jordan's father in *For Whom the Bell Tolls;* like Mr. Harris, Jordan is lost in his morbid thoughts:

> I'll never forget how sick it made me the first time I knew he was a *cobarde*. Go on, say it in English. Coward. It's easier when you have it said and there is never any point in referring to a son of a bitch by some foreign term. He wasn't any son of a bitch, though. He was just a coward and that was the worst luck any man could have. (338–39)

The interlinguistic game of *For Whom the Bell Tolls* is reminiscent of "Homage to Switzerland," while the "cowardice" of the father—perhaps of all father figures— haunts Mr. Harris who may be wondering, like Jordan, if he would be made "a *cobarde* . . . the way second generation bullfighters almost always are" (*FWBT* 338), and if, in a biblical but also Freudian echo, "The sins of the father are to be laid upon the children" (*The Merchant of Venice* 3.5.1).

The other two sections of "Homage to Switzerland" end with the belated yet inevitable arrival of the train; this section ends with the death of the father and we are reminded that

> all stories, if continued far enough, end in death, and he is no true-story teller who would keep that from you. Especially do all stories of monogamy end in death, and your man who is monogamous while he often lives most happily, dies in the most lonely fashion. There is no lonelier man in death, except the suicide, than that man who has lived many years with a good wife and then outlived her. If two people love each other there can be no happy end to it. (*DIA* 122)

The ending of Part III creates ties to Part I and Mr. Wheeler; his stepping onto the platform and the beam light of the approaching train (238: 9–10) creates the ominous image of a man who may not be waiting for the train only to board it but possibly to throw himself under it.

The absence of a pronoun at the beginning of the sentence gives the revelation a strange familiarity further reinforced by the stoic and sarcastic comment "oddly enough" (331:14). That comment is reminiscent of the hard-boiled humor of a number of Hemingway's characters and also of his sister Madelaine's comment about his morbid reaction to his father's death: "He was half jesting, half serious. The thought seemed quite unlikely" (Miller 115).

331:15–17 **I am sure his loss was a blow. . . . "Science took it awfully well"**: The grim humor displayed by Mr. Harris is expanded by the old man's awkward condolences. He associates the family and science in a zeugma that links family and science in a strange grammatical structure, which, though correct, results in a comical effect. Mr. Harris's reply is a prosopopoeia, a figure that personifies science while abstracting the event of the suicide and its trauma. For a second, pain and fear have appeared from under the gloss of social conventions, but humor immediately recreates an ironic protective distance.

331:18 **This is my card:** Mr. Harris gives the man his card where his initial "E. D." (E for Ernest?) appear; his father's initials were "E. J.", which further establishes the continuity between father and son. When "the gentleman" reciprocates the gesture, his odd identity seems to be entirely contained in his membership with the National Geographic Society (331:23–24).

331:22 **DR. SIGISMUND WYER, PH.D.:** The man's name gives the story its final Freudian twist. Sigmund Freud was at the time of the publication of the story at the height of his popularity and influence (see entry for 328:40). Wyer is therefore a direct evocation of the Austrian psychoanalyst; for Mr. Harris, he becomes a father figure, as his being called the "old man" suggests. The apparently trivial and comical conversation turns out to be a talking cure that leads Mr. Harris finally to say out loud—though through the veil of irony—that his father committed suicide. The conversation with Dr. Sigismund Wyer, like a classic psychoanalysis, thus leads the patient to mention the elements of his repressed past, in particular, those linked to the family and the father.

The reprinting of the card in its original form is one last strange turn of the story. The story is not merely the text of the card but the thing itself, a reification of the card, just as the card reifies Mr. Wyer's identity.

331:25 **I will keep it very carefully:** Harris's reply is both ironic and serious. On the one hand, it sounds like the "Isn't it pretty to think so?" of the end of *The Sun Also Rises* (251), for the card gives no real indication about the man to whom he has just spoken. On the other hand, given the epiphany the conversation has led to, Harris may be keeping the card the way he may keep the card of his doctor for future consultation.

NOTES

1. Paul Smith is right when he says that direct trains from Italy no longer stop at Territet (253). However, the Orient Express used to be a favorite destination for wealthy international tourists, the British in particular, which is why that train used to stop there. Territet featured several luxury hotels, one of the oldest funiculars in the country—the Territet–Caux railway opened in 1883—and special amenities such as tennis courts exclusively reserved for tourists.

2. "To do things 'railroad fashion' is now the byword; and it is worth the while to be warned so often and so sincerely by any power to get off its track. There is no stopping to read the riot act, no firing over the heads of the mob, in this case. We have constructed a fate, an *Atropos*, that never turns aside. . . . The air is full of invisible bolts. Every path but your own is the path of fate. Keep on your own track, then" (Thoreau 83).

3. *The Einstein Theory of Relativity, 1923,* produced by the Fleischer Studios, https://vimeo.com/9832926.

4. The automobile features prominently only in Hemingway's late works such as *Across the River and into the Trees* or posthumous works like *The Garden of Eden* or *The Dangerous Summer,* where it starts to assume an important aesthetic and symbolic function.

5. Many modernist artists were powerfully influenced by Einstein's theory that radically upset time and space and, therefore, the very idea of being. In "Description without Place" (1945), Wallace Stevens writes, "It is possible that to seem—it is to be, / As the sun is something seeming and it is. The sun is an example. What it seems / It is and in such seeming all things are."

6. The Romansh language has been Switzerland's fourth language since 1938. It is spoken by a small speakers' community in the eastern parts of the country near the Austrian border. Although it appears on official documents of the Swiss Confederation, it does not have the same official status as German, French, and Italian, the other languages spoken in Switzerland. All four official languages, especially Swiss German, are composed of many dialects; the waitress says she speaks "the dialects" (322:21; 324:40; 328:34), which draws attention to the linguistic complexity that the deceivingly flat English of the narration covers with its cultural and economic hegemony.

7. The US dollar was worth about five Swiss francs in 1930, but it lost one-fourth of its value against the Swiss franc when the crisis spread worldwide, something Hemingway and Mr. Wheeler would have been acutely aware of. According to the Bureau of Labor Statistics consumer price index, the dollar experienced an average inflation rate of 3.14 percent per year between 1930 and 2019, meaning the real value of a dollar decreased. Seventy-five dollars in 1930 is equivalent in purchasing power to about $1,100 in 2019. In the United States of 1930, a loaf of bread cost nine cents, a pound of hamburger twelve cents, and the average new car cost some $760. The average US wage in 1935 was $474; clearly, the money at stake is not insignificant. As in the case of languages, the effect of power takes place in the *translation*, that is, in the conversion of the US currency into European currencies.

8. In 1930 in Switzerland, a pound of potatoes cost twelve centimes, a pound of bread twenty-four, and six eggs twenty-one centimes. In the 1930s, income for employees in the hotel and restaurant sector lost some 19 percent, due mostly to the steady decrease of tips (Leuthold 18).

9. Hemingway had already portrayed such an anonymous waitress in "Cross-Country Snow" where Nick and George tease her. In that story, the waitress is pregnant, and there is no indication that she has a husband or a fiancé. The economic, social, and sexual vulnerability of the waitress in "Homage to Switzerland" resonates with the one in "Cross-Country Snow."

10. Earlier examples of this dichotomy include Liz in "Up in Michigan," Jig in "Hills Like White Elephants," and the American wife in "Cat in the Rain."

11. Whether Hemingway thought that this absence of care for women aligned the men who behaved thus with homosexuals is a hypothesis worth exploring; such indifference is displayed toward Brett by the gay men in the *bal musette* scene in *The Sun Also Rises* (28), and Jake's anger against them might come from his feeling "like" a homosexual. Smith notes that, before the deletion of the passage that explicated Wheeler's homosexuality, "Hemingway might have been thinking of more than a 'metaphysical' meeting of the various 'Wheelers' . . . in Territet (253).

12. For the composition and publication history of "Homage to Switzerland," see Smith 252–53.

13. In the phrase, "Oui, Monsieur," the word meaning "sir" in English should be capitalized in the polite form, as in "Dear Sir"; the same thing occurs with the word "mademoiselle (326:38).

14. The correct sentences should be *Connaissez-vous les Champagnes?* And *Il faut/faudrait les connaître.*

15. Champagne is masculine in French, that is, *le meilleur champagne*; in his reply the porter both translates and corrects Mr. Johnson's "clowning with language."

16. Smith proposes "a period in the late spring of 1932" (252).

APPENDIX: A TRANSLATION OF THE FOREIGN-LANGUAGE PASSAGES
IN "HOMAGE TO SWITZERLAND"

323:1 **Fräulein** German; miss
323:18 **Mademoiselle** French; miss
323:42 **Mademoiselle** French; miss
324:3 **Au revoir, Mademoiselle** French; Good-bye, miss
325:8 **Signorina** Italian; miss
325:36 **Wollen Sie trinken?** German; polite form singular and plural; [literally] Do you want to drink?; Would you like a drink?
325:37 **Oui, monsieur** French; Yes, sir
325:39 **Oui, monsieur** French; Yes, sir
325:40 **Connais-vous des champagnes?** French; incorrect; Do you know Champagnes?
325:41 **Non, monsieur** French; No, sir
325:42 **Faut les connaître** French; informal; Gotta know them
325:42 **Fräulein** German; miss
325:45 **Laquelle est le best?** French; incorrect; Which one is the best?
326:1 **Le meilleur** French; The best
326:17 **fête** French; party
326:34 **Mais vous êtes encore jeune** French; But you are still young
326:35 **Monsieur n'a que trente-cinq ans** French; The gentleman is only thirty-five
326:38 **mademoiselle** French; miss
327:7 **Prosit** German; Cheers!
327:8 **A votre santé, monsieur** French; Cheers, sir!
327:9 **Salut!** French; hi, hello; incorrect for "cheers"; transposition from Spanish ¡Salud! cheers!
327:12–13 **La Suisse romande** French; French-speaking Switzerland
327:23 **Oui, c'est normal[e]** French; misspelled; Yes, that's normal
327:24 **Et vous, monsieur?** French; And you, sir?
327:25 **Ça va** French; I'm ok; it's all right
327:26 **Pour moi, . . . ça ne va pas** French; I'm not fine; things aren't well for me

WORKS CITED

Baker, Carlos. *Hemingway: A Life Story.* Scribner's, 1969.
Barnes, Julian. "Julian Barnes Reads 'Homage To Switzerland' by Ernest Hemingway" *Guardian Short Stories Podcast,* 10 Dec. 2007, https://www.theguardian.com/books/audio/2010/dec/08/julian-barnes-ernest-hemingway-podcast.
Berman, Ronald. *Modernity and Progress: Fitzgerald, Hemingway, Orwell.* U of Alabama P, 2005.
Bishop, Elizabeth. "In the Waiting Room." *The Norton Anthology of American Literature, vol. E,* 9th ed., edited by Amy Hungerford, Norton, 2017, pp. 66–68.
Carroll, Lewis. *Alice's Adventures in Wonderland and Through the Looking Glass.* Bantam Doubleday, 1992.
Cirino, Mark. "'You Don't Know the Italian Language Well Enough': The Bilingual Dialogue of *A Farewell to Arms.*" *Hemingway Review,* vol. 26, no.1, 2006, pp. 43–62.

Donaldson, Scott. *Fitzgerald and Hemingway: Works and Days*. Columbia UP, 2009.

Eliot, T. S. "The Love Song of J. Alfred Prufrock." *The Complete Poems and Plays, 1909–1950*, Harcourt, Brace & World, 1952, pp. 3–7.

Faulkner, William. *Requiem for a Nun. Novels: 1942–1954*, Modern Library, 1994, pp. 471–664.

Fitzgerald, F. Scott. 1925. *The Great Gatsby*. Scribner, 2004.

Freud, Sigmund. "Negation." 1929. *Standard Edition of the Works of Sigmund Freud*, translated and edited by James Strachey, Hogarth Press and Institute of Psycho-analysis, pp. 335–39.

Frost, Robert. "Stopping by Woods on a Snowy Evening." *Robert Frost's Poems*, Washington Square, 1946, p. 194.

Hemingway, Ernest. *The Complete Stories of Ernest Hemingway: The Finca Vigía Edition*. Scribner's, 1987.

———. *Death in the Afternoon*. 1932. Scribner's, 1960.

———. *A Farewell to Arms*. 1929. Scribner's, 1995.

———. *For Whom the Bell Tolls*. 1940. Scribner's, 2003.

———. *The Letters of Ernest Hemingway: Volume 3 (1926–1929)*. Edited by Rena Sanderson, Sandra Spanier, and Robert W. Trogdon. CUP, 2015.

———. *The Letters of Ernest Hemingway: Volume 5 (1932–1934)*. Edited by Sandra Spanier and Miriam B. Mandel.

———. *A Moveable Feast*. 1964. New York: Scribner's, 1995.

———. *The Sun Also Rises*. 1926. Scribner's, 2003.

James, Henry. "The Art of Fiction." *Tales of Henry James*, selected and edited by Christof Wegelin and Henry B. Wonham, Norton, 2003, pp. 375–94.

Kipfer, Barbara Ann, and Robert Chapman, eds. *Dictionary of American Slang*. 3rd ed. Collins, 1995.

Leuthold, H. "Le revenu national suisse" [The Swiss National Income]. *Revue syndicale suisse: organe de l'Union syndicale suisse*, vol. 32, no. 1, 1940, pp. 12–20.

Miller Hemingway, Madelaine. *Ernie: Hemingway's Sister "Sunny" Remembers*. Crown Publishers, 1975.

Meyers, Jeffrey. *Hemingway: A Biography*. Macmillan, 1985.

Nakjavani, Erik. "Repetition as Design and Intention: Hemingway's 'Homage to Switzerland.'" *Hemingway's Neglected Short Fiction: New Perspectives*, edited by Susan F. Beegel, U of Alabama P, 1989, pp. 263–82.

Reynolds, Michael. "Ernest Hemingway, 1899–1961: A Brief Biography." *A Historical Guide to Ernest Hemingway*, edited by in Linda Wagner-Martin, OUP, 2000, pp. 15–52.

Shakespeare, William. *The Norton Shakespeare*. 2nd ed. Edited by Stephen Greenblatt. Norton, 2008.

Smith, Paul. *A Reader's Guide to the Short Stories of Ernest Hemingway*. G. K. Hall, 1989.

Stevens, Wallace. "Description without Place." *The Collected Poems of Wallace Stevens*. Vintage Books Edition, 1990, pp. 339–46.

Thoreau, Henry David. *Walden, Civil Disobedience, and Other Writings*. Edited by William Rossi. Norton, 2008.

Wender, Jessie. "Meet Grandfather Flash, the Pioneer of Wildlife Photography." *National Geographic*, 20 Nov. 2015, https://www.nationalgeographic.com/photography/proof/2015/11/20/meet-grandfather-flash-the-pioneer-of-wildlife-photography/.

Williams, William Carlos. "The Red Wheelbarrow." *The Norton Anthology of American Literature, vol. D*, 9th ed., edited by Mary Loeffelholz, Norton, 2017, p. 288.

A DAY'S WAIT

Verna Kale

"A Day's Wait" is one of Hemingway's shortest stories and follows a typical progressive plot structure: the narrator's young son is sick, and a doctor is summoned. The doctor takes the boy's temperature and announces it to be 102 degrees. The boy lies in bed and seems withdrawn and unable to focus, but he also refuses to sleep. The boy tells his father that he doesn't have to stay if "it" is going to bother him. His father goes out bird hunting and, when he returns, takes the boy's temperature again. Only then does the boy reveal what has been troubling him: his classmates in France have told him that a person cannot survive a temperature greater than forty-four degrees, so, with 102, he has been waiting all day to die—a fate the father unknowingly left him to experience alone. The father explains the conversion from the metric temperature scale and the boy relaxes. By the next day, he is on the mend and crying at small things like any other sick child.

With its plot twist, the story shares more in common with the kind of fare Hemingway enjoyed as a young reader—such as he read in *St. Nicholas* and *Harper's* magazines (Brasch and Sigman 10)—than with what he was otherwise writing in the early 1930s, the genre-flouting *Death in the Afternoon* and the gritty stories that make up the rest of *Winner Take Nothing*. It is the only one of Hemingway's stories I've ever heard of being taught in elementary or middle school—you can purchase lesson plans for it on the Teachers Pay Teachers website, and it has appeared in a widely adopted middle-grade textbook published by Prentice-Hall. It is also one of only two Hemingway short stories—"Cat in the Rain" being the other—that I've personally found suitable to read with my daughter, who, nine years old at the time of this writing, is the same age as the child in the story. That is not to say, however, that "A Day's Wait" is a children's story, for it is more appropriately placed in *Winner Take Nothing* than it might initially seem.

The text of the story is stable, offering few mysteries to the textual scholar besides its exact date of composition. Versions include a manuscript with few corrections (located in the archives at Princeton University) and a typescript that served as the setting copy for *Winner Take Nothing* (in the Ernest Hemingway Collection at the John F. Kennedy Presidential Library). Unlike several other stories in the collection, it was not previously published in a magazine. Hemingway told editor Maxwell Perkins that he could have sold the story to a magazine for a dollar per word, but he wanted to make sure that *Winner Take Nothing* offered readers unpublished stories (*Letters vol. 5*, 437). Hemingway claimed to Perkins that it was among those stories written "absolutely as they happen," and the story appears to have gone through very few revisions (*Letters vol. 5*, 541–42). The events on which the story was modeled occurred in December 1932. Paul Smith suggests that the "earliest date of composition could not have been before late January 1933" because "Hemingway spent most of January on the road" and that it was completed by March (302). However, it is possible that Hemingway started working on the story right away in December 1932, and it is also possible (though less likely) that it was the "simple story of action" he aimed to write in April 1933 (*Letters vol. 5*, 369). It may also have been written during a period of productivity in February. In any case, it was among the last in the collection to be completed, save one, "Fathers and Sons" (*Letters vol. 5*, 451).

Always experimenting and pushing himself as an artist, but also hyperconscious of himself as a professional who provided customers a product worth their money, Hemingway wanted readers to feel that they were getting a good value for their purchase. Somewhat defensively, Hemingway offered to give Arnold Gingrich, publisher of *Esquire*, his money back when Gingrich sent Hemingway his ratings of each story in the collection and awarded two out of five stars to "A Day's Wait" and "The Mother of a Queen" (and only one star to "One Reader Writes") (*Letters vol. 5*, 531). Hemingway defended the story, telling Gingrich it is better than Gingrich thinks, and he irritably suggests that Gingrich send him a receipt for the book and Hemingway will give him his money back. Perhaps not wishing to anger his new magazine's most prominent contributor, Gingrich wisely backed off in his reply, admitting that "A Day's Wait" is a good story and noting that his wife liked it very much. It's easy to imagine that Gingrich, aspiring to reinvent American masculinity for the "genuine adult male" who "prefer[s] old wine and new stories . . . good clothes and strong language" might have overlooked the quiet devastation hidden in the simple story, while Helen Gingrich, homemaker and mother to the couple's five-year-old son with another baby on the way, comprehended it (Advertisement).

Reviews of the collection were lukewarm, expressing fatigue with Hemingway's fixation on death and violence, and very few of them mention "A Day's Wait" by name—those that do overlook its importance. T. S. Matthews in *The New Republic* declares Hemingway's worldview to be one of "bitter adolescence" and compares the writer to an aging football player who "after graduation continues to see life in terms of off-tackle plays" (24). Perhaps because he already reads the collection as somewhat childish, Matthews finds "A Day's Wait" one of the few worthwhile stories in it, but the praise is qualified: he recommends the story to "all 'Penrod' enthusiasts"—that is, readers who enjoy the misadventures of Booth Tarkington's eponymous 'tween hero. Matthews, apparently (and wrongly), thinks "A Day's Wait" is supposed to be funny. Harry Hansen in the *New York World-Telegram* says merely that the story is about "[a] lad worrying about his temperature" and obliquely suggests it counts among the "slight sketches—bits jotted down out of an unusual memory."

There are notable exceptions that recognize the story's impact. A review by John H. Harvey in the *Minneapolis Star* praises the story: "For sheer artistry and simple treatment, 'A Day's Wait' cannot be surpassed. The mere idea of a nine-year-old boy stoically facing death and then weeping at nothing when he finds he is not going to die is more than a mere idea when Hemingway takes it" (17). More prominently, Louis Kronenberger, in the *New York Times Book Review,* writes, not disparagingly, of Hemingway as a sentimentalist whose work betrays a "nostalgia" for "a world filled with much more dubiety and anguish." Kronenberger names "A Day's Wait" as one of the stories in the collection that "get[s] close to that world . . . however casual or gruff or gingerly the approach" (6). Yet even these reviewers seem not to have grasped the enormity of the miscommunication between father and son.

Secondary criticism of the story, too, is limited. Scholars have generally agreed that the story is "sentimental"—though there is less agreement in what role sentimentality plays in how we are to interpret the relationship between father and son. Sheldon Norman Grebstein locates in the story "a potentially sentimental situation" and credits Hemingway for handling it without "pathos" but rather "from a series of observations, gestures and dramatic metaphors" (9–10). Peter L. Hays calls the story "sentimental," if self-consciously so, and the boy's stoicism "juvenile heroics . . . and a little silly" (25). Hays argues that the story is Hemingway poking fun at his own already familiar code of conduct. Linda Gajdusek reads the story as being not so much about the boy's experience but the father's own "pained realization" of the boy's interiority (300).

Scholars, too, have examined the story's narrative patterns of inside/outside (Grebstein) and up/down (Gajdusek), these contrasts serving as an attempt "to define the nature of contradictory human experience . . . through a sequence of ironies" (Monteiro 301). Joseph Flora, too, notes that the conflict in the story stems from the father and son's differing subjectivity: "No person knows fully the experience of another" (219). Both Monteiro and Flora point out that the hunting interlude offers an adjacent life-and-death drama between the man and the birds that contrasts with the sick boy waiting inside to die (Flora 220; Monteiro 301). Susan Beegel identifies the boy's and the father's taciturnity as a source of conflict, one that reaches beyond "the superficial . . . Fahrenheit/Centigrade confusion" (536). Beegel diagnoses the "central problem" to be "Schatz's silent endurance, and the father's blindness to a child's fear" (536). Their masculine stoicism, she argues, is "directly responsible for the linguistic and emotional isolation of father and son" (537). We can, unironically, add Schatz to the list of Hemingway heroes who face death alone.

332:1–2 **He came into the room . . . I saw he looked ill:** The story opens with a personal pronoun, "he," and there are two people, "we," in the bed. The second person in bed, presumably the narrator's wife and the child's mother, does not appear again in the story. (Those who read the story strictly biographically will note that the other person in bed, Pauline Pfeiffer, is actually a stepmother, ill with flu herself). The narrator here might be Nick Adams, though he is never expressly identified as Nick in this story, and Philip Young chose not to include the story in his "chronological" collection of Nick Adams stories and previously unpublished fragments. If we assume the father *is* Nick, the father's failure to comprehend the boy's confusion takes on additional weight, as other stories tell us that Nick Adams is a doctor's son, a writer, and someone who, too, has lain in bed afraid to sleep lest he meet death. As Flora and Gajdusek have observed, the first-person limited point of view emphasizes the father-son relationship while allowing for the miscommunication to go unrecognized by the reader until it is revealed to the father (Flora 218; Gajdusek 294).

332:2–4 **He was shivering . . . and he walked slowly as though it ached to move:** A sudden onset of chills and aches, along with fever, is a typical presentation of influenza (Meara 217).

332:5 **What's the matter, Schatz?:** Meaning literally "treasure" in German and used as a term of endearment, much like "sweetheart" or "darling," Schatz is the boy's nickname rather than his proper name, which, like the narrator's, is never given in the story. Schatz was one of the nicknames given to Hemingway's eldest son, John Hadley Nicanor Hemingway, the only child Hemingway had with his first wife, Hadley Richardson Hemingway. John Hemingway was more commonly known by the nickname "Bumby" in childhood and "Jack" in adulthood, but the nickname Schatz, though less frequently used, shows up in his father's letters across decades. "Schatz" may have been bestowed on Bumby as early as 1925 when the Hemingways made their first trip to Austria to ski and placed him in the care of a local German-speaking nanny; it was certainly in regular use by 1926 (Baker 177; Diliberto 222; Reynolds 33). Schatz was a nickname that Hemingway would continue to use with Jack as late as 1956 (Letter to Jack) and he used it occasionally with other family members as well. The name can be found in two other Hemingway works of fiction. In *For Whom the Bell Tolls*, the nickname appears in the context of romantic or erotic love as Robert Jordan thinks to himself, "Sweetheart, *cherié, prenda,* and *schatz.* He would trade them all for Maria. There was a name" (167). In *Islands in the Stream* (published posthumously in 1970), the eldest son of protagonist Thomas Hudson, young Tom, is also sometimes called Schatz. Like Hemingway, Hudson has three sons; Tom is the eldest, from his first marriage, and two younger boys, Dave and Andy, are from a second marriage. In manuscripts for "Fathers and Sons" (though not in its published form), the boy is called "Schatz," providing further evidence for including "A Day's Wait" among the Nick Adams cycle (Smith 304).

332:8–14 **"No. I'm all right."** . . . **"I'm all right," he said:** Even before Schatz believes he is dying, he is already performing toughness for his father, insisting that he is "all right" and refusing to go back to bed.

332:11 **a very sick and miserable boy of nine years:** Born 10 October 1923, John Hemingway was nine years old in December 1932 when the events on which the story is based took place.

332:15–17 **When the doctor came he took the boy's temperature.** . . . **"One hundred and two":** The father and the doctor have this part of the conversation in front of the boy before moving downstairs, out of the boy's earshot, to discuss the prescriptions. There is no exposition between the doctor's reading of the temperature and the shift to the next scene, downstairs. The boy's reaction, if any, goes unnoticed by the father/narrator. This lack of awareness is not from a lack of caring. The father has taken the illness seriously enough to summon a doctor that same morning. As Beegel points out, Hemingway had witnessed firsthand the particularly gruesome manner of death wrought by "Spanish influenza," the 1918 influenza pandemic, and had written about it in "A Natural History of the Dead" in *Death in the Afternoon*, revised and included in *Winner Take Nothing* (Beegel, "Love" 39). By all indications the father understands the seriousness of the illness, even in otherwise young and healthy people, and does not hesitate to get the boy immediate medical attention.

332:18–21 **Downstairs, the doctor left three different medicines.** . . . **The germs of influenza can only exist in an acid condition, he explained:** Common fever reducers in the 1930s would have included salicylic acid (aspirin), antifebrin (a precursor to what we know today at acetaminophen), antipyrine (somewhat similar to today's NSAID drugs, like ibuprofen, but with more side effects), and phenacetin (a drug later banned for its carcinogenic effects) and were prescribed in combination with sodium bicarbonate, an alkaline salt that neutralizes acid (commonly known as baking soda) (Meara 218–22; "Sodium Bicarbonate"). The "purgative" (332:20) is likely a laxative such as calomel, Seidlitz powder, magnesium citrate, or Epsom salts (Meara 231; cf. Brown 13). One textbook recommends giving small doses of these medicines in capsule forms at frequent intervals to avoid toxic side effects (Meara 219). Thus, the prescription the doctor gives is standard protocol for its time. To both the reader and the father, the doctor appears knowledgeable if somewhat abstruse. Like Doctor Adams in "Indian Camp," this doctor does not communicate directly with the patient at all or demonstrate any concern for anything but the patient's physical condition because it is "not important" (*CSS* 68). The father, exhibiting no medical expertise of his own, aside from his general solicitude as a concerned parent, accepts the doctor's prescriptions because the doctor "seemed to know all about influenza" (332:22), and, though he's a dutiful parent who makes "a note of the time to give the various capsules" (332:26–27) and offers to sit with the child, he fails to pick up on the boy's fear. The boy is left completely out of the conversation, overhearing only enough to convince himself that he is dying.

332:23–25 This was a light epidemic of flu and there was no danger if you avoided pneumonia: Public health records validate Hemingway's claim. A vital statistics report in *The American Journal of Public Health* in 1933 notes "such epidemics [of influenza] as occurred in 1931 and 1932 were distinctly minor" (734). Federal mortality statistics for 1932 indicate that death rates from influenza were higher for cases with "respiratory complications specified" (Murphy 12); in 1932, eleven children ages 5–9 in Arkansas are recorded in the mortality statistics reported by the Department of Commerce for having died of influenza with "respiratory complications not specified" (Murphy 179). This is indeed a "light" epidemic compared to that of 1918, which was twenty-five times more deadly than a typical influenza outbreak and killed enough people to shave twelve years off the average US citizen's life expectancy (Beegel, "Love" 36). As Meara writes in a textbook on infectious diseases, revised to include a chapter on "epidemic influenza" considered separately from "grip," "Influenza pneumonia has a high mortality, which differs in different epidemics," and the 1918 epidemic "fell upon us with all the horrors of a medieval plague" (227, 236). Neither the doctor, nor the father (nor the absent other parent), appears concerned that the boy's illness is unusually serious. Only the boy, with his misinformation, worries.

333:3 I read aloud from Howard Pyle's *Book of Pirates*: Published posthumously in 1921, *Howard Pyle's Book of Pirates* is a collection of adventure stories by American author and illustrator Howard Pyle (1853–1911) that had previously appeared serially in *St. Nicholas* (1894–95). In a 15 November 1932 letter to Maxwell Perkins, Hemingway recalls reading the stories as a child and asks Perkins to send it to him for Bumby (*Letters vol. 5*, 272). In the same letter, he notes that he has ten stories ready for a collection and needs two or three more. The book would arrive, as requested; Bumby would fall ill; and Hemingway would have the basis for another story. The influence of the book is more than circumstantial: Beegel has noted that the book provides an "allusive subtext" for understanding how the story "questions the very values of male stoicism and taciturnity that it seems to extol" ("Howard Pyle" 536). Beegel points to the story "With the Buccaneers," in particular, in which a teenage runaway comes under enemy fire when the captain commands him to steer the ship and becomes aware of the possibility of "sudden and violent death" (95, qtd. in Beegel, "Howard Pyle" 538). Afterward, "he was nearer crying than laughing," much like Schatz at the end of "A Day's Wait" (96, qtd. in Beegel, "Howard Pyle" 538).

333:8–12 **It would have been natural for him to go to sleep, but when I looked up he was looking at the foot of the bed, looking very strangely. . . . "I'd rather stay awake":** This passage recalls two of Hemingway's World War I stories. "A Natural History of the Dead" is ironic and graphic in its depiction of what is "natural" in death. With the Spanish flu, "you drown in mucus, choking, and how you know the patient's dead is; at the end he shits the bed full" (*DIA* 139). The line is revised in *Winner Take Nothing*, and though Hemingway preferred the original expression (*Letters vol. 5*, 481), read against "A Day's Wait," the revision is particularly evocative: "how you know the patient's dead is: at the end he turns to be a little child again, though with his manly force, and fills the sheets as full as any diaper" (146). Influenza, Hemingway writes in both books, is, apart from loss of blood, the "only natural death" he had ever seen (*DIA* 139, 338:25). Schatz's case is not so severe, and, with his fever controlled, he should have been able to sleep. However, like Nick Adams in "Now I Lay Me," he is determined to avert death by staying awake: "I . . . did not want to sleep because I had been living for a long time with the knowledge that if I ever shut my eyes in the dark and let myself go, my soul would go out of my body" (*CSS* 276). Unlike young Nick in "Indian Camp," who is "quite sure that he would never die" (*CSS* 70), Schatz is aware of his mortality and faces it with a quiet resolve that his father interprets as lightheadedness.

333:13–15 **"You don't have to stay in here with me, Papa, if it bothers you." "It doesn't bother me":** The full emotional impact of this story lies not in the twist, when the boy comes to realize that he is not going to die, but rather here, with the ambiguous pronoun "it" and the lapse in communication between father and son. There is no antecedent for "it." The boy bravely tells his father that he need not stay if *the boy's death* is going to bother him. The father, the audience realizes, just thinks the boy is slightly addled by fever and takes the ambiguous "it" to mean spending time in the sick room or the illness in general. His reply, "It doesn't bother me," is meant to be reassuring but is certainly taken by the boy to mean *your death* doesn't bother me. Perhaps it takes a reader for whom English is a foreign language to question the antecedent of an ambiguous pronoun that Anglophone readers accept as idiomatic. In 1957, German scholar Werner Hüllen rightly noted that "*it war im Sinne des Jungen das Sterben,*" (*it* was, for the boy's purpose, death) and the conversation between father and son was a "ganze Reihe von Satzen" (a whole series of sentences) belonging to "zwei verschiedenen Gedankenketten" (two different chains of thought) (434, translation mine). The story is not just about the boy's personal bravery when facing what he believes to be his impending death but also his bravery even as he believes this imminent death *does not bother* his father. Or, Beegel notes, the boy may believe that his dying *does* bother his father, badly enough to make him leave, thus "corroborating Schatz's worst fear about his illness"

("Howard Pyle" 537) and a child's fear of abandonment. Thus the story should be included with "Hills Like White Elephants," "A Canary for One," "Cat in the Rain," and other stories of fractured domestic life and lapses in communication, and with "The Snows of Kilimanjaro" for its study of the individual's confronting his own mortality. In *Winner Take Nothing*, "A Day's Wait" is certainly the emotional equal of "Fathers and Sons."

333:17–18 **I thought perhaps he was a little lightheaded . . . I went out for a while:** Mild delirium was also a commonly recognized symptom of influenza (Meara 217). The father *thinks* the boy is lightheaded. He, of course, does not share that judgment with the child, who believes he is behaving as bravely and rationally as possible. With this conflicting sets of beliefs, and just having told his son that the boy's death does not bother him, the father leaves.

333:19–21 **It was a bright, cold day, the ground covered with a sleet that had frozen so that it seemed as if . . . the bare ground had been varnished with ice:** Quail season opened in Arkansas in 1932 on 1 December, and the first significant amount of sleet fell on 9 December 1932, with temperatures dipping into the teens ("Veritable Hunter's" and "Sleet"). On 10 December 1932, the *Fayetteville Daily Democrat* reported that the state Game and Fish Commission was requesting farmers to "scatter a little grain for the birds" who were at risk "if the mixed coating of snow and sleet now general over the state lasts over 36 hours" ("Sub-Freezing").

333:21–22 **I took the young Irish setter for a little walk:** Hemingway arrived in Piggott on 29 November and went hunting several times during this period. On 10 December, the day after the sleet storm, he hunted alone with the purebred bird dog Hoolie belonging to his sister-in-law Virginia "Jinny" Pfeiffer. His hunting journal notes that the ground was frozen and covered with sleet. He killed two quail on this outing ("Notebook"). Using this external information and reading biographically, we can date the events that inspired the story to around 10 December 1932.

333:23–25 **it was difficult to stand or walk on the glassy surface . . . dropping my gun and having it slide away over the ice:** This outdoors scene, which contrasts starkly with the sickroom, also evokes the father's fallibility, and his unsure grip on the gun contrasts with the boy's unrelenting grip on his own consciousness.

333:30–33 **Coming out while you were poised unsteadily on the icy, springy brush they made difficult shooting . . . happy there were so many left to find on another day:** Though Hemingway would claim the story was written straight from life, this passage marks a significant difference, and the discrepancies are thematically significant. Though the narrator enjoys his morning spent shooting in the chilly air and manages to shoot two quail and then two more while missing five, Hemingway had been disappointed by the freezing conditions that interfered with bird season. In mid-December 1932, he wrote to his mother, sister Madelaine, and brother Leicester that the shooting was "*nil*—all lakes frozen—no feed for ducks—they all leaving—Worst duck shooting I've ever seen" (*Letters vol. 5*, 297). Hemingway's hunting journal shows only one duck killed that week; quail were more numerous: he records shooting an average of six per day, though he killed only two (not four, as the story suggests) on 10 December.

The reality of the 1932 Piggott visit was overwhelmingly negative in other ways as well: not only did Bumby and Pauline have the flu, but so too did Jinny, and this illness, coupled with the bad weather, interfered with plans for a hunting trip on the White River. Meanwhile, both Patrick and Gregory had whooping cough, and a barn on the premises, which Hemingway had been using as guest quarters and a workroom, burned with his books, clothing, and several guns lost in the fire (*Letters vol. 5*, 229). Overall, the mood at the Pfeiffer home was not a happy one. It is essential to the emotional impact of the story, however, that the father is out enjoying himself and that the enjoyment hinges partially on an imagined future, while the boy believes himself to be dying. The hunting interlude also reminds the reader of a theme recurring in Hemingway's work, that death is both indiscriminate and unavoidable: the narrator kills some birds, and those spared live to be killed another day.

333:34–36 **At the house they said the boy had refused to let any one come into the room. "You can't come in," he said. "You mustn't get what I have"**: Where is his mother, the other person lying in bed in the story's opening sentence? Who are the other members of the household whom he worries about infecting? Had they too left the boy on his own during his daylong ordeal? In an October 1933 letter to Pauline, her mother, Mary Pfeiffer, writes that "A Day's Wait" was very moving and factually accurate, but she seems to regret the incident that inspired it: "We had to grapple with present problems, plague and fire and cold and all the evils attendant thereon. But it is past, we will forget it" (qtd. in Hawkins 55).

333:40–334:2 **I took his temperature. . . . "It's nothing to worry about"**: Here, either the father is trying to assuage the child's nervousness, which he has finally understood, or he truly is not very concerned. To the boy, the father's imprecise language still refers to a lethal temperature, and he begins to let on to his father what he fears. Years later, the "Scott Fitzgerald" chapter of *A Moveable Feast* will offer a comic version of a similar scene in which Hemingway takes the hypochondriac Fitzgerald's temperature with a bath thermometer and reassures him his temperature is "thirty-seven and six tenths" as Hemingway "was trying to remember whether thirty-seven six was really normal or not. It did not matter, for the thermometer, unaffected, was steady at thirty" (145–46). Whether Hemingway recalled this 1925 episode with Fitzgerald when writing "A Day's Wait" or if he later recalled "A Day's Wait" as he was writing the memoir is uncertain, but each uses unfamiliarity with the temperature scale conversion to expose a character's vulnerability, albeit to very different effect in each account.

334:4–6 "Don't think, I said. "Just take it easy." . . . He was evidently holding tight onto himself about something: Schatz's hold on himself recalls the protagonist in "A Very Short Story" who "went under the anaesthetic holding tight on to himself so he would not blab about anything during the silly, talky time" (*CSS* 107) and Nick Adams in "A Way You'll Never Be" who can't control what he says to the Captain even as he is "trying to hold it in" (314:2). In "A Day's Wait" the ambiguous pronoun "it" means something different to father and son. The father is advising the boy to relax, but the boy regards the suggestion as an admonishment to take death easily. The "something" he holds tightly to is his own fear, and, like Hemingway's other protagonists, the boy is fighting not only against the weakness of his own body but against the language that reveals that weakness to others.

334:14–18 "About how long will it be before I die?" . . . "What's the matter with you?" . . . "That's a silly way to talk": When Schatz cannot stand the wait any longer and finally puts his fear into words, the father's initial response reinforces the code of behavior the boy has tried so valiantly to maintain. The father is at first incredulous and then dismissive. The particular word choice, "silly," connotes foolishness and childishness and may even be gendered feminine (*OED*). The miscommunication has not yet been cleared up, and so, to the boy, the father's response is not comforting but is rather an admonishment of his weakness.

334:19–21 "At school in France the boys told me you can't live with forty-four degrees. I've got a hundred and two." He had been waiting to die all day: A degree on the Celsius scale corresponds to 1.8 degrees on the Fahrenheit scale. The average human body temperature is 37 degrees Celsius and 98.6 degrees Fahrenheit. ("SI Units"). A fever of 44 degrees Celsius would correspond to 111.2 degrees Fahrenheit and would indeed be deadly. Bumby's mother and Hemingway's first wife, Hadley Richardson Hemingway, had primary custody of Bumby. She had remained in Paris following their 1927 divorce, and Bumby was enrolled in school there (Diliberto 253). Schatz's recounting of the conversation he has had with his French schoolmates is the moment that both the father and the reader realize what has been troubling the boy. It's an a-ha! moment typical of short stories, but not typical of Hemingway's short stories (with notable exceptions, such as "A Canary for One"). The twist here makes it one of the more accessible stories in the book. Hemingway wrote to Perkins that a collection needs a certain number of stories that people can understand easily because an easy story "gives [readers] the necessary confidence in the stories that are hard for them" (*Letters vol. 5*, 369). Both the father and the reader momentarily know more than the boy, and they are both amused and moved. However, as Hemingway claimed to Gingrich, there's more to the story than this gimmick, and the boy's suffering becomes wholly apparent later, upon rereading.

334:22–27 **"You poor Schatz" . . . "It's like miles and kilometers . . . in the car":** This exchange illustrates the care the father has for his son. As Flora and others have noted, any hurt he has inflicted is unintentional, and now that the father understands what is troubling the boy, he gently explains the situation, invoking the boy's nickname not once but twice and reassuring him—"Absolutely" (334:26).

The difference is one of scale: the first thermometers were developed in the seventeenth century, and different instruments produced different scales for measurement (Treese 840–41). Daniel Gabriel Fahrenheit innovated the use of mercury in thermometers and devised a scale with a 240-degree range between ice water and boiling water. The scale was refined and widely adopted in England and its colonies. Meanwhile, in 1742, Anders Celsius proposed a 100-point scale between the freezing (100) and boiling (0) points of water. Divisions on this scale were called "degrees centigrade," and the scale was adopted into the metric system in the late eighteenth century as governments and scientists recognized the usefulness of a common scale (Beauchamp). As Schatz's father explains, the metric system in continental Europe measures temperature degrees centigrade (or "Celsius" as the scale has been officially known since 1948) and distance in meters, while the English system, used in England and the United States, measures temperature in degrees Fahrenheit and distance in miles (Treese 843). The father has explained this concept to the boy during their travels together, and he educates him with an explanation and familiar example the boy can understand.

334:28 **"Oh," he said.** The boy's response, however, the one-word "Oh," indicates that the boy is still "holding tight" (see entry at 334:6). He still hesitates to express his emotions.

334:29–31 **But his gaze at the foot of the bed relaxed slowly. . . . and he cried very easily at little things that were of no importance.** The story resolves with the parent-child dynamic restored and the catharsis of the boy's easy and ironic tears: the boy, who has stoically faced death, now cries easily at nothing—or at what his father believes to be nothing. Even now, with the initial traumatic misunderstanding resolved, the father fails to understand his son. "A Day's Wait" neatly illustrates how subjectivity can alter even factual information, like the reading on a thermometer, and how easily a person can misunderstand the subjective experience of another.

Advertisement for *Esquire*. *The Indianapolis Star,* 17 Oct. 1933, p. 5.

Baker, Carlos. *Hemingway: A Life Story*. Scribner's, 1969.

Beauchamp, Zack. "Why Americans Still Use Fahrenheit Long after Everyone Else Switched to Celsius." *Vox,* 4 June 2015, https://www.vox.com/2015/2/16/8031177/america-fahrenheit.

Beegel, Susan. "'Howard Pyle's Book of Pirates' and Male Taciturnity in Hemingway's 'A Day's Wait.'" *Studies in Short Fiction,* vol. 30, no. 4, 1993, pp. 535–41.

———. "Love in the Time of Influenza: Hemingway and the 1918 Pandemic." *War + Ink: New Perspectives on Hemingway's Early Life and Writings,* edited by Steve Paul, Gail Sinclair, and Steven Trout, Kent State UP, 2014, pp. 36–52.

Brasch, James Daniel, and Joseph Sigman. *Hemingway's Library: A Composite Record*. Garland, 1981.

Brown, Jeremy. *Influenza: The Hundred-Year Hunt to Cure the Deadliest Disease in History*. Touchstone, 2018.

Diliberto, Gioia. *Hadley*. Tichnor & Fields, 1992.

Flora, Joseph M. *Hemingway's Nick Adams*. LSU Press, 1982.

Gajdusek, Linda. "Up and Down: Making Connections in 'A Day's Wait.'" *Hemingway's Neglected Short Fiction: New Perspectives,* edited by Susan Beegel, UMI Research P, 1989, pp. 291–302.

Grebstein, Sheldon Norman. *Hemingway's Craft*. Southern Illinois UP, 1973.

Hansen, Harry. "The First Reader." *The New York World-Telegram,* 28 Oct. 1933.

Harvey, John H. "Hemingway Tales Brutal in Humor, Forcefully Told." *The Minneapolis Star,* 30 Dec. 1933, p. 17.

Hawkins, Ruth. *Unbelievable Happiness and Final Sorrow: The Hemingway-Pfeiffer Marriage*. U of Arkansas P, 2012.

Hays, Peter L. "Self-Reflexive Laugher in 'A Day's Wait.'" *Hemingway Notes,* vol. 6, 1980, p. 25.

Hemingway, Ernest. *The Complete Short Stories of Ernest Hemingway: The Finca Vigía Edition*. Scribner Paperback Fiction, 1987.

———. *"A Day's Wait" manuscript*. Ernest Hemingway Collection, C0068, Manuscripts Division, Department of Rare Books and Special Collections, Princeton University Library.

———. "A Day's Wait" setting copy. Ernest Hemingway Collection, box MS33, item 222. JFK Library, Boston.

———. *Death in the Afternoon*. 1932. Scribner's, 1996.

———. *For Whom the Bell Tolls*. 1940. Scribner's, 1995.

———. *Islands in the Stream*. Scribner's, 1970.

———. *The Letters of Ernest Hemingway: Volume 5 (1932–1934)*. Edited by Sandra Spanier and Miriam B. Mandel. CUP, 2020.

———. Letter to Jack Hemingway, 22 and 28 Jan. 1956. *Maurice F Neville Collection of Modern Literature (Part II)*, item 354, Sotheby's, 2004.

———. *A Moveable Feast: The Restored Edition*. Edited by Seán Hemingway. Scribner's, 2009.

———. *The Nick Adams Stories*. Edited by Philip Young. Scribner's, 1972.

———. "Notebook: Hunting Book, 1930–1934." Ernest Hemingway Collection, box OM14, JFK Library, Boston.

———. *Winner Take Nothing*. Scribner's, 1933.

Hüllen, Werner. "Gespräche ohne Verstehen: Versuch einer Deutung von Ernest Hemingway's Kurzgeschichten 'A Day's Wait' und 'Cat in the Rain.'" *Die Neueren Sprachen*, 1957, pp. 432–39.

Kronenberger, Louis. "Hemingway's New Stories and Other Recent Works of Fiction," *The New York Times Book Review*, 5 Nov. 1933, p. 6.

Matthews, T. S. "Fiction by Young and Old." *The New Republic*, 15 Nov 1933, pp. 24–25.

Meara, Frank Sherman. *The Treatment of Acute Infectious Diseases*. 2nd ed. Macmillan, 1921.

Monteiro, George. "Hemingway, O. Henry and the Surprise Ending." *Prairie Schooner*, vol. 47, no. 4, 1973, pp. 296–302.

Murphy, T. F. *Mortality Statistics 1932*. US Department of Commerce. United States Government Printing Office, 1935.

Reynolds, Michael. *Hemingway: The Homecoming*. W. W. Norton & Company, 1999.

"SI Units—Temperature." Weights and Measures, National Institute of Standards and Technology, US Department of Commerce, https://www.nist.gov/pml/weights-and-measures/si -units-temperature.

"silly, adj., n., and adv." *OED Online*, Oxford University Press, September 2020.

"Sleet, Light Rain Heralds New Drop; 16 Today's 'Low.'" *Fayetteville Daily Democrat*, 9 Dec. 1932, p 1.

Smith, Paul. *A Reader's Guide to the Short Stories of Ernest Hemingway*. G. K. Hall, 1989.

"Sodium bicarbonate." *Wikipedia: The Free Encyclopedia*, 29 June 2019, https://en.wikipedia. org/wiki/Sodium_bicarbonate.

"Sub-Freezing, Sleet Covers Entire State." *Fayetteville Daily Democrat*, 10 Dec. 1932, p. 6.

Treese, Steven A. *History and Measurement of the Base and Derived Units*. Springer, 2018.

"Veritable Hunter's Paradise Promised in State This Fall." *Harrison* [Arkansas] *Daily Times*, 15 Sept. 1932, p. 1.

"Vital Statistics." *American Journal of Public Health*, vol. 23, no.7, 1933, pp. 733–37.

Young, Philip. *The Nick Adams Stories*. Scribner's, 1972.

A NATURAL HISTORY OF THE DEAD

Ryan Hediger

"A Natural History of the Dead" proposes to anatomize a topic that profoundly resists analysis, as Hemingway well knew. That essential problem, the challenge of the topic, motivates much of the piece, including not only Hemingway's selection of material but also his techniques for treating it. With its withering critique of "humanists" and other optimists, this piece treats death in a sophisticated and arresting way. That complexity is deepened when we recognize the story's position in *Winner Take Nothing*, a collection that wears its skepticism about familiar paradigms of selfhood on its cover, in its title. "A Natural History of the Dead" follows "A Day's Wait," which also considers the topic of death, though there it is death dreaded but never arriving, as the boy Schatz, ill in bed, misunderstands the meaning of his fever temperature. But in "Natural History," death has come and is present in every scene. The story is also reminiscent of "The Snows of Kilimanjaro," which evokes the strange presence of death in the room and the powerful otherness of death with its ability to unmoor us from the familiar, which is at the heart of the meaning of "A Natural History of the Dead" too.

That uncanny presence motivated the composition of "A Natural History of the Dead" in several ways. First, the piece clearly grows out of Hemingway's own experiences as an ambulance driver for the American Red Cross in Italy in World War I, confronting the carnage and death such a position entails and suffering his own grave wounds. More immediately, though, this piece is also motivated by the suicide of Clarence Hemingway, Ernest's father, on 6 December 1928. Having just returned to his home in Key West, Florida, from his father's funeral in Oak Park, Illinois, Hemingway interrupted his revision of *A Farewell to Arms* to draft "a sketch about another wounded soldier on the Italian front" (Forsythe 131; also see Smith 231). This sketch would become the final, narrative section of "A Natural History of the Dead," presenting the debate between the doctor and the artillery officer about how to treat the gravely wounded soldier. The natural history parody that opens the final version was written later, and, as Paul Smith reports, that section was even more directly motivated by Hemingway's efforts to make sense of his father's death (231–32). Smith writes, "It was Dr. Clarence Hemingway, after all, who was the first natural historian to instruct his son in the observation of nature, inform it with the idealism of the nineteenth century, and then blow it all away with a bullet in his head" (238). As Hemingway revised the piece, however, he steadily edited out what had been direct references to parental suicide, instead generalizing its focus and accenting other foci, many of which are examined by Susan F. Beegel in her 1988 study *Hemingway's Craft of Omission* (for example, 47).

But what is "A Natural History of the Dead"? Perhaps it makes sense to call it experimental fiction, as Beegel does and as do Charles Stetler and Gerald Locklin in *Hemingway's Neglected Short Fiction*. In particular, we can read the piece in light of postmodernist fiction, in which one technique is the mixing of genres and discourses. However, like Beegel, I prefer to accent its status as genre-*defiant* (*Craft of Omission* 32). I agree with Hemingway's editors and critics who suggest this piece defies ordinary categorization as a short story (Stetler and Locklin 248).[1] Its experimental status operates at the level of genre, then, much as *Green Hills of Africa* and *A Moveable Feast* do. Stetler and Locklin note, for instance, that these works anticipate "the New Journalism" (252), the style of news writing that was developed in the 1960s and '70s by writers such as Tom Wolfe, Hunter S. Thompson, and Joan Didion, in which the subjective position and attitude of the writer are an explicit part of the work. Indeed, the piece was first published as part of *Death in the Afternoon* (1932), Hemingway's nonfiction book about bullfighting.

Beyond a mere exercise in categorization, determining the genre of such work is key to understanding its purposes and effects. In the case of "A Natural History of the Dead," Hemingway demonstrates how the facts and presence of death defy human understanding, making the resistance to genre effectively part of that point.[2] Categories and forms of understanding cannot do justice to the experiences this piece considers. In this way, the piece's criticism of humanists and humanism deserves to be recognized as a forerunner to what many today call posthumanism, an intellectual movement that gathered steam in the late twentieth century and beyond, that displays skepticism about—but still some trust in—human reason and human power in comprehending and existing in the natural world. Posthumanist theory, alongside ecocriticism and other rising modes of interpretation, lends new value to often-neglected genres like natural history, nature writing, and the like, and it seems most faithful to Hemingway's purposes in "A Natural History of the Dead" to read it in that context.

As Forsythe notes, the opening natural history "parody proved difficult to compose, undergoing more extensive revision than the [concluding] sketch over a longer period of time" (134). Hemingway worked hard to get the satirical voice right, to engage carefully with natural history conventions. Beegel explains that Hemingway contemplated returning to the satirical voice at the close of the piece before deciding against that, settling on the narrative ending that appears in *Winner Take Nothing* (*Craft of Omission* 41–49). He relies on many of the techniques of nature writing, such as careful observation and description and the drawing of general conclusions from particular observations. But, of course, the dark joke is that Hemingway's focus is a somewhat understudied but universal element of nature: death and more especially the dead. Furthermore, rarely is the human observer—as an element of nature—the explicit focus of such writings; the human typically inhabits a safe position, outside the cycles of nature. Hemingway's purpose in "A Natural History of the Dead," by contrast, is quite the opposite.

If this piece can be read as a kind of natural history, it is an unconventional one, one that deserves a distinct name. I would call it something like "uncanny natural history." Consider the graphic descriptions of bodies "blown into pieces which exploded along no anatomical lines" (337:16–17) and the natural-history-voiced declaration that the "dead grow larger each day until sometimes they become quite too big for their uniforms" (337:29–30). Both accounts depict the body in monstrous ways that might seem inexcusable or too direct in a work of conventional fiction. When Robert Herrick compared Erich Remarque's important novel about World War I *All Quiet on the Western Front* to Hemingway's *A Farewell to Arms,* the comparison was not flattering to Hemingway. Herrick particularly criticized Hemingway's presentation of "pictures of mangled flesh" (qtd. in Smith 235).

In *Hemingway's Craft of Omission,* Beegel argues that "A Natural History of the Dead" was written partly as a response to Herrick's review (35–36); in this piece, Hemingway doubles down on his explicit and unnerving treatment of bodily injury. The "uncanny" in "uncanny natural history" is also clearly exemplified in such usages as Hemingway's phrase "the quality of unreality" (337:4) that attended to the experience of collecting the "fragments" (336:42) of the dead at the munitions factory. After all, the entire premise of nature writing is trust in the rational human's ability to convey precise *reality;* hence, the careful descriptions, collected together by the likes of Mungo Park into a deep trust in the very structure of reality itself, a reality *intended* (by its Creator) to buoy up the doubting and suffering traveler. Park—or his ghostwriter, as discussed below—finds the small moss-flower to be assembled with astonishing care, despite being, from his humanist's perspective, "of so small importance" (335:17). He therefore concludes that the Supreme Being *must* care for an entity like himself, so obviously more important than the plant.

In a cosmic sense, that presumed importance is simply humanist bias. When Hemingway applies this same scrutiny to the dead, however, he and others experience not trust and hope but a strange form of "unreality." Careful study of such realities, in other words, confuses and unsettles rather than affirms and inspirits. This deeper insight into the position of the human on planet Earth not only undermines the core assumptions of much humanistic nature writing, it anticipates other similarly skeptical work of more recent vintage, such as Robert Sullivan's *The Meadowlands* (1998), a piece of uncanny nature writing that investigates pollution and corruption near New York City, or much of the recent writing on climate change, the Anthropocene, and other human-caused disasters. Nature and the natural, trust in goodness, belief in the inspiriting value of careful description: all these become infected with doubt in this later work, as in Hemingway's "A Natural History of the Dead." By the end of Hemingway's piece, as we see below, he goes beyond mere satire, beyond sharp jokes: the destabilization is much more total.

335:1–3 **It has always seemed to me . . . the flora and fauna of Patagonia:** Hemingway opens by assuming the voice of the naturalists he goes on to name and satirize, writing uncharacteristically long sentences in the rhythms of earlier times and including such diction as "charming," "interestingly," and "furnish" to reproduce the style.

335:4 **W. H. Hudson:** Hemingway seems to position his piece alongside predecessors by citing those he purportedly follows. The first writer named, W. H. Hudson (1841–1922), was a novelist and nature enthusiast with special admiration for birds. Born in Patagonia and dying in England, Hudson was also the target of Hemingway's satire in *The Sun Also Rises,* with reference to Hudson's novel *The Purple Land* (1885), and in *The Garden of Eden,* with reference to Hudson's novel *Far Away and Long Ago* (1918), a book Hemingway actually recommended to young writers.

335:4 **Gilbert White:** Gilbert White (1720–93) is best known for his *Natural History and Antiquities of Selborne* (1789), a study of an English village. White is noted here for writing about the "Hoopoe" (335:5), a rarely seen bird of dramatic appearance, with black and white stripes on the lower body and an orange or pinkish head with a notable crown of feathers.

335:6 **Bishop Stanley:** Bishop Stanley (or Edward Stanley, 1779–1849) joins Hudson and White in exemplifying a love for nature. All these writers' work predates World War I, which accounts for some but not all their perspective. Their interest in birds and plants is intended to contrast sharply with Hemingway's proposal in this piece to study the dead.

335:7–8 **Can we not hope. . . . I hope so:** If the reader has not already caught the dissonance of Hemingway's title to this piece, it becomes unmistakable by the end of the first paragraph, when the sentence begins, "Can we not hope to furnish the reader with a few rational and interesting facts," only to land like a bomb with the word "dead," full stop. "I hope so" might first seem merely funny, blackly funny. But it is just the opening salvo.

335:9–13 **When that . . . caught his eye:** Stylistically, the parody is already in full swing, with word choices like "persevering" and the long, complex sentences, uncharacteristic of Hemingway. He uses the second and third paragraphs (discussed below) to enlarge and extend his critique, which moves from potentially silly to serious. Like the other writers named in the first paragraph, Mungo Park (1771–1806) wrote in a different age. He was a Scottish man famous for his exploration of Africa and his travel book *Travels in the Interior Districts of Africa* (1799).

335:13–21 **"Though the whole plant . . . not disappointed.":** The words here are quoted from Park's book, and Hemingway uses them to expose the deficiencies of what he regards as an unrealistic, pious faith in God's benevolent plan. After all, Hemingway implicitly reasons, if all goes according to God's plan, how are we to account for the horrors regarding the dead that the remainder of the piece will detail? Ironically, as discussed by John Portz, these words, ostensibly by Park, were more likely composed by Byron Edwards, who ghostwrote part of Park's book. In fact, Portz further explains, Park himself tended to write in a Hemingway-esque, "plain, unpretentious, practical style" and conducted his life more generally in the stoical ways Hemingway himself tended to admire. So, Hemingway's targeting of Park here is particularly unfair—especially since, Portz avers, Hemingway perhaps did not read the full Park book in question (32–33).

335:22–26 **With a disposition . . . from the dead:** Borrowing the language of hope and piety to be found in some natural history, which can only produce "increasing . . . faith, love and hope" (335:23–24), Hemingway brings the end of this paragraph again to "the dead" (335:26), producing another argument-ending grammatical full-stop with those words. Formally, then, at the paragraph level, Hemingway is engaging idealistic perspectives, only to answer them in the end with the challenging reality of death. Similarly, the bluntness of diction here—"the dead"—is a signal of the larger approach of this piece, which uses frank and graphic descriptions not just to deeply undermine faith and hope but also to offer a harsh truth, even as it suggests that this genre-defying approach via uncanny natural history may be a better general method to do so.

335:27–336:8 **In war . . . less hardy horse:** This paragraph applies the logic and methods of naturalist description, as promised, to the dead, producing more of the dissonances that indicate the effectiveness of Hemingway's approach. It is jarring to discuss human dead so objectively as bodies, male or female, and to do so alongside discussions of dead mules and horses. The move pulls the human down from our humanist pedestal, sorting us instead among the other animals, all exposed to death, presaging the theme that Hemingway explicitly states later: in war, people die "like animals" (338:14). Thus, I read these scenes, with their discussions of animals, not as Matthew Forsythe does as "inconsistent" or in error (143) or as Smith does as "digression" (234), but rather as essential to the point of the text. Indeed, the tendency among this story's critics to dismiss discussions of animal suffering and death in war seems to participate in the problematic humanism that Hemingway is clearly and directly attacking in this piece. The humorous bent of the piece takes a lighter tone in the stock mule joke of this paragraph ("whether these animals were really mortal" [336:3–4]), before returning brutally at the paragraph end to the game-ending fact of death in war.

336:9–11 **Most of those mules . . . road of their encumbrance:** This paragraph intensifies the piece's incipient catalog of horrors. Using the methods of natural history—drawing inferences about the past, about nature, and about animal behavior (including humans) by way of close observation—Hemingway presents the horrible case of mules pushed off cliffs and declivities in order to clear the road. This is an aptly grim example of the position of animals in modern war more generally, with the war machine writ large dispatching with anything and everything in its way. Again, this image strikes a stark and dramatic contrast with the hopeful image of the flower associated with Mungo Park.

336:13–15 **at Smyrna. . . . the shallow water to drown:** Then Hemingway digs deeper still, with his anecdote about the terrible events in the Greek city of Smyrna in 1922, located at a strategically important position on the Aegean Sea. Near the end of the Greco-Turkish War (1919–22), the city of Smyrna was engulfed in flames, fires set at least partly by the Turks, driving thousands of people, horses, mules, and goods to the waterfront over a ten-day period. Turkish troops committed additional atrocities, including theft, rape, and massacre, culminating in the deaths of some 10,000-to 15,000 Greeks and Armenians, or perhaps more (Naimark 52). This horrible episode, practically ending the war, is evoked by Hemingway here with reference only to the drowned horses and mules, whose miserable and monstrous deaths echo his other discussions of animals in war, whose suffering evokes the more general horrors. A similar version of this anecdote about Smyrna appears in the earlier Hemingway story "On the Quai at Smyrna" in *In Our Time* (1925).

336:16 **called for a Goya to depict them:** In the version of the Smyrna episode told in *In Our Time*, Hemingway lets the image of mules with broken legs speak for itself as the end of the grim vignette about war; here, he insists on its power via different means, by suggesting that the sight was one worthy of a Goya depiction. Francisco de Goya (1746–1828), a major Spanish painter of his day, produced a number of notable works on the horrors of war, including *The Third of May 1808*, about Spanish resistance to Napoleon. One effect of this reference to Goya is to evoke the challenges of depicting this horror in language, calling for another medium—and a recognized master in it—to evoke the horror.

336:17–21 **Although, speaking literally, one can hardly say . . . alleviate their condition:** But then Hemingway goes deeper, collapsing both Goya and the artifice of Hemingway's own metaphor of "call" ("called for a Goya" [336:16]) into the monstrous and powerful otherness of death. Death overwhelms all human sense and interpretation, so that the paragraph turns away from artifice back to the sheer reality of vulnerability, one shared by humans and animals alike. The animals, he reports, would not have called "for pictorial representation" (336:19–20). Instead, they would have called for "some one to alleviate their condition" (336:21). Thus, rather than an erroneous "tangent" (Forsythe 143), this discussion of animal suffering and mortality in war is precisely central to Hemingway's point.

336:22–26 **Regarding the sex . . . Milan, Italy:** This paragraph transitions to another element in a natural history of the dead by treating the sex of the bodies, already evoked in the opening of the fourth paragraph ("male of the human species" [335:27]). The logical procession, in other words, depends on understanding the observed in ostensibly scientific and rational terms, here by sex category. This scene references and summarizes a horrific episode that occurred in Hemingway's own life in 1918 after an explosion at a munitions factory outside Milan. As biographer Carlos Baker reports, Hemingway himself understood the experience as his "first baptism of fire," using those words on a postcard he wrote shortly afterward (40).

336:26–29 **We drove . . . by the trucks:** The account of this explosion's aftermath in "A Natural History of the Dead" highlights the contrast in modes of engaging with nature—pious naturalism or Hemingway's brutal realism—by reporting the narrator's inability to "clearly observe" much of the "minute animal life" (336:28, 336:27–28). The scientific diction of "minute" and the premise of "clear observ[ation]" are both undercut by the "dust" of the moving vehicles (336:29, 337:9), another apt and understated figure for war, an example of how the conditions of war prevent precisely the kind of clear and calm observation of life that the naturalist takes for granted. The very premise of calmly observing wildlife as a mode of being in the world is also overwhelmed here, as few would think to do so in the context of so grim a disaster as a munitions explosion.

336:41–42 **after we had searched quite thoroughly for the complete dead we collected fragments:** Language has become a strange instrument in this line. A search for "the complete dead" is both logical—that is, a sensible first step in a disaster recovery—and defiant of ordinary sense or interpretation. What a phrase: "complete dead." However, in the context of natural history, it is standard to search for complete specimens. Likewise, the collection of fragments, were we discussing the collapse of an old and rare tree or a dinosaur fossil, would seem like ordinary science. But "fragment" applied to newly exploded human bodies is monstrous. Hemingway sustains this dusty dissonance throughout this paragraph by relying on scientific language in an unsettling way to catalog this horror. It is easy to miss this dissonance and to pass over Hemingway's technique in action because the sheer facts of the subject are themselves so overwhelming (this point underscores the intelligence of Hemingway's selection of material here).

336:42–337:1 **Many of these . . . the tremendous energy of high explosive:** The sentence engages in a passive construction (fragments "were detached" [336:42]) and thus advances the scientific frame with the objective voice, in which parts of human bodies "illustrated only too well the tremendous energy of high explosive" (336:45–337:1). From a rational and scientific perspective, the power of the explosion is indeed the focus, and this sentence names it effectively in that scientific and even decorous voice. But the declaration rings with unstated horror—*especially* its decorousness— precisely because it is so much the wrong thing to say and the wrong way to say it. Focusing on "the tremendous energy" of the explosion is exactly inappropriate and entirely inhumane or, better, unfeeling. The use of such an objective perspective to understand this event makes the observer monstrous and also blind; thus, Hemingway again exposes the utter failure of an optimistic natural historian's framework to *see* and interpret the events of war, affirming instead the methods and style of a brutal, indecorous realism Hemingway practiced. As discussed in the introduction, Robert Herrick's criticism of this realism motivated Hemingway's composition of this piece. At the root of Hemingway's brutal style, however, is a reckoning with, an exposure of, and finally a challenging of the brutality of war itself. The stylistic brutality is motivated by Hemingway's insistence on facing events with an aggrieved, bitter empathy. This is not brutality for its own sake. Hemingway's technique of gruesome, ironic natural history here epitomizes the kinds of transformations to art and literature often understood to be driven by the horrors of the Great War.

This technique of understatement, using a phrase ironically to expose its own insufficiency, would be used to similar effect by Kurt Vonnegut to treat the same subject of the horrors of war in his 1969 novel *Slaughterhouse-Five,* about World War II. There, his phrase "so it goes" is repeatedly used to describe events that cannot possibly be accepted so blithely by feeling human beings. Vonnegut thus exposes, like Hemingway had before him, how simply accepting such horrors as inevitable or as part of "science" or ordinary reality is entirely inhumane, inhuman, or unfeeling.

Hemingway's narration of this Italian scene leaves implicit that the fire near the munitions plant presents the constant hazard of new explosions. The possibility that those cleaning up the "fragments" of bodies might themselves become fragments looms over the scene. Considered in that light, the proximity of the living to the dead becomes surreal, as though the boundary between life and death wavers or becomes porous; at every moment there is the terror that the horrors of the carnage are about to envelop one. And again, that is a kind of synecdoche of the experience of war more generally, in which the observer sees atrocity after atrocity—the seeing is itself unbearably bad—and the observer is at constant risk of being engulfed by those very horrors. The horrors fail to remain observable objects outside the self at a safe remove; instead, they breach the safe enclosure of selfhood and become uncanny, infecting the self, like Hemingway's sentences undermining natural history by performing it.

337:3–6 **On our return . . . much greater:** That terrifying, uncanny, and unnerving prospect is made explicit in the transition to the next paragraph, as the participants in the cleanup are said to find a "quality of unreality" (337:4) to the scene. Having "no wounded" (337:4–5) is explicitly understood to lessen the horror, but when placed in a narrative and viewed from a distance, the fact of utter decimation and loss of life involved in a scene of "no wounded," only fatalities, deepens the horror in a different way.

337:6–8 **Also the fact . . . from the usual battlefield experience:** That same uncanny technique of detachment is advanced further with the point that "it had been so immediate" (337:6) that the event had just occurred, so that the bodies had not yet begun to rot or smell. This suggestion anticipates the next paragraph, and it further justifies Hemingway's satirical technique throughout the piece. The natural historian's voice—understanding such a scene and such tasks as cleaning up the "fragments" of newly destroyed women's bodies—is, in a strictly rational way, making sense. The bodies are less disgusting. But what does "less" really mean here? Being so close in time and space to such newly wrought destruction is monstrous and terrifying, evoking a porosity now of time, as though the immediate and fatal past is very nearly the present, as though it might become present. Again, the alive/dead distinction wavers. The phrase "as little unpleasant as possible" (337:7), naming the immediacy of the newly dead, is in that sense unfathomably understated, horribly decorous in tone, demonstrating again the need for a different frame of interpretation than one offered by the mentality, language, and rhetorical techniques of the natural historian.

337:8–14 **The pleasant . . . unexploded munitions:** The mention of "the beautiful Lombard countryside" (337:9) as "a compensation for the unpleasantness of the duty" (337:10) has the unsettling effect of making beauty terrible and untrustworthy; clearly, as evidenced by the persistence of Hemingway's memory of these events and his recounting of them here, the horrors were not so easily dispatched by beautiful scenery. Indeed, the talk of "compensation" relies on a rational, Enlightenment worldview, with a safe, practically impregnable self that receives "impressions" of exterior events and can, from that position of safety, calmly trade one thing for another, horrible views for pretty ones. That worldview, its style of speech and thought, is ironized, satirized by this sentence about the Lombard countryside, testifying to a selfhood not of balance and rationality but of trauma and dread. That dread is reiterated in the ironically decorous language about it being "indeed fortunate" (337:11–12) that the fire had not quite reached the "huge stocks of unexploded munitions" (337:14). Had it done so, the cleanup would have been immeasurably worse and more hazardous.

337:14–18 **We agreed too . . . high explosive shell:** Note the further stylistic satire, with the grossly understated usage "extraordinary business" (337:15). The unbiological explosion of this sentence, with bodies "blown into pieces which exploded along no anatomical lines" (337:16–17) is yet another way of exploding the former attitudes, of casting radical doubt on the natural, logical, and pious attitude of the humanist and the natural historian. Instead, bodies are understood in the terms of military equipment; they "divided as capriciously" (337:17) as a shell. People become mere munitions, objects to explode.

337:19–24 **A naturalist . . . presence of the dead:** The previous discussion of the newly dead prepares for the material of this paragraph. Now we face the long dead, made that way due to the horribly absurd activities of large-scale wars in which an advance and then a retreat occurs, "so that the positions after the battle were the same as before except for the presence of the dead" (337:23–24). They have died for no reason, higher or otherwise, which undermines one's Mungo Park-like faith.

337:25–41 **Until the dead . . . impressions one retains:** The natural historian's method is again employed to macabre and ironic effect, as observed entities are described in minute detail. We confront bodies made monstrous not by sudden force of explosion but by the power of slow decay, turning color, swelling, and then being defiled by the living, who raid the corpses of anything valuable to be found in their pockets, overturning the bodies to leave these human beings in an "ultimate position" of chaos. Such diction, "ultimate position" (337:34), joins with the objective, scientific voice that undermines itself again. The clarity and command of that voice are undone by what they describe: a tangle of bodies utterly wasted and violated. The conditions that would drive other people to treat the dead this way—the conditions of war—are further exposed in their horror by this scene, the strangeness of which is evoked by the presence of the paper, itself an oddly striking sign of depravity in war. These "impressions" are much more than superficial.

337:41–338:2 **The smell . . . cannot be recalled:** As in previous paragraphs, this one concludes with darker horrors, as Hemingway marks a failure of memory, the inability to recall the "smell of a battlefield in hot weather." War exceeds representation and even recall. To mark this foulness, Hemingway references the more ordinary horrors of war—"the smell of a regiment" (337:43–44)—which are akin to some of the more foul odors present in ordinary life. Those we can imagine. But that more terrible battlefield smell is far worse. Further, in the final sentence, Hemingway likens such traumatic experience to its mirror opposite, that of extreme joy in love, which also "cannot be recalled" (338:2). So much for the natural historian's ability to clearly report all realities in nature: two of the most essential ones, love and death, lie beyond the capacity of memory to recall or language to evoke directly.

338:3–12 **One wonders . . . His own image:** This paragraph makes clear many of the somewhat submerged themes enacted in previous paragraphs by way of craft and technique. Hemingway displays in the war landscape the stabilizing verities of poppies and trees, which might reassure us, but they are all infected by the presence of guns, the exploded earth, the shelled houses, and the smell of the previous paragraph, which Hemingway wafts back over readers by this paragraph's end. Such realities, Hemingway underscores in the final sentence, call into question the Christian notion that humans are made in, and act in accordance with, God's own image. He thus redoubles his critique of the kind of views he attributes to Mungo Park and other faithful naturalists.

338:13–17 **The first thing . . . break the skin:** Hemingway makes more explicit one of the implicit ideas animating earlier paragraphs: the likenesses between humans and other animals in death. The point about "little wounds" evokes the strange and surprising power of mortality, which can defy our expectations by arriving even due to unexpected causes, a theme Hemingway also explores in "The Snows of Kilimanjaro," in which protagonist Harry dies from what began as a minor scratch.

338:17–24 **Others would die . . . I saw one:** Conversely, some survive for "two days" despite suffering gruesomely severe injuries that a person could seemingly never endure, a claim that sets the stage for the narrative section that ends "A Natural History of the Dead," beginning on 339:26. This paragraph seems for a moment to sustain a traditional humanist concept, the foundational and generalized difference between all other "animals" and "men," in life as in death. The long-standing assumption is that there is some absolute and universal difference between human animals and all other animals, an idea related to Enlightenment trust in the dignity and rationality of humans. Yet, by the end of the paragraph, Hemingway has undercut that distinction too: he writes that he had "never seen a natural death, so called, and so I blamed it on the war" (338:21–22). That is, he blamed his sense of the horrors of death on the war and *its* horrors, reserving a traditionally humanist place for decency in death. But then, he writes, he "saw one" (338:24), a "natural" death, a topic he addresses in the next paragraph.

338:25–30 **The only natural death . . . he's gone:** "Spanish influenza" (338:26) killed from fifty- to a hundred-million people in 1918–19, five to ten times the number— ten million—who died directly due to military conflict in World War I (Rice 12). The example of death by the 1918 flu, then, is offered here to demonstrate how horrible "natural death" can be (338:25). Some readers may blanch at Hemingway's explicit details of uncontrollable waste evacuation, but we should recall that the natural historian's method central to this piece justifies and even requires such fulsome detail. By showing us what this device of careful detail can do to unsettle us, Hemingway advances his larger project of dismantling rational humanism and the beliefs that undergird it. In his account, the disease inverts other familiar planks of humanism and rationality, making a man "a little child again" (338:28) and violating the stable boundaries of his body, which cannot contain or control its contents as he drowns in his own bodily fluids.

338:30–38 **So now I . . . the children of decorous cohabitation:** Satire turns to direct and powerful invective, a move that unsettles some readers and critics because it runs contrary to many of Hemingway's most famous literary techniques, including his characteristic understatement and omission of material via the iceberg principle. Hemingway violates the prevailing forms not only of his own fiction, then, but of fiction more generally. This is another reason to read this piece as something other than fiction. Hemingway would insist on testing and violating those norms of fiction in a number of other works in the 1930s with the novelized nonfiction book *Green Hills of Africa* (1935) and the nonfiction bullfighting book *Death in the Afternoon,* where he first published a version of "A Natural History of the Dead." This experimentation was not a passing fancy; later work included the nonfiction novel about his second African safari, written in the 1950s, *True at First Light,* later republished as *Under Kilimanjaro.* We should understand genre-testing writing as a major element of Hemingway's work.

Hemingway's case in these sentences makes a nearly personal attack on humanists, insisting that their exposure to death, and potentially painful and humiliating death, radically undermines their philosophy because such exposure is universal. Every human faces such an end, the potential indignity and unavoidable weakness of death. Hemingway's insult, calling humanists "the children of decorous cohabitation" and thereby suggesting their parents lacked physical passion in intimacy (338:37–38), can appear gratuitous (Forsythe calls it a diversion "from his primary subject" [144]). But, in fact, it makes an additional and powerful argument. Underscoring that every life (or nearly every life, in the age of artificial insemination) grows out of sex—ideally, Hemingway implies, "indecorous," perhaps passionate sex—Hemingway advocates a dramatically different vision of the human animal.

Insisting on the importance of this debate about the character and nature of human lives and revealing his personal anger about what he sees as humanism's misleading philosophy, Hemingway expresses a wish to "see the finish of a few" humanists (338:38–39), permitting him to assess their dignity in death. That personal anger derives in part from his very personal stake in the matter. According to Forsythe, the "suicide of Clarence Hemingway looms in the background" of this larger composition (142), since, as noted above, it was partly the ideology of humanism that Ernest Hemingway felt had failed his father Clarence and contributed to his suicide (Smith 238). Writing this piece in the immediate wake of Clarence's death, Hemingway had powerful feelings about the issue. It is telling that earlier drafts included specific references to "the death of one's parents" (Forsythe 142; also see Smith 231–32), personal matters that Hemingway mostly excised from the final version.

338:38–40 **But regardless . . . all their lust:** Hemingway ends the paragraph by alluding to lines from Andrew Marvell's 1681 poem "To His Coy Mistress," in which Marvell criticizes the logic of sexual purity, a poem Hemingway also uses in *A Farewell to Arms* (154). In the poem, a "long-preserved virginity" shall, if persisting until death, finally be tried by "worms," a perverse image of sexual intercourse, the like of which Marvell insists is inevitable as our bodies will be consumed by other organisms as we decompose in death. In other words, sexual norms would be overwhelmed by the reality of human biology, wherein the integrity and ostensible purity of the body will collapse back into the wilder procreative facts of nature and ecology that make human life possible in the first place, including worms. This paragraph's final sentence aligns the "sterility" of that humanist mindset with forms of composition ("quaint pamphlets") and modes of discourse ("foot-notes") that are bound to fail for their denial of larger realities (338:40), making for a waste of human efforts ("gone to bust" [338:40]) akin to Marvell's claim in the poem that the logic of virginity will finally turn "into ashes all my lust" (l. 30). That is, in death, the love and passion of the poem's speaker will uselessly return to dust. That inevitable end of the body is one Hemingway imputes onto his humanist targets directly in his own mocking footnote here, calling them already "extinct" (338:42). He thus satirizes the footnote mode of composition even as he declares its users victims to a natural process (extinction) that is far stronger than humanist philosophies.

338:41–339:6 **While it is . . . mouths have been:** Hemingway reiterates his claim of the previous paragraph that talk of humanists is merely academic. Many of those who died, especially who died in youth in war, were not at all informed about these sorts of intellectual debates. This move emphasizes the piece's logic, privileging the importance and final inevitability of the biological realities of life and death over intellectual squabbles and philosophical niceties.

339:6–10 **It was not . . . bury them again:** Logically, this sentence resumes the structure established by the discussion of bodies bloating in the heat (337:19–338:2), moving—

after Hemingway's aside over three-plus paragraphs to clarify several themes and to attack humanists (338:3–339:6)—from death in the heat to death in other weather conditions. In rain, the bodies can seem to be benignly treated, being "washed . . . clean" (339:7), with the rain making "the earth soft" (339:8) so that burial is easier. However, those benign conditions can themselves go too far, so that the ground becomes *too* muddy and soft; the rain "washed them out" (339:9), requiring reburial. This excess of a good thing intensifies Hemingway's critique of idealism and of notions of a balanced, stable, godly nature. Even too much of a good thing becomes bad. Life and death in nature are precarious. Furthermore, the reappearance of buried dead bodies is yet another form of monstrous and unsettling proximity between the living and the dead; avoiding dead bodies is one of the reasons for burial itself.

339:10–15 **Or in the winter . . . by a sniper:** Another answer to the horrors of decaying bodies in heat is death in cold, particularly in the mountains. Might that not solve the horrors of decay? Not entirely, for here too are new forms of monstrosity, with the need to bury bodies in the snow—because the frozen ground prevents more conventional burial—leading, again, to their reappearance in the spring, requiring reburial. Note the unnatural perversity of dead bodies emerging in spring, customarily a season of rebirth; instead, we have something closer to re-death. This sour note sets up Hemingway's sarcastic declaration that "war in the mountains is the most beautiful of all war" (339:12–13); "A Natural History of the Dead" has relentlessly undermined the possibility of any war being beautiful. Thus, going on, Hemingway discusses, for example, a seemingly beautiful and peaceful burial ground in the mountains at Pocol, a village and ski resort in northeast Italy, near Venice. In this cemetery, several thousand war dead are buried, many unidentified. Hemingway effectively disinters one of the buried, "a damned fine general" (339:20) who was killed not in glorious fashion, but "by a sniper" (339:14–15), arguably a form of murder that demonstrates no courage or talent other than marksmanship. Being a general cannot save him from being sorted in a cemetery with the unnamed dead of modern war.

339:15–25 **This is where . . . in such things:** To clarify the indignity of the general's death, Hemingway again gives us a naturalist's details, the small hole in the front of the general's head where the murdering bullet entered and the explosively large hole in the back of his head where the bullet exited. The actual general referenced here is Antonio Tommaso Cantore (Mandel 173–74). Hemingway pairs this death with that of General von Berrer (misspelled as von Behr), commander of the Bavarian Alpenkorps (Alpine corps, or mountain troops) in the German army. Believing a false report of victory, he drove ahead of German forces and directly into Italian Bersagliari bicycle troops, who shot and killed him (Lewis and Roos, 223). This story demonstrates the perversity of exposure in war (339:22), when even those who excel at their craft can die in an otherwise successful effort. Hemingway uses these examples to call into question war clichés—such as the notion that generals die comfortably, in bed, rather than brutally on the battlefield like their soldiers. To make this case, Hemingway proposes a revision to the title of the book *Generals Die in Bed,* a popular 1930 antiwar novella about World War I by Charles Yale Harrison (1898–1954), a Canadian.

339:26–33 **In the mountains too . . . and a day:** Hemingway uses the notion of the mountains to transition from his natural history parody to the narrative account of the dying soldier amid the already-dead, which he uses to end this piece and reiterate the arguments made so far. The gruesome image of the badly injured soldier, his head broken like a "flower-pot" (339:30), is a familiar type by this point, reiterating the precarity of life. His shattered head belies his remaining alive, like the long-lived, injured cat discussed earlier, and the man's uncanny, even unnatural survival upsets observers.

339:33–38 **The stretcher-bearers . . . I mean:** The stretcher-bearers, who have obviously witnessed other horrors, are particularly upset by this case; that fact underscores its extremity, again along lines presented above, with the unsettling intermingling of the living and the dead threatening to undermine familiar notions of selfhood and decency. And again, emphasizing the challenge of conveying these horrors in writing, Hemingway calls for Goya to evoke the scene of the doctor inspecting the fatally injured man amid the many other corpses in the cave in the winter night.

339:39–340:4 **After looking at him. . . . Captain Doctor":** Such a scene of horror, however, cannot move the injured and jaded doctor to agree to the stretcher-bearers' request to move the dying man out of the cave of the dead, even after the stretcher-bearers profess not to mind having to move the injured man twice. This prospect of moving a dying man in, then out, and then back into the cave of the dead itself expresses the almost absurd exposure to death in wartime, a vignette akin to the case discussed above, in which an Austrian offensive advanced and then retreated back to its former position, leaving nothing changed but creating many new dead (337:22–24). The doctor, we imagine, has seen so much carnage that he cannot easily be moved to care about this case, regarding the injured man in a reductive, binary way as dead or dying, with the only other option being alive and hoping to survive. In this sense, the doctor's categories for analysis have been radically, violently simplified, much as his actual vision has been dramatically and painfully compromised by the conditions of war. The high hopes of Enlightenment sight and rationality are reduced by modern war to something more akin to binary computer code.

340:5–10 **"No," said the doctor. . . . shoot him yourself.:** After the doctor asserts his authority in the case of the dying man, rejecting the stretcher-bearers' plea for decency in the face of grave injury, the artillery officer suggests another solution, an overdose of morphine. The officer shares the doctor's perspective insofar as both recognize the injured man's death as inevitable, but the officer suggests a merciful and painless solution. The doctor's reply, insisting on other needs for morphine, needs that *also* demonstrate concern for the suffering of the (others) injured, reiterates the horrible conditions of war and doctoring in war, a point already concisely rendered with the earlier detail about the "doctor's eyes," "red" with "the lids swollen, almost shut from tear gas" (339:35–36). While the doctor does seem jaded and it can be easy to side with arguments for mercy, he also makes powerful arguments against the artillery officer's suggestions: morphine is indeed precious in wound treatment in war, perhaps too precious to use in an overdose. If it is a question of putting the injured man out of his misery, the doctor tells the artillery officer, "shoot him yourself" (340:10).

340:11–15 **"He's been shot" . . . you like these?":** The doctor's solution—"shoot him"—however, seems too brutal for the artillery officer, who insists that the injured man has already been shot and therefore should not be asked to suffer more of that same fate. Morphine would be a gentler though ultimately similar solution. Then, noting the seeming callousness of the doctor regarding this badly injured man, the artillery officer raises the stakes of the debate by implying that, if doctors were exposed to gunfire more often—"If some of you doctors were shot" (340:11–12)—they would be more empathetic about such injuries. The doctor's reply, "What about these eyes?" indicates that he too is exposed to the weapons of war (340:14).

340:16–20 **"Tear gas." . . . "You are crazy.":** But there again is a point for further dispute, as the artillery officer calls such injuries as the doctor's eyes minor, indeed "lucky" (340:16). The doctor returns the personal form of insult by saying that tear gas is understood as lucky only because it permits soldiers to leave the dangerous frontlines; by contrast, the doctor's injured eyes do not earn him a reprieve from his duties. Indeed, the doctor suggests that soldiers "rub onions" in their eyes to appear injured by tear gas (340:18). The artillery officer backs down, refusing to take the bait in an escalating dispute, blaming the insult instead on the doctor's own condition of seeming exhaustion or madness: "You are beside yourself" (340:20).

340:21–30 **The stretcher-bearers came in. . . . not a human being.":** The stretcher-bearers reappear but are dispatched forcefully by the upset doctor, as the artillery officer, thinking over his options, accepts the doctor's suggestion: "I will shoot the poor fellow" (340:25). The doctor agrees, but with a threat: if the artillery officer does so, the doctor will report him, exposing the illegal act. The officer's response, "You are not a human being" (340:30), reiterates the key term "human," underscoring that the status of the human, the humane, and the humanist is precisely the central question of "A Natural History of the Dead." In that way, Hemingway helps earn his joining of the parodic first half of this piece with its fictional vignette conclusion, despite the objection that the two sections do not cohere (see Portz 37).

340:31–341:2 **"My business is. . . . F— your sister. . . .":** The debate returns to the question of what it means to "care for" the wounded man, with the doctor, in effect, arguing that he cannot help the man in any meaningful way, in light of all the constraints of his duty to care for other injured soldiers. Nor can he allow the artillery officer to shoot the man, as dispatching suffering men by shooting them would be a violation of the Hippocratic Oath, the oath medical professionals take to attest to their commitment to assist, not hurt, the injured. An honest doctor in command of a situation could not readily assent to the killing of another soldier, even a gravely wounded one. When the artillery officer suggests yet another solution, sending the injured man "down on the cable railway" (340:35), the doctor does not respond in kind but instead simply asserts his authority in the larger military hierarchy. The tension is a signal one, as the artillery officer's questions and suggestions regularly defy the standards of law and medical practice in favor of a notion of individualized mercy, norms be damned. The doctor fields (and rejects) these suggestions until, it seems, he can take no more, asking the rhetorical question, "Who are you to ask me questions?" (340:36) to assert his power of military authority. One framework is personal; the other is official. Requiring a response from the artillery officer drives the latter only *more* deeply into a personal mode. His response, "F— yourself" (340:42) couples with his act of standing and approaching the doctor, continuing to curse the doctor in a widening set of *personal* insults involving his mother and sister, appearing to bring about the expected physical confrontation.

341:3–10 **The doctor . . . you know I am the boss:** The doctor responds to the artillery officer's aggression with a tool of his medical practice, iodine, rather than with a fist fight. While the artillery officer believes he is blinded, it is probably only a temporary effect (Smith 237), as the doctor later says: "Your eyes will be all right" (341:28). After throwing the iodine, the doctor redoubles his exertion of authority, kicking the officer and taking his pistol. When the officer persists in his personalized mode of vitriol, threatening to kill the doctor in vengeance, the doctor once again shifts the framework back to the official, away from the personal, insisting on his superiority in the command hierarchy: "I am the boss" (341:9). The doctor attempts to resolve the personal dispute permanently, saying, "All is forgiven since you know I am the boss" (341:9–10). The doctor wields an implicit threat of military discipline against the artillery officer, but even as he does so, he forgives and commands the end to the dispute, which is in the best interest of the artillery officer in at least that strictly military sense.

341:10-11 **Adjutant! Adjutant!:** When the doctor then calls for the sergeant and the adjutant (an assistant to a commanding officer), he is seeking help from within the military command structure. While the return to order might first seem to restore faith in large structures and traditional verities, the unease of everyone involved in the situation exposes again how such systems are often clumsy at best or dangerous at worst. The doctor's appeal to another force of authority, the adjutant, fails here, as does his assertion of being in command before the officer attacks him, an additional example of the larger dynamics of this narrative vignette. Instead, the doctor must use every means at his disposal to resolve the situation. There is no outside solution to the dilemma, not only of the dispute between the doctor and the artillery officer but also to the suffering of the badly injured soldier. As Beegel writes in *Hemingway's Craft of Omission,* there is also no expected intervention by a benign deity (40).

341:12-17 **"The adjutant . . . a little delirious.":** The doctor, in accord with his military duty, then gives commands (341:13-14, 341:17) and begins to treat the officer's injury despite his protests, requiring others to hold the officer "tight" (341:17), and we have no reason to believe he does so unprofessionally.

341:18-33 **One of the stretcher-bearers. . . . Hold him very tight.":** When the stretcher-bearers report—defying the doctor's repeated command that they leave—that the gravely injured man had finally died, the doctor can explain that he was correct in his medical assessment of him, that the whole dispute was "about nothing" (341:25). "Nothing" is a key term in this collection of stories, earning a position in its title and importance in famous stories like "A Clean, Well-Lighted Place." Beegel underscores the ironic meanings of "nothing" here, which, in contrast to its surface meaning, also evokes "death," the terrifying cause of this entire dispute. The dispute was about something that does not matter, then, or that matters immensely, strangely, because it does not matter. The prospect of becoming mere material, unanimated, a corpse, is to be about nothing, to be nothing, a horrifying prospect (*Craft of Omission* 40). Language has again become a strange, uncanny instrument, naming such contrary states at once.

Further, there is a signal that the doctor's statement is even more true than first appears, since it is likely that the stretcher-bearers appeared on the previous page (340:21) to announce the death. Had the doctor permitted them to say so, the subsequent escalation of the dispute, leading to the iodine attack, would have been avoided. We have war in miniature here in several ways. The possibility of altogether avoiding conflict is manifestly present, as it often is, but impatience and exhaustion on the doctor's part facilitates the growing tension. His specifically military-derived power in this situation enables the doctor's order that the stretcher-bearers "get out" and thus aggravates the situation; military hierarchy disables communication and intensifies conflict. What's more, the fight, like so many battles, including ones discussed earlier, produces no change in larger events, only temporary pain on the officer's part, a kind of metaphor for the injuries and death wrought by often futile battles. The effort to render a specific scene so carefully that it evokes the whole of which it is part—war—is a classic Hemingway method.

To the extent that this scene dramatizes questions about the best response to challenging circumstances, about grace under pressure in the Hemingway catch-phrase often used as a Rosetta Stone for his work, the doctor has proved quite able, as argued by Joseph Flora, Wirt Williams, and Arthur Waldhorn (qtd. in Smith 237). Many readers want to align the doctor and the officer with either humanists or their antagonist, as Forsythe does (137), making them allegorical figures. But, as Smith reports, Gerry Brenner suggests that this vignette is not intended to favor the doctor over the artillery officer but instead to dramatize their conflicting perspectives, to show that, in such complex situations, there are multiple important perspectives (237). We might call that mode of understanding "narrative realism."

Everyone in the scene inhabits a position much like that of the artillery soldier, having to endure—even being forcibly held in a position of endurance by those around one. The artillery officer is being held still not just to receive physical treatment for his wound but also to prevent his dangerous outrage in the face of inhumane suffering, which has so enflamed him that his life and the lives of the doctor and perhaps others are at risk. The officer is raging against the horrible truths of war, wanting to end them by whatever means he can find. And while the officer is literally constrained to endure, the other figures in the scene are likewise constrained in parallel ways. The doctor is constrained by his observers and his professional duty, and the stretcher-bearers are also constrained, having to abide by the military command structure. These forms of constraint, resulting in the limited and painful vision of the doctor and the temporary absence of vision in the artillery officer present the realistic counterpoint to the idealized form of vision introduced in the figure of Mungo Park and the optimistic humanistic and Enlightenment tradition he represents.

NOTES

1. See Forsythe, especially 139, for a summary of critical discussion of the genre of this piece.

2. In her analysis *Hemingway's Craft of Omission: Four Manuscript Examples,* Susan F. Beegel also emphasizes the challenges presented by attempting to interpret death (for example, 34, 40).

Baker, Carlos. *Ernest Hemingway: A Life Story.* Scribner's, 1969.

Beegel, Susan F. *Hemingway's Craft of Omission: Four Manuscript Examples.* UMI Research P, 1988.

———. Introduction. *Hemingway's Neglected Short Fiction: New Perspectives,* edited by Susan F. Beegel, U of Alabama P, 1989, pp. 1–18.

Forsythe, Matthew. "Fragmented Origins of 'A Natural History of the Dead.'" *War + Ink: New Perspectives on Ernest Hemingway's Early Life and Writings,* edited by Steve Paul, Gail Sinclair, and Steven Trout, Kent State UP, 2014, pp. 131–49.

Hemingway, Ernest. *The Complete Short Stories of Ernest Hemingway: The Finca Vigía Edition.* Scribner's, 2003.

———. *A Farewell to Arms.* Scribner's, 1929.

Lewis, Robert W., and Michael Kim Roos. *Reading Hemingway's* A Farewell to Arms. Kent State UP, 2019.

Mandel, Miriam B. *Hemingway's* Death in the Afternoon: *The Complete Annotations.* Scarecrow P, 2002.

Marvell, Andrew. "To His Coy Mistress." *The Norton Anthology of Poetry,* 5th ed., edited by Margaret Ferguson, Mary Jo Salter, and Jon Stallworthy, Norton, 2005, pp. 478–79.

Naimark, Norman M. *Fires of Hatred: Ethnic Cleansing in Twentieth-Century Europe.* Harvard UP, 2001.

Portz, John. "Allusion and Structure in Hemingway's 'A Natural History of the Dead.'" *Tennessee Studies in Literature,* vol. 10, 1965, pp. 27–41.

Rice, Geoffrey W. "A Disease Deadlier than War." *The New Zealand Medical Journal,* vol. 126, no. 1378, 2013, pp. 12–14.

Smith, Paul. *A Reader's Guide to the Short Stories of Ernest Hemingway.* G. K. Hall, 1989.

Stetler, Charles, and Gerald Locklin. "'A Natural History of the Dead' as Metafiction." *Hemingway's Neglected Short Fiction: New Perspectives,* edited by Susan F. Beegel, U Alabama P, 1989, pp. 247–53.

Vonnegut, Kurt. *Slaughterhouse-Five, or The Children's Crusade: A Duty Dance with Death.* Dial, 2009.

WINE OF WYOMING

Susan Vandagriff

In late July 1928, a month after the birth of his first child with Pauline Pfeiffer, Ernest Hemingway headed to Wyoming to finish *A Farewell to Arms* and to fish in the Bighorn Mountains with his friend Bill Horne. By August 18, he wrote to Guy Hickok, a journalist and a friend from his time in Paris, that he was getting "good wine" from "a nice French family (bootlegger) where we sit on the vine shaded porch" (*Letters vol. 3*, 428). The family was Charles and Alice Moncini and their two sons August and Lucien who lived in Sheridan. Like the Fontans, the Moncinis made and sold wine from their home (*Letters vol. 3*, 428n) He introduced them to Pfeiffer when she joined him there, and the experience served as the inspiration for "Wine of Wyoming." Hemingway would later write to editor Maxwell Perkins that the story was "nothing but straight reporting of what [I] heard and saw when was finishing A Farewell To Arms out in Sheridan and Big Horn" (*Letters vol. 5*, 541).

On October 11, 1928, Hemingway wrote to Perkins that he had "a story about ¾ done" (*Letters vol. 3*, 467), but the story was not published until August 1930 in *Scribner's Magazine*. Hemingway submitted the story to Perkins for the magazine in May, confidently defending his decision not to translate the French in the story: "Don't let anyone tell you . . . [it] has too much French in it. Everyone that reads Scribners [Magazine] knows some French or knows somebody that knows some French" (*Letters vol. 4*, 298).

The story was the first finished of *Winner Take Nothing* and received some of its kindest critical attention. Critics felt that the story stood out for its simplicity, sensitivity, and subtlety in a collection that many found grisly, brutal, and deliberately shocking. However, it later fell out of favor, as some have speculated, due to an increasing shortage of French readers among the American public (Martin 364).

It has subsequently received less scholarly discussion than other stories from the collection (most notably the Nick Adams stories); but, among what discussion there is, clear themes have emerged of intolerance, immigration, communion, marriage, and the differences between the Old World and the New. Joseph Flora's *Hemingway's Nick Adams* examines the marital themes of the story while arguing that the story ought to be included as one of the Nick Adams works, citing its placement near "A Day's Wait" and "Fathers and Sons" as Hemingway's "inviting his readers to consider the oldest story of the collection . . . as part of a late Nick trilogy" (234). Sheldon Norman Grebstein also focuses on the narrator, but, rather than debating his identity, he explores the implications of the fluidity of the narrator's role as both detached storyteller and significant actor. Grebstein, like others, observes the story's repeated contrast between the refinement of the Old World and "boorish Americans and the corruptions of American life" (65). Lawrence Martin, too, writes about the story's illustration of "the contrast of European generosity and native American crudity" (363). Kenneth G. Johnston examines the story's political undertones and its inclusion of Al Smith's failed 1928 presidential campaign as illustrating "the thwarted prospects of the 'foreigner' in America" (163). More recently, H. R. Stoneback writes about the story's depiction of Catholicism and its themes of "communion and dryness (in its several senses)" (210). Ann Putnam looks at how the story fits within Hemingway's personal and fictional understanding of the West, especially in the story's "ambivalence about place in general, and the West in particular," which, Putnam finds, closely mirrors Hemingway's own feelings (18). George Monteiro describes "Wine of Wyoming" as a story of "sheer transparency," where "[t]here appears to be nothing left unsaid" (129), while Catherine Keyser discusses the story's culinary representation of race, immigration, and culture.

"Wine of Wyoming" has four major sections distinguished by the section breaks that occur after lines 344:6, 348:2, and 350:29. A nameless narrator (returning to America from an expatriate life in France) shares wine and food with a French immigrant family living in northern Wyoming, but, on the last night of his stay, fails to come to the goodbye party they throw for him. Although critics like Monteiro have remarked on the story's straightforwardness, "Wine of Wyoming" is not as simple as it appears. Hemingway plays with and comments on narration and storytelling through the writer-narrator's choices to reveal and conceal throughout the story. The story also takes a complicated view of the American dream, highlighting the hypocrisy, intolerance, consumption, and destruction that plague the frontier and its inhabitants. Despite its bygone Prohibition plotline, the story's themes of immigration and intolerance and environmental decay and destruction feel sadly relevant to a modern reader. "Wine of Wyoming" offers a small tragedy with grander implications, as a cast of characters relate the disappointments of bigotry, solitude, scarcity, and debauchery yet seem unable to recognize or prevent contributing to their continuation.

Title: Other titles considered were "Il Est Crazy Pour Le Vin" [He Is Crazy about The Wine], "A Lover of Wine," "Pichot Est Crazy Pour Le Vin" (in earlier drafts Pichot was the family name, not Fontan), "September," and "The New Country" (Smith 218). Many of these titles focus on Fontan and foreshadow his eventual shame, but they fail to capture the context. "Wine of Wyoming" alludes to the story's crisis but emphasizes the importance of its setting. Like the wine the title references, the story is the product of the specific location and time.

342:1 **It was a hot afternoon in Wyoming**: The story is set in Sheridan, Wyoming, in what seems to be mid to late September, judging from one of Hemingway's rejected titles (see entry above) and Mme. Fontan's story of the Labor Day picnic (345:12). Although August would have been more biographically true to Hemingway's experience, setting the story in September establishes an early autumnal mood, where the uncomfortable heat of summer lingers, but the growth and plenty have already ended.

342:2 **the mountains were a long way away:** The story opens on a familiar backdrop in Hemingway's fiction, the mountain viewed across a plain. Sheldon Norman Grebstein points out that the same landscape appears in *The Sun Also Rises*, "Hills Like White Elephants," and "The Snows of Kilimanjaro" (164). The first line is also reminiscent of the opening of *A Farewell to Arms*: "In the late summer of that year we lived in a house in a village that looked across the river and the plain to the mountains. . . . beyond the plain the mountains were brown and bare" (3). Not only is the topography of each setting similar but also the season and the heat and dryness that accompany it. The story's mountains are the Bighorn Mountains to the west of Sheridan. The narrator's view of the mountains is returned to three other times in the story (348:9–13, 350:44–351:4, 353:43–45), and, as is typical of Hemingway's work, our understanding of the narrator's emotions often derives from his perceptions of his surroundings.

342:2–6 **you could see snow on their tops . . . baking in the sun. There was a tree made shade over Fontan's back porch:** The story's first impression is one of extreme heat and dryness, which is intensified by the legal dryness of Prohibition. But it's an environment that is immediately contrasted with the Fontans' oasis, the lone spot of shade in the scene.

342:6 **I sat there at a table:** Although the narrator is never named in the story and Philip Young does not include it in *The Nick Adams Stories,* Joseph Flora argues that it should be included among those stories, even granting that it "does not have the verbal or exact situational echoes of earlier Nick stories" (223). The narrator shares several parts of his identity with Nick: a writer, an expat with a preference for European culture, and an avid hunter and fisher. Of course, these are also all traits that the narrator shares with other Hemingway protagonists, as well as with Hemingway himself.

342:12 **He's at the mines:** M. Fontan most likely works at the mines at Dietz, a few miles from Sheridan, which opened in 1893 (Linford 356). As railroad companies moved across the United States in the late nineteenth century, the demand for coal grew, and, in Wyoming, "[m]iners were imported from all parts of the United States and foreign countries" (Linford 349). It is unclear from the story when exactly the Fontans immigrated to America. However, it is possible that the recent horrors of World War I, coupled with the demand for Fontan's skills from his upbringing in Saint-Étienne (see entry at 344:12–13) might have prompted them to move their family to Wyoming.

342:14 **Ain't got any beer. That's a last bottle. All gone:** The first scene introduces the reader to the central conflicts of the story: Prohibition and the illegal nature of the Fontans' product and their selective hospitality. The narrator is allowed to continue drinking and to enjoy the shade, while the two drunk men are turned away.

The first readers of the story when it appeared in *Scribner's Magazine* in 1930 would still have been living under Prohibition, whereas many readers of *Winner Take Nothing*, published in October 1933, might have been legally drinking after the Twenty-First Amendment passed in early December of that year.

342:28–29 **She spoke French . . . and some English constructions:** Although in other works Hemingway chooses to represent foreign language in English while retaining its particular constructions, idioms, and syntax to indicate translation, in "Wine of Wyoming" he does not translate at all (for more on Hemingway's representation of other languages, see Mark Cirino's "You Don't Know the Italian Language Well Enough"). Hemingway was not always successful in his translations, but for this story he took the story to Lewis Galantière (a friend from Paris and a renowned translator and playwright) in New York to check his work before it was first published in *Scribner's Magazine*. According to Baker, "It was the work of a few minutes" (211), and Hemingway rewarded Galantière with a knife. The translation is largely correct, and any errors are possibly intentional, meant to indicate how the Fontans have changed in their new country and to represent the family's unique patois. See entry at 346:30.

The Fontans' French serves dual purposes within the story. For readers who are not native French speakers, it forces a point of empathy with the Fontans, who are themselves surrounded by a language they do not speak easily. However, as Kenneth G. Johnston points out, this line also reveals how America has changed the Fontans, since "the purity of the [French] language is gone" (161). The Fontans, like their mixture of French and English, do not truly belong to either France or America and have been unable to completely preserve the culture and traditions they brought to their new country.

343:2 **il est crazy pour le vin:** [he is crazy about wine.] "Crazy pour" is one of Mme. Fontan's oft-repeated phrases. Some variation of the phrase is used seven times throughout the story (343:4, 343:34, 346:31, 348:40, 349:4). Her description of her husband's passion for wine was also a title Hemingway considered before settling on "Wine of Wyoming" (see Title entry). The line also was echoed in a conversation between the narrator and his wife that Hemingway eventually eliminated, describing Mme. Fontan's passion for her husband: "Elle est crazy pour lui" [She is crazy about him] ("Wine of Wyoming" ms. 837). See entry at 353:34.

The distinction between passion and insanity, represented by the repeated word "crazy," plays an important role, as a line is repeatedly drawn between a refined love for something and an unchecked passion that leads to overindulgence. America and Americans seem to specialize in the latter throughout the story, be it books, churches, hunting, or drinking. Even the construction of the phrase, French interrupted with the one English word—the American idiom of "crazy"—suggests a unique Americanness in the kind of love that blends into destructive insanity.

343:5–6 **She was a plump old woman . . . the house was very clean and neat.** The narrator repeatedly calls attention to the order and cleanliness of the Fontans' home and clearly views it and Mme. Fontan fondly in these descriptions. His attention to this detail is reminiscent of the older waiter in "A Clean, Well-Lighted Place": "It is the light of course but it is necessary that the place be clean and pleasant" (291:3–4). Like the café, the Fontans' home takes on role of an oasis of order, hospitality, and cleanliness: with shade from the sun (342:5–6), bountiful food and drink (344:30–32), and people who exhibit traditional European values and appreciation for this order.

343:6–7 **She came from Lens:** Marie Fontan comes from an industrial town in the north of France, near the Belgian border, which explains her fondness for beer over the wine her southern husband favors (343:4). Like her husband's home of Saint-Étienne (see entry at 344:12–13), this region was known for its mining. Lens and the surrounding area were practically destroyed during World War I, adding to the sadness of Mme. Fontan's loss of home in America. Were she to return to France, much of the city she remembered would be gone.

343:19 **mangé les *beans* en *can:*** [eats beans in a can.] Although a fine meal for Nick Adams in the first part of "Big Two-Hearted River" (*CSS* 167), here the meal of beans from a can is meant to contrast Mme. Fontan's good cooking, hospitality, and care of her husband with the daughter-in-law's negligence (in Mme. Fontan's eyes, at least).

343:24–25 **All the time she reads . . . stay in the bed and read books:** The details Mme. Fontan gives suggest the American daughter-in-law is the opposite of what Mme. Fontan evidently expected: a working, cooking, fertile woman. One of Mme. Fontan's daughter-in-law's many shortcomings, and one she sees in all Americans, is an excessive fondness for books. Here, Mme. Fontan merely indicates that they lead to sloth, although later in the story a type of detachment seems like a more damaging consequence (see entry at 346:44–45). The love of books also ties into an ongoing critique of American overindulgence.

343:33 Why doesn't he get a divorce?: Flora points out that the narrator's question is an inappropriate one for one Catholic to ask another and plays into the often dark view of "the mysteriousness of sex and love" in *Winner Take Nothing* (223). Although the narrator and the Fontans profess shared Catholic and traditional European values in the face of modern American immorality, this exchange between Mme. Fontan and the narrator shows how, like the "Polack catholiques" (347:26) that Mme. Fontan criticizes for their inconsistency, their Catholicism matters only to a certain point. The narrator's offhand question also gains significance when it is revealed that he is married, despite his saying nothing of his wife in his narration or his conversation with the Fontans. See entry at 347:20.

343:34 Besides, il est *crazy* pour elle: [Besides, he is crazy about her.] In this exchange we also see the repetition of "crazy pour" seen earlier at 343:2. However, the use of italics in this instance suggests that Mme. Fontan speaks of her son's love for his wife as a more literal craziness than she views M. Fontan's love of wine.

343:41 She's Indian all right: The revelation that the Fontan's daughter-in-law is a Native American colors the older woman's disapproval of and expectations for her. Neither the exotic primitive nor the hard-working and docile wife Mme. Fontan expected, the unnamed daughter-in-law calls attention to unspoken assumptions about Native Americans and America itself. Gina Rossetti points out that modernism's use of Indigenous peoples often serves as a critique on modern society: "the primitive's so-called simplicity is a much needed antidote to the problems of modern culture" (58). Rossetti argues that, in some of Hemingway's works, he "presents a far more critical approach to primitivism" (58), but here the daughter-in-law simply inverts the stock primitive character by embodying what Mme. Fontan sees as the problems of modern culture. Her race itself seems mostly symbolic, as she has no tribal affiliation, only a monolithic Native American identity. An Indigenous, or true, American, she can be read as a representation of the country itself, and she complicates the immigrant dream (and paternalistic European vision) of the American West. Much as they did not get the American daughter-in-law they expected, the Fontans did not get the wild, fertile, prosperous, and accommodating country they expected.

The Fontans, displaced from their own homes, should feel more sympathy with the daughter-in-law, who, as Catherine Keyser points out, is the victim of "forced exile that predated World War I" (106). Her presence adds an additional layer to the narrative's depiction of bad guests, as all European settlers (the narrator and the Fontans included) are themselves uninvited and egregiously ill-behaved guests on Indigenous lands. See entry at 350:19.

344:8–9 there was a clean tablecloth . . . still tasted of the grapes: The narrator's appreciation for the order and cleanliness of the Fontans' home is apparent, but the second section also establishes the themes of hospitality and communion that run through the story. The religious nature, both of the conversation surrounding Catholicism (see 347:7–8, 347:20) and of the imagery of communion, as food and wine are shared, elevate this order and the manners of both parties to a matter of ceremony and ritual. Their significance is not felt, however, until the rules of hospitality and communion are broken in the final sections of the story. Similarly, the description of the "clear and good" (344:9) wine suggests the yet unsullied purity of what is being shared.

344:12–13 from the Centre near Saint-Etienne: Sam Fontan is originally from a French industrial town in the southeast of France, specifically the Rhône-Alpes region. Fontan would have grown up in an area "known for its culinary excellence" and near the Beaujolais and Burgundy wine regions (Northcutt 255). Despite its proximity to agriculture, Saint-Étienne was known in the nineteenth century for its coal mining, textile mills, and metallurgy. Fontan was likely already a miner before moving to Wyoming.

Hemingway appears to be confused in his geography by placing Saint-Étienne near "the Centre." The Centre region is not even adjacent to the Rhône-Alpes region. However, Hemingway might have meant simply the center of the country, or at least more central when compared with Lens, which is not far from the Belgian border.

344:14 I worked on my book: In Hemingway's biographically equivalent experience, the book in question would have been *A Farewell to Arms*.

344:26 No. Give me the whole quarter. I'll get it changed on the way: Flora writes that André, the Fontans' younger son, is "obviously on the way to becoming Americanized," but the narrator is "entertained" by his enthusiasm and boyish antics (227). This interpretation seems shaky given the number of times "shrill" is used to describe the boy during his later conversation with the narrator, conveying more irritation than amusement. However, Flora's perception of his Americanization is accurate, as the boy displays a disregard for traditional virtues of honesty or generosity, tricking his way into a lower movie fare and pocketing the change.

344:30–32 "You haven't eaten anything." I had eaten two helpings of chicken . . . and two helpings of salad: Hemingway makes a comic contrast between Mme. Fontan's concern that her guest has not eaten enough and the narrator's evidently hearty consumption. However, the abundance here contrasts with the story's repeated idea that eating well has been lost in America, from Mme. Fontan's distrust of American restaurants (343:14–16), the "*beans* en *can*" served by the Fontans' daughter-in-law (343:19), and the narrator's elegiac comment, "Mais on ne mange pas très bien. D'antan, oui. Mais maintenant, no" [But we don't eat very well. In the past, yes. But now, no.] (345:41–42).

344:41–42 **If you work all day in a book-factory you get hungry:** Mme. Fontan's misunderstanding of English is used for comedic effect as she repeatedly mistakes what the narrator does for a living. Flora interprets this misunderstanding in particular as pleasing to the narrator because it shows that the Fontans "care nothing about his fame or critical reputation" (226). However, this is complicated by Marie's negative feeling toward books and their proliferation in America. See entry at 346:44–45.

345:8–9 **He was very tolerant . . . and worldly knowledge:** M. Fontan is contrasted with his wife as the knowledgeable, worldly veteran (344:44–345:1) to her rustic, naïve housewife. Flora points out that "save for Madame Fontan, there are no positive images of women in the story" (233). Given the story's attention to good and bad marital pairings, her own naïveté, unceasing hospitality, and unwillingness to criticize her husband serve not only to contrast her lazy, overly well-read daughter-in-law (343:24) and the controlling wife of the "nice fella" who sneaks over to the Fontan's for beer (350:16) but also implicitly the narrator's own absent wife. However, this traditionally feminine, nurturing, and docile ideality comes to readers through the eyes of male beholders, who view the world with a decidedly nostalgic perspective.

345:12 **Clear Creek:** A tributary of Powder River, itself a tributary of the Yellowstone River.

345:12 **Oh, my God:** This is the fifth of twenty-three times that Mme. Fontan will appeal to a deity over the course of the story. Although the exclamation "mon Dieu" is common in French speech and is portrayed as humorous idiosyncrasy throughout the story, this constant invocation of God plays into the story's motifs of Catholicism and communion.

345:13–14 **Tout le monde est allé dans le truck:** [Everybody went in the truck.] The Labor Day picnic story appears in the second section of the story, and while it remains a happy story that represents the partial fulfillment of the immigrant dream of America, within it are the first strains of the darkness and disappointment that color the last two sections of "Wine of Wyoming." Mme. and M. Fontan's story speaks of the community of immigrants, and initially there is a feeling of inclusivity even in a foreign land, captured by Mme. Fontan's cheerful hyperbole, translated literally to mean that "all the world" is in Charley's truck.

345:14–15 **C'est le truck de Charley:** [It's Charley's truck.] This line may be an oblique reference to the real family that inspired the story. Charles Moncini was a truck driver, not a miner like Sam Fontan.

345:16–17 **On a mangé, on a bu du vin, de la bière, et il y avait aussi un français qui a apporté de l'absinthe:** [We ate, we drank wine, beer, and there was also a Frenchman who brought absinthe.] The picnic is marked by many of the story's now familiar signs of good times: abundant food, plenty to drink, and the presence of other French people. The Fontans meet a fellow Frenchman who lives in California and who has brought absinthe with him. Although France was not under mass prohibition laws like the United States, the production and sale of absinthe were prohibited from 1915 until 2000 (Difford). Absinthe would have been a familiar drink to the Fontans, as its popularity in France peaked in the late nineteenth century, especially with soldiers, such as Sam Fontan, who then introduced it to their families on returning home (Conrad 6).

Absinthe appears in other Hemingway works, such as *The Sun Also Rises*, where a depressed Jake drinks it to the point where, he observes "I was very drunk. I was drunker than I ever remembered having been" (*SAR-HLE* 178). Absinthe also appears in "Hills Like White Elephants," where Jig remarks, "Everything tastes of licorice. Especially all the things you've waited so long for, like absinthe" (*CSS* 212). However, unlike Jig's statement, which evokes both the forbidden and dark nature of the strongly alcoholic drink and the nihilism and numbness that Jig feels in a life of drinking one thing after another, Fontan's listing of absinthe is, by comparison, quite casual and lighthearted. For the Fontans, this is simply a special treat from the French past, even if, for the American narrator and for Hemingway, the drink carries tones of annihilation and extremity.

345:18–23 **There's a farmer comes to see what's the matter . . . and after a while they went away:** The picnic seems especially rosy as it remains untouched by the Prohibition laws that taint the rest of the Fontans' American experience. However, the melting pot ideal represented by food and drink shared by the French immigrants and the American farmer who joins them has its limits. Italians, Mme. Fontan tells the narrator, wanted to join the group too but are unwelcome, are insulted without their knowledge (345:20–21), and finally leave when it's clear the group would "have nothing to do with them" (345:22). This is the first we see of the Fontans'—particularly Mme. Fontan's—bigotry toward other immigrants. See entries at 345:43 and 347:23.

345:31–32 **Et le lendemain il ne reste rien:** [And the next day, there was nothing left.] The picnic contains the first hint of the story's tragic end, when M. Fontan and the other men are also unable to stop drinking and save any wine for the next day.

345:35–39 **Good trout, all right, too. . . . All the same size; half-pound one ounce:** Additionally, in this story we see the first limits of the abundance of the American West, as the Fontans can only catch a few fish, and the trout are so small that it even gives the narrator pause, asking Mme. Fontan to repeat, "How big?" (345:37).

Historically, dam building, overfishing, the introduction of nonnative species (often bigger and considered more attractive), the subsequent mistreatment and mismanagement of less-valued native species, and industrial and agricultural changes to the landscape all affected trout populations. Here, the narrator, himself a wildlife tourist typical to the region at the time, appears to have bought into the trout-fishing mythology perpetuated by many Western writers and publications like *Field and Stream* (which Clarence and Ernest Hemingway read [Reynolds 80]). Tales of Rocky Mountain fishing promised incredible fish in incredible numbers but often ignored the unnatural realities of hatcheries and stocked waters. For more on how fishing mythology created and supported the unrealistic ideal of Western America, see Jen Corrine Brown's book *Trout Culture: How Fly Fishing Forever Changed the Rocky Mountain West.*

345:41–42 **Mais on ne mange pas très bien. D'antan, oui. Mais maintenant, no:** [But we do not eat very well. Yesterday, yes. But now, no.] When asked about his feelings for America, the narrator offers this cryptic and mournful response. His response reiterates the story's portrayal of America as a place where no one eats well, as opposed to Europe. See also 344:30–32 and 352:27–28. However, this line describes the narrator's perception of the entire country as bygone, perhaps explaining the story's later revelation that the narrator is only visiting America and lives as an expatriate in France.

The line is also reminiscent of one in "Fathers and Sons" when Nick thinks back on his teenage romance with Trudy and begins to ponder the decline of the Ojibway: "They all ended the same. Long time ago good. Now no good" (376:10–11).

346:2 **Et, my God, ils sont sales, les Polacks:** [And, my god, they are dirty, the Polacks.] Mme. Fontan continues her bigotry toward other immigrants, in this instance, Polish immigrants, whom she refers to using the slur "Polack" and depicts as slovenly. Much like the Italians at the Labor Day picnic (345:20) and the two men at the start of the story (342:8–28), the Polish are excluded from the Fontans' good opinion and company. The Fontans' selective society is similar to many cliques and friendships in Hemingway's writing that seem to be founded on a shared value system but dependent on others being deliberately and viciously excluded, such as the fictitious Order that Colonel Cantwell and Renata belong to in *Across the River and into the Trees* (56) or the "one of us" Brett includes the Count among in *The Sun Also Rises* (26) (see also Vandagriff "The Scapegoat's Scapegoat"). Exclusivity heightens the sense of community between the Fontans and the narrator but makes both parties' eventual failure to live up to the unspoken rules that govern their bond all the more devastating.

346:3 **It is fine for hunting and fishing:** Despite the repetition of this claim by M. Fontan (347:40), the narrator's statement is contradicted by almost every instance of hunting or fishing within the story, from the puny trout the Fontans catch on Labor Day (345:38–39) to the narrator and his wife's disappointing prairie chicken hunting trip where they end up shooting at the prairie dogs (350:37–42). Similar to Mme. Fontan's expectations for her Native American daughter-in-law, the belief of plentiful game and fish in the American West is portrayed as a myth or at best something that was once true but is not anymore.

346:11–12 **Ils sont des sauvages, les boys, vous savez. . . . Ils veulent shooter les uns les autres:** [Boys are savages, you know. . . . They want to shoot each other.] M. Fontan calls André a savage, evoking both the opposite of the old-fashioned, European values the Fontans and the narrator embody and somewhat contradictorily—by its associations with the traditional European depictions of Native Americans—the disappointingly modern daughter-in-law. His fears about letting the boys hunt alone are also reminiscent of Mme. Fontan's later complaints about Polish Catholics, with M. Fontan arguing the boys would just shoot each other, much as Mme. Fontan claims that Polish Catholics "go to church, then they fight with knives all the way home and kill each other all day Sunday" (347:24–25). However unmodern and un-American the Fontans remain, their children have not inherited their values.

346:30 **On peut looker. On ne fait pas del mal. On peut looker:** [I can look. I'm not doing any harm. I can look.] André's French is not perfectly correct here, as "looker" is not French. The word counts on the listeners' understanding of both English (look) and French (an-er infinite verb ending) to make sense of it. It is possible that Hemingway simply mistranslated, but the word makes sense coming from André. He is an American teenager raised by French parents, and, while fluent in English (see 346:34–35), his French reveals his American upbringing.

346:31 **Il est crazy pour le shooting:** [He is crazy about shooting.] André wants desperately to hunt on his own, with muskrats and water vermin as his prey of choice. The American "crazy" reappears, reminding readers of the distinction between a fine passion and an unchecked indulgence; André appears to fall into the latter category.

The adolescent boy's overeagerness to hunt and unwillingness to surrender the gun to his father take on a darker tone if the story's discussion of hunting is read as an allusion to sexual fulfillment, a parallel Flora points out is present in several other stories, including "The Doctor and the Doctor's Wife" (234). See entry at 354:5–9.

346:34–35 "**When I'm bigger I'll shoot the muskrats . . . he said in English:** Perhaps in addition to André's less-than-charming behavior and interests, the most compelling sign of his thorough Americanization is his perfect English, so perfect that the narrator calls attention to it, pointing out that this is not his own translation.

346:41 **It was a library book—*Frank on a Gunboat*:** *Frank on a Gunboat* is one in a series of books written by Harry Castlemon (né Charles Austin Fosdick, 1842–1915) and was published in 1868. Fosdick published fifty-eight boys books, many of them featuring his most popular character, Frank, who first appeared in *Frank, the Young Naturalist* (1864). Frank's manly outdoor adventures ranged from a glorified and idealized service in the Civil War to exploring the Rocky Mountains. Fosdick himself lived in New York and had not seen much of the West he described in his novels ("Charles Austin Fosdick"). In response to criticism of the quality of his work, Fosdick said, "Boys don't like fine writing. What they want is adventure" (qtd. in Anderson 102). "Wine of Wyoming," too, seems at odds with the romanticized West that Fosdick and others presented in their dime novels. The story is certainly not what one might expect of a Hemingway Western. "Wine of Wyoming" was frequently praised and criticized for being a finer story of "emotional truth" (Gregory E5), with what admirers found a more mature, comic, and sensitive style and what critics found sentimental and full of "all the old nostalgias" (Troy 570).

346:44–45 "**Books are all right,**" . . . "**But too many books are bad.**": As M. Fontan tries to remind his wife in this passage, the narrator is a novelist, but, while she concedes books aren't inherently bad, it can be overdone. Flora argues that Mme. Fontan's point cannot simply be dismissed as humor: "The Fontans raise the issue not only about the relationship between reading and living, but between writing and living. Can the writing of books also take one away from the feasts that life affords?" (228). Flora's reading of the narrator's career and Mme. Fontan's dislike of books offers a different understanding of the narrator's eventual choice not to attend the fête. The narrator reports the Fontans to readers as a writer does, amused and pleased with their characters, idiosyncrasies, and anecdotes, but not recognizing their full humanity and capacity to be hurt by his actions. Similarly, Grebstein notes that the narrator occupies a hybrid space within the realm of Hemingway's nameless narrators because he functions as both a witness and a protagonist who is "effacing himself for much of the story" but "one of his actions . . . precipitates the story's crisis" (64). This hybrid narrator plays into one of the story's recurring motifs, as characters fail to recognize their role in the decline and trouble around them. Mme.

Fontan complains of bigotry against Catholics but dismisses Polish Catholics as dirty murderers, and M. Fontan is disgusted by the overindulgent Americans but cannot stop himself from drinking all the wine. Given the story is one that Hemingway described as highly autobiographical—"'Wine of Wyoming' is nothing but straight reporting of what [I] heard and saw" (*Letters vol. 5*, 541)—the story can be read as indicative of Hemingway's own concern with his position as both an author and as a participant in life. See entry at 353:12.

347:7–8 **En Amérique il ne faut pas être catholique. It's not good to be catholique:** [In America you must not be Catholic.] Although it certainly doesn't feel like it to the Fontans, Catholicism grew rapidly due to the "mass immigration of nearly 9 million Roman Catholics between 1890 and 1925," making it "the largest denomination in the United States" (Olson 101). However, this increased visibility led to increased intolerance and "triggered another round of anti-Catholicism, led by the American Protective Association in the 1890s and the Ku Klux Klan after World War I" (101).

347:9 **It's like the dry law:** Fontan's cousin makes a perceptive connection between the intolerance for Catholics in America and the dry laws that seem designed to target Catholic immigrants' religious practices and traditional agriculture and cuisine. Historian Norman H. Clark observes a "kind of class-conscious hostility to non-Protestant foreigners which . . . had occasionally gripped Prohibitionists when they observed the drinking habits of recent immigrants—'the ignorant horde,' a Prohibitionist newspaper reported, 'that Europe sends over here to rule America'" (80).

347:17 **On dit que Schmidt est catholique:** [People say that Schmidt is Catholic.] Schmidt refers to Al Smith (1873–1944), the 1928 Democratic presidential candidate, who lost to Herbert Hoover after, as Johnston points out, multiple attacks on his Catholic faith, which "clearly revealed that ancient prejudices had flourished in the new world" (162). Smith was Irish American, the grandchild of immigrants, and, Johnston writes, "political analysts agree that his origins and Catholicism were major factors" in his loss to Hoover, receiving only eighty-seven electoral votes to Hoover's 444 (163). The story's readers, first in *Scribner's Magazine* in 1930, then in the 1933 collection, would already be aware of Smith's eventual defeat, lending an odd dramatic irony to the story as the American narrator (knowing his country too well) and the reader (knowing the real results of the election) both recognize the futility of the Fontans' hopes for a president who represents the Catholic immigrant population. For more on Smith's campaign and its presence in "Wine of Wyoming," see Johnston.

347:20 **We are catholique:** This line marks the first reference to the narrator's wife, however obliquely. The Fontans show no surprise, but, for readers, the line makes a startling, if oblique, revelation. At no point does Hemingway identify the narrator's companion as his wife, or even as female. The gender of the unnamed companion appears in conversation that was cut from the story's manuscript (see entry at 353:34), making apparent Hemingway's conscious decision to not include any identifying information. Not until the end of the story does this unnamed character get to speak, but the wife's absent presence can be read as a self-aware extension of the iceberg technique Hemingway is known for, as Hemingway creates a writer character who narrates a story that is made remarkable by what it leaves out.

The word "catholic" possesses two definitions. One is denominational, referring to members of the Catholic Church, but "catholic" can also mean universal or common. This second definition offers another understanding of the narrator's statement and of the Fontans and their troubles. Although it could have been easy for Hemingway's original readers to dismiss the struggle of an immigrant family, whose Catholic faith was unpopular at the time, their disappointment and disillusionment with the American dream and the modern world are a common story.

The narrator's interjection is also interesting and critical in its contradictory presentation of the community of Catholicism. "We are catholique," states the narrator, in solidarity with the Fontans, but, despite the plurality of the pronoun, he visits them alone, his wife curiously absent. Although the Fontans are part of the largest religious denomination in America at the time, they remain geographically and ethnically separated from others of their faith. See entry at 347:23–28. Even before the disastrous fête, the communion of these fellow believers appears broken.

This statement proclaiming their Catholicism was also biographically true of Hemingway at the time of writing, having converted to Catholicism, at least "nominally" (Baker 185), in order to marry Pauline Pfeiffer.

347:21 **Sure, but you live in France:** Soon after the shock of discovering that the narrator is married, the reader also discovers he is an expatriate living in France and only a visitor to the American West. This, the reader might suspect, is why the Fontans have been so eager to feed and welcome the narrator, who provides a connection to their lost homeland. However, as Putnam points out, he ultimately remains "this American who had once lived in France" (23), his carelessness regarding the Fontans' feelings revealing him to be like any other American in the story. As Mme. Fontan's somewhat dismissive tone in this line indicates, the narrator, for all their shared faith and language, has no real understanding of the Fontans' situation. The Prohibition laws and anti-Catholic sentiment are minor inconveniences to him, rather than daily disappointments and hardships, and he can easily swallow the hopelessness of Smith's candidacy (348:2) because it will matter little to him who is elected.

347:23–28 **Les Polacks sont catholiques. . . . One catholique is like another:** [The Polacks are Catholics.] Mme. Fontan's bigotry shows again here, with her belief that Polish Catholics are not real Catholics. Nationalism and ethnocentric religious belief were common among Catholic immigrants in the late nineteenth and early twentieth century to the point where "the nationality parish" had become necessary to prevent ethnic schisms from dividing the Catholic Church and leaving the "new" immigrants (often from Eastern and Southern Europe) open to conversion into Protestants (Olson 103).

Her specific critique of Polish Catholics is that they are hypocritical in their faith, going to church but committing murder on the way home, an image that echoes the Grangerfords and Shepherdsons family feud in Mark Twain's *Adventures of Huckleberry Finn*. Hypocrisy, however, seems to be more common than Mme. Fontan admits: the Catholic narrator casually recommends divorce (343:33); M. Fontan shamefully drinks all the wine, like the overindulgent American "cochons" that he criticizes (349:45–350:3); and the narrator proves himself to be truly American after all by disrespecting the friendship and hospitality the Fontans offer. As Fontan concludes, "One catholique is like another" (347:27–28). The real hypocrisy, the story indicates, lies in the belief that one can, in the Old World or the New, escape the taint of modernity and callousness.

347:45–348:2 **"Il est catholique,"** . . . **"No," I said:** [He is Catholic] These lines conclude the second section of the story with a pessimistic prediction. Mme. Fontan's hopeful refrain, "My God, Schmidt est catholique" [My god, Smith is Catholic] (347:45), aligns with the sentiment Johnston argues many immigrant families felt, that "his political prominence and early success symbolized the immigrant's dream come true" (163). For a moment, it seems possible that there might be a home for Catholics and "new" Americans in the United States after all, but the American-born narrator immediately recognizes this outcome as impossible and has already abandoned the country the Fontans are trying to build their future in.

348:11–13 **There were furrowed brown mountains. . . . The snow looked very white and pure and unreal:** In the mountains' second appearance, the snow, which had previously been distant but visible (342:2–3), now is qualified as both idealized and intangible. As an opening to the third section, this description indicates that the good, pure things that the narrator and the Fontans long for are ultimately unattainable, in part because they never truly existed, despite the two previous sections' promise of fellowship, community, and shared values.

348:20–22 **"Schmidt," she said . . . "Sure," I said. "Trust Schmidt.":** Johnston ties this exchange to narrator's view of the pure but unreal snow (348:13). Mme. Fontan wants to believe that, if Smith is elected, their dry law troubles will be over, but, as Hemingway and readers knew, "despite his campaign promises to change the dry laws," Smith's official platform promised to uphold them (Johnston 165). The narrator's unenthusiastic answer, coming after his pessimistic view the night before, shows his nihilistic view of American life: change is unlikely to come, and if it does, it will not make any difference. For the narrator, the promise and opportunity of American life is unreal.

348:23–33 **Already we paid seven hundred fifty-five dollars. . . . They put Fontan in jail and they take seven hundred fifty-five dollars:** Unlike the Fontans' other more laughable troubles, such as their gun-crazy teen and their book-crazy daughter-in-law, this anecdote sets this section of the story apart as it brings to light the seriousness of their situation. The Fontans have already paid heavy fines, and M. Fontan went to jail. Wyoming's fines for violating the dry laws were initially closer to $200 but by 1929 (believing the punishment was not severe enough to deter anyone) the state legislature passed penalties that went as high as $10,000 and up to five years in jail (Larson 441).

Mme. Fontan cannot understand the simple illegality of something that seems so trivial and commonplace as good wine and beer. She explains irrelevantly to the narrator that their product is well made and reasonably priced when its existence was the crime.

348:36–349:10 **"Vous savez, il est crazy pour le vin. . . . C'est bon, la bière. C'est très bon pour la santé.":** [You know, he is crazy about wine. . . . Beer is good. It's very good for your health.] These stories show the Fontans' relationship with alcohol, which is at once casual and connoisseurial. Mme. Fontan's story of learning to love and savor beer as a young girl in France depicts drinking as a natural part of growing up and expanding one's palate, but it also grounds drinking in community. She and her sister grew up surrounded by fields of hops and close to a major brewery. Beer, to Mme. Fontan, is part of home, making its illegality in America another way she is separated from that home in her new country. M. Fontan is depicted, at every opportunity, to savor wine: putting it in his coffee (348:39–40) and wanting his rabbit cooked in it (349:4–7). "Son pays est comme ça" (348:41), Mme. Fontan observes: It's like that where he comes from. Just as beer represents home to her, wine is home to him. Their eagerness to recapture those memories of home is tangled in their illegal product, which heightens the stakes around their ability to keep making it and the meaning of their decision to share it with this narrator and not with others.

349:12–349:23 **"But there was a thing here that I never saw. . . ." "They're bad when they're drunk.":** The Fontans' homesick and epicurean appreciation of wine and beer is contrasted with Americans, who drink for no other reason than to get drunk. They pollute the Fontans' pure products with whiskey to make boilermakers, to Mme. Fontan's shock and horror. Not only do the Americans ruin the

Fontans' good beer with their whiskey, but they are out of control, drinking until one woman vomits on the table and in her shoes (349:19). The Americans disrupt the clean, orderly home of the Fontans and, what's more, disrespect the hospitality they are offered by simply viewing the Fontans' home as a place where they can get liquor and "have another party the next Saturday" (349:20–21).

Despite her confidence that the narrator hasn't "ever seen [this behavior] either" (349: 13), the narrator's reply must be taken as verbal irony. "No," he says (349:15), feigning to match her level of disbelief, but clearly the narrator has seen this done before, later even explaining the rationale behind the Americans' behavior (see next entry). The narrator's own living situation, an American expat in France, suggests that he might be committing a similar crime in the Fontans' home country.

349:30 **They want to get sick, so they'll know they're drunk:** Unlike Mme. Fontan, the narrator understands what drives his fellow Americans' self-destructive behavior. Unable to appreciate the finer qualities of what they consume, the Americans must go to extremes, like the book-crazy daughter-in-law, the shooting-crazy son, and the church-crazy nation. The pattern suggests that Americans do not experience anything, from books to wine to religion, except in its magnitude and, even then, miss the point.

349:31–41 **One time a fellow comes here. . . . 'Not for hundred fifty dollars.' My God, no:** Again, the Americans are contrasted with the Fontans and, implicitly, the Old World values they represent. They arrive drunk, which as Mme. Fontan notes at the beginning of the story (342:26–28) puts the Fontans at risk for arrest and fines. Beyond that, they have brought "their girls" (349:32–33) with them but fail to treat them with the chivalry Mme. Fontan and her husband seem to feel they deserve, as she remarks that these are "nice girls too, all-right girls" (349:36). They spike the wine with liquor and refuse to take care of the girls who become sick from drinking. Their insistence that the girls "were all right right there at the table" (349:39) is disrespectful to the sick women, who are not allowed the dignity of privacy, and also to the Fontans, whose home is treated with callous disregard. The wine is just a way to get drunk, not something crafted with care and deserving of appreciation, and the Fontans' house is just a place to get alcohol and have parties, not someone's home.

Mme. Fontan tells the narrator about the next time she locked these guests out (349:40), the second time she has mentioned locking the door against bad guests (349:21–22). Reminiscent of the first scene in the story where the narrator may stay and drink while the other men are turned away, the enjoyment of the Fontans' hospitality and company is only extended to those who, the Fontans perceive, deserve it. It also foreshadows the story's end, with Fontan locked out of his own wine (See entry at 352:34–35).

349:45–350:5 **"Cochon," he said delicately. . . . He was glad to speak of something else:** Fontan, somewhat apologetically, terms that kind of visitors "pigs." The narrator vehemently agrees however, going even further to call them "Salauds" [bastards] (350:3). However, the narrator's additional coarseness doesn't seem to please or reassure Fontan, whom the narrator observes finds it "distasteful" and is "glad to speak of something else" (350:4–5). Similar to the narrator's suggestion of divorce (343:33) or Mme. Fontan's retort to his claims of solidarity—"Sure, but you live in France" (347:21)—this moment, though small, foreshadows that, for all their shared beliefs, the narrator is somehow out of sync with the genteel Fontans.

As he explains his own strong language, Fontan returns to what becomes the refrain of the stories of American customers: their sin is "vomir sur la table" [to vomit on the table] (350:1–2). This attention to the table points to the disgusting manners of their customers, who vomit where they eat, but, given the story's repeated communion imagery and discussion of religion, the table takes on a more significant role as the altar where communion is served. Americans respect no part of the ritual, polluting the sacrament and debasing the altar.

350:7–9 **"There are officers from the fort. . . . Everybody that was ever in France they want to come and drink wine. They like wine all right.":** The Fontans describe some of their better customers who share one significant trait with the narrator: they have also spent time in France. Like the narrator, their connection to France separates these officers from the rest of America and, in Fontan's mind, enables them to appreciate wine. Fontan's "all right" can be read to mean both that these military gentlemen greatly enjoy the wine and that they enjoy it the right way.

The fort likely refers to Fort Mackenzie, close to Sheridan, which was built in 1898 to suppress Native American resistance to white settlement (Junge 2). Although it was one of the last occupied forts in Wyoming, by the time this story takes place, it would have been a hospital for veterans, rather than an operating military fort. The post was abandoned in 1918 but instead was transferred to Public Health Service and eventually to the Veterans' Bureau. President Warren G. Harding signed over the funds to make the final conversion into a hospital, and in 1922 the hospital began to serve its first patients, with "its particular function being treatment of patients with neuropsychiatric disorders" (Junge 9).

It's unclear from the Fontans' phrasing if they are referring to officers who were stationed at Mackenzie and continue to live in the area or to officers currently being treated at the hospital, which would understandably continue to be called a "fort" by the public who knew its original purpose. However, the fact that these officers are familiar with France does suggest the latter, as they would likely be veterans of World War I.

350:10–18 **"There was one man".** . . . **"He's always in bed when his wife gets back from the show.":** Mme. Fontan goes on to relate the story of one man who sneaks out of his house at night to drink a beer at the Fontans'. Its inclusion alongside the officers at the fort and the Fontans' consensus that he's "a nice fella" (350:16) indicates the Fontans do not view this behavior in a negative light, seeming to appreciate the man's passion ("he comes straight down here, sometimes in his pyjamas" [350:12]) as well as his moderation and manners, sitting and drinking a beer, presumably with the Fontans, whom he knows by name. Then he goes back to bed before his wife can discover his absence, careful not to cause trouble, unlike the other Americans who court it. His behavior falls on the good side of "crazy," like Fontan adding wine to his coffee, showing a charming and moderate irrationality.

350:19 **Crow Reservation:** The narrator and his wife are driving north, into Montana to hunt on the Crow Indian Reservation. This area of what is now northern Wyoming and southern Montana is the land of the Očeti Šakówiŋ (more commonly known as Sioux), the Cheyenne, and the Apsaalooké (Crow) (*Native Land* n.p.). A Crow Territory was established in the area in 1851, but, as prospectors and other white settlers came west, the US government eventually forced the Crow to live on a reservation. This reservation was the site of the Battle of Little Bighorn in 1876. The tension between settlers and displaced tribes lingered and was explicitly cited in the US War Department report as the rationale for establishing Fort Mackenzie in Sheridan twenty-two years later (Junge 2–3). However, as Mark Junge speculates, these tensions may have been inflamed deliberately to convince whites of the need for the protection of a fort that was also economically promising for Sheridan (14–15). Junge also admits that "even by the late 1920's [sic] the memory of Indian-white conflict was relatively fresh" (14), suggesting the daughter-in-law has far more racism to contend with in Sheridan than just that of her in-laws.

350:28–29 **"We count on you," Fontan said. "Good night," I said:** Fontan's final line of this section, "We count on you" (350:28), serves as the reader's indication of how hungry the Fontans are for the company and understanding this writer has come to represent. Similar to the illegal wine and beer, this writer is also a connection to the faith and homeland the Fontans have lost in America. The narrator fails to respond to, and implicitly to recognize, the significant emotion of M. Fontan's statement, instead closing the conversation.

350:31–35 **The day before we had had good shooting.** . . . **The sun was high and the patch of shade was very small:** In the opening of the fourth section the narrator and his wife have a disappointing day of hunting, and the description of the trip recalls the narrator's time at the Fontans'. Just as the narrator explained to Fontan, "Mais on ne mange pas très bien. D'antan, oui. Mais maintenant, no" [But we do not eat very well. In the past, yes. But now, no.] (345:41–42), this passage begins by saying that yesterday's hunt was good, but on that day "we had not seen a prairie-chicken." In line with the rest of the story's treatment of hunting and fishing in the American West, we hear of past abundance but never actually see it, as the narrator chooses to resume his story after the day of plenty has already passed. Adding to the sense of scarcity, the day is hot and dry and the land without much shade. The discomfort of the narrator and his wife contrasts with the comfort he experienced at the Fontans, where "a tree made shade over Fontan's back porch" (342:5–6) and suggests that such comfort is hard to find in Wyoming.

350:37–42 We came up behind a prairie-dog town and stopped the car to shoot. . . . we did not want to get in trouble from stray bullets going toward the house: The narrator's shooting, not for sport or for meat but simply out of boredom, ought to awaken readers' fears for the narrator, as his behavior shows the same careless-ness that readers expect from other Americans. Game is not plentiful and eventu-ally, Hemingway seems to argue, will be gone from the West entirely. The idea is explored more explicitly at the end of the story when the narrator and his wife discuss the Fontans' future prospects. See entry at 354:5–9.

350:44–351:4 Across the plain we could see the mountains. . . . and from a long way away it shone very brightly: The story returns for a third time to the narrator's view of the mountains. Not only does Smith find the mountains reminiscent of the titu-lar hills in "Hills Like White Elephants" (see entry at 353:40–45), but the description of the old snow, in particular, he finds reminiscent of François Villon's "Ballade des dames du temps jadis" with its *ubi sunt* refrain of "Mais où sont les neiges d'antan?" or as Dante Gabriel Rossetti translated it, "Where are the snows of yester-year?" (Villon 3). The narrator's tone is in line with Villon's elegiac refrain, observing that "summer was ending" and all that is left is the fragile, glasslike snow of the past, with no new snow coming to replace it. What was before so "pure" and "unreal" is now doomed.

Hemingway is blunter in a later allusion to the same poem, as Richard Cantwell muses in *Across the River and into the Trees*, "Où sont les neiges d'antan? Où sont les neiges d'autre fois? Dans le pissoir toute la chose comme ça" (107), which Mark Cirino translates to "Where are the snows of other times? In the pisser like all other such things" (*Reading ARIT* 107).

351:5–6 We wanted something cool and some shade. We were sun-burned and our lips blistered from the sun and alkali dust: The dryness of Wyoming in the story is both the literal aridity of Wyoming's summer and also the dry laws that plague the Fontans. The Fontans' name, Stoneback points out, was revised from the original inspiration Moncini to Pichot to Fontan, the final name reflecting "a rich cluster of associations with *fontaine*—fountain, spring, source—and *fonte*, thawing snow"

(220). However, the reader must wonder, like the frail glassy snow from the past year (351:1–2), how long the Fontans can last in the landscape the narrator describes: burnt, hot, dry, dusty, and, given the alkali, corrosive. Fontan is also the name of a village in the Provence-Alpes-Côte d'Azur region, an area that was frequented by Hemingway's friends, including F. Scott Fitzgerald and Pablo Picasso.

351:18–19 **You come tonight. Fontan will have the wine. We'll make a fête before you go:** All three of Mme. Fontan's statements fail to come true, as the narrator and Fontan betray the behavioral code that dictates their friendship. Mme. Fontan's choice of "fête" conveys multiple meanings about the planned celebration. *Fête* literally means feast, and, while many parties could fall under the category, the story's repeated emphasis on the importance of abundance, hospitality, and good food and drink in the scarce and unwelcoming modern America gives this feast added significance, similar to the oasis in the desert that the Fontans' shady porch has become. Additionally, for French Catholics, fêtes are also the celebrations of the saints, a time of religion, tradition, and fellowship with other Catholics. This final dinner with the Fontans also alludes to the biblical Last Supper, as a final act of community and communion between those with shared beliefs, complete with the sharing of Fontan's new wine.

351:24–25 **We did not want a foreign language:** Of all the excuses the narrator makes for why they did not return to the Fontans that evening, this one feels most honest and most cutting. Unlike the beginning of the story, where the narrator cheerfully dismisses the language barrier between himself and Mme. Fontan, saying, "She spoke French, but it was only French occasionally, and there were many English words and some English constructions" (342:28–29), the narrator now argues the divide is real and exhausting. He is American after all. Despite their religion, the appreciation of wine and food, and the time spent in France, for all that he has in common with the Fontans, they are ultimately not his people; their language is not his own. Monteiro points out that, after this point in the story, "the Fontans speak no more Franco-English or French" (130).

351:32–36 **"We must go and say good-by to the Fontans," I said. . . . "I wish we'd gone.":** The narrator and his wife are relatively flippant about their broken promise, especially when compared to their exchange after visiting the Fontans for the last time (353:32–34). The narrator says, "I'm afraid they expected us last night" (351:34), as though he somehow still believes there is a possibility that they did not expect them; and his wife replies easily, "I suppose we could have gone" (351:35). Even the narrator's slight regret, "I wish we'd gone" (351:36) pales in comparison to their later, fully realized sense of guilt and failed duty: "We ought to have gone last night" (353:33). Their casualness is emphasized by the narrator's surrounding description of their departure. Despite telling Mme. Fontan, "We have to leave in the morning" (351:18), the narrator goes on to describe how they pack their things and have lunch (351:29–31), visit with other friends in town (see next entry), and only then make their way to the Fontans' to say goodbye.

351:37–38 **We said good-by to the man at the desk at the hotel, and to Larry and our other friends in the town, and then drove out to Fontan's:** This line seems particularly odd, referencing people that the reader has never heard mentioned before and lingering over the mundanities the reader does not care about (even the unnamed "man at the desk" warrants a mention), wanting instead to get to the Fontans.

Some of its oddity derives from the fact that the narrator is providing some insight into his own life, a switch in a narrative that has, until only a few paragraphs prior, been exclusively focused on the Fontans and taken place at their home. This subtle shift in focus, much like the absent presence of the wife, calls readers' attention to what the narrator is avoiding talking about, and, for once, it is the Fontans. The passage gives the sense that, both in the moment and in his later construction of the narrative, the narrator is deliberately avoiding the fallout from his absence at the Fontans' home.

Larry, a named character, makes no other appearance in the published narrative but had a more significant role in earlier drafts, functioning as part of another couple with Martha, whom Hemingway excised from the story entirely (Smith 217). However, the decision to keep this reference to Larry, and in such a way that implies we ought to know who Larry is, seems like a deliberate attempt to draw our attention to the narration itself and what we aren't being told. The name "Larry" may be a reference to Lawrence Nordquist, who owned the ranch Hemingway stayed at in Wyoming.

351:41–42 **We thought you would come last night. . . . When you did not come he drank it all up:** Sam Fontan's wine drinking has prompted a number of different interpretations. Fontan, Grebstein argues, "demonstrates that he is prey to the same animal appetites that he despises in those American 'cochons'" (65). Smith disagrees with Grebstein's reading: "Fontan, as the story and its rejected titles indicate, is 'crazy for the wine'—his addiction and his final shame are a little less than cultural" (220). Putnam sides with Grebstein, in that Fontan "succumbs to the qualities he has learned to despise in those Americans who come to his place," but holds that it is ultimately the narrator's decision not to come to dinner that "has betrayed them" (23), as this breaking of the unspoken code that dictated their friendship is what prompts the disappointed Fontan to drink all the wine.

Despite Smith's defense of M. Fontan's drinking as typical to his character, Mme. Fontan does not attempt to explain his behavior by describing him as "crazy pour le vin" here, as she has previously. There is a difference in what she lovingly seems to excuse, Fontan's passion shown in his careful attention to the wine process and his adding it to every food, and this uncontrolled consumption that she seems to pity.

352:2 **There is no wine. You drank it all up:** Fontan's excessive consumption cannot even be wholly unexpected after his story about Labor Day, where "Mais nous avons tout bu" and "Et le lendemain il ne reste rien" [But we drank everything. And the next day, there was nothing left.] (345:31–32). Mme. Fontan and the narrator and his wife are all embarrassed for M. Fontan, and Fontan's own devastation at his actions indicates that he, at least, views his actions in light of the excessive drinking he witnesses in Americans.

352:12–13 **You'll like that wine. . . . You can drink it for supper tonight:** The now broken relationship between the narrator and the Fontans shows clearly in the changed expectations of M. Fontan, who seems at once desperate to give the wine he promised but also resigned to the fact that it is no longer something they'll share together.

352:26–28 **Looking through the window I could see where the wine was stored. . . . It smelled sweet and sickish like an Indian house:** Although the desired wine is in sight, Fontan cannot reach it, the locked, untidy house reenacting the denial and exclusion the Fontans have felt in their American life. Their son's home, and implicitly the future, is chaotic and dirty, lacking the order the Fontans have worked hard to cultivate, and the fruits of their labor are kept out of reach.

Flora points out the narrator's description of the smell of the son's home as "sweet and sickish like an Indian house" is similar to Nick Adams's description of "the sick sweet smell [Native Americans] get to have" in "Fathers and Sons" (376:9). Nick's memory of the smell occurs in an elegiac passage about the ultimate decline of the Native Americans as he sees it, the sick sweet smell coming as "they ended" (376:10). The Fontans' order ends in the son's house, but the shared language with "Fathers and Sons" suggests the ending of other people and traditions of the American frontier as well. Smell is a recurring sensory detail associated with Native Americans in Hemingway's work, such as when Nick attempts to "get rid of the smell" of his father by walking through the Ojibway camp in "Fathers and Sons."

352:34–35 **We tried the key and it did not work. It turned half-way in either direction:** Fontan is locked out of his own wine, a punishment reminiscent of the Fontans' own policy toward overindulgent Americans (see entry at 349:31–41).

352:40 **"No," I said. "That man would see. Then they would seize it.":** Fontan's desperate attempts to access his own wine have moved beyond disappointing to dangerous. Putnam points out that the story is structured so it suddenly reveals, to the reader and the narrator, how "the welfare of the French couple is put into jeopardy by the thoughtless gesture of this American who once lived in France" (23). Although the narrator tries to remedy the situation he has created by going with Fontan to get more wine, he soon realizes, as does the reader, that his mistake cannot be unmade and that Fontan's disappointment and frustration can and will bear consequences lasting beyond what the narrator could foresee.

353:5 **Where did that crazy go?:** This is the last appearance of the word "crazy" in the story and marks the first time it is used as a noun and outside the phrase "crazy pour." The term is now purely derogatory with no element of love or passion attached. Presumably, this house belongs to Fontan's son and daughter-in-law. (The Fontans speak of the woman whom they had assumed would be home with familiar contempt, and the narrator's observation of the "empty tin cans" [352:16], which recalls Mme. Fontan's complaints about her, and a smell the narrator associates with Native Americans.) The daughter-in-law must take all the blame for a situation she had nothing to do with and for doing exactly what her mother-in-law complains she never does: leaving the house. However, for Fontan or the narrator to accept responsibility for their own behavior would require an admission that the values they have been espousing and the significance they attach to "[e]verybody that was ever in France" (350:7–8) are unreal and unsubstantial.

353:12 **Madame Fontan looked sad:** The narrator tells rather than shows Mme. Fontan's sadness, a deviation from Hemingway's usual objective style and from the conventions of good writing. The narrator repeats this literary faux pas again at 353:26 ("She felt badly for Fontan"), 353:27 ("We all felt very badly"), 353:28–29 ("They stood together sadly on the porch"), and finally repeating the line itself at 353:29–30 ("Madame Fontan looked sad."). The narrator is no longer able to function as a writer or a purely objective observer of the disappointment and pain he has had a hand in causing, and, as his detachment slips, so does his skill as a writer. The moment highlights what Cirino calls "the central tension of Hemingway's fiction" between the "excess of thought on the part of the intelligent, introspective, and creative man" and "the burden with which such cognition saddles the protagonist" (*Thought in Action* 7). A writer needs to be sensitive to the motivations and emotions of the characters they represent, but the narrator and thus the narrative become overwhelmed as the narrator can no longer maintain authorial distance from his subjects.

353:14–17 **"You can come back next year?" . . . "You see?" Fontan said to her:** Similar to Fontan, readers cannot truly believe the narrator's promise to return in two years. Putnam points out that the narrator suffers from incredible "ambivalence" about the home the Fontans' house and company has come to represent: "Feeling both the urge to stay, and . . . an equally urgent desire to leave, the narrator defiles this clean well-lighted place" (23). This ambivalence about place and belonging can be seen both in the narrator's current situation as an expatriate, who is at home in neither country, but also in the narrator's choice to focus the story so deliberately away from his home life by detailing the Fontans' lives and speech so clearly while leaving himself and his marriage in the dark.

353:19–20 **He knew when he was ruined:** Fontan is "very upset" (352:3), "desperate" (352:20), "incoherent and crushed" (352:43), "disgraced" (353:12), and finally "ruined" when it becomes clear that the wine is inaccessible and the narrator will never taste it. Although "ruined" seems extreme to describe Fontan's situation, Fontan's inability to preserve and share this representation of his cultural values with the modern narrator (and as it appears, with either of his Americanized children), Fontan himself becomes a part of the past that will not carry on without pollution or decay. In the end, Fontan cannot preserve tradition and has himself become so American that he too is barred from returning home, even through the wine he makes.

353:34 **Yes, we ought to have:** Following this line an interesting section of dialogue was cut:
"They're the best people ~~in Wyoming~~ we know."
"Yes. They're the best people," she said.
~~"How do you feel?"~~
~~"I feel just like you do."~~
~~"Elle est crazy pour lui."~~
~~"I hope they have a lot of good luck."~~
~~"They won't have," I said. "And they won't elect Schmidt president either."~~
                                                    ("Wine of Wyoming" ms. 837)
Smith attributes "Elle est crazy pour lui" [She is crazy about him] to the narrator's wife in his discussion of this deleted conversation (218, 221); but, from the rest of the conversation, it appears that this line is the narrator's. This reading makes more sense as the narrator would be aware of Mme. Fontan's unique phrasing of "est crazy pour" that is alluded to here. Instead of Smith's claim that the highly perceptive wife "sees that Madame Fontan is 'crazy pour lui'" (221), this excised dialogue seems to mark the disconnect between the narrator's realized guilt and his wife's parroting and platitudes.

353:37 **It looked like Spain, but it was Wyoming:** The story returns for the last time to the narrator's view of the mountains, and the dream of achieving the Old World in the New is brought into a harsh and realistic light. The mountains could look like Spain, but "it was Wyoming." The past and its values and traditions, like Fontan's wine, can no longer be reached.

By contrast, Johnston points out the similarities the narrator sees between Spain and Wyoming may not be purely positive ones, despite the story's often nostalgic view of Europe, noting, "as far as opportunities for success, happiness, and 'good luck' are concerned, there is little to choose between Europe and America" (166).

The line is also reminiscent of the opening of "God Rest You Merry, Gentlemen," where the narrator describes how "Kansas City was very like Constantinople" (298:3). In both instances, time and space are collapsed between Old and New World locations; for better and worse, America resembles Europe.

353:38–39 "I hope they have a lot of good luck." " . . . and Schmidt won't be President either.": This final allusion to Smith's campaign (and its eventual failure) suggests that the narrator's surety in the Fontans' future misfortunes is grounded in his similar surety in the continued intolerance and corruption of America. It also contrasts the wife's more abstract and facile understanding of what has occurred and what the Fontans face, with the narrator's more pessimistic and concrete vision of the future.

Readers in 1933 would be certain of both of the narrator's predictions, knowing that Smith would lose the 1928 election by a landslide and that only bad luck would follow with the 1929 stock market crash and the Great Depression.

353:40–45 The cement road stopped. . . . They were farther away now and they looked more like Spain than ever: Smith compares the last descriptions of the mountains to the girl's view of the Spanish hills in "Hills Like White Elephants" (221), especially in the way that the narrator seems to see the failed and ruined future of the West and of the Fontans in the mountains, just as the girl, surveying the land remarks, "And we could have everything and every day we make it more impossible" (*CSS* 213). Like Jig's observations of the hills beyond the river, the mountains are consistently described as far away and, in this last instance, seem even more distant than before. Looking back to the previous descriptions of the mountains, what they offer is the potential for shade and refreshment that does not reach the plain below ("they made no shadow" [342:3], the "snow looked very white and pure and unreal" [348:12–13]). Given the Fontans' precarious financial and legal situation and the realization that the community and friendship that promised relief in an inhospitable land has been spoilt beyond repair, the renewal implied by the mountains seems more out of reach than ever. The mountains belong to another place and time entirely, as they could not exist in this modern country.

354:5–9 "It's a fine country for la chasse, Fontan says." . . . "There's nothing to prove he won't be," I said: In this final conversation, the narrator briefly attempts to be optimistic, as optimistic as the story can manage at least, by returning to Fontan's assertion that America has good hunting. However, the wife's question confirms the inklings of doubt that the poor fishing and hunting seen throughout the story have created; the promised abundance cannot and will not last forever. Yet the narrator speculates, somewhat hopefully, that the Fontans will be dead before the game is entirely gone. Even in this hope, however, is the promised end of both the Old World and the New and distinct pessimism for the prospects of André.

Flora points out the possibility for another reading of the story's discussion of game and hunting, as Hemingway use of "the parallels between hunting and sexual fulfillment" in other stories such as "Fathers and Sons," "The Snows of Kilimanjaro," and "The Short Happy Life of Francis Macomber" (234). The Fontans' marriage is a detailed and happy one, and, from the narrator's comparative silence regarding his own marriage, readers may assume his is otherwise. The narrator does say that "we had had good shooting" (350:31–32) but, like many of the better times in the story, it occurs in the past.

354:10–11 "We ought to have gone last night." "Oh yes," I said. "We ought to have gone.": Although Grebstein proposes that the narrator "does not totally admit his own part in the deterioration" of the Fontans or of the West (67), but this repetition of the wife and the narrator's exchange, coming immediately after their discussion of the dwindling game, suggests at least awareness, if not admission. By the end of the story, the narrator and his wife are finally cognizant of the unintended consequences of his broken promise.

The exchange also shifts its meaning in the second occurrence because it is no longer necessarily about the Fontans. The first occurrence of the conversation occurs immediately after the couple has left the Fontans' home and is preceded by the narrator's observation: "They felt so badly. Fontan felt terribly" (353:32). In that instance, it is understood that they ought to have gone to prevent the Fontans' feeling badly. Repeated without that context, the exchange suggests that they ought to have gone for themselves.

APPENDIX: A TRANSLATION OF THE FRENCH IN "WINE OF WYOMING"

343:2 Il fait de la vendange. Oh, my God, il est crazy pour le vin. He's harvesting the grapes. Oh, my God, he is crazy about wine.

343:4 Oui j'aime la bière, mais Fontan, il est crazy pour le vin. Yes, I love beer, but Fontan is crazy about wine.

343:10 Mangez ici. Il ne faut pas manger à l'hôtel ou au restaurant. Mangez ici! Eat here. You don't need to eat at the hotel or the restaurant. Eat here!

343:18–19 Et mon fils il est marié avec une américaine, et tout le temps il a mangé les *beans* en *can*. And my son he is married to an American, and all the time he eats beans in a can.

343:24–25 Rien que des books. Tout le temps elle stay in the bed and read books. Nothing but books. She stays in bed all day and reads books.

343:34 **Besides, il est *crazy* pour elle.** Besides, he is crazy about her.

343:40 **Elle est Indienne?** She is an Indian?

344:16 **Un roman** A novel

344:27 **Il faut revenir tout de suit après le show** You must return right after the show

344:30 **Mangez!** Eat!

344:34–35 **Mangez du fromage. Mangez du crimcheez. Vous n'avez rien mangé.** Eat cheese. Eat the cream cheese [rendered phonetically]. You haven't eaten anything.

344:37 **Mais j'ai rudement bien mangé.** But I had a terribly good meal.

344:38 **Mangez! Vous n'avez rien mangé.** Eat! You haven't eaten anything.

344:43 **Elle ne comprend pas que vous êtes écrivain.** She doesn't understand that you are a writer.

345:6 **Mangez! Je vais chercher de la bière.** Eat! I'm going to get some beer.

345:13–15 **Tout le monde est allé dans le truck. Nous sommes partis le dimanche. C'est le truck de Charley.** Everybody went in the truck. We left on Sunday. It's Charley's truck.

345:16–17 **On a mangé, on a bu du vin, de la bière, et il y avait aussi un français qui a apporté de l'absinthe. . . . Un français de la Californie!** We ate, we drank wine, beer, and there was also a Frenchman who brought absinthe. . . . A Frenchman from California!

345:18 **My God, nous avons chanté.** My God, did we ever sing.

345:25–26 **Très peu. . . . Nous avons chanté, vous savez.** Very few. . . . We sang, you know.

345:27–28 **toutes les femmes ont dormi dans le truck. Les hommes à côté du feu.** all the women slept in the truck. The men by the fire.

345:31–32 **Mais nous avons tout bu. . . . Et le lendemain il ne reste rien.** We drank everything. . . . And the next day, there was nothing left.

345:34 **Nous avons pêché sérieusement.** We fished seriously.

345:41–42 **Mais on ne mange pas très bien. D'antan, oui. Mais maintenant, no.** But we don't eat very well. In the past, yes. But now, no.

345:43 **On ne mange pas bien.** We don't eat well.

345:43–346:2 **Et aussi, il y a trop de Polack. Quand j'étais petite ma mère m'a dit, 'vous mangez comme les Polacks.' Je n'ai jamais compris ce que c'est qu'un Polack. Mais maintenant en Amérique je comprends. Il y a trop de Polack. Et, my God, ils sont sales, les Polacks.** And also, there are too many Polacks. When I was little my mother told me, 'You eat like the Polacks.' I never understood what a Polack was. But now in America, I understand. There are too many Polacks. And, my God, they are dirty, the Polacks.

346:4–5 **Oui. Ça, c'est le meilleur. La chasse et la pêche. . . . Qu'est-ce que vous avez comme fusil?** Yes, that's the best. Hunting and fishing. . . . What kind of rifle do you have?

346:7 **Il est bon, le pump.** The pump is good.

346:8 **Je veux aller à la chasse moi-même.** I want to go hunting by myself.

346:10 **Tu ne peux pas.** You can't.

346:11–12 **Ils sont des sauvages, les boys, vous savez. Ils sont des sauvages. Ils veulent shooter les uns les autres.** Boys are savages, you know. They are savages. They want to shoot each other.

346:13 **Je veux aller tout seul.** I want to go by myself.

346:15 **Je veux aller tout seul. . . . Je veux shooter les rats d'eau.** I want to go by myself. I want to shoot muskrats.

346:30 **On peut looker. On ne fait pas de mal. On peut looker.** I can look. I'm not doing any harm. I can look.

346:31–32 **Il est crazy pour le shooting. . . . Mais il est trop jeune.** He is crazy about shooting. . . . But he is too young.

346:37 **C'est vrai. . . . Il a tué un jack.** That's true. . . . He killed a jack[rabbit].

346:42 **Il aime les books** He likes books.

346:44 **Monsieur il fait les books.** Monsieur [the narrator] writes books.

347:1–4 **Ici, c'est une maladie, les books. C'est comme les churches. Ici il y a trop de
churches. En France il y a seulement les catholiques et les protestants—et très peu de
protestants. Mais ici rien que de churches. Quand j'étais venu ici je disais, oh my God,
what are all the churches?** Books are a sickness here. Like churches. Here there are too
many churches. In France, there are only the Catholics and the Protestants—and very few
Protestants. But here nothing but churches. When I came here I said, oh my God, what
are all the churches?

347:5 **C'est vrai. . . . Il y a trop de churches.** It's true. . . . There are too many churches.

347:7–8 **En Amérique il ne faut pas être catholique.** In America you must not be Catholic.

347:12–13 **Ce n'est pas bon de changer sa religion.** It's not good to change your religion.

347:15–16 **Mais je reste catholique.** But I am still a Catholic.

347:17 **On dit que Schmidt est catholique.** People say that Schmidt [Smith] is Catholic.

347:18 **On dit, mais on ne sait jamais.** They say, but we never know.

347:21–22 **Je ne crois pas que Schmidt est catholique.** I don't think Schmidt [Smith] is
Catholic.

347:23 **Les Polacks sont catholiques** The Polacks are Catholics

347:30 **Moi, je ne crois pas.** As for me, I don't think so.

347:31 **Il est catholique** He is Catholic

347:33 **My God, il est catholique.** My God, he is a Catholic.

347:34–35 **Marie va chercher de la bière. . . . Monsieur a soif—moi aussi.** Marie, go get
some beer. Monsieur is thirsty—I am too.

347:40–41 **C'est un bon pays pour la chasse. . . . J'aime beaucoup shooter les canards.** It's a
good country for hunting. . . . I really like to shoot ducks.

347:42 **Mais il y a très bonne chasse aussi en France** But there is also very good hunting in
France

347:43 **C'est vrai. . . . Nous avons beaucoup de gibier là-bas.** It's true. . . . We have a lot of
game there.

347:45 **Il est catholique. . . . My God, Schmidt est catholique.** He is Catholic. My God,
Schmidt [Smith] is Catholic.

348:17 **C'est jolie, la neige.** The snow is pretty.

348:26–27 **Il n'a jamais fait de mal à personne.** He never hurt anyone.

348:36–37 **Vous savez, il est crazy pour le vin.** You know, he is crazy about wine.

348:40–41 **Dans son café, vous savez! Il est crazy pour le vin! Il est comme ça. Son pays
est comme ça.** In his coffee, you know! He is crazy about wine. He's like that. His country
is like that.

348:44 **Je n'aime pas les houblons.** I do not like hops.

349:4 **il est crazy pour le vin** he is crazy for the wine

349:8–10 **'La sauce est meilleure que le jack.' Dans son pays c'est comme ça. Il y a beaucoup de gibier et de vin. Moi, j'aime les pommes de terre, le saucisson, et la bière.
C'est bon, la bière. Cest très bon pour la santé.** 'The sauce is better than the jack[rabbit].'

Where he comes from, it's like that. There is a lot of game and wine. Me, I like potatoes, sausage, and beer. Beer is good. It's very good for your health.

349:16–17 **Oui. . . . Et aussi une femme qui a vomis sur la table!** Yes. . . . And a woman vomited on the table!

349:18 **Comment?** How?

349:19 **C'est vrai. Elle a vomis sur la table. Et après elle a vomis dans ses shoes.** It is true. She vomited on the table. And afterward, she vomited in her shoes.

349:35–36 **'On va être malade!' 'Oui,' il dit.** 'They'll be sick!' 'Yes,' he says.

349:45 **Cochon** Pig

350:1–2 **C'est un mot très fort. . . . mais vomir sur la table** It's a very strong word. . . . but to vomit on the table

350:3 **Cochons . . . cochons. Salauds.** Pigs . . . pigs. Bastards.

350:6 **Il y a des gens très gentils, très sensibles, qui viennent aussi.** There are very nice people, very fine, who also come.

350:16 **C'est un original . . . mais vraiment gentil.** He's eccentric, but very nice.

351:19 **fête** feast or party

354:5 **la chasse** hunting

WORKS CITED

Anderson, Vicki. *The Dime Novel in Children's Literature.* McFarland Publishing, 2004.

Baker, Carlos. *Ernest Hemingway: A Life Story.* 1969.

Brown, Jen Corrine. *Trout Culture: How Fly Fishing Forever Changed the Rocky Mountain West.* U of Washington P, 2015.

"Charles Austin Fosdick." *Dictionary of American Biography.* Scribner's, 1936.

Cirino, Mark. *Ernest Hemingway: Thought in Action.* U of Wisconsin P, 2012.

———. *Reading Hemingway's* Across the River and into the Trees. Kent State UP, 2016.

———. "You Don't Know the Italian Language Well Enough: The Bilingual Dialogue of *A Farewell to Arms.*" *Hemingway Review,* vol. 26, no. 1, 2006, pp. 106–14.

Clark, Norman H. *Deliver Us from Evil: An Interpretation of American Prohibition.* Norton, 1976.

Conrad, Barnaby, III. *Absinthe: History in a Bottle.* 1988. Chronicle Books, 1997.

Difford, Simon. "Why Absinthe Was Banned." *Difford's Guide,* https://www.diffordsguide.com/g/1102/absinthe/why-absinthe-was-banned.

Flora, Joseph. *Hemingway's Nick Adams.* LSU Press, 1982.

Grebstein, Sheldon N. *Hemingway's Craft.* Southern Illinois UP, 1973.

Gregory, Horace. "Ernest Hemingway Has Put on Maturity." *The New York Herald Tribune,* 29 Oct. 1933, p. E5.

Hemingway, Ernest. *The Complete Short Stories of Ernest Hemingway: The Finca Vigía Edition.* Scribner's, 2003.

———. *A Farewell to Arms.* Hemingway Library Edition. Edited by Seán Hemingway. Scribner's, 2012.

———. *The Letters of Ernest Hemingway: Volume 3 (1926–1929).* Edited by Rena Sanderson, Sandra Spanier, and Robert W. Trogdon. CUP, 2015.

———. *The Letters of Ernest Hemingway: Volume 4 (1929–1931)*. Edited by Sandra Spanier and Miriam B. Mandel. CUP, 2017.

—— *The Letters of Ernest Hemingway: Volume 5 (1932–1934)*. Edited by Sandra Spanier and Miriam B. Mandel. CUP, 2020.

———. *The Sun Also Rises*. The Hemingway Library Edition. Edited by Seán Hemingway. Scribner's, 2014.

———. "Wine of Wyoming" manuscript, item 837, Ernest Hemingway Collection, John F. Kennedy Library, Boston.

Johnston, Kenneth G. "Hemingway's "Wine of Wyoming": Disappointment in America." *Western American Literature* vol. 9, no. 3, 1974, pp. 159–67.

Junge, Mark. *National Register of Historic Places Inventory—Nomination Form: Fort Mackenzie*. National Parks Service, 1978, https://npgallery.nps.gov/NRHP/GetAsset/NRHP/81000612_text.

Keyser, Catherine. *Artificial Color: Modern Food and Racial Fictions*. OUP, 2018.

Larson, Taft A. *History of Wyoming*. U of Nebraska P, 1965.

Linford, Velma. *Wyoming, Frontier State*. Old West Pub. Co, 1947.

Martin, Lawrence H. J. "Crazy in Sheridan: Hemingway's "Wine of Wyoming" Reconsidered." *New Critical Approaches to the Short Stories of Ernest Hemingway*, edited by Jackson J. Benson. Duke UP, 1990, pp. 360–72.

Monteiro, George. *The Hemingway Short Story: A Critical Appreciation*. McFarland, 2017.

Native Land. Native Land Digital, native-land.ca.

Northcutt, Wayne. *The Regions of France*. Greenwood P, 1996.

Olson, James S. *Catholic Immigrants in America*. Nelson-Hall, 1987.

Putnam, Ann. "'Wine of Wyoming' and Hemingway's Hidden West." *Western American Literature*, vol. 22, no. 1, 1987, pp. 17–32.

Reynolds, Michael S. *Hemingway's Reading, 1910–1940: An Inventory*. Princeton UP, 1981.

Rossetti, Gina M. "Native Encounters: Examining Primitivism in Hemingway and London's Short Fiction." *Studies in American Naturalism*, vol. 11, no. 1, 2016, pp. 55–68.

Smith, Paul. *A Reader's Guide to the Short Stories of Ernest Hemingway*. G. K. Hall, 1989.

Stoneback, H. R. ""Mais Je Reste Catholique": Communion, Betrayal, and Aridity in 'Wine of Wyoming.'" *Hemingway's Neglected Short Fiction: New Perspectives*, edited by Susan F. Beegel, U of Alabama P, 1992, pp. 209–24.

Troy, William. "Mr. Hemingway's Opium." *The Nation*, 15 Nov. 1933, p. 570.

Vandagriff, Susan. "The Scapegoat's Scapegoat: A Girardian Reading of *Across the River and into the Trees*." *The Hemingway Review*, vol. 36, no. 2, 2017, pp. 95–111.

Villon, Francois. "The Ballad of Dead Ladies." *Ballads Done into English from the French of Francois Villon*, translated by Dante Gabriel Rossetti. T. B. Mosher, 1907, pp. 3–4.

THE GAMBLER, THE NUN, AND THE RADIO

Nicole J. Camastra

The penultimate story in *Winner Take Nothing*, "The Gambler, the Nun, and the Radio," depicts the conversations among three characters in a hospital, set in the fictional town of Hailey, Montana. The narrative begins after a Mexican gambler, Cayetano Ruiz, is brought in with a gunshot wound; he is tended to by a nun, Sister Cecilia, who also takes care of Mr. Frazer, a writer being treated for a broken leg after falling off his horse. The triangulation of these three people develops different perspectives of pain and reactions to it. The first two characters correspond to their eponymous labels, indicating their simpler thematic function than Frazer's. Limited primarily to his point of view, the third-person narration comes to describe his relationship with the radio, a device that offers more ambient noise than anything else, because it signals the philosophical weight of acknowledging the recurrence of pain and the necessity of blunting it.

Frazer's broken leg bears some resemblance to the actual injury Hemingway sustained from a car accident, a broken arm, which forced him to remain in St. Vincent's Hospital in Billings, Montana, for several weeks beginning 1 November 1930. During this time, he could not write. He was tended to by a nun, Sister Florence, and he befriended some Mexicans in the ward. It is unclear, according to Paul Smith, exactly when Hemingway began sketching the story after the incident that provided its raw material. Smith claims the process may have begun as early as "the summer of 1931" because the author at that time was "accustomed" to composing narratives soon after the event that prompted them (289). Intermittent work on "Gambler" continued throughout 1932, concentrated more so during the latter half of that year, when Hemingway wrote his editor, Maxwell Perkins, in November that he had "four stories ready to be typed." He described them as "very good" (*Letters vol. 5*, 271). Final work on the story was likely done by February 1933, according to Carlos Baker (141n), and "Gambler" would be published by *Scribner's Magazine* in May 1933 before it appeared in *Winner Take Nothing* in October of that year. The original iteration of it in *Scribner's* was titled "Give Us a Prescription, Doctor"; had eleven, not nine, distinct sections; contained geographical references to Portland, Oregon, that later became Seattle, Washington; and had a different ending. Despite his belief that "Gambler," along with other stories in *Winner*, was "excellent" (*Letters vol. 5*, 293), the collection sold poorly compared to his previous one, *Men Without Women* (Trogdon 126).

Horace Gregory regarded the story as "beautifully simplified and pure," saying that it showed a "sudden expansion" of the author's "range" (Stephens 140). William Troy used "Gambler" to highlight the strengths and weaknesses of *Winner Take Nothing*. On one hand, he held it to be "the most successful" piece "in the book." On the other hand, he claimed it to represent potential shortcomings for the author's craft, which he thought relied too heavily on superficiality and thematic action "as a catharsis and not an expression" (Stephens 146–47). After its original publication, the story was collected in *The Fifth Column and the First Forty-Nine Stories* (1938), reprinted in *Great Modern Catholic Stories* (1942) and in *The Snows of Kilimanjaro and Other Stories* (1962). *Winner Take Nothing* is no longer printed as such and is available only as part of the Finca Vigía Edition of *The Complete Short Stories of Ernest Hemingway* (1987).

"Gambler" received renewed, albeit brief, attention when it was adapted for TV by Hemingway's friend A. E. Hotchner, who discussed the project with the *New York Times* right before it aired in May 1960. Identified by the *Times* as a "wiry writer with a virtual monopoly in adapting Hemingway works for television" (Schumach), Hotchner mistakenly dates Hemingway's hospital stay, and the genesis of the story, to 1932 instead of 1930, which might also undermine his credibility as the author's media proxy. Nevertheless, the generally favorable review of Hotchner's production describes the tale as "unusual," in part, because of its "sentimental" overtones. The reviewer seemed most struck by the fact that "Mr. Hemingway" told a "story in which sweetness and light overwhelmed the powers of darkness. The novelty value alone was remarkable" (Shanley). However, seeing "sweetness and light" as mutually exclusive to the "powers of darkness" might be too simplistic; both ends of the spectrum exist in the story, the tone of which is perhaps more complicated and demands more scrutiny than most readers allow. Suffice it to say that the attention garnered by the story has focused largely on tone to understand what many insist is either Hemingway's increasing nihilism and disdain for religion (Morton) or his underrated sense of humor (Whittle).

Despite being one of the most neglected stories in a collection that is itself neglected, in "Gambler," as in some others, Hemingway manipulated perspective especially well, perhaps as a musical composer might hear variations on a theme or fugue. Music proffers valuable inroads to discover the complexities of his métier; Hemingway's comments to Lillian Ross in 1950 on using the word *and* "the way Mr. Johann Sebastian Bach used a note in music when he was emitting counterpoint" and writing "like Mr. Johann sometimes—or, anyway, so he would like it" (50) offer enough material to proceed down that exegetical path (Camastra). In "Gambler," references to popular songs are no doubt important indicators of cultural climate and attitude, but the music Frazer listens to serves an ancillary function; it is the radio, not the songs on it, that helps him bear the reality of "a condition that requires illusions," to quote Karl Marx (69), a looming figure at the end of the story.

The denizens of the hospital in "Gambler" provide one illustration of disappointment; physically broken but convalescing, they all must reinvent themselves following injury. Even if they succeed, they lose something of themselves in the process. As David Wyatt has put it, "A price paid by the body [has] to be lived out by the spirit." For Hemingway, Wyatt contends, "Winning . . . proved difficult to distinguish from losing" (81); the same holds true in his fiction. Frazer knows this since he had "been through all this before" and braces himself to go through it again. "Fathers and Sons," which follows "Gambler" and ends *Winner Take Nothing*, deals also with similar concerns. Nick's son knows that he "ought to go to pray at the tomb of [his] grandfather" (376:42), and Nick knows that he ought to take him. Reproach, for actions or inactions, ends the collection and seems a natural extension of "The Gambler, the Nun, and the Radio," what Hemingway called a "study in pain and the discouragement" that accompanies it (*SL* 418).

Title: Paul Smith notes that Hemingway's earliest manuscripts of the story bear the working title "Three Ambitions" (289). The original magazine publication appeared as "Give Us A Prescription, Doctor," which changed again to "The Gambler, the Nun, and the Radio" before Hemingway published it in *Winner Take Nothing*. The revision sounds better, if for no other reason than it evinces the characteristic staccato sound and rhythmic cadence of Hemingway's prose. Thematically, the tripartite title calls specific attention to the cultural milieu in which it was published, linking it more closely to the political and economic climate of the time than his other works. Hemingway, however, avoided being a political writer. He wrote to the Russian critic Ivan Kashkin in 1935 that an author "owes no allegiance to any government" and that, if any good, "he will never like" the one "he lives under." Limiting one's artistic eye to class consciousness, for example, demonstrates a limited talent because "all classes are [the writer's] province" (*SL* 419). Nevertheless, the story is arguably one of his most implicitly political, for Hemingway *was* conscious of the difficulties many Americans faced in the early 1930s. He indicated as much in a letter to Guy Hickok, composed during his hospital stay in Billings, where he acquired the experience for "Gambler": "An average of 63 banks a day failed in Arkansas," even though things remained "pretty prosperous" in Billings because of "the sugar beet racket," but "everyone else in America is unemployed" (*Letters vol. 4,* 427).

By May 1933, when the story first appeared in *Scribner's Magazine,* gambling, religion, and entertainment all provided a kind of psychological escape from the difficult economic constraints of the Great Depression. The primary vice, alcohol, was still prohibited. Although the Blaine Act was introduced in February 1933, repeal of the Eighteenth Amendment would not happen until December of that year. Between the beginning of Prohibition in 1919 and when the Twenty-First Amendment was ratified in December 1933, gangsters like Al Capone in Chicago had built empires from bootlegging. At the same time, figures like Bernarr Macfadden had grown a publishing behemoth by capitalizing on his success as self-proclaimed minister of physical culture, denouncing formal Western medicine and dedicating himself to showcasing the natural strength of the human body. Religious sects, particularly the Pentecostals, maintained their popularity and even grew their numbers.

Despite economic hardship, entertainment, like other vices, continued to appeal to people, demonstrated by demands for concert tickets. The number of philharmonics in the United States "increased from seventeen before World War I to 270," according to one survey from 1939. Outcomes from similar studies were higher (Horowitz 397). Moreover, many American homes had radios, a device that emblematizes the decade, not least of all because of President Franklin Delano Roosevelt's fireside chats. The radio provided the literal and figurative mouthpiece for this period in American history. That Frazer listens to it places him among the majority, as one of the people who relies on an opiate, in the parlance of the story, but his decision to use it as background noise belies its popular appeal and prompts his meditation on the need for opiates, or "an anesthetic," in the first place.

355:1–3 **They brought them . . . heard the Russian:** Other than foregrounding a conflict without any explication, this opening sentence subtly acknowledges the focus on displacement evident in the preceding and following stories. We move from the previous story's end in Wyoming, which, according to the narrator, "looked more like Spain than ever" (353:45), to the setting for "Gambler" in Montana, named after the Spanish word for mountain, *montaña*. Despite the suggestion of Iberian landscape and language, the narrators in both "Wine of Wyoming" and "Fathers and Sons" live in France. Mr. Frazer in "Gambler" lies in an American hospital, but his story initially concerns an indeterminate "they" with an emphasis on the Russian. This singular identification suggests at least his nominal difference from "them."

Further differentiating voices in the story, the third-person narrator is never identified, and some critics have suggested that it is really Hemingway's voice, echoing the supposed nihilism. Paul C. Rodgers argues that the "key to the story is the ironic viewpoint of the narrator" (439), that "all the inclusions, emphases, and implications" are his. . . . He provides the specter of final absurdity" in the narrative (443). Rodgers reaches the conclusion that "Frazer *is* a radio. He is . . . nerveless and immobile and insignificant. His knowledge is a paralyzing opiate" (449). Rodgers's argument is interesting, but logical only if one accepts his claim that Hemingway's "pessimism during the early 1930s reached its nadir in the *nada* prayer of 'A Clean, Well-Lighted Place' and in the 'opium' meditation" of the present story (439). Alternately, there is evidence to suggest that Hemingway was not capitulating to despair but, rather, extending his experiments with narrative point of view, for *Winner Take Nothing* follows directly on the heels of *Death in the Afternoon,* the author's first nonfiction work and a book about "learning how to see" (Wyatt 99).

355:6 **What about the other one?:** The brief dialogue between Frazer and the night nurse in these early lines of the story introduces Frazer and provides a somber dimension to the opening conflict: one of the men brought in might die. Acknowledgment of "the other one" also underlines the inadvertent triangulation that occurs throughout the story: there is typically someone "other" who does not understand the conversation or the situation or the implication of what is going on.

355:10 **They were both beet workers:** The paper identifies both the Mexican and the Russian as "beet workers," but we later learn that the "paper was mistaken" about some things (see entry at 365:42). Their presumed occupation is plausible because both Mexicans and German Russians were brought to Montana to work for major companies, such as Great Western Sugar, cultivating and harvesting sugar beets. The American West provided vast amounts of land for this lucrative crop, the foundation of which "was the irrigation infrastructure that captured and delivered the region's scarce water resources to monoculture farms" (Johnson 323); the problem was acquiring enough labor. According to one estimate, the "amount of labor required to grow an acre of sugar beets" was "about ten times that . . . for an acre of corn or wheat" (Kipp 36n). The industry, therefore, paid to transport its workers, comprised at first of mostly Chinese, Japanese, and German Russian peoples; but, by the 1920s, the workers were almost entirely Mexican.

Though Hemingway's narrator refers to one of the characters in the opening sentence only as "the Russian," he is likely a German Russian, or Volga German, those Germans whose immigration to Russia followed the invitation of Catherine the Great, herself of German descent. Under her rule from 1762 to 1796, this group was exempt from taxes and military service that were otherwise mandatory. The influx of Germans, especially in religious minorities such as the Mennonites, continued well into the nineteenth century until Alexander II ended the exceptions they lived under. Many of them came to the United States, especially to the Great Plains and Upper Midwest, where they worked as beet laborers and were often despised for the way they made their children work in the fields with them. They did, however, enjoy some of the advantages available "during the [sugar beet] boom period of the late 1910s"; if they worked hard enough, they could "rent or buy their own farms," which promised some measure of economic independence and security (Kipp 35). Many availed themselves of this opportunity and, consequently, there was a notable shift "toward Mexican labor," especially after 1920 (Kipp 35), when the industry lobbied on behalf of Mexican immigrants because it needed them. By then, the immigration quotas put in place restricted many people, including Eastern Europeans, from entering the States.

Their living conditions were often cramped and strenuous. Great Western, for example, built adobe houses behind their factory in Billings. Quite spartan in appearance and known as "the colony," it was where Mexican families lived while they worked. Many brought musical instruments with them, and, socially, they did not cross the proverbial and literal railroad tracks in town. Being segregated only encouraged the racism that was already directed toward them ("Montana Mosaic"). The gambler in Hemingway's story, along with those who subsequently visit him, likely lives in such a place. Befriending Mexicans in St. Vincent's Hospital would have exposed Hemingway to the cruel and exploitative practices of the sugar beet industry, perhaps prompting him to describe it as a "racket" (*Letters vol. 4, 427*).

355:14–15 **That was what the paper said:** The ostensibly objective explication of the conflict given in this paragraph is provided by "the paper," making it seem more reliable than other accounts but certainly the most elliptic, for the paper captures only the events and not their meaning or the motive behind them. In this way, as in almost everything that follows pertaining to the actual gunfight, there is either context, in the characterization of Cayetano, or there is text, the so-called facts of what happened. As is typical of Hemingway's prose, however, the event that prompted the story occurs before the timeline of the narrative, so we do not see it. We have no objective view, only different perspectives of it. How we see an event has almost everything to do with how we understand it. Manipulating point of view in this way extends beyond the benchmark characteristics of modernist fiction, which had shifted from using a reliable third-person narrator to illustrate an objective worldview such as works of realism and naturalism assumed. Hemingway's specific use of a more subjective point of view speaks to his growing facility with ironic distance and, as David Wyatt has argued, emotional vulnerability.

355:16–17 **The Mexican . . . believed it to be an accident:** The third-person perspective suggests the objective truth that the Mexican's unfortunate situation stemmed from bad luck, just being in the wrong place at the wrong time.

355:20 *cabrón:* A Spanish obscenity with several English translations that include "asshole," "dumbass," and "bastard." The dialogue between Cayetano and the detective sergeant furthers the idea that, despite the pretext of communication, much goes unsaid. The two men speak to each other through an interpreter, but one side has a clear disadvantage; the detective knows no Spanish. The interpreter, presumably another native Spanish speaker, perhaps another Mexican, feels some solidarity with the wounded Ruiz and so protects him by offering the detective the version Cayetano wants him to have. Cayetano trusts the interpreter based on his ironic gibe, that it was an "accident [his assailant] hit [him] at all, the *cabrón*" (355:20).

There are several similar moments in this story where the Spanish word is used instead of its near-English equivalent. Since Hemingway has Cayetano speak English and Spanish, often in the same sentence, the choice to present only some ideas in his native tongue is interesting. It sometimes requires translation but often does not. Hemingway's lexical choice suggests an emotional more than an intellectual response. Even if we are not familiar with *cabrón*, we can guess from the context that it is meant pejoratively (see 356:10). This sentiment lies at the heart of Hemingway's theory of omission, or iceberg theory, that he articulated on several occasions and that, by the early 1930s, he had started to move away from, according to David Wyatt. In substituting foreign idiomatic expressions for their English equivalents, he still leaves something out, for much gets lost in translation. He does this in his early work, including *The Sun Also Rises* (1926) and *A Farewell to Arms* (1929), but he continues it more deliberately in the 1930s. His fourth novel, *For Whom the Bell Tolls* (1940), involves Spanish characters fighting for a cause tied to the Iberian land and cultural ethos. In this dynamic context, many things are said and felt that depend on an ethnic sensibility. Robert Jordan, the American protagonist, "had lived parts of ten years in Spain before the [Spanish Civil] war," and he knows the people "trusted you on the language, principally. They trusted you on understanding the language completely and speaking it idiomatically" (*FWBT* 135). Though Hemingway seems to be violating the theory of omission by identifying the ways he intends to characterize Jordan as one whom the others can trust, he nevertheless refuses to translate everything Jordan says or hears. Consequently, we empathize with Jordan in ways that we might not logically understand. In using language this way, one could argue that Hemingway did not move away from his iceberg theory so much as he transformed the way he conceived of it.

355:23 **He says it was an accident:** The interpreter's voice is highlighted here, and it clearly indicates his sympathy for the Mexican. He also seems committed to Cayetano's claim not to "know who shot him" because they "shot him in the back" (355:28–29). That he says this "confidently, to the detective" (355:28) suggests his impartiality, but he is wrong since, as the detective protests, all "the bullets" went "in the front" (356:1–2). The interpreter's answer that "Maybe he is spinning around" (356:3) provides comic relief, but it also proffers a visual image of the way information is being spun in this three-way conversation where one party cannot understand the other two. Saying one thing while meaning the opposite is not only ironic, but it also continues to triangulate information. Some characters appear to grasp the truth because they literally speak the same language, while others, like the detective, cannot penetrate that barrier. Hemingway, famous for his omission of dialogue attribution, deftly turns that practice on its head as he literally plays with the game of "he said, she said."

356:10 **Mandarlo al carajo:** Frustrated with the interpreter, the detective turns to Cayetano, hoping to appeal to his sense of justice: "Don't you want the man who shot you to be punished?" (356:7–8). The Mexican's response indicates his resolve. He knows the man won't be punished, at least not in any technical sense. Instead, Cayetano curses that man, sending him to hell. According to Allen Josephs, the phrase uttered by Cayetano literally translates as "send him to the foreskin." In English, this makes no sense. Josephs identifies the phrase as a "Cubanism, though not exclusively. It's an idiom which has no literal translation." Josephs reads it as "go to hell" or "fuck you/him." Cayetano could be cursing the detective *or* the man who shot him.

356:13 **Ask him who shot the Russian:** Turning his attention toward the Russian, the detective seeks answers using a different bait. Cayetano feels sorry for the "Poor Russian" who "give cries when they shoot him" and has been "ever since" (356:14–16), but he refuses to name the assailant. This defiance marks him, for many critics, as a code hero, one who exhibits stoicism and grace even under the direst pressure. Seth Bovey claims that "Hemingway's code was influenced in some way by his knowledge of the West" because it belonged to "cowboys of the Great Plains during the late nineteenth century" (86).

356:20 **You don't have to act like a moving picture:** Growing ever more frustrated, the detective challenges Cayetano by accusing him of pretense. Instead of the unreal and dramatic context of Chicago or Hollywood, the hospital in Hailey, Montana, is quite real. The detective wants to find the shooter, lest he "shoots a woman or a child" (356:22–23). The dramatic irony, unbeknownst to Hemingway when he composed "Gambler," lies in the fact that the story itself became fodder for the Hollywood grist mill in 1960 when A. E. Hotchner oversaw the production of it for television.

356:26 **Listen, amigo:** The tone of Frazer's imperative command mimics that of the detective, but Frazer refers to Cayetano as "amigo," signaling a different rapport between these two men than the one established with the detective. This is the first time Frazer addresses the Mexican directly. His amiability is subtle but important, nonetheless. All the way through Frazer's translation, he makes it clear that he translates for the detective, "He says," etc. In other words, Frazer is not acting as interlocutor or agent, merely a friend, an "amigo."

356:38 **How did you break your leg?:** Cayetano learns why Frazer is in the hospital, from "a fall off a horse" that broke his leg. The real account of Hemingway's car accident was put in a letter to Guy Hickok. Owing to his broken arm and inability to write, Hemingway dictated the letter to his wife, Pauline Pfeiffer. He explains they were

> Coming into Billings . . . en route to Piggott, had a spill brought on by loose gravel and Saturday night drivers and six days later when the doctor operated on my upper arm to fasten the bone together by boring a hole through it and then lashing the end with kangaroo tendon. . . . So now it is all fine except that it is lousy and has hurt like holy hell ever since it happened. . . . any trouble is in the nerves. (*Letters vol. 4*, 427)

Hemingway describes here the details of what happened, but he provides a more subjective account of the pain in *Green Hills of Africa* (1935). He writes that his right arm had been

> broken off short between the elbow and the shoulder, the back of the hand having hung down against my back, the points of the bone having cut up the flesh of the biceps until it finally rotted, swelled, burst, and sloughed off in pus. Alone with the pain in the night in the fifth week of not sleeping I thought suddenly how a bull elk must feel if you break a shoulder and he gets away. (148)

He quickly resolved that, when hunting, he would "shoot as long as [he] could kill cleanly" (*GHOA* 148). Empathy demonstrates the first exercise in perspective, one that the author would develop in "Gambler."

356:45 **then held himself still:** The Mexican identifies Frazer's accident as "bad luck" (356:40), which makes the two men *simpatico* since the gambler believes he has "no luck" (365:34). With the tacit acknowledgment that they both understand what it means to bear "much pain; enough pain" (356:43), Cayetano excuses himself from conversation, so he can hold "himself still." Holding still or "holding tight" provides a core Hemingway image; it bears the metaphysical correlative of grace under pressure. Ann Putnam posits that the story "becomes a study in the art of winning, the choreography of holding steady" (160). As early as *In Our Time,* the idea appears in "A Very Short Story" as the protagonist goes "under the anaesthetic holding tight on to himself so he would not blab anything during the silly, talky time" (*CSS* 107). Variations of it recur such as when Nick sees the trout move in "Big Two-Hearted River": "He watched them holding themselves with their noses into the current." Watching, "Nick's heart tightened as the trout moved" (*CSS* 163, 164).

357:9 **Outside in the corridor:** This second section is separate from the first part of the text in its literal locale. The conversation still involves the identity of Cayetano's assailant, but the victim is absent. Hemingway's signature dialogic ambiguity plays out, requiring the section to be reread to understand who is speaking which line. Though the sergeant claims he wishes he could "talk spick" (357:13), he also admits that he gets no "fun out of asking that spick questions" (357:15–16). His contempt for Cayetano and his language only furthers the divide between the sergeant and the rest of them. The interpreter's attempt to reassure him that he does not need to learn Spanish, given his services, only frustrates the sergeant. This section demonstrates Hemingway's exercises in tone. The detective is frustrated and cynical; Frazer is ironic ("Why don't you learn?" [357:14]); and the interpreter is faithfully literal ("I am a very reliable interpreter" [357:17–18]).

357:29 **Sister Cecilia:** Commonly known as the patron saint of music and musicians. It is reported that, at her wedding, "while the musicians played, Cecilia sang to the Lord in her heart" (Walsh 388). Despite the general association between her and music, *Butler's Lives of the Saints* focuses primarily on her proselytizing and acknowledges her musical quality as an incidental characteristic, certainly ancillary to her life and martyrdom. This proportion is reflected in Hemingway's story as well since it emphasizes Sister Cecilia's staunch faith and music serves a secondary function compared to the existential quality of white noise it resembles as it is emitted from the radio. Hemingway's character exhibits other similarities to her namesake; the real Cecilia was not only "brought up a Christian," but she remained steadfastly devout in the face of defeat, such as being given "in marriage to a young patrician named Valerian," who subsequently, along with his brother, converted, was baptized, and dedicated himself to doing "good works" (Walsh 387). Cecilia's feast day is November 22, which may suggest one practical reason Hemingway chose this particular namesake for Frazer's caregiver. His hospital stay began in November 1930.

Hemingway used Cecilia's name, suggesting an association between it and the role of music in the story, but he modeled his character on Sister Florence, who tended to Hemingway during his hospital stay in Billings. George Monteiro notes that the author "had written a religious story" for her and believes it illustrates an "apologia" for his "nervous acedia in the fifth week of his confinement" at St. Vincent's (134). Subsequently, Monteiro holds it is not to be taken as "a key to the author's own prevailing spiritual state" (134). Refusing to see the nun or Frazer's response to her as caricatural, he posits that "Gambler" is a "skeptic's act of homage to the Virgin Mother" (133). (See entry at 359:41–42.)

The third section that introduces Sister Cecilia focuses entirely on her perspective of the Mexican, which makes her another kind of interpreter for the injured gambler. She brings "news of him" to Frazer "each morning" (357:28–29). In so doing, she makes clear her admiration for the Mexican who experiences tremendous pain yet "doesn't make a sound" (358:2–3). Her devoted act of prayer for an ostensible lost cause signals her true faith; she has compassion for the sinner because she views him separately from his sin. Though her optimism attributes a certain naïvete to her character, she is nonetheless a good Catholic, something Hemingway, though he started identifying as "catholic" in the 1920s, never felt himself to be, even though some of his protagonists strive toward faith (*Letters vol. 3,* 13). Cayetano is presumably Catholic since he promises "to say his prayers" (357:36); however, he refuses confession even though "they thought he could not live" (357:30–31), having developed peritonitis.

Because he has been shot "[t]wice in the abdomen" (355:9), the bullet ruptured his peritoneum, the membrane that envelops the abdominal cavity. Severe pain would normally follow as the organs are exposed to bacteria and become inflamed, and the condition is life-threatening. The mystery surrounding his situation endears the nun to him, for she knows Cayetano is "a bad one" (357:41). The condition of Cayetano's "beautiful" hands (357:31), for instance, leads Sister Cecilia to believe that he is definitely "not a beet worker" (357:43). As Frazer learns later, he makes his living gambling. Clearly, he is the eponymous gambler and she the nun, representing two extremes on the moral spectrum, but neither is dismayed by their respective disappointments, as it becomes clear later that the gambler will continue to hope his luck will change and the nun will persevere to achieve sainthood. The next section of the story introduces the radio, which suggests another perspective of such naïve optimism.

358:6 **a radio:** While the radio was already popular before the Great Depression, by 1939, "eighty-eight percent of all American homes were said to possess one of twenty-five million radios; destitute families valued . . . [them] over refrigerators, furniture, and bedding." The "cultural flagships" of the airwaves "included the New York Philharmonic, Metropolitan Opera, and NBC Symphony on Saturdays, and the *Ford Hour* on Sundays" (Horowitz 398). Serving also as the mouthpiece for Franklin Delano Roosevelt's New Deal optimism, the device epitomized the decade.

The first two sections introduce the reader to Cayetano, followed by Sister Cecilia in the third section; the paragraph that opens the fourth section introduces Frazer's radio. The radio is inoperable for most of the day due to X-Rays and "ore in the ground or something about the mountains" (358:7–8), but at dusk it operates "beautifully" (358:9). The beauty of it, in Frazer's view, lies in its ability to transport him mentally "farther west" (358:10), from Minneapolis to Seattle and back again at "six o'clock" when "you could get the morning revellers" in the Minnesotan city (358:13–14).

Traveling west might recall Archibald MacLeish's poem "American Letter" (1930) in which the speaker describes the sun rising, following it over the "low east" to the "high plains of Wyoming" and finally hitting the "far Pacific" (ll. 56–64). He exclaims that America is "West and the wind blowing" (l. 37); it is "a shining thing in the mind" (l. 40). Hemingway had dedicated *Winner Take Nothing* to MacLeish, and the intertextual resonance here emphasizes the displacement felt acutely by the speaker in MacLeish's poem who senses "it is a strange thing to be an American" (l. 27) and wonders how "a wise man [can] have two countries" (l. 23). Above all, he is alone, for, in America, people do not "live together in small things" (l. 75). Rather, it is "one man and another and wide" (l. 79). Frazer, similarly dislocated, lies in a hospital bed, amid others who are broken and alone in their beds, pining for a view, whether a physical one granted by the window or a figurative one sketched by the sequence of radio stations. That Frazer forges connections with the nun and the gambler indicates the resolve among some hospital patients to "live" together or risk living "only as shadows," as MacLeish's speaker knows he must learn to do (l. 91).

358:26–27 **This does not sound so funny now but it was very funny then:** Hemingway's characteristic irony depicts a vignette, that of Frazer getting "knocked out by the leaded base of the lamp hitting the top of his head. It seemed the antithesis of healing" (358:30–31). The humor of the situation, according to Frazer, lies in the attending doctor's attempt to direct everyone's attention out the window, toward the pheasants. Instead of a beautiful and natural tableau, Frazer gets hit in the head "just as in a comic section" (358:29–30). The other level of irony lies in the fact that Frazer refers to the lamp as a reading light, a device that should allow him to see things more clearly but instead renders him unconscious. The resulting laughter prompts the narrator to conclude, "Everything is much simpler in a hospital, including the jokes" (358:33–34).

358:36 **Dawson mountains:** This paragraph that focuses on the scenery extends the previous introduction of the importance of a view and point of view. Dawson County, located in the easternmost part of Montana, contains at least thirteen named mountains. However, it is over two hundred miles from Billings in Yellowstone County where Hemingway recovered from his car accident at St. Vincent's Hospital. Both counties produce sugar beets, owing to their proximity to the Yellowstone River, but Yellowstone County yields several tons more, according to recent agricultural data and crop profiles (Mikkelson and Petroff). Although some readers believe that Hemingway set the story in fictional Hailey in recognition of his friend Ezra Pound's birthplace of Hailey, Idaho, there is no evidence for this claim. More likely, he substituted Hailey for Billings since Yellowstone County, though taking up a slightly larger geographical area of 2,600 square miles, had over 30,000 citizens in 1930. The larger size of Billings makes it a more probable place for someone, as the detective suspects Cayetano of doing, to try to be a "gangster" and "act like a moving picture" (356:19–20) and would seem to negate Frazer's sense of isolation and desire for the outside world. Regardless, the prevalence of mountains in Montana would provide plenty of natural beauty for Frazer to ponder, no matter where he is.

358:37 **the two views:** From his hospital bed, Frazer has two views, one of the Dawson mountains, which look quite real with "winter snow on them" (358:37) and the other of "the town, with a little smoke above it" (358:35–36). More philosophically, Frazer comments on the "great value" of a view (358:44), that it "becomes very important and you would not change it, not even by a different angle" (358:44–359:1), so long as it is from "a room the temperature of which you control" (358:40). Frazer depends on the view from his room to reconcile with his current state as a writer who cannot write and whose nerves had "become tricky" (363:31). Maintaining some control over the conditions of the viewing adds an invaluable measure to it.

The paragraph that opens this fourth section is bookended by prepositional phrases that foreground setting; they suggest its function as an integral component of Frazer's state of mind. Moreover, their rhythm and cadence—"In that hospital . . . early in the morning" (358:6–21)—sound uncannily similar to the way Hemingway describes setting at the end of "Indian Camp," where Nick Adams "[i]n the early morning . . . sitting in the stern of the boat . . . felt quite sure that he would never die" (*CSS* 70). Setting, and its power to regulate and modulate emotion, is a powerful character in its own right throughout Hemingway's work.

359:3 **The best tunes they had that winter:** Frazer likens the value of his vista to the figurative view afforded by songs on the radio. The internal perspective they offer reflects the attitudes, acceptances, and allowances of the early 1930s. Frazer mentions four songs. His familiarity with them depicts a certain landscape, "Just as" his window does (359:1). For him, the "best tunes. . . . that winter were 'Sing Something Simple,' 'Singsong Girl,' and 'Little White Lies.' No other tunes were as satisfactory" (359:3–5). That winter would have been the time of Hemingway's stay in St. Vincent's, from 1 November through 21 December 1930 (*Letters vol. 4*, lxxx), and all the songs Frazer mentions are from 1930, except for "Sing Song Girl," recorded in January 1931, indicating that the music Frazer listens to likely provided the soundtrack for Hemingway's convalescence. Bruce Morton contends that the songs Frazer mentions here all contain lyrics that describe a "flirtatious hypocrisy which reveals Frazer's cynical response to Sister Cecilia and her faith" (82) and, arguably, suggest a kind of misogyny directed at her. Although Morton angles the textual evidence to support this view, it does not bear scrutiny in the overall context. Frazer enjoys the nun's company, and there is more evidence demonstrating this fact than there is undermining it.

359:3–4 **"Sing Something Simple":** written by Herman Hupfeld in 1930 and recorded by several performers, including The Revelers, the name of which recalls Frazer's imaginative picture of the "morning revellers in Minneapolis" (358:13–14). The song focuses its lyrics on the simplicity of singing nonsense: "the words are silly, the song is simple," so much so that a "[d]unce can memorize the thing."

359:4 **"Singsong Girl":** Recorded by Ben Pollack and His Orchestra on 21 January 1931, the song describes the superficial affection a man has for a love interest from China. Referring to her as his "Little Yella Cinderella," he asks her to entertain him by singing. Altogether, the three named songs describe silliness, lies, and entertainment, the very illusions sought by a listening public eager to remedy the harsh reality of American life in the early 1930s. That the singer wants to be entertained by a "Yella Cinderella" connotes the pronounced racial and class stratification in America during this time. A Cinderella figure is one who works for free, almost an indentured servant, and her skin color, yellow, recalls the immigration quotas in place for Chinese laborers. Her racial difference also points to the difficult labor conditions of another ethnic group in this story, the Mexican beet workers who were exempted from the immigration quotas, in large part because of the sugar beet industry that relied on their cheap labor for production. Chinese laborers, however, had been banned from entering the United States since at least 1882, when the Chinese Exclusion Act was passed. Before that, the Page Act of 1875 banned Chinese women from entering the country for fear that they would come here to work as prostitutes. "Sing Song Girl" evokes a type of male fantasy that is built on exploitation and racial stereotype. This is not to suggest that the tune reflects Frazer's fantasy but, instead, that of a public eager for palliation.

359:4 **"Little White Lies":** Walter Donaldson, who composed the music for "My Blue Heaven" and "How Ya Going to Keep 'Em Down on the Farm?," wrote "Little White Lies," which was recorded on 16 September 1930 by Seger Ellis; its lyrics highlight the "[d]evil in [the] heart" of a lover, whose deceptions are hidden by the cover of "those lips" and "those eyes." The devil may be the entertainment itself that distracts listeners or provides white noise to keep them from thinking at all.

359:5 **"Betty Co-ed":** Frazer admits that "Betty Co-ed" was "a good tune too, but the parody of the words which came unavoidably into Mr. Frazer's mind, grew so steadily and increasingly obscene that there being no one to appreciate it, he finally abandoned it and let the song go back to football" (359:5–9). It was a 1930 hit sung by Rudy Vallée (Morton 81n) that celebrates the prototypical college girl who cheers on her favorite NCAA team, whether Yale or Harvard or Purdue. Despite the affectionate attention from "every college boy," she loves the singer. Bruce Morton connects the last lines of this song with what he calls Sister Cecilia's "coy hypocrisy": "She did the same at old Notre Dame. Her line is good for years: Roguish eyes, telling lies, breathing sighs. Betty Co-ed" (qtd. in Morton 82). Morton contends that this song particularly, coupled with the nun's "retreat to the chapel in order to pray for a Notre Dame victory," emphasizes Frazer's "ironically relevant attitude toward Sister Cecilia and the religious faith which she represents" (81–82). Given a larger context, this is untrue, for Frazer likes Sister Cecilia, whose namesake, as Morton points out, is the patron saint of music.

Going "back to football" (359:8–9) as Frazer is wont to do after parodying "Betty Co-ed," figuratively suggests that the writer, and Sister Cecilia, longs for a narrative with a clearer definition of triumph and defeat. Similar to the one-dimensional entertainment provided by silly songs, American football provides a simple context within which one finds a clear winner and loser on a strategic "battlefield." Compared to the slow strategy of baseball, for example, the emotional experience of listening to a football game proffers immediate gratification in terms of emotional catharsis.

359:17 **necessary to turn off the radio:** The fifth section begins by bringing the narrative back into the present time of the story, with the entrance of Sister Cecilia and the exit of the radio as they begin to use the X-Ray equipment in the hospital. The competing frequencies prove too much, and the device stops working. They discuss Cayetano, and the nun expresses disdain for "all those Mexicans" (359:25) who haven't come to see him; she believes he will die alone.

359:27 **the game this afternoon:** Frazer invites Sister Cecilia to listen to a football game with him. She knows nothing about the sport, unlike baseball, which she understands well. The match he refers to took place on 6 December 1930, and "in a clash of undefeated teams, slight underdog Notre Dame crushed Southern California 27-0 to win a third national championship for coach Knute Rockne" (Murolo 53). The nun declines Frazer's request seven times, "No. No. No. No. No. No. No" (360:25) and offers her prayers instead. Based on the outcome of the actual game, they appear to have worked, and Cecilia triumphantly declares the morning after the game that she knew "they couldn't beat Our Lady" (360:33).

359:32 **The world series:** Sister Cecilia here refers to the 1930 World Series between the Philadelphia Athletics and the Saint Louis Cardinals. She prayed often during the game, and the excitement of it "nearly finished" her (359:32). Frederick L. Murolo identifies the game's outcome, the Athletics beating the Cardinals for their "second consecutive championship," as evidence that the nun's prayers were answered. He tempers this conclusion, however, by stating that this is the case from *her* perspective. He also illustrates that not *all* her prayers were answered, for despite her "pleas," Bing Miller "struck out . . . with the bases loaded in game three" (52). Overall, Murolo seeks to demonstrate that the nun's faith is not so naïve as most critics believe it to be, citing the Athletics' victory, the win of "Our Lady" (359:40), Notre Dame, and the subsequent recovery of Cayetano to conclude that a nun "who goes three for four" comes close to "affirming the power of prayer" (53), which provides a good balance to the perceived pessimism of the story.

359:41–42 **I wish you'd write something sometime for Our Lady:** Before praying for the Notre Dame football game in the fifth section of the story, Sister Cecilia makes this request of Frazer. Although Hemingway composed "Gambler" for Sister Florence, Frazer finds it a difficult challenge to accept, probably because he lacks his caregiver's optimism. Despite Sister Cecilia's disappointments, she persists in her devotion to the Holy Mother and in praying and caring for the wounded.

360:33–34 **Cayetano's better too:** Sister Cecilia makes the connection between Notre Dame's victory and Cayetano's progress. She says that, now, he is "much better" (360:34). Her prayers have been answered. We learn that, frustrated by the lack of visitors for the Mexican, the nun visited the Police Headquarters and asked that "some Mexicans" be sent up to Cayetano (360:38). She believes he will continue to improve once he knows that he is "not forgotten by his own people" (360:36). This idea of one's people runs through *Winner Take Nothing*, especially in its recurring thematic engagement with displacement and community. The three Mexicans who come to visit reappear in subsequent sections.

361:6 **It is from Red Lodge:** After asking to be seated, the three Mexicans enjoy a drink with Frazer. He offers them "the bottle . . . from Red Lodge" (361:5–6), which his visitors agree is "the best . . . Much better than that of Big Timber" (361:7–8). Red Lodge, Montana, was a coal mining town that, as a result of the Great Depression, had turned to bootlegging to compensate for lost revenue. The smaller town of Big Timber, Montana, is located about eighty-five miles northwest of Red Lodge and along the Northern Pacific Railroad. A fire in 1908 destroyed much of the town, suggesting that by 1932 Red Lodge may have indeed been better able to produce illegal liquor. They all drink except "the thin one" who claims that alcohol "mounts to [his] head" (361:3). Instead of drinking, he asks Frazer about the radio, how many tubes it has, and how much it cost. Frazer does not know its price since it "is rented" (361:14). This lack of possession suggests that the device is perhaps more incidental than some readers have wanted to admit. It also indicates that he is not as tethered to it as he might otherwise be to a personal possession.

361:36 **He is a card-player:** When the Mexicans explain Cayetano's apparent skill as a cardplayer, Frazer seems impressed, for Cayetano has won large sums of money from his opponents, including the visitors. One lost "one hundred and eighty dollars" (361:39–40), and the other parted with "two hundred and eleven dollars" (361:42). The fat one "never played with him" (361:44). Frazer suggests that Cayetano is "very rich" (361:45), but the visitors clarify that he is "poorer than" they are, with only "the shirt on his back" (362:1–2), which, Frazer jokes, as a result of the bullet holes, is "of little value" (362:3). For all his skill, Cayetano has no material possessions; he is poor and may die. Furthermore, the assailant who shot him had clearly lost a sum of money as he was not a cardplayer but "a beet worker" (362:7). Following his actions, he "had to leave town" (362:7). Both men are displaced by circumstances of their own doing. The scenario is entirely likely, given the segregated communities of Mexicans who came to work for the sugar beet companies in the Yellowstone Valley. There was often crime among them since, owing to pronounced racism, they rarely mingled with the non-Mexican denizens of Billings.

362:8–9 **He was the best guitar player ever in this town:** The dialogue shifts now to music, a primary concern in the story, given the title. The one who shot Cayetano was apparently a gifted musician. The adverb *ever* implies that the men, including Cayetano, have been in the town a long time and are not merely visitors. This is also plausible since many Mexicans who were transported to work for companies like Great Western Sugar stayed on in urban areas where they could find work that would last until the next sugar beet season began. Although Cayetano's assailant was the last of the great guitarists, there remains "an accordion player who is worth something" (362:14), according to the thin Mexican. After confirming that Frazer likes music, the Mexicans vow to "come one night with music" (362:19), guessing that the nun "would allow it" because she seems (362:19–20), at least to one of them, "very amiable" (362:20). Frazer agrees, believing the sister would permit it if Cayetano was "able to hear it" (362:21).

362:34 **I thought marijuana was the opium of the poor:** Frazer's response to the thin Mexican's Marxist axiom is a veiled cultural stereotype. By the early 1930s, marijuana use among whites had "been increasing" for "more than a decade" (Johnson 331), leading some to see it as a viable substitute for alcohol during Prohibition (Hay). Nevertheless, many Americans associated it not only with the poor but particularly with Mexicans and African Americans. The American jazz song "Reefer Man" was written in 1932 by J. Russel Robinson and first recorded by African American entertainer Cab Calloway and his orchestra for the 1933 film *International House*. Racist fears, along with the propaganda film *Reefer Madness* (1936), helped stigmatize the drug. In the context of Frazer's conversation, his statement connects to the history of Mexican beet workers in the American West.

After the Mexican Revolution began in 1910, the smokable form of the drug was brought into the country via Texas by Mexicans escaping violence; in 1914, El Paso became the first city to have an ordinance outlawing it (Hay). Many immigrants ended up as beet workers in Montana. In some ways, Frazer is literally correct that "marijuana is the opium of the poor," for the *betabeleros,* Mexican and Mexican American beet workers, used it as others might use opium. This may explain why one of the Mexicans asks him if he has ever smoked "opium" (362:35). In the "landscape of Western agriculture," which was comprised largely of sugar beet farms, many Mexicans and Mexican Americans "planted a patchwork of illicit marijuana, selling and using it to offset some of the hardships imposed on them by the exploitative nature of commercial farming" (Johnson 324). This practice was widespread enough to prompt companies to act. The *Sanders County Independent Ledger* reports in October 1931 that, in the following year, growers would add a clause to laborers' contracts "specifying that the Mexican forfeits his contract money should marijuana be found growing on land contracted by him" ("Mexican 'Dope' Weed Is Found"). Nick Johnson maintains that the drug was grown, sold, and used to alleviate two chronic problems replete in the *betabeleros* community: the incredibly painful physical conditions that resulted from their "hard labor" and "poverty" (332).

As a literal and figurative opium, marijuana was an integral part of the Mexican farming community that built the American West. That Frazer issues this statement does not reflect his racism; rather, it fits in with the overall theme of the story that opiates are everywhere, used by almost everyone, and include ethnic stereotyping.

362:29 **acolyte:** One who assists the celebrant in Mass. More than just a member of a congregation, the acolyte would be akin to a deacon, one who is well versed in the ritual and order of the Mass and its significance. Going from acolyte to apostate, the thin Mexican now "distrust[s] all priests, monks, and sisters" (362:27). He questions Frazer about the nun, asking if she is "a little crazy" (362:22). Given his political leanings, it is no surprise that he "is very strong against religion" (362:40), that he "believe[s] in nothing" (362:29). Frazer anticipates this, of course, and in response to questions about the nun's sanity, he replies sincerely that she "is a fine woman of great intelligence and sympathy" (362:25-26). Some critics, such as Bruce Morton, read Frazer's response to the Mexican's question as ironic, but Frazer's tone is sincere. He likes Sister Cecilia, and there is no consistent evidence in the story that he dislikes or distrusts her. In fact, the thin Mexican is an antagonist here, one with whom Frazer does not agree about many things. Frazer's tone in response to the thin Mexican's claim of believing in nothing *is* ironic. When the latter insists he does not go to Mass, Frazer ironically asks, "Why? Does it mount to your head?" (362:31). His opponent does not detect the irony, for he insists on correcting Frazer, stating that it is alcohol, not religion, that mounts to his head. The effects of the former are incidental and inconvenient. The philosophical weight of the latter is quite grave: he believes religion "is the opium of the poor" (362:32-33) and that religion "is a vice" (362:38). His small companion seems to apologize for his friend's rancor by saying that he is "very strong against religion" (362:40). Frazer's response that "[i]t is necessary to be very strong against something" is said "politely" (362:41-42). Here, "politely" emphatically signals Frazer's disagreement with his adversary. He agrees with being "strong against something" only to be polite (362:41), and his manners have guided the entire exchange so far, from offering them a drink to asking them about their presumed friend, Cayetano to suggesting they come back to play music. Moreover, the thin Mexican's condescending statement that he respects "those who have faith even though they are ignorant" (362:43) only exacerbates his own ignorance of the complexities of faith, of the people around him, and of the world in which he lives where there are all kinds of "opiums of the poor," including myopic philosophical beliefs.

363:5 *copita:* Spanish diminutive for "glass," "cup," or "shot." Frazer is offering the men a small glass or shot of Red Lodge liquor. They say no, partly because they feel they are "robbing" (363:7) Frazer of his booze and, for the thin Mexican, because it would go to his head. Just before leaving, the big Mexican extends the same kind of courtesy by asking Frazer if they can bring him anything when they return. Even though *copita* is italicized in this passage, indicating semiotic difference from the rest of their exchange, Frazer seems to be speaking Spanish, making them comfortable despite personal differences, particularly in the case of the thin Mexican.

363:16 **Denver Post:** This periodical has been in circulation since 1892. Its founding by Democratic supporters of Grover Cleveland meant that it assumed a politicized stance. This bias may have been one reason the paper ceased production in 1893. Fundraising campaigns revived the paper two years later, and its new iteration depended on sensationalism and exaggeration, otherwise known in the 1890s as yellow journalism, to engage a wide audience. Frazer may subtly be acknowledging the paper's lack of credibility when he admits he "could see Denver from the *Denver Post*" but then "correct the picture from *The Rocky Mountain News*" (363:15–16).

363:16 **The Rocky Mountain News:** Now defunct, this newspaper, established in 1859, was the primary rival of the *Denver Post.* At the end of the nineteenth century, it appeared to be more concerned with fighting crime in the Denver area than with resorting to yellow journalism, as did the *Denver Post,* to increase its audience. By the 1920s, both papers relied on promotions and giveaways to boost their sales.

363:28 **Seattle, Washington:** The paragraph that ends section five, perhaps the longest of the story and falling right in the middle of it, provides some metacommentary on the exchange Frazer just experienced. Seattle had very "wet" tastes and resisted Prohibition and the "vice law" ordinances in that city. In fact, "war on vice" arrests "were widespread" (Samuels). Moreover, the city was a haven for alcohol smugglers because of its "proximity to Canada and long coastline amenable to smuggling" (Samuels). The "war on vice, liquor, and gambling was declared on October 16, 1932 and resulted in 32 publicized arrests within the first week" (Samuels). Frazer might have grown "very fond of Seattle" (363:28) for its penchant for resistance and revolution, for its love of vice and refusal to surrender it willingly. This is exactly the type of environment the thin Mexican despises since it is full of opiates.

However, the reference to Seattle was changed from Portland in the original story published in *Scribner's Magazine.* Edward Stone makes the point that, because

Frazer imagines himself driving in a taxi cab *from* Seattle, after the radio stations sign off, *to* "the roadhouse on the Canadian side where he followed the course of parties by the musical selections they phoned for" (363:23–24), then that drive must be a reasonable distance (378). Changing the city to Seattle means traveling only about a hundred miles, certainly manageable for a devoted debauchee.

363:29 **but it was not good:** The sixth section of the story is comparatively short and develops thematic tension by emphasizing binary elements of Frazer's environment. The Mexicans came with beer, but "it was not good"; though Frazer saw them, he did not "feel like talking" (363:30), and after their departure, he knew "they would not come again" (363:31). Frazer's resignation is shaped by his "bad" nerves (363:32), which, after five weeks, "had become tricky" (363:31). His reference to the "same experiment" (363:34), along with what he had "been through . . . before" (363:35), initially seems unclear. Marion Montgomery has seized on this uncertainty as the primary weakness of the story. She claims Sister Cecilia has "the dream of sainthood as an opium to help her bear the drudgery of her devotion; Cayetano, the gambler, has his dream of money . . . to help him bear the misfortunes of chance. But Mr. Frazer—the writer (?), bronco-buster (?), revolutionary (?)—has whiskey and radio to help him bear what pain?" (210). Edward Stone identifies Frazer's relative pronoun *this* as "the Nothingness that underlies pain, failure, and disillusionment alike" (380). Given the recurring thematic treatment of metaphysical pain in Hemingway's work, Stone's suggestion seems more plausible than Montgomery's, which implies a "problem" with the story, as she puts it in the title of her essay. Frazer has experienced this type of, in Hemingway's words, "discouragement" before (*SL* 418); the "only thing which was new to him was the radio" (363:35–36). Later, Cayetano claims he would use the radio to camouflage the noise of his pain, whereas Frazer uses it to silence the noise inside his head. He was "learning to listen to it without thinking" (363:37–38), arguably using it to avoid thinking at all. Choosing the radio as ambient noise might signal Frazer's resignation, a subtle extension of the mood that opens the paragraph. He has been through pain and disappointment. The radio is new only in its capacity to palliate the pain by distracting him.

363:41 **the mail:** Frazer's enthusiastic response to Sister Cecilia grows from his observation that she is "very handsome" (363:40), but it also relates to the mail she brings, which is "more important" (363:42). It connects him to "a different world" (363:42), the one outside the hospital. Ann Putnam sees the story as primarily concerned with the dichotomy between community and isolation; that separation is developed in degrees with the illustration of the ward compared to Frazer's private room and, on a bigger scale, with the news from "a different world" and the happenings of his immediate, microcosmic one. But Frazer's mail holds nothing "of any interest" (363:43), possibly because it is the same place that produces the songs he hears on the radio, tunes that entertain by depicting silliness. He can modify the conditions of his view from inside his room, whereas the outside world presents itself unmediated in the mail he reads.

364:1 **You look *so* much better:** The focus on how they look and feel here further underscores the importance of perspective and the tension between appearances and the stark reality they may hide. The nun's admission of desiring sainthood strikes Frazer. Such personal and, perhaps, egotistical desire directly opposes the tenet of humility central to Catholic faith. Frazer is only "a little taken aback" (364:4), however. The measure of his surprise matters, because contrary to the view of many readers and critics, Frazer never rejects the nun or her faith. Morton contends that "Sister Cecilia is, for Frazer, a burlesque of her saintly namesake" (85), but his genuine interest in seeing her suggests otherwise.

364:5 **A saint:** In Catholic discourse, *saint* refers to both the faithfully departed in heaven and to those formally canonized by the Church. All Saints Day, 1 November, is a Holy Day of Obligation that typically focuses on those whom the Church has beatified, even though, according to catechetical teaching, those who reach heaven are already saints. We cannot know who actually comprises that group, but some are formally recognized by the Church according to certain criteria that require, among other things, miracles performed during and after the person's life on earth; such events indicate divine presence and assistance through that individual. Alternately, martyrdom provides another path. For instance, the historical Saint Cecilia performed no miracles but was executed for her faith. In rare cases, such as that of Mother Teresa, one can be called a saint while still living if her life is deemed a holy one. In Hemingway's story, Sister Cecilia lives a devout life and will likely reach heaven, which may explain why Frazer gives her pretty good odds at "three to one to be a saint" (364:26). Beyond that, her emphatic desire probably indicates her will to serve others, and healing Cayetano through perpetual prayer may be her chance to demonstrate God's grace through miraculous intervention.

Becoming a saint has been the nun's dream since childhood. Like any other lifelong desire, hers involved a certain amount of repudiation of the world around her, a solitary journey into the convent, and the promise of fulfillment. Despite not having gotten what she wanted after she "renounced the world" (364:7), she continues to believe sainthood remains a possibility. Though her personal aim seems fantastic compared to the inmates of the hospital, it is not so different from that of most people: seize on a goal, identify a course of action, make sacrifices, achieve momentary promise of triumph only to discover disappointment, and be faced with the choice to capitulate to despair or recover. Although the nun's social position may make her life's ambitions seem unique, they are probably no different from Frazer's, for a writer must face the same course of action and threat of disappointment for a similarly elusive goal. Hemingway put it in starker terms during his Nobel Prize acceptance speech: a writer, if any good, "must face eternity, or the lack of it, each day" ("Banquet Speech").

Marking sainthood as an ambition seems ironic, for it defies the requisite humility to become one. Many of the most renowned saints, such as Mother Teresa, rejected the title, claiming their own doubt a barrier to such an honor. Pride may be Sister Cecilia's sin, but her desire recalls Hemingway's original title for the story, "Three Ambitions" (Smith 289).

364:15 **Everybody gets what they want:** Frazer may recognize an affinity with Sister Cecilia, and his efforts to encourage her are real, not merely an attempt to placate her. Frazer's gibe here demonstrates what he and Frederic Henry ultimately realize: "You never got away with anything" (*FTA* 320). Henry articulates this worldview during the complications of his wife's childbirth. He says, "They threw you in and told you the rules and the first time they caught you off base they killed you" (327). *Their* punitive actions reach beyond those who transgress "the rules," however; "stay around and they would kill you" too. What Henry understands is the same "experiment" that Frazer experiences (363:34); it is what he has "been through . . . before" (363:35): suffering is an integral component of existence.

Sister Cecilia likely shares this knowledge of inevitable and indiscriminate suffering, but she palliates it with an unabashed optimism, partly demonstrated by her love of sports. Helping her cope is the fact that her prayers *do* get answered, as Frederick Murolo points out: "She prays avidly for her favorite teams in two sporting events of 1930" (52; see also 359:28 and 359:33). Murolo contends her prayers are heard for a third time when Cayetano recovers. If the nerve in his leg regenerates entirely, perhaps she can claim the miracle as her own. This view provides an alternative to the critical supposition that Frazer rejects the nun's faith.

364:29 **How's your friend Cayetano?:** From discussing her chances of sainthood, Frazer shifts the conversation to Cayetano. Similar to Nick Adams's frequent habit of deflecting by saying "nothing" or Jake Barnes asking Brett if they should "have another Martini" (*SAR* 249), this abrupt shift in tone and subject matter tends to occur in Hemingway's work when characters realize they are at an impasse, that there is nothing more to say, or that they do not agree with what is being said. Frazer's worldview presupposes that the nun's chances of sainthood are quite low, not because she is at fault but as a result of the "game," which is rigged. If biography is any indication, Hemingway admitted as a Catholic that he thought it a good rule "they make a definite time limit before we can become Saints." It seemed "damned" important "to give people an impartial square deal in criticism than to try and get them canonized here on earth" (*Letters vol. 3*, 13). The process for becoming a saint typically cannot commence until five years after a person's death. In an ideal world, that "square deal" would counter a fixed game any day.

Frazer's discussion with the nun shifts the focus to Cayetano, and he learns that the gambler is paralyzed because "[o]ne of the bullets hit the big nerve that goes down through his thigh" (364:30–31). Frazer's hope that the nerve may regenerate is belied by his cynicism about things turning out for the best. What "they always tell" you seems to be untrue (364:15–16); it is only, as David Bourne knows years later in *The Garden of Eden,* "the stuff they feed the troops" (230). However, if Sister Cecilia is successful, if she can perform the requisite miracle for sainthood, then perhaps her prayers can regenerate the nerve completely. The nun asks Frazer to see Cayetano, but he likely does not want to buck the gambler up any more than he himself wanted to be bucked up by Sister Cecilia. She brings him in regardless.

364:40 *Hola, amigo! Qué tal?:* [Hello, friend! How are things?] At the nun's request, Cayetano is wheeled in to see Frazer. They converse in Spanish, signaled by the gambler's salutation. Frazer's response is presumably given in Spanish even though it appears in English: "As you see . . . And thou?" (364:41). The English archaic form of the nominative second-person pronoun indicates his speaking in Spanish, with *thou* representing his use of the formal Spanish pronoun *usted* which lacks a modern English equivalent. After the men discuss Cayetano's paralytic leg, Frazer offers encouragement by saying that "the nerve can regenerate" (364:43). Cayetano's reply is similar to Frazer's earlier claim that "Everybody gets what they want" (364:15). Both men recognize the empty promise of such things and the sure disappointment that comes from believing in them too readily. They commiserate. That Sister Cecilia observes their exchange "happily" (365:4) signals her contentment and willingness to occupy a space outside their private world marked by shared language and experience.

365:13 *Hombre, sí:* Literally, "Man, yes," but the colloquial translation in this context might more aptly be "for real." Inquiring about the other's pain, Cayetano tells Frazer that, if he "had a private room and a radio," he would be "crying and yelling all night long" (365:10–11). Frazer doubts it because, thus far, the Mexican has dealt with his discomfort stoically. Not only does Cayetano insist "yes, for real," but he believes such expression is "very healthy" (365:13). The men continue to speak in Spanish, even though Cayetano gives some phrases in English, which he speaks, "but badly" by his own admission; he understands "it all right" (356:38). Frazer's fluency in Spanish is as important here as it was in the opening of the story, for it allows him to forge a connection that would otherwise be difficult or impossible; some things inevitably get lost in translation. More than experiencing similar discomfort, the men can express it to each other.

365:31 **I am a poor idealist. I am the victim of illusions:** Cayetano's admission means he perpetuates his condition willingly, for it likely provides the only bulwark against an indifferent and cruel world. He is not, therefore, a "victim" but a willing participant. The gambler, like the nun, is an optimist who hopes that, if he lives long enough, "the luck will change" (366:4). Regardless of his idealism, he realizes the implacability of his situation; he has "no luck" (365:34). The psychological position is untenable, for how can one be both victim and participant in one's own delusions? It proves safer to choose one or the other side.

365:36 **I am completely without luck:** Cayetano further reiterates the phenomenon of his bad luck, illustrated by the accident that lands him in the hospital. The *cabrón,* the bastard, who shot him "could not hit a horse if he were holding the stirrup" (365:40). Cayetano's injury demonstrates the indiscriminate nature of suffering, as does Frazer's and that of the rest of the inmates of the hospital.

365:42 **The paper was mistaken:** This detail seems incidental but, in the larger scheme of the story, emphasizes the notion of narrative perspective. "Gambler" opens by implicitly codifying the objective truth of the paper, which provides many details about the event we do not witness, the assault on Cayetano and the Russian. We might believe what we are told because that "was what the paper said" (355:14–15), but we then learn that it was false.

365:44–45 **With my luck, if I carried a gun I would be hanged ten times a year:** The gambler's resolve not to carry a weapon signals his firm belief that he will continue to have bad luck. The hyperbolic claim provides humor, and, in the context of Hemingway's story, his optimism for eventual good fortune signals the positive affirmation of his fate's course. Though he always loses, and will logically continue to do so, Cayetano hopes that living long enough will change his luck, and then he will "be rich" (366:5).

366:18 **You are a philosopher:** The final passage in the penultimate section of the story highlights the philosophy of confronting pain, using Cayetano's injury and willingness to endure despite it as a metaphor. Frazer calls his friend "a philosopher" (366:18), to which Cayetano replies that he is only a "gambler of the small towns" (366:19). The juxtaposition underlines one of Hemingway's recurring credos, that knowledge is different from education and that it is hard earned from experience, not books. The two men finally discuss their pain; Frazer admits he is not tired from talking, despite his initial reluctance to speak with Cayetano in the beginning of the section; and Cayetano also admits he is not fatigued. When asked about his leg, the gambler appears not to be troubled by its paralysis because he has "no great use" for it (366:26). He can still "circulate" (366:27) going to "[o]ne small town, then another, another, then a big town, then start over again" (366:19–20). Like Frazer, he had been "through this all before" (363:35); this time, Cayetano must try to experiment without the leg. When the gambler asks Frazer about his pain, the writer replies, "It will not last, certainly" (366:30). He remains certain that it will pass, but he also knows it will return, which is why he can dismiss it as "of no importance" (366:30). He presents a paradox; how he confronts his pain is everything, the way forward. He cannot grant it more weight than it deserves, however, or it will have defeated him. This recalls Dr. Adams's statement to young Nick Adams in "Indian Camp" when the doctor performs a Caesarean on an Indian woman without anesthetic; her screams bother Nick, but his father does not hear them because "they are not important" (*CSS* 68). Allowing the screams to bother him would interfere with his ability to maintain a necessary clinical distance from which he can perform his duty. There is always pain. As such, there is no conquering it, only confronting it and hoping that "it passes quickly" (366:31).

366:33 **That night the Mexicans played:** This paragraph opens the ninth and final section of the story. The aural musicality of this passage, along with the fact that they are playing music described as "cheerful" (366:34), underlines the notion of repetition, of having "been through this all before" (363:35). As such, it provides a fitting recapitulation to the thematic focus on the cyclical nature of pain, but, instead of Frazer's pain, we learn about the pain of the others in the hospital. The musicality of the opening sentence of this final section establishes a certain aural expectation based on repetition: "That night the Mexicans played the accordion and other instruments in the ward and it was cheerful and the noise of the inhalations and exhalations of the accordion, and of the bells, the traps, and the drum came down the corridor" (366:33–36). The sounds of words and phrases here mimic the function of the instrument they describe, so the accordion made "the noise of the inhalations and exhalations" (366:34–35). These thirteen syllables contain repeated unstressed and stressed syllables that mimic the long draw of the instrument as it expands and contracts. Alternately, the "bells, the traps, and the drum" are given just one syllable in quick succession (366:35), suggesting their rhythmic function in the ensemble. The repeated use of the conjunction *and* denotes a rhythmic volition that suggests the sequence and cadence of syllables will continue.

The subsequent sentences all start nearly the same way and treat similar material, suggesting a type of fugue. Wirt Williams maintains that "Gambler" illustrates the author's "transference of fugal form to fiction," which is to say that Hemingway treats a singular melody, pain, in "three character keys" that are "distinct and highly formalized" (101). *Fugues,* however, have traditionally been considered didactic and academic, whereas *variations* are supposed to be more lighthearted. Their entertaining quality grew from the demonstration of "variety that could be achieved in embellishing a basic idea" (Burkholder, Grout, Palisca 274). The humor in the story offers such embellishment (Camastra 101).

Relying on the repetition indicative of both fugue and variation, the roll call of hospital patients implies circularity, especially through its aural qualities. We learn that "there was a rodeo rider" (366:36) and "[t]here was a carpenter" (366:40) and "[t]here was a boy" (366:43), and "[t]here was Cayetano Ruiz" (366:44–45), and that the "Mexicans were having a good time" (367:2–3)—so good, in fact, that they "came twice more to play at night of their own accord" (367:5). The repeated expletive phrase "there was" suggests that there will always be, in perpetuity, those the world breaks who try afterward to recover despite the possibility that they will be broken again.

367:9 **Cucaracha:** On this final night that the Mexicans visit the hospital, they play "noisy, bad music," and Frazer "could not keep from thinking" (367:7). He asks the musicians to play "La Cucaracha." The Spanish folk song is centuries old, but different verse lyrics, added over time, indicate various social and political contexts. For example, the song became very popular during the Mexican Revolution in the early part of the twentieth century when its politicized words articulated the grievances of both sides, of those who fought with Pancho Villa and those who sided with Victoriano Huerta. One such iteration refers to marijuana and presumably describes Huerta, Mexico's dictator who famously loved it and alcohol: "The cockroach, the cockroach / can't walk anymore / because it doesn't have, because it's lacking / marijuana to smoke." The song recalls Frazer's earlier reference to the cultural stereotype that marijuana was used only by communities of color and the contemporaneous belief that savage and sexual violence typically ensued from its use.

The indeterminate nature of the song's origins speaks to a bigger theme in Hemingway's story: the power of repetition, of having been through "this all before" (363:35). Most folk songs rely on repetition as a mnemonic device, for the more times a lyric is sung, the easier it is to memorize. Therefore, the shape of the melody is repetitive. Oral cultures ensured the life of their stories the same way, through circularity, not linearity. "La Cucaracha" in Hemingway's narrative serves two functions: one, it undergirds the structural notion of repetition, of variation, and the notion of storytelling from different perspectives; and two, it emphasizes the thematic focus on revolution as a catharsis, an opportunity to purge the self of the opiates needed to deal with life in the first place. That the musicians play the tune "with emotion" (367:10) speaks to its thematic function. But regardless of the cathartic nature of revolution, as Frazer puts it, the song itself is also an opiate, for it has the "sinister lightness and deftness of so many of the tunes men have gone to die to" (367:9–10). Men can rush to their death with the sound of revolution in their ear. The music, as opiate, blunts the possibility that they may die for nothing, for there will always be another revolution, according to Frazer's logic.

367:13 **Mr. Frazer went on thinking:** Though the song stirs Frazer's emotions, the feeling is only superficial because he "went on thinking." Frazer typically avoids thinking because it heightens both his physical and metaphysical experience of pain. He thinks only when he writes because his trade demands it. His thoughts now focus not on writing but on "what the little" Mexican, the Marxist, "had said" (367:15–16).

367:17 **Religion is the opium of the people:** Though the allusion to Karl Marx is obvious, Hemingway avoided being a political writer because, in his words, "a thousand years makes economics silly and a work of art endures forever, but it is very difficult to do and now it is not fashionable" (*GHOA* 109). Writing to the Russian critic Ivan Kashkin in 1935, Hemingway admits that "everyone tries to frighten you now by saying or writing that if one does not become a communist or have a Marxian viewpoint one will have no friends and will be alone. . . . I cannot be a communist now because I believe in only one thing: liberty. . . . The state I care nothing for. . . . I believe in the absolute minimum of government" (*SL* 419). Frazer, like Hemingway, knows that "it isn't all in Marx nor in Engels" (qtd. in Baker 198), and he, too, believes in "the minimum of government, always less government" (367:28).

Frazer ponders different opiates of the people. What prompts him, however, is the thin Mexican's earlier reference to one of Karl Marx's most famous axioms, that religion is the opium of the people. It comes from the Prussian philosopher's Introduction to *A Contribution to the Critique of Hegel's Philosophy of the Right* (1844). The relevant section reads:

> *Religious* suffering is, at one and the same time, the *expression* of real suffering and a *protest* against real suffering. Religion is the sigh of the oppressed creature, the heart of a heartless world, and the soul of soulless conditions. It is the *opium* of the people.
>
> The abolition of religion as the *illusory* happiness of the people is the demand for their *real* happiness. To call on them to give up their illusions about their condition is to call on them to *give up a condition that requires illusions*. (69).

If we recognize religion as just one label in a taxonomy designed to make sense of the world, particularly its indifferent cruelty, then the rational mind sees the dual nature Marx assigns it: that it is simultaneously "expression" of and "protest" against "real suffering." Frazer likely agrees with this, but Marx also cedes, by the end of the paragraph, that such illusions are necessary. Frazer's real issue with the thin Mexican's Marxist antics is not that he is necessarily wrong but that he believes his education about such things makes him right. As with other Hemingway protagonists, knowledge and erudition stand on opposite ends of the spectrum.

367:17 **dyspeptic:** Frazer underlines his disgust with the Mexican's perspective by using this adjective that, though it signals the man's overall gloominess, focuses on the root of it: dyspepsia, a condition characterized by indigestion. The implicit suggestion is that he does not enjoy the sensual pleasures of life because, in his worldview, they all represent an ignorant belief in vice as escape. The Mexican's knowledge of the world is abstract, not phenomenological. Maintaining mental clarity seems important to him, hence his refrain from alcohol, which "mounts to [his] head" (361:3). Despite the Mexican's striving for clarity, there are many things that do not occur to him, such as other opiates synonymous with religion. Among them, Frazer includes music, economics, patriotism, sex, drink, the radio, ambition, and the belief in "any new form of government" (367:27). Clearly, any of these can be substituted in the above passage from Marx to the same effect because the primary tenet dictates that our condition requires such illusions about religion or booze or sex or music or whatever else we might use to blunt the pain of having "been through this all before" (363:35).

367:29 **Liberty . . . a MacFadden publication:** *Liberty,* a popular culture magazine, was launched in 1924. Despite its popularity, it lost money and was bought in 1931 by Bernarr Macfadden (1868–1955). As an early and well-known proponent of American physical culture, Macfadden began *Physical Culture* magazine in 1899 and grew his publishing organization from there to eventually include such titles as *True Detective, True Story, The New York Graphic, SPORT,* and *Liberty. Liberty* provided him with a mouthpiece through which he promoted the presidential candidacy of Franklin Delano Roosevelt by proclaiming he was physically fit for office. Macfadden himself was a guru of physical health who competed in bodybuilding competitions, advocated for fasts and special diets, and believed the human body, were it strong enough, could cure itself of disease without the use of pharmaceuticals (Adams). Macfadden ultimately turned his attention toward politics and, in a 1932 article for *Liberty,* suggested martial law and dictatorship as solutions to the country's economic Depression (Stone 383).

The irony of advocating for dictatorship under the auspices of liberty is too obvious to belabor, although Frazer admits "[w]e believed in that," presumably Macfadden's publication and the role of the media in shaping thought; but "they had not found a new name for it yet" (367:30). Believing the media's narrative is an opium too and, like drinking, a "sovereign" one (367:23). This might recall Frazer's insistence on the value of a point of view, even if it stems from habit instead of intentional design. Like songs on the radio, the prevailing narrative is just one that "you become fond of . . . and resent the new things" (359:2–3). Regardless, the more subtle point of the Macfadden reference emphasizes the range of opiates that Frazer contemplates and showcases his conclusion that everything, were it used or abused, would be an instrument to blunt pain. What Frazer finally identifies "Bread" (367:37) as "the real, the actual, opium of the people" (367:31–32), an epiphany that implies the absolute necessity of an opiate, for we cannot live without it. (Incidentally, Macfadden virulently opposed the consumption of white bread, which he called the "staff of death" [Copeland].)

Frazer ponders the source of true opium and finds the staff of life, a spiritual imperative, and so his meditation on opiates brings him back to the premise in Marx: "To call on them to give up their illusions about their condition is to call on them to *give up a condition that requires illusions*" (69). There is no escaping the need for an opiate. The human condition is such that an opiate is required, much the same way "anæsthetic" is needed for an operation (367:45). Adrian Bond suggests that "Gambler" illustrates the author's epiphenomenalism, the doctrine that consciousness is a secondary symptom of physical being, of physiological processes, and, as such, has no power to change or alter these processes. Bond notes about Frazer that "the chronic sufferer is notably a writer, hence a recording consciousness. . . . As if in an out-of-body experience, the mind confronts the stranger of the body, seeming to hover some place above it—watching, making notes—and, in doing so, assumes a marginality belied by its apparent authority" (372). Frazer's perspective is integral to the story precisely because it occupies a detached space from which it observes the conditions of life that mark its recurring and inevitable pain.

367:42 **It is a historic tune:** Having had something of an epiphany, Frazer asks the nurse to "[g]et that little thin Mexican in here" (367:38–39). When the latter asks Frazer what he thinks of "La Cucaracha," he also tells Frazer that it "is a historic tune . . . of the real revolution" (367:42–43). However, in some ways, the tune chronicles a series of revolutions, which, according to Frazer's logic and that of the story, are doomed to recur.

367:44–45 **Why should the people be operated on without an anæsthetic?:** Frazer means this metaphorically. Adrian Bond calls attention to this rhetorical question and states that Frazer understands "anæsthetic[s]" as "those things [people] embrace in order to keep their minds off the operation of daily existence. In the parlance of French existentialism, these activities constitute 'divertissement'" (375). In the context of Hemingway's story, such palliation is a requisite part of life if one is to hold tight and brace one's self against its current (see entry at 356:45).

368:3 **They should be rescued from ignorance:** In order to accomplish this for the people, the Mexican believes that he should reveal their illusions to them. He knows that, in Marx's words, "the abolition of religion as the *illusory* happiness of the people is the demand for their *real* happiness" (69), so he believes in his goal of liberating them from their own ignorance. He does not realize, however, that the human condition requires illusions; nor does he see that his fervor is merely another opiate. Frazer understands this, though, as he tells the Marxist, "Education is an opium of the people" (368:4), and the Mexican has "had a little" (368:5).

368:15 **tyranny:** The reference to "tyranny" as a way to extend the cathartic pleasure of revolution recalls Macfadden's claim that America needed martial law and a dictator to rise out of the Depression. Opiates, by contrast, are for "before and for after" (368:16). The cycle is inescapable and so, therefore, is the need for an anesthetic.

368:16–368:20 **He was thinking . . . could hardly hear it:** Paul Smith notes that the manuscripts indicate "*four* tentative conclusions" (290). In the first one, Frazer has left the hospital and indicates his wish to visit Portland, which later becomes Seattle; the second one ends with his roll call of hospital patients who have been broken by the world and are "damned twice" presumably by their broken body and then their fractured spirit, which can partially be renewed by the radio; but, nevertheless, Frazer concludes that economics cannot satisfy as an answer. Still another attempt ends with Frazer's request for "La Cucaracha." The fourth ending is found in the magazine version, and the fifth comes "when he added it to the tear sheets" from that version (Smith 290).

These last three sentences were added between publication of the story in *Scribner's Magazine* and then in *Winner Take Nothing* later that year. "Give Us a Prescription, Doctor" implies a governing force in the dispensation of pain relief, a doctor. Similar to God, deference to such a being would imply that Frazer, too, is at the mercy of a larger force. In the original ending, there is only the acknowledgment that "opiums are for before and for after" (368:15–16). In the revised version, Frazer chooses his opium, a "spot of the giant killer" (368:18–19), and the radio. The fact that Frazer has to think well to determine he does not want to think at all actually precipitates this agency; the opiates he chooses are not the result of blind choice or happenstance. He settles on the "sovereign opium" (367:23). "[T]he giant killer" was Hemingway's euphemism for booze, and it appears in other of his works. In a 1950 letter, Hemingway identifies "alcohol . . . as the Giant Killer" and admits he "could not have lived without [it] many times; or at least would not have cared to live without" (*SL* 690). At the end of "Gambler," Frazer takes a "spot" of the "giant killer" (368:18–19), just enough to soften the hard edges of that "well-lighted part of his mind" (367:33).

WORKS CITED

Adams, Mark. *Mr. America: How Muscular Millionaire Bernarr Macfadden Transformed the Nation Through Sex, Salad, and the Ultimate Starvation Diet.* Harper Collins, 2009.
Baker, Carlos. *Hemingway: The Writer as Artist.* 3rd ed. Princeton UP, 1963.
Bond, Adrian. "Being Operated On: Hemingway's 'The Gambler, the Nun, and the Radio.'" *Studies in Short Fiction,* vol. 34, no. 3, 1997, pp. 371–78.
Bovey, Seth. "The Western Code of Hemingway's Gambler." *North Dakota Quarterly,* vol. 58, no. 3, 1990, pp. 86–93.

Burkholder, J. Peter, Donald Jay Grout, and Claude V. Palisca. *A History of Western Music.* 8th ed. Norton, 2010.

Camastra, Nicole J. "A Study in Pain: Musical Variations and Ernest Hemingway's 'The Gambler, the Nun, and the Radio." *Critical Insights: American Short Story,* edited by Michael Cocchiarale and Scott D. Emmert, Salem P, 2014, pp. 99–113.

Copeland, Libby. "White Bread Kills: A History of a National Paranoia." *Slate,* 6 Apr. 2012, www.slate.com/human-interest/2012/04/a-review-of-white-bread-a-new-book-about -our-nations-fear-of-flour.html.

Gregory, Horace. "Ernest Hemingway Has Put on Maturity." Stephens, pp. 139–40. Originally appeared in *New York Herald Tribune Books,* vol. 10, 29 Oct. 1933, pp. vii–5.

Hay, Mark. "Marijuana's Early History in the United States." *Vice,* 31 Mar. 2015, *https://www. vice.com/en_us/article/xd7d8d/how-marijuana-came-the-united-states-456.*

Hemingway, Ernest. *The Complete Short Stories of Ernest Hemingway: The Finca Vigía Edition.* Scribner's, 1987.

———. *The Letters of Ernest Hemingway: Volume 3 (1926–1929).* Edited by Rena Sanderson, Sandra Spanier, and Robert W. Trogdon. CUP, 2015.

———. *The Letters of Ernest Hemingway: Volume 4 (1929–1931).* Edited by Sandra Spanier and Miriam B. Mandel. CUP, 2017.

———. *The Letters of Ernest Hemingway: Volume 5 (1932–1934).* Edited by Sandra Spanier and Miriam B. Mandel. CUP, 2020.

———. "Ernest Hemingway—Banquet Speech." *Nobelprize.org,* 10 Dec. 1954, nobelprize.org /nobel_prizes/literature/laureates/1954/hemingway-speech.html.

———. *Ernest Hemingway: Selected Letters, 1917–1961.* Edited by Carlos Baker. Scribner's 1982.

———. *A Farewell to Arms.* 1929. Scribner's, 2003.

———. *For Whom the Bell Tolls.* 1940. Scribner's, 1995.

———. *The Garden of Eden.* Scribner's, 1995.

———. *Green Hills of Africa.* Scribner's, 1935.

———. *The Sun Also Rises.* 1926. Scribner's, 1954.

Horowitz, David. *Classical Music in America: A History of Its Rise and Fall.* Norton, 2005.

Johnson, Nick. "Workers' Weed: *Cannabis,* Sugar Beets, and Landscapes of Labor in the American West, 1900–1946." *Agricultural History,* vol. 91, no. 3, 2017, pp. 320–41.

Josephs, Allen. "*Mandarlo al carajo.*" Email to Nicole J. Camastra, 30 June 2018.

Kipp, Dustin. "'We Were Beet Workers, and That Was All': Beet Field Laborers in the North Platte Valley, 1902–1930." *Great Plains Quarterly,* vol. 31, 2011, pp. 23–38.

MacLeish, Archibald. "American Letter." *The American Tradition in Literature,* edited by George Perkins et al., vol. 2, 6th ed., Random House, 1985, pp. 1164–66.

Marx, Karl. "Critique of Hegel's Philosophy of Right." *Theories of Religion: A Reader,* edited by Seth Daniel Kunin and Jonathan Miles-Watson. Rutgers UP, 2006, pp. 69–70.

"Mexican 'Dope' Weed Is Found." *Sanders County Independent Ledger,* 7 Oct. 1931, p. 3, image 3, www.montananewspapers.org.

Mikkelson, Martha, and Reeves Petroff, comps. "Crop Profile for Sugar Beets in Montana," https://ipmdata.ipmcenters.org/documents/cropprofiles/MTsugarbeet.pdf.

"Montana Mosaic: Ethnic Diversity—Migrants Make Montana Produce." *PBS Learning Media,* 2006.

Monteiro, George. *The Hemingway Short Story: A Critical Appreciation.* McFarland, 2017.

Montgomery, Marion. "Hemingway's 'The Gambler, the Nun, and the Radio': A Reading and a Problem." *Forum,* vol. 3, no. 9, 1962, pp. 36–40. Reprinted in *The Short Stories of Ernest Hemingway: Critical Essays,* edited by Jackson J. Benson, Duke UP, 1975, pp. 203–10.

Morton, Bruce. "Music and Distorted View in Hemingway's 'The Gambler.'" *Studies in Short Fiction,* vol. 20, no. 2–3, 1983, pp. 79–85.

Murolo, Frederick L. "Another Look at the Nun and Her Prayers." *Hemingway Review,* vol. 4, no. 1, 1984, pp. 52–53.

Putnam, Ann L. "Opiates, Laughter, and the Radio's Sweet Lies: Community and Isolation in Hemingway's 'The Gambler, the Nun, and the Radio.'" *Hemingway Repossessed,* edited by Kenneth Rosen, Greenwood, 1994, pp. 159–68.

Rodgers, Paul C., Jr. "Levels of Irony in Hemingway's 'The Gambler, the Nun, and the Radio.'" *Studies in Short Fiction,* vol. 7, 1970, pp. 439–49.

Ross, Lillian. *Portrait of Hemingway.* Rev. ed. Modern Library, 1999.

Samuels, Kathryn. "The Rainy City on the 'Wet Coast': The Failure of Prohibition in Seattle." The Great Depression in Washington State Project, 16 Oct. 2018, depts.washington.edu/depress/prohibition_seattle.shtml.

Schumach, Murray. "Hemingway Aide Discusses Writer." *New York Times,* 19 May 1960, p. 45.

Shanley, John P. "The Gambler, the Nun and the Radio." *New York Times,* 20 May 1960, p. 63.

Smith, Paul. *A Reader's Guide to the Short Stories of Ernest Hemingway.* G. K. Hall, 1989.

Stephens, Robert O., ed. *Ernest Hemingway: The Critical Reception.* Burt Franklin & Co., 1977.

Stone, Edward. "Hemingway's Mr. Frazer: From Revolution to Radio." *Journal of Modern Literature,* vol. 1, no. 3, 1971, pp. 375–88.

Trogdon, Robert W. *The Lousy Racket: Hemingway, Scribners, and the Business of Literature.* Kent State UP, 2007.

Troy, William. "Mr. Hemingway's Opium." Stephens, pp. 145–47. Originally appeared in *The Nation,* 15 Nov. 1933, p. 570.

Walsh, Michael, ed. *Butler's Lives of the Saints.* Concise ed., rev. and updated. Harper, 1991.

Whittle, Ambery S. "A Reading of Hemingway's 'The Gambler, the Nun, and the Radio.'" *Arizona Quarterly,* vol. 33, 1977, pp. 173–80.

Williams, Wirt. *The Tragic Art of Ernest Hemingway.* LSU P, 1981.

Wyatt, David. *Hemingway, Style, and the Art of Emotion.* CUP, 2015.

FATHERS AND SONS

Donald A. Daiker

There is near unanimity that "Fathers and Sons," the concluding story of *Winner Take Nothing* and the final Nick Adams story to appear in Hemingway's lifetime, is one of his best and most important. Hemingway called it a "[d]amned good story" (Bruccoli 192), and his Scribner's editor Maxwell Perkins agreed, writing, "I do not think you ever wrote a better story than 'Fathers and Sons'" (Bruccoli 204). . Hemingway read passages from "Fathers and Sons" at a meeting in 1937 at Sylvia Beach's bookstore in Paris (Baker, *Life* 312–13), a sign of his enduring pride in the story. James Mellow considers it "one of Hemingway's most personal and revealing stories" (259), just as Carlos Baker and Robert Paul Lamb describe it as "very moving" (Baker, *Writer as Artist* 130) and "powerfully moving" (Lamb, *Short Story* 84).

Hemingway signaled the story's importance through placement, always a vital consideration for him. "In making a book of short stories readable," Hemingway wrote to Perkins, "there is a hell of a lot to having them placed properly in relation to each other" (Bruccoli 268). As soon as he had written "Fathers and Sons," Hemingway knew that it had to be placed toward the end of his volume: "it will be either next to last or last," he wrote to Perkins (Bruccoli 192). Just as he concluded *In Our Time* (1925) and *Men Without Women* (1927) with the key Nick Adams stories "Big Two-Hearted River" and "Now I Lay Me," respectively, so he chose "Fathers and Sons" to anchor *Winner Take Nothing*.

The "Fathers and Sons" manuscripts bear witness to the story's personal importance to Hemingway, not surprising since it marks the first time he had made fictional use of the suicide, five years earlier, of his father, Dr. Clarence E. (Ed) Hemingway. According to Paul Smith, "No other [Hemingway] manuscripts show more extensive and detailed revisions and additions through so many versions than do those for 'Fathers and Sons'" (*Reader's Guide* 310). In a detailed and persuasive analysis of the manuscripts, John Beall illustrates "Hemingway's careful and complex process of drafting and revising his story" through "six different stages of composition" (119). Moreover, as Robert Fleming has demonstrated, the "manuscripts show evidence of the emotional turmoil that [Hemingway] suffered while he was writing the story" (*Mirror* 61).

According to Smith, Hemingway may have begun writing "Fathers and Sons" as early as 1929, the year after his father's suicide (*Reader's Guide* 307). Hemingway said that he began the story in mid-November 1932 (*Letters vol. 5*, lxix), but it was not until 13 June 1933 that he could write to Perkins, "finished 24 page story yesterday" (*Letters vol. 5*, 408). On 26 July, as he was getting ready for his long-delayed trip to Africa, Hemingway wrote to Perkins, "Have everything pretty well cleared now and will start re-writing The Tomb of My Grandfather today" (*Letters vol. 5*, 451). Three days later he sent Perkins the rewritten story (*Letters vol. 5*, lxxiv).

There is consensus on the story's tone and major theme as well. Kenneth Lynn is clearly in the minority in characterizing its tone as "brooding" (34). Many more readers see it as meditative, reflective, and nostalgic, something like a secular evensong. For Wirt Williams, "the tone is superbly elegiac" (105). For Sheridan Baker, "the story is a moving meditation on the impossibility of good fatherhood" (39). And for Richard Hovey, "The story is a poem in prose, subtle, humorous, warm, poignant, reminding us perhaps of a mood evoked by some of Tennyson's lyrics" (44). As for theme, Charles Oliver is right in stating that "the predominant interpretation" is that "Fathers and Sons" is a story of "father-son reconcilement" (136). Joseph DeFalco writes that "Nick finally becomes at one with the father and thereby becomes the father himself." Thus, "Nick's acceptance of his own father is tantamount to his becoming a self-realized man" (218). "One great skill of the story," Carlos Baker writes, "is its compression of generations of men, until the whole Adams clan of grandfather, father, son, and son's son are seen in a line, each visible over his son's shoulder" (*Writer* 89). Paul Hendrickson represents a minority view in contending that there is less reconciliation than misunderstanding: "Fathers and Sons" is "a psychologically layered tale about the inability of fathers and sons to understand each other" (272).

Much of the commentary on "Fathers and Sons" focuses on its central character: Nicholas Adams. Specifically, it tends to center on Nick either as a version of Hemingway himself or as a recurring character in Hemingway's short fiction. I've read nothing that disputes the contention that Nick is "Hemingway's frequent alter ego" (Paul 10) and that "Fathers and Sons" is an "autobiographical" (Donaldson 179) and even "heavily autobiographical" (Dudley 58) story. According to Hovey, "Fathers and Sons" "appears to be so close to the facts and so frankly confessional that it is hard not to take this piece as one of Hemingway's most explicit efforts to set down his feelings about his own father" (44). "Nick Adams and Hemingway are not identical twins," Arthur Waldhorn has said, "but they are intimately related. They share like—sometimes exact—experiences and recall obsessively whatever has scraped their sensibilities" (53). No one has defined their relationship more insightfully than James Mellow:

The invention of Nick Adams was one of the most vital inspirations of Hemingway's career. . . . That Nick Adams—in some ways the better self—had a less bitter life, was a different persona in which Hemingway could acknowledge fear and failure, lust and tenderness, a more measured resentment against his mother. It was as if, in the fictional alter ego of Nick Adams, Hemingway had created the sensitive, ironic, perhaps even more intellectual, persona he would seldom allow himself to be in life. In the fiction, he risked a different self. (267–68).

Perhaps because he is his alter ego, Nick Adams is the character Hemingway returned to most frequently. From "Indian Camp" (1924) through "Fathers and Sons" (1933), he appears in fourteen published stories—and more if stories like "A Very Short Story," "An Alpine Idyll," "A Day's Wait," and "Wine of Wyoming" are included (see Daiker, "In Search," and Flora, *Nick Adams*). Even when Hemingway apparently thought he was through with Nick after publishing "Fathers and Sons," he couldn't let go. Some two decades later, in his fifties, Hemingway began what turned out to be his longest Nick Adams story, "The Last Good Country," the unfinished and posthumously published tale of a teenaged Nick's flight from pursuing lawmen with his younger sister Littless.

Scholars, beginning with Philip Young, have long agreed that Hemingway's work "extends forward and backward" (52). This interconnectedness is nowhere more apparent and more important than in the Nick Adams stories. Looking back on his short fiction, Hemingway told Perkins in 1938 that "there is a line in all the Nick stories that is continuous" (Bruccoli 267). In his groundbreaking *Hemingway's Nick Adams Stories,* Joseph Flora demonstrates that "Hemingway has a sense of Nick's career—and he intends that the careful reader should too." Indeed, the "reader who elects not to let story comment on story will miss a great deal" (216). Flora contends that three of the final stories in *Winner Take Nothing*—"A Day's Wait," "Wine of Wyoming," and "Fathers and Sons"—"form a Nick trilogy" (Flora, *Nick Adams* 234), perhaps comparable to the marriage tales ("Mr. and Mrs. Elliot," "Cat in the Rain," "Out of Season," and "Cross-Country Snow") in the second half of *In Our Time*. There are numerous links between "Fathers and Sons" and earlier Nick stories, most obviously in the characterization of Nick's father and of Nick's girlfriend Trudy. Paul Strong rightly posits "the subtle, extraordinarily detailed interconnectedness of Hemingway's fiction" (50), which means that later Nick Adams stories like "Fathers and Sons" sometimes clarify their predecessors.

Title: Before choosing "Fathers and Sons," Hemingway considered several other titles, including "Long Time Ago Good" and "Indian Summer" (Bruccoli 199). The first complete draft is titled "The Tomb of My Grandfather." But Hemingway may have come to see its inappropriateness because it suggests that the central relationship is between a grandfather and grandson when it is, in fact, between a father and son. The phrase "Long time ago good" appears verbatim in the story (376:10–11), as well as in a contemporaneous letter (*Letters vol. 5,* 314), but perhaps suggests a pessimism that belies the story's tone. Michael Reynolds (*Young Hemingway* 111) and James Meredith are in the minority in viewing the title as ironic. Meredith writes that "Hemingway used the title ironically because the story reveals more emotional rifts than moments of bonding between these fathers and sons" (190). Most critics find that the story includes more moments of affection than rifts, and they point to Nick's concluding memory of love-making with Trudy followed by his extended conversation with his son as signs of the story's affirmative ending. When Hemingway asked Perkins if he preferred a title other than "Fathers and Sons," Perkins said no but with his usual discretion and sensitivity: "We have kept that title ('Fathers and Sons'). We think it throws back into the past and future the way the story does more than any of the others, though 'Tomb of a Grandfather' is a fine title" (Bruccoli 204).

Hemingway told his German publisher Ernst Rowohlt that "a title should always be a poem in its-self. In Our Time, Men Without Women, The Sun Also Rises, A Farewell to Arms—those all make poems in themselves in English. The title is as important as the book" (*Letters vol. 4*, 234). Presumably, Hemingway might have found the titles "Fathers and Sons" and *Winner Take Nothing* poems in themselves as well.

Fathers and Sons is the title of an 1862 novel by the Russian writer Ivan Turgenev, who also provided the title for Hemingway's parody *The Torrents of Spring* (1926). But, aside from the title, the Turgenev novel bears little resemblance to the Hemingway story. Turgenev was one of the writers—Stendhal, Flaubert, de Maupassant, and Tolstoy were others—that Hemingway imagined as opponents in a heavyweight world championship of writing (Lynn 549). In *The Sun Also Rises* (1926), a "very drunk" Jake Barnes reads "a book by Turgenieff" called "A Sportsman's Sketches." "I had read it before," Jake says, "but it seemed quite new" (118). Hemingway frequently borrowed *A Sportsman's Sketches* (1852) from Sylvia Beach's rental library at her Paris bookstore, Shakespeare and Company (Lynn 154).

369:1–7 **There had been a sign . . . were not met:** Hemingway's biographers agree that the germ of the story is an actual trip that Hemingway made in November 1932 with his nine-year-old son John, nicknamed Bumby. They drove from Key West, Florida, to Piggott, Arkansas, an arduous 1,300-mile journey through Alabama and Mississippi, in order to join Pauline Pfeiffer, Hemingway's second wife, and their two younger sons, Patrick and Gregory, for the Thanksgiving holidays at the Pfeiffer family home. Piggott is located in the northeast corner of Arkansas, close to the Missouri border.

The story reveals no specifics about Nick's destination. Instead, its "brilliant opening paragraph" (Flora, *Nick Adams* 236) begins with Nick's decision to ignore "a sign to detour" (369:1) and to drive straight through an unidentified town. It's what Reynolds calls a "depression-era town" (*1930s* 137): its traffic lights that blink on and off "would be gone next year when the payments on the system were not met"

(369:6–7). For Paul Strong, the traffic lights suggest "a controlled, orderly world" (51). For others, it's the detour *not taken* that is significant; in an insightful essay, Richard McCann writes that the image of the untaken detour "suggests that this story will lead into a center usually driven by" (267). It may also suggest that Nick knows how to read and interpret signs—not only by what they say but by how others have read them. That Nick successfully avoids the detour may serve as a metaphor for his ability to navigate the turns and complexities of his life. Nick's belief that the detour indicates "some repair which had been completed" (369:3) may also suggest that time and distance have allowed him to repair his troubled relationship with his father—signaled by the very telling of this story. In opposition to this affirmative reading, Kenneth Johnston finds that the story's initial setting foreshadows its major theme: "like father, like son. Despite the detour sign and the flashing red lights, despite the warning signals from the past, Nicholas Adams, figuratively speaking, is going down the same street, the same road, as did his father" (185).

The story's central character is identified as "Nicholas Adams" in the opening sentence (369:3–4), one of the rare instances—"Now I Lay Me" and "Summer People" are other exceptions—in which his full name appears. For Meredith, Hemingway's late decision to use Nick's full name "has an arresting effect on experienced readers of Hemingway's fiction who are all too familiar with the less formal, adolescent nickname. The formality of using Nick's full name does more than underscore a sense of present-day maturity; it demonstrates the depths of Nick's self-identification with his father" (191).

Hemingway's "Cross-Country Snow" begins not with "a sign to detour" but with the necessity of stopping: Nick Adams and his friend George can no longer continue up the ski slope because their bucking funicular is finally halted by snow that had "drifted solidly across the track" (*CSS* 143). Just as Nick drives straight through the detour sign, so George and Nick continue their skiing trip by immediately jumping from the car, executing a jump turn, and heading down the slope. Neither Nick will be deterred by external forces.

369:7–12 **on under the heavy trees . . . on both sides:** The "heavy trees of the small town" affect natives and strangers quite differently (369:7). Hemingway often highlighted differing responses to places; in *The Sun Also Rises,* Jake, who has made Paris his "town" (10), loves the place, whereas Robert Cohn, who is "more enthusiastic about America" (7), does not even like it. According to Carlos Baker, "Few writers have been more place conscious than Hemingway" (*Writer* 49).

Hemingway likened the forward motion of an automobile journey into new and unknown regions—"It was not his country" (369:12)—to the backward movement into adolescence and childhood: "Starting out to drive in a part of the country you do not know, the distances all seem longer than they are, the difficult parts of the road much worse than they are, the dangerous curves more dangerous and the steep ascents have a greater percentage of grade. It is like going back into your childhood or early youth" (*DS* 92). Aside from the link between driving unknown roads and retreating into the not-fully-known past, this passage helps explain Nick's sense of relief and relaxation when the run is almost done and the final destination in view. For Flora, the story "has a subtle rhythm as the movement of the journey counter-points the action" (*Nick Adams* 236).

369:12–22 **It was not his country . . . which way they would fly:** When we learn that what Nick sees from the car windows "was not his country" (369:12), it becomes clear that the story is set not "in the upper Midwest" (Pottle 370) nor is this Nick's "father's country" (McCann 266). The "red dirt" (369:11), the "cotton" (369:14), and the "red sorghum" (369:15), a heat-loving plant that grows best in areas with long summers, identify the South as the story's setting. Hemingway had told Edmund Wilson "that they stopped in northern Mississippi on the final night of the journey" (Baker, *Life* 605).

The elegiac, relaxed tone of the story is in part established by the phrase "the day's run made, knowing the town he would reach for the night" (369:16–17). No longer required to worry about his driving, about directions or detours, Nick is now able to pay close attention to the countryside—the corn fields and thickets and cabins. Even more important, he now has the leisure, with "his son asleep on the seat by his side" (369:15–16), for "hunting the country in his mind as he went by" (369:19–20). A much younger Nick in "Now I Lay Me," the final story of *Men Without Women*, had done much the same thing, fishing the "whole length" of a trout stream, he says, "very carefully in my mind" (*CSS* 276). But in the earlier story Nick's mental activities were designed to keep him awake since he had then believed that, if he ever shut his eyes, "my soul would go out of my body" (276). The older Nick has no such fears. "The story takes place in mid-autumn, evoking harvest and reward," Flora has written. "Its rhythms are appropriately mellow, the sentences tending to be long and even languid" (*Ernest Hemingway* 46). Fall had always been a special time for Hemingway and Nick because of hunting season. "The Three-Day Blow," set as "the fall wind blew through the bare trees" (*CSS* 85), concludes with a teenage Nick and his best friend Bill happily heading across a meadow with "two shotguns" and "a box of shells" (*CSS* 92). "Best quail shooting ever . . . country lovely in the fall," he wrote to Perkins (*Letters vol. 4*, 614). The inscription on a memorial to Hemingway in Ketchum, Idaho, begins, "Best of all he loved the fall" (Dearborn 627).

"Fathers and Sons" emphasizes midpoints and centeredness. It takes place during "the middle of fall" (369:12–13) in the middle of the country as darkness falls, a midpoint between night and day. It begins at a junction on "the main street" in "the center" (369:2) of an unnamed town. Appropriately, Nicholas Adams is navigating his role—his midpoint—between two generations: the father who will be introduced in the next paragraph and the son who sleeps beside him.

With the exception of one brief reference to the car (374:35), the story never returns to its contemporary time or place settings. Nor is there another mention of Nick's sleeping son until his words begin the dialogue with his father that concludes the story (376:16). Because Nick is "self absorbed in his memories" (Lamb, *Short Story* 84), the story instead moves steadily into the past.

369:23–28 **In shooting quail . . . down into the thicket:** Hunting the country in his mind reminds Nick of his earlier experiences shooting quail, a clear link to "A Day's Wait" where the unnamed narrator, presumably Nick, "flushed a covey of quail" and "killed two" (333:26, 333:27) while his son, nicknamed "Schatz," like Hemingway's son Bumby, lies, not next to Nick in a car seat, but in bed with a fever. In an early draft of "Fathers and Sons," Nick addresses his son as "Schatz" (*SS-HLE* 412).

What may be especially significant in "Fathers and Sons" is the sudden shift to second person ("you must not get between them and their habitual cover" [369:23–24]) and the challenges quail hunting presents, metaphorically, to all of us: the quail may "come pouring at you" (369:24–25), forcing you "to turn and take them over your shoulder" (369:27). "Like quail," Paul Strong has written, "memories have their 'habitual cover,' and unless approached with care, they flush and come at us in ways we do not expect and cannot control" (52). They may force us to "turn" in unanticipated ways, as Nick does at the end of the story in response to his son's persistent pleas. In his excellent analysis of "Fathers and Sons," Sheldon Norman Grebstein points to the story's "intricate syntactical and sound patterns" (143), especially in the sentence beginning "In shooting quail," which produces a "'whoosh' effect, the phenomenon of a flying object which seems to gain speed as it approaches, attaining a movement so rapid it blurs at precisely the instant it is closest to us and thus produces a sensation of suspended animation" (145).

At his best, Hemingway's style informed the content and theme of the text. As Meredith has argued, "In an experience common with highly self-conscious, middle-aged men, Nick is not only thinking about his father; Nick is actually thinking like his own father, as the momentary shift from the third to second person perspective in this passage suggests" (191).

369:28–370:7 **Hunting this country . . . as an eagle sees, literally:** This passage includes the first specific mention of Nick's father, one of the two fathers (Nick is the second) of the story's title. We learn that Nick's father has been his teacher and mentor: Nick hunted for quail "as his father had taught him" (369:29). The father's teachings are so crucial to Nick's identity that, for the only time in Hemingway's fiction, the full name of "Nicholas Adams" is repeated (369:29). In earlier stories like "Indian Camp" and "The Doctor and the Doctor's Wife," Nick learned much from his father but nothing more important than the grace under pressure that his father had demonstrated in performing an emergency Caesarean under primitive conditions and then in responding to his wife's unjust accusations with calm detachment. What we next learn about Nick's father in this wonderfully descriptive passage and in several succeeding paragraphs is his "great gift" (370:6), his remarkable eyesight that enables him to count individual sheep when Nick himself sees only "a whitish patch on the gray-green of the hill" (370:20). The eyes of Dr. Adams, his "very valuable instrument" (370:5), are like those of Dr. Hemingway, one of the many signs of the story's autobiographical basis. According to Ernest's older sister Marcelline Hemingway Sanford, "Daddy's eyes were so perfect that as a young man he had been given the name 'Ne-tec-ta-la,' which meant 'Eagle Eye,' by the Indians in the Smoky Mountains. Daddy had 20/20 vision and never needed glasses until he was past fifty, and then only for reading" (52). The perfect eyesight of Dr. Adams contrasts markedly with his wife's inability to see. Although Mrs. Adams is not mentioned in this story—she appears in only three Nick Adams stories and is never found close to Nick—she apparently suffers from the same sensitivity to light that plagued Mrs. Hemingway (Sanford 50–51): we see her in "The Doctor and the Doctor's Wife" in a "darkened room" with "the blinds drawn" (CSS 75).

370:8 **He would be standing with his father on one shore of the lake:** Nick stands with his father here, just as he stands with him emotionally throughout the story. The "lake" is Walloon Lake, where the Hemingway cottage known as "Windemere" was located. It is in Michigan's northern lower peninsula just south of the city of Petoskey, which is named in the Nick Adams story "Ten Indians."

370:11 **it's your sister Dorothy:** This is the first time in a Nick Adams story that a sister is mentioned. She will be mentioned later in the story but never again in Hemingway's fiction. A younger sister, Littless, is a central character in the unfinished and posthumously published "The Last Good Country." Hemingway had an older sister, Marcelline (1898–1963), and three younger sisters: Ursula (1902–66), Madelaine (Sunny) (1904–95), and Carol (1911–2002).

370:14 **the point that guarded the bay:** The point that Nick sees across the lake is the setting of "The End of Something" as well as Bill and Nick's destination at the end of "The Three-Day Blow." It is located on Lake Charlevoix, close to the town of Horton Bay, mentioned by name as "Horton's Bay" in "The End of Something," the story where Nick breaks up with his girlfriend Marjorie. By contrast, the Hemingway children often picnicked and occasionally spent the night at Murphy's Point on Walloon Lake, just a quarter mile away from Windemere (Miller 27).

370:22–37 **Like all men . . . bringing him to know it:** If his eyes "were the great gift his father had" (370:6), this paragraph focuses on the greatest gift Nick's father bestows upon Nick: his love for fishing and hunting, "a passion that had never slackened" (370:36). Readers had earlier experienced that passion in stories like "The

End of Something," "The Three-Day Blow," "Big Two-Hearted River," and "A Day's Wait." It may be significant that it's when we learn that Nick still "loved" to shoot and fish that his age—"thirty-eight" (370:35)—is revealed, perhaps an indication that his identity is closely bound to his father's teaching him how to hunt and fish. For his father's gifts of hunting and fishing, Nick twice says that he is "very grateful" (370:30, 370:37). Hendrickson writes, "There is such love and gratitude in the story for what his father has bequeathed in terms of the natural world" (290).

370:23–24 **he was sentimental, and, like most sentimental people, he was both cruel and abused:** The more problematic portion of this paragraph is Nick's rather vague characterization of his father as "sentimental," as "cruel," and as "abused." If Dr. Adams is cruel—Marcelline writes that Dr. Hemingway "was never cruel" (31)—we do not see cruelty in the stories (see Daiker "Ten Indians"). We do see him abused—by Dick Boulton and Mrs. Adams in "The Doctor and the Doctor's Wife" and again by Mrs. Adams in "Now I Lay Me." But it's difficult to know exactly what Nick means when he calls him "sentimental" and then adds that "[a]ll sentimental people are betrayed so many times" (370:27). No commentator I know has addressed those lines, although Jackson J. Benson has written that the judgment "all sentimental people are betrayed so many times" applies to Jake Barnes of *The Sun Also Rises* ("Literary Allusion" 27).

370:26–27 **they had all betrayed him in their various ways before he died:** Nick is not much more specific in this claim. Perhaps by not defending Dr. Adams against his wife's charges Nick is apparently blaming himself as well as his sisters—Dorothy in this story, Littless in "The Last Good Country." But the manuscripts make clear that, at least in Nick's mind, Mrs. Adams is the culprit. In a manuscript passage he eventually deleted, Hemingway had written that "There is only one thing to do if ~~you are~~ a man is married to a woman with whom he has nothing in common, with whom there can be no question of justice but only a gross fact of utter selfishness and hysterical emotionalism and that is to get rid of her. He might try to whip her first but that would probably be no good" (*SS-HLE* 413–14). According to Reynolds, this passage shows that Hemingway "wants to blame the father's death on the mother . . . whom he cannot forgive for being alive. . . . But when he said it, he knew he could not let it stand, because she will read it. No matter how much he wants to hate his mother . . . he cannot hurt her that directly" (*1930s* 114). In *For Whom the Bell Tolls*, Robert Jordan charges his father with cowardice, reasoning that "if he wasn't a coward he would have stood up to that woman and not let her bully him" (339).

370:27–28 **Nick could not write about him yet, although he would, later:** This is the first time in the story that Nicholas Adams is identified as a writer. Nick never voices the possibility of writing about his mother.

370:38–45 **While for the other . . . the ball of the thumb:** Nick had said that his father was as "sound" on hunting and fishing as he "was unsound on sex" (370:31) but that Nick "was glad that it had been that way" (370:32). In the earliest story manuscript, Nick refers to his father's sexual advice as "nonsense" (*SS-HLE* 405), suggesting that he never took it seriously. Here Nick explains why: no matter where you live, in the country with opportunities to hunt and fish or the city without any, "each man learns all there is for him to know about it [sex] without advice" (370:39–40).

371:3–4 **His father looked and said, "Suck it out clean and put some iodine on when you get home.":** This passage is Hemingway's late addition to the text, and one of the few indications, since he is never called "Dr. Adams" in the story, that Nick's father is a physician who tends to his son both as doctor and father.

371:8 **A bugger is a man who has intercourse with animals:** Nick's father is incorrect, confusing bestiality with sodomy. The *OED* traces the word back to 1540 and defines it as "[a] person who penetrates the anus of someone during sexual intercourse."

371:12 **none seemed attractive or practical:** The tone of this exchange, and the "mashing" exchange that follows illustrating the father's unsoundness on sex has been understood in contrasting ways. Jackson J. Benson, for example, argues that Nick's father responds "coldly" to Nick's questions and that Nick recalls their discussion "with bitterness" (*Writer's Art* 11). According to Jeffrey Meyers, the "father fiercely represses the son's awakening desires by threatening him with the horrors of venereal disease" (249). Paul Strong writes that these and later paragraphs make clear that Nick both "loved *and* hated" his father (55).

   However, I side with those who find these scenes broadly comic, even "splendidly comic" (Beegel, "Second Growth" 81). Young Nick's inability to find an animal "attractive or practical" (371:12) enough for sex and his resolve to "try mashing at least once" (371:21–22) reveal Hemingway at his humorous best.

371:14–15 **Enrico Caruso:** An Italian tenor (1873–1921), internationally famous for his voice and for his dramatic performances at opera houses around the world. He also had a reputation for molesting women. In an early draft of *The Sun Also Rises,* Hemingway calls Caruso "a great one" and likens him to Cayetano Ordóñez, the model for Pedro Romero in *The Sun Also Rises* (211). In *A Farewell to Arms,* Frederic Henry brings his friend Rinaldi some Caruso records (135–36).

371:16 **mashing:** Essentially frottage, mashing involves bumping or rubbing against a stranger or nonconsenting person for sexual gratification. In 1906, Caruso was charged and found guilty of pinching the buttocks of a married woman in the monkey house of the Central Park Zoo in New York City. Caruso claimed a monkey did the bottom-pinching ("Signor Caruso"). For Hovey, the passage on Enrico Caruso's mashing is "one of the most delicious bits of humor in all of Hemingway" (45). Beall writes that this "comical portrait of Nick's sexual education" (126), especially the punning on *mashing*, is indebted to the "Sirens" chapter of James Joyce's *Ulysses*.

371:20 **Anna Held:** (1872–1918): Polish-born French and later Broadway star, noted for her beauty and vivacity. She did appear, with bare shoulders, on the inside cover of wooden La Flor De cigar boxes.

371:23–24 **masturbation produced blindness, insanity, and death:** However, we interpret the tone of Nick's memories, it's wise to keep in mind Debra Moddelmog's point that the views of Nick's father were mainstream at the time (360). If Nick's father was unsound on sex, Nancy R. Comley and Robert Scholes write, he was "like most parents of his day" (76).

371:24–25 **a man who went with prostitutes would contract hideous venereal diseases:** In "A Very Short Story," Nick "contracted gonorrhea from a sales girl in a loop department store while riding in a taxicab through Lincoln Park" (*CSS* 108). See Daiker, "In Search of," below.

371:27–28 **Nick had loved him very much and for a long time:** Critics of Nick's father—he is not called Dr. Adams in this story nor, as George Monteiro points out, is his medical profession even mentioned (135)—have difficulty with this line. "Love" is a word that does not come easily to Nick. Erik Nakjavani writes that "the expression of love for his father constitutes the constant in Nick's narrative" (99). Hemingway himself could be less than loving in his comments: he wrote to playwright Laurence Stallings, "My father, who was a marvelous shot at grouse, ducks, quail and clay birds, shot himself with equal success last year" (*Letters vol. 4*, 261).

371:41–42 **It was a good story but there were still too many people alive for him to write it:** This is the story's first paragraph to identify Nicholas Adams as "a writer by profession" (Grimes 69) and to intimate that his father had committed suicide. The two are linked in that Nick thinks that he will eventually write about the suicide in order to "get rid of" thinking about it (371:30), although there are "still too many people alive for him to write it" (371:41–42). For Hovey, these lines make clear that "Hemingway is . . . conscious of using his art as therapy" (46). From his brilliant analysis of the manuscripts, Beall concludes that "Hemingway's revisions by hand evoke Nick's inner conflicts as a writer—between the catharsis of his pain that writing could bring and the pain that his writing could bring to others—hence, making it 'too early' for Nick to write the story yet" (131). For Fleming, "Implicit in the reference to 'many things' that Nick must purge by writing are his wartime experiences, a probable [second] divorce, and his shaky relationship with his own son" (*Mirror 7*). In *For Whom the Bell Tolls* Robert Jordan thinks that he "will get rid of all that [the evils associated with war] by writing about it. . . . Once you write it down it is all gone" (165). The earlier Nick Adams story "Big Two-Hearted River" had identified Nick as a writer who journeys alone to Michigan's Upper Peninsula in order to put "the need to write" (*CSS* 164) temporarily behind him.

"Remember us writers have only one father and one mother to die," Hemingway told Scott Fitzgerald less than two years before writing "Fathers and Sons." "But don't poop away such fine material," he cautioned (*Letters vol. 4*, 490). "Fathers and Sons" is Hemingway's first but not last allusion to his father's death by suicide: in *For Whom the Bell Tolls,* Jordan says that his father "shot himself" (66), just as Ed Hemingway had. Toward the end of that novel, lying wounded and alone as Fascist troops advance along the road that Jordan's beloved Maria had used to escape, he says to himself, "I don't want to do that business that my father did" (*FWBT* 469). According to Susan Beegel, "Fathers and Sons" does "not present the real father any more than the undertaker presents the real face." Instead, Hemingway gives us "a father prepared for public viewing" ("Second Growth" 83).

371:43–372:1 **Nick's own education . . . through the slashings to the camp:** This paragraph focuses on the site where Nick learned about sexual matters: "the hemlock woods behind the Indian camp" (371:43–44). The route there begins with the Adams's "cottage" (371:45), evidently the same "cottage" that appears in "The Doctor and the Doctor's Wife" (*CSS* 75) and in "Ten Indians" (*CSS* 255). In "Ten Indians," the site is the source of pain for Nick because it is in the "woods" by the Ojibway camp where he learns from his father that his girlfriend Prudie had earlier that day been "threshing around" and "having quite a time" with a boy named Frank Washburn (256). But such unhappy memories do not intrude into "Fathers and Sons."

372:1–2 **Now if he could still feel all of that trail with bare feet:** The third sentence of this paragraph is an apparently unintended sentence fragment. It appears as a complete sentence in the untitled typescript: "Now he could feel all of that trail with bare feet" (*SS-HLE* 418), but the 1933 *Winner Take Nothing* prints the fragment.

372:5 **You crossed the creek on a log:** The focus on remembered pleasures is intensified by the pronoun shift to the second-person "You" of walking barefoot through the hemlock woods, crossing creeks, climbing fences, and finally reaching the main road.

372:8 **sorrel and mullen:** Both are edible grassland plants. Sorrell, a relative to rhubarb and buckwheat, was named for its *sorrel* (French for sour) taste. Mullen was used medicinally as an herbal remedy for pulmonary illness. Neither plant is native to the United States.

372:9 **killdeer plover:** a common bird that gets its name from its shrill, wailing *kill-deer* call.

372:10 **Below the barn:** The "barn" that Nick passes is apparently the same Garner "barn" (*CSS* 255) as in "Ten Indians."

372:15: **jack-lights with for spearing fish at night:** A jacklight is a portable lantern, by Hemingway's time electric, often used (as it is here) to lure game. In "Three Shots," the original opening of "Indian Camp," later deleted, Nick's father and his Uncle George fish with "a jack light" on a large, unnamed lake in Michigan's Upper Peninsula (*NAS* 3).

372:16 **Then the main road went off to the left:** On a metaphorical level, McCann sees Nick's turning off the "main road" as a sign of his traveling "back into his deepest self" (270).

372:17 **shale:** fine-grained, clastic sedimentary rock composed of mud that is a mix of flakes of clay minerals, quartz, and calcite.

372:18–19 **the hemlock bark the Indians cut:** In "Indian Camp," the earliest Nick Adams story, Dr. Adams, Uncle George, and young Nick follow a "logging road" to "the shanties where the Indian bark-peelers lived" (*CSS* 67).

372:21–22 **They left the logs . . . they did not even clear away:** Once Nick remembers leaving the main road, turning into the woods, and encountering "the hemlock bark the Indians cut" (372:18–19), the nostalgic tone of the earlier paragraph gives way to anger at the devastation "[t]hey"—the enemy in Hemingway often appears as an impersonal "they"—have caused, with the cool forests replaced by "open, hot, shadeless, weed-grown slashing" (372:24–25).

372:23 **Boyne City:** The tannery site at the southeast end of the eastern branch of Lake Charlevoix, the lake across which bark is hauled in winter. In "The Three-Day Blow," Nick would like to take the British writers G. K. Chesterton and Hugh Walpole "fishing to the 'Voix tomorrow" (*CSS* 88).

372:25 **weed-grown slashing:** As Hendrickson has pointed out, "the word 'slashing' is a Hemingway obscenity" (288), and Nick Adams curses its prevalence as he and his sister escape northward from the Adams cottage in "The Last Good Country." "During Hemingway's childhood," Beegel has written, "Michigan was the scene of a forestry holocaust" ("Environment" 238). For Marc Dudley, "The Indian woods, stripped and gutted as they are," become "a reminder of [the white man's] own culpability in crimes against the red man" (59).

372:26 **But there was still much forest then:** The introduction of Nick's girlfriend Trudy and her brother Billy is appropriately prefaced by a movement backward in time from the contemporary "slashing" to the earlier era of the "virgin forest" as well as by a return to the second-person voice.

372:28–29 **it was cool on the hottest days:** Nick's memory of the forest includes this recurrent detail in Hemingway's fiction that betokens intense, unalloyed pleasure. An older Nick remembers that Luz, the woman in "A Very Short Story" whom he loves and wants to marry, is "cool and fresh in the hot night" (*CSS* 107). Jake Barnes looks forward to vacationing in San Sebastián because it "is always cool and shady on certain streets on the hottest day" (*SAR-HLE* 188). Nick's father welcomes his walk into the hemlock woods at the end of "The Doctor and the Doctor's Wife" because it "was cool in the woods even on such a hot day" (*CSS* 76).

372:32–38 **"You want Trudy again?" . . . He my brother.":** Nick has obviously rejected his father's warning that "the thing to do was to keep your hands off of people" (371:25–26); what we learn first about Nick and Trudy is that theirs is a sexual relationship. They have just had sexual intercourse and will do so at least twice more before the day is out. Trudy is willing; she replies "Un Huh" (372:34) to Nick's asking, "You want to?" (372:33). In the manuscripts she is more eager: "Like it so much," she says (*SS-HLE* 404).

There is general critical agreement—Roger Whitlow is the exception (101)—that the "Trudy" of "Fathers and Sons" is the same character called "Prudence Mitchell," "Prudie," and "Prudence" in "Ten Indians—and "Trudy" (*CSS* 513) in "The Last Good Country." Whether called Trudy, Prudie, or Prudence, she is clearly based on an Ojibway girl that Hemingway knew and perhaps loved.

Prudence Boulton was the daughter of Dick Boulton, namesake of the bullying Indian in "The Doctor and the Doctor's Wife." An Ojibway, Prudence was two to three years younger than Ernest, and she helped in his mother's kitchen at the Walloon Lake cottage (Baker, *Life* 140). In the posthumous "The Last Good Country," Trudy is called Nick's "girl." Nick's father figure, the admirable John Packard, says, "She was a beautiful girl and I always liked her" (*CSS* 523). Nick says, "So did I." Then in an apparent reference to Trudy's cheating on Nick in "Ten Indians," Nick says, "None of it was her fault. She's just built that way. If I ran into her again I guess I'd get mixed up with her again" (524). According to Smith, Hemingway "never forgot" Prudence ("Tenth Indian" 67). It is not known whether Hemingway knew that, at the age of sixteen, Prudence committed suicide with her lover Richard Castle by swallowing strychnine (A. Strong 326). See entry at 375:43–376:11.

372:39–44 **Then afterwards they sat . . . very long barrel:** Nick, Trudy, and Billy are "listening for a black squirrel" (372:39); in "The Doctor and the Doctor's Wife," Nick and his father walk into the "hemlock woods" looking for "black squirrels" (CSS 76) but not to shoot them since they do not bring a gun along.

373:43 **only three cartridges a day:** Another reference to the father as teacher, who limits Nick's shots so as to teach him the value of economy and selectivity.

373:5–6 **Nick was feeling hollow and happy.** Billy is far more interested than Nick in killing squirrels. Nick, in postcoital contentment, feels "hollow and happy." In "Ten Indians," Nick "felt hollow and happy inside himself to be teased about Prudence Mitchell" by the Garner boys (CSS 254).

373:7 **Eddie says he going to come some night sleep in bed with you sister:** Nick's sense of happiness and well-being is shattered by Billy's announcement that his older half brother Eddie wants to "sleep in bed" with Nick's sister Dorothy. It is immediately met by Nick's angry and incredulous "What?" (373:9).

373:7–8 **you sister Dorothy:** We know that she is Nick's sister, but we don't know if she is younger or older than Nick. Since Eddie Gilby is the "older half-brother" of Billy and Trudy (373:12), perhaps Dorothy is older than Nick. According to school records from 1914, when Ernest was fifteen, Trudy was twelve, her brother Billy nine, and her brother Eddie seventeen (St. John 83).

373:28 **Don't you kill him, Nickie:** In "The Last Good Country," Nick's sister Littless, told that the Evans boy is making trouble for them, says, "I know it, Nickie. But don't you kill him" (CSS 542).

373:30–36 **"After I scalped him I'd throw him to the dogs." . . . "Nickie!":** When Nick then threatens not only to kill Eddie but to scalp him and throw him to the dogs, Billy becomes "very depressed" (373:31), and Trudy starts to cry (373:35). Although Flora characterizes this extended passage as "an amusing account" with Nick becoming "comically traditional" (Nick Adams 242), that's not the way many others have read it. What's certain is Nick's insensitivity to his girlfriend and her brother. Although Billy speaks "gloomily" (373:31), Trudy tries to distract Nick by first putting her hand in his pocket, then "exploring" with her hand (373:21), and then jumping on top of Nick, choking him, and crying out, "No. No. No" (373:36). Nick is so into his wrath that he will not understand their fears for their half-brother: "What's the matter with you?" he accuses (373:37).

373:45–46 **Nick had killed Eddie Gilby . . . and he was a man now:** We may find an equally insensitive and self-centered Nick in "Summer People" (see Daiker "What to Make"), but Constance Cappel Montgomery is right in asserting that, in "Fathers

and Sons," "Nick is furious . . . the angriest that we ever, ever see him." But Montgomery believes Nick, engaging in what Benson calls "chivalric make-believe" (11),
"is enjoying" his manly role in this racist fantasy as defender of his sister's virtue
against an outsider, a "half-breed renegade" (Montgomery 105). For Dudley, Nick's
murderous thoughts constitute "perhaps the author's most forceful expression of . . .
latent racial anxiety" (12): "Hemingway's purpose is clear as he deliberately juxta-
poses Nick's sexual 'taking' of young Trudy Gilby (in his memories of experimental
play) with his later, quite violent defense of his own sister's maidenhood from Eddie Gilby (Trudy's half brother)" (12), making the story one of Hemingway's "bold
explorations of race and marginalization" (28).

374:4 **You can take the gun. There's one shell:** The scene ends as it began, with
reference to squirrel shooting, underlining—in Paul Strong's words—"the curious
way sexual and hunting imagery merge" (56). When young Nick apportions one of
his two remaining shells to Billy, he continues his putative manhood by assuming
the adult role his own father played in limiting his daily allotment of shells.

374:7–34 **Then, later . . . said Trudy:** After the intensity of the previous scene with
its talk of scalping, killing, choking, and tearing to pieces, Nick's postcoital memory
seems mundane by comparison. There is a sharp contrast between Nick and Trudy.
Whereas Trudy, wondering if she has just become pregnant, folds her legs together
"happily" and rubs against Nick (374:9), Nick himself has "gone a long way away"
(374:9–10). Much the same happened to Nick after sex with Kate in "Summer People": "His mind was working very hard and clear. He saw everything very sharp
and clear" (CSS 503). It's what British novelist Ian McEwan describes as "the clarity
that comes with a sudden absence of desire" (162). Nick wonders if Billy has shot a
squirrel, whereas Trudy doesn't care at all. It is Nick, of course, who ends their afternoon, despite Trudy's objections, because he's "[g]ot to go home" (374:21). And it
is Nick who declines Trudy's invitation to return after supper with a sharp, definite
"No" (374:30). This scene makes two things clear: Nick is the one who controls their
relationship, and Trudy cares more for Nick than he does for her, the same pattern
with Nick and Marjorie in "The End of Something." Is that one reason why, seeking
greater affection and commitment, Trudy/Prudie meets Frank Washburn in the
woods behind the camp in "Ten Indians" (CSS 256)?

This scene also makes clear that Nick and Trudy are really kids. Trudy may
be able to come and go as she pleases, but Nick has family obligations: he has to
get home for supper because he is expected there. He has only three cartridges a
day for shooting because that's the number his father allots him. Whitlow only
slightly overstates the case when he writes that "Nick, Prudence, and Trudy are
hardly more than children. Nick can be no older than his early teens, and the girls
may be younger yet. They are only engaged in the innocent sexual experimentation

of childhood" (102–03). In response to Reynolds's calling Trudy "soft and pliant" (*1930s* 137), Whitlow counters that Trudy is "quite aggressive in her sexual activity, even childishly shameless. . . . Trudy is certainly not submissive and the childish libertinism which makes up much of her character provides considerable 'individual personality'" (104).

374:29–34 **"Come out after supper?"** . . . **"on the face," said Trudy:** Some readers see problems in these lines:

l. 29: "Come out after supper?"
l. 30: "No."
l. 31: "How you feel?"
l. 32: "Good."
l. 33: "All right."
l. 34: "Give me kiss on the face," said Trudy.

It seems clear that lines 29 and 31, as well as line 34, are spoken by Trudy. It seems equally clear that lines 30 and 32 are spoken by Nick. But who is the speaker of line 33? Who says, "All right"? It is unusual for the same speaker to speak in consecutive, indented paragraphs in a line enclosed by quotation marks. The manuscripts offer no guidance.

374:35–375:5 **Now, as he rode along . . . not towns his father knew:** The narrative shifts, briefly, from the woods and the past to the highway and the present with the last specific reference to the car carrying Nick and his son through the growing darkness to their unnamed destination. Although Nick thinks that he is "all through thinking about his father" (374:36), he isn't. "All through" lasts only two short sentences before "[h]is father came back to him" (374:38–39) in one of the most evocative and poetic passages Hemingway would ever write. Flora notes the "lyrical tone" of this "intensely moving passage" (*Nick Adams* 242); Beegel calls it "one of the most beautiful in the Hemingway canon" ("Second Growth" 89). For Mellow, it is one of "the most poignant and sensitive tributes to another man Hemingway would ever write" (33). Beall writes that Nick's "elegy is rhythmically rhapsodic, poetically memorializing how a variety of seasonal scenes helps Nick . . . as a father see *his* father" (133).

The point is that Nick's father comes "back to him" throughout the year: not only "in the fall of the year, or in the early spring" (374:39), but with everyday sights like "shocks of corn," a "lake," or "a horse and buggy" (374:40–41) or when an eagle—evoking, as Beall notes, the eagle-eyed father (133)—drops "through the whirling snow" (374:43). Nick emphasizes that his father not only comes back to him but continues to be forever present in the phrase "His father was with him."

The poignant specificities of Nick's memories of his father pick up references in earlier Nick Adams stories. When Nick says that his father comes back to him "if he ever saw a horse and buggy" (374:41), it recalls the scene from "Now I Lay Me" when Dr. Adams, returning home from a hunting trip, "got down from his buggy and hitched the horse" (*CSS* 278). The "deserted orchards" (375:1) of Nick's memories remind us of the "bare trees" in the "orchard" that Nick traverses in "The Three-Day Blow," just as the memory of "open fires" (375:4) recalls the fire that Nick sees at the beginning and end of "The Battler."

375:5 **After he was fifteen he had shared nothing with him:** This paragraph ends with what Flora calls "the saddest line in the story" (*Nick Adams* 143). The phrase "he had shared nothing" is also a warning not to overestimate the autobiographical nature of the Nick Adams stories. Although Hemingway's longtime friend Bill Smith remembered Ernest telling him the shotgun story that follows (Mellow 40), Ernest shared a great deal with his father long after he turned fifteen, as his letters make clear. In an affectionate letter of March 1925, for example, Hemingway, grateful for his father's approval of "The Doctor and the Doctor's Wife," shared with him what he shared with few others, his central writing goal: "You see I'm trying in all my stories to get the feeling of the actual life across—not to just depict life—or criticize it—but to actually make it alive" (*Letters vol. 2*, 286).

375:6–27 **His father had frost . . . not help a man:** Once again, the sentence that seems to dismiss his father from Nick's consciousness serves rather to lead Nick into further characterizing him as a man who loved manual labor in the outdoors and then introducing one of his most poignant memories, the moment when a young Nick, whipped for lying, angrily contemplated killing his father with a shotgun blast. According to Grebstein, "Nick's act of discarding his father's underwear because it smelled repugnant to him (although it had been freshly laundered) is directly related to the rejection of his father's constricted morality and his subsequent sexual initiation by the Indian girl" (157). Both paragraphs here focus on Nick's acute sense of smell, a counterpoint to his father's keen eyesight, in each instance "a faculty that surpasses human requirements" (370:22). If his father's eyesight went hand in hand with his nervousness, Nick's sensitivity to smell led to his separation from all his family members, all the "others" (375:25) except one, a favored sister, unnamed, like Littless in "The Last Good Country." However useful keenness of smell may be for a bird dog, "it did not help a man" (375:26–27).

Nick's memories of his father are visual as well as olfactory. As he contemplates shooting his father, he sees him "sitting on the screen porch reading the paper" (375:19–20). In "Ten Indians," another story in which Trudy figures prominently, Nick sees "his father sitting by the table, reading" (*CSS* 255). Like his father, Nick turns out to be a reader. In "The Doctor and the Doctor's Wife," Nick's father finds him "sitting with his back against a tree, reading" (*CSS* 76). In "The Three-Day

Blow," Nick and Bill discuss the books they've read by George Meredith, Maurice Hewlett, Hugh Walpole, and G. K. Chesterton. In *The Sun Also Rises,* Nick's doppelgänger Jake Barnes brings a stack of books wherever he travels (188).

375:23–25 **There was only one person in his family that he liked the smell of; one sister. All the others he avoided all contact with:** There is no way of knowing whether Dorothy is this sister or not. But there is a link between this "one sister" and Littless of "The Last Good Country" because Littless also speaks of her family members as "the others" (*CSS* 514). Young Nick's "incestuous attraction to his sister" that Beegel locates in "Fathers and Sons" ("Second Growth" 93) becomes more pronounced in "The Last Good Country," where Nick and Littless kiss and where she wants to "get married" and become his "common-law wife" (*CSS* 537). Meyers asserts that it is Hemingway's sister Madelaine who is Dorothy (10), while Lynn suggests that Ursula is the model for Littless (56). No sister of Nick's ever again appears in a published Hemingway story.

375:28–42 **"What was it like" . . . "But what were they like to be with?":** The final portion of "Fathers and Sons" opens with the first words spoken by Nick's son, unnamed here but identified as "Schatz" in an early manuscript (*SS-HLE* 412). Nick's son addresses him as "Papa," the same way the nine-year-old Schatz, another of Hemingway's nicknames for his son Bumby, addresses his unnamed father in "A Day's Wait" (333:14), which both Philip Young and Joseph Flora consider a Nick Adams story. By contrast, Nick always called his own father "Dad" or "Daddy" (*CSS* 67, 68).

The son's asking Nick about hunting with the Indians melds nicely with Nick's earlier thoughts and memories. Nick's father is present again in his role as mentor, doling out only three shells daily so as to teach Nick to be a responsible hunter. Nick's telling his son, "We used to go all day to hunt black squirrels" (375:32–33) echoes the end of "The Doctor and the Doctor's Wife" when young Nick and his father head into the hemlock woods together looking for "black squirrels" (*CSS* 76). Nick tells his son that Billy Gilby and his sister Trudy were Ojibways and "very nice" (375:41), but, when pressed to say "what were they like to be with" (375:42), he is as reticent to speak concretely about sexual experience as his own father had been. It seems that it was only a single summer, "one summer" (375:37), that Nick, Billy, and Trudy spent together in the woods. From "The End of Something," we learn that Nick spent much of a later Michigan summer with a young girl named Marjorie. If the unnamed soldier of "A Very Short Story" is Nick Adams, then he and Luz enjoy a summer of love in Padua. In "Summer People," set during a still later Michigan summer, we see Nick, called "Wemedge," one of Hemingway's favorite nicknames, with Bill, Carl (Odgar), the Ghee, and, most vividly, Kate. Nick has had an active love life, especially during the summer.

375:43–376:11 **"It's hard to say."** . . . **Now no good:** But the words Nick does not speak to his son, the long sentence beginning "Could you say she [Trudy] did first what no one has ever done better" (375:43–44) are among the most quoted in all of Hemingway. According to Mellow, this is "a steamy flashback . . . regarded by most critics and biographers as the mature man's elegy to a young man's initiation into the sexual act" (33). Where critics and biographers cannot agree is the autobiographical basis of the relationship. Carlos Baker speaks for the skeptics: "Ernest's fictional accounts of sexual initiation with Prudy Boulton were more likely the product of wishful thinking than of fact" (*Life* 26).

Wishful thinking or not, Hemingway's prose has been brilliantly analyzed by Grebstein, who identifies the "technique of communicating sexual action through stylistic pattern." For Grebstein, the passage "combines incremental repetition, syntactical montage, and accelerating staccato rhythm to gain its effects." What Hemingway does, Grebstein continues, is to frame "the rapturously unthinking moments of the sex act with a coherent prose of reason, leading us from reflective memory into acutely empathic re-experience, down to the awakening and back to the point of initial awareness" (150–51). Hemingway uses many of the same stylistic patterns in *For Whom the Bell Tolls* when Robert Jordan kisses Maria for the first time and "suddenly, holding her against him, he was happier than he had ever been, lightly, lovingly, exultingly, innerly happy and unthinking and untired and unworried, and only feeling a great delight (72). In a letter to American writer George Albee, Hemingway wrote that depicting sexual intercourse "is probably the hardest thing to do in all writing" (*Letters vol. 4,* 517).

In his reading of this passage, Robin Gajdusek focuses on the phrase "the great bird flown like an owl in the twilight" (376:3–4) as one instance of the "frequent association" in Hemingway's work between "the flight of birds . . . and the orgasmic moment of fully completed love" (178). For Gajdusek, "Hemingway has invested birds, their beauty, their flight, and their role as mediators between the earth and the heavens, with mythological and psychic significance" (179).

In the earliest story manuscript, handwritten in pencil and told in the first person, Trudy is called "Prudy Gilby," and there is no mention of either brother Billy or half brother Eddie (*SS-HLE* 404). In that manuscript, Nick answers his son's second question, "What happened to her?" with a line that appears nowhere in the published story: "She went away to be a hooker" (404). In the posthumously published "The Last Good Country" when John Packard asks, "What became of your girl?" a teenage Nick says much the same thing: "Somebody said she was working up at the Soo" (*CSS* 523). The "Soo" is Sault Ste. Marie, Ontario, Canada, long known for its many accessible brothels. This early manuscript opens with the words "My father was" (*SS-HLE* 404), a clear indication of what was to remain the story's central focus.

Nick's memories glide easily from one sensory experience to another, "the sweetgrass smell, the smoke smell" (376:7) that characterizes any "place where Indians have lived" (376:5). But Nick's thinking of places once inhabited by the Ojibways invariably leads to thoughts of their demise: "Long time ago good. Now no good" (376:10–11). In "The Last Good Country," when Mrs. Tabeshaw is complimented on her looks, she responds, "Long time ago" (CSS 526).

For Nick in the unpublished "The Indians Moved Away," "Indians all smelled alike. It was a sweetish smell that all Indians had" (NAS 34). Once again Nick's thoughts link Native American smells to Native American extinction: "There were no successful Indians" (35). When the sons of Simon Green, who had once operated a profitable farm, sell the farm to buy a poolroom, "They lost money and were sold out. That was the way the Indians went" (36). But the smell did not go with them, at least according to Hemingway's younger sister Madelaine: "We even loved the smell of the Indian camp. The odor of their camping grounds remained in the area for a few years after they all pulled out" (Miller 26).

376:12–17 **And about the other. . . . "But I think you would.":** The opening four words are a puzzling fragment, at least at first, since what pairs with "the other" is not immediately clear. But apparently "the other" picks up the son's earlier question: "What it was like . . . to hunt with the Indians?" (375:28–29). Since the previous paragraph focused on Indians, this much shorter one comments on hunting.

376:18–22 **And my grandfather . . . live with them?:** Hemingway's younger brother Leicester (1915–82) wrote, "During one summer Father spent three months with the Sioux Indians of South Dakota, absorbing nature lore and gaining a great admiration for Indian ways" (20). According to Marcelline, their father spent many free hours as a boy exploring old Native American mounds along the Des Plaines River. With his brothers, he pretended to be members of a mythical tribe known as the Skowhegans (Sanford 21, 22, 28). He collected arrow heads, clay bowls, and flints for his prized collection of artifacts. In *For Whom the Bell Tolls,* Robert Jordan remembers "the cabinet in [his] father's office with the arrowheads spread out on a shelf" (336). In "Now I Lay Me," Nick remembers his mother burning his father's "stone axes and stone skinning knives and tools for making arrow-heads and pieces of pottery and many arrow-heads" (CSS 278). Like the Native Americans he admired, Hemingway's father could make fire with the flints he collected. His fascination with Native Americans seems to have been lifelong.

376:24–27 **"How old will I be. . . . soon enough.":** Nick's son will "soon enough" be twelve years old. Hemingway's and Hadley Richardson's son, John Hadley Nicanor Hemingway, was born on 10 October 1923 (Baker, *Life* 117), so he would have been almost ten when Hemingway was completing "Fathers and Sons" (Smith, *Reader's Guide* 307–10).

376:28 **"What was my grandfather like?:** From this point on, every word spoken by Nick's son is directed at reconnecting with his dead grandfather. In "A Day's Wait," Nick's son had been to "school in France" (334:19). From "Cross-Country Snow," we can gather that he had been conceived in Europe but that Nick and his wife Helen had decided to "go back to the States" (*CSS* 146), just as Hemingway and Hadley had decided to fly back across the Atlantic to take advantage of superior North American medical facilities. The boy was born in Toronto, Canada.

These gifts can be taken as signs of the grandfather's kindness and generosity, perfectly appropriate gifts from a grandfather remembered for his marksmanship and for commenting on sister Dorothy's running up a flag outside the family cottage (376:29), and appropriate as well for a boy raised in France and too young for a real rifle.

376:34 **his father:** This is the story's first and only reference to Nick's grandfather, a fourth generation of Adamses. Hemingway's paternal grandfather, Anson T. Hemingway, was a Civil War veteran who ran a successful real estate business in Chicago and who raised his family in Oak Park, a Chicago suburb, where Ernest was born. When Hemingway's father committed suicide in 1928, he used Anson's Union Army pistol (Meyers 2).

376:40 **It's a long way from here:** Hemingway's father was buried in Forest Home Cemetery in Oak Park (Reynolds, *Homecoming* 211), approximately 460 miles from Piggott, Arkansas.

377:4 **I don't want to be buried in France:** Although Nick is tentative in most of his responses, he is direct and forceful on this point. In "Wine of Wyoming," the antepenultimate story in *Winner Take Nothing*, Madame Fontan says that the narrator, an unidentified "I" and possibly Nick Adams, "live[d] in France" (347:21). The narrator says, "Mais il y a très bonne chasse aussi en France" (347:42), which translates as "But there is also very good hunting in France."

377:5–9 **Well, then . . . to the ranch:** On 13 July 1930, Hemingway, his second wife Pauline, and his and Hadley's son Bumby, then almost seven, moved into a cabin on the L Bar T ranch, owned by Lawrence Nordquist, in northern Wyoming, just inside the Montana state line (Baker, *Life* 211–12). Pauline and Bumby lived there for two months. Ernest stayed longer. On 1 November, he fractured his arm in an automobile accident and spent almost two months recuperating in St. Vincent's Hospital in Billings, Montana (Baker, *Life* 216), an experience that forms the basis for "The Gambler, the Nun, and the Radio," the story that immediately precedes "Fathers and Sons" in *Winner Take Nothing*.

Smith notes that the issue that has divided most critics is the story's resolution—its nature and permanence—"for few disagree that Nick Adams has achieved some sort of accommodation with the past" (*Reader's Guide* 312). Smith further observes that readers who consider "Fathers and Sons" an integral part of the Nick Adams canon are likely to find its ending more affirmative than those who "place the story within the psychic history of American culture or Hemingway himself" (313).

Larry Grimes believes that the "hint of procrastination in Nick's response to his son's plea" means that "Nick will not visit the grave" (70). But most commentators accept McCann's view that in "agreeing that they will visit his grandfather's tomb, Nick seems to agree to some acceptance of his father and of that past" (272). With the promised journey as a bond of their love," Paul Strong writes, "one is left feeling hopeful for father and son" (58). For Flora, "The ending of the story is edged in love and forgiveness" (*Nick Adams* 248).

According to Carlos Baker, the title *Winner Take Nothing* "contained just the hint of cynical acceptance of the human condition which [Hemingway] felt the stories embodied and illustrated" (*Life* 241). It's true that in "After the Storm," "A Clean, Well-Lighted Place," "The Sea Change," and "The Gambler, the Nun, and the Radio," the "winner" literally takes nothing. But "Fathers and Sons" is quite different. With Nick as a "rounded, humane, and complex character," Beall has written, the story "brings *Winner Take Nothing* to a close with a far less cynical figure than the loners and misfits that generally populate the collection" (140).

Both Nick and his son are winners in this story—Nick because he has mined his past for memories that clarify his present; his son because he has helped his father reconnect with *his* father. "In telling Nick's story," Fleming writes, "Hemingway had himself done what Nick was not yet able to do: he had sorted out many of his feelings about his own father and, through the technique of omission, had implied much more" (*Mirror* 65). The volume with the downbeat title ends on a distinctly upbeat note.

NOTE

I thank Frederic Svoboda, University of Michigan-Flint, and Jack Jobst, Michigan Tech, for helping me with Michigan geography. I am deeply grateful to John Beall of the Collegiate School in New York City for reading and significantly improving an earlier version of this chapter. His essay "Hemingway as Craftsman: Revising 'Fathers and Sons'" is the best I've read.

Baker, Carlos. *Ernest Hemingway: A Life Story.* Scribner's, 1969.

———. *Hemingway: The Writer as Artist.* Princeton UP, 1956.

Baker, Sheridan. *Ernest Hemingway: An Introduction and Interpretation.* Barnes & Noble, 1967.

Beall, John. "Hemingway as Craftsman: Revising 'Fathers and Sons.'" *MidAmerica,* vol. 43, 2016, pp. 118–43.

Beegel, Susan F. "The Environment." *Ernest Hemingway in Context,* edited by Debra A. Moddelmog and Suzanne del Gizzo, CUP, 2013, pp. 237–46.

———. "Second Growth: The Ecology of Loss in 'Fathers and Sons.'" *New Essays on Hemingway's Short Fiction,* edited by Paul Smith. CUP, 1998, pp. 75–110.

Benson, Jackson J. *Hemingway: The Writer's Art of Self-Defense.* U of Minnesota P, 1969.

———. "Literary Allusion and the Private Irony of Ernest Hemingway." *Pacific Coast Philology,* vol. 4, 1969, pp. 24–29.

Bruccoli, Matthew J., ed. *The Only Thing That Counts: The Ernest Hemingway-Maxwell Perkins Correspondence, 1945–1947.* Scribner's, 1999.

"bugger, n.1." *OED Online,* OUP, September 2020.

Comley, Nancy R., and Robert Scholes. *Hemingway's Genders: Rereading the Hemingway Text.* Yale UP, 1994.

Daiker, Donald A. "In Search of the Real Nick Adams: The Case for 'A Very Short Story.'" *The Hemingway Review,* vol. 32, no. 2, 2013, pp. 28–41.

———. "'I Think Dad Probably Waited for Me': Biography, Intertextuality, and Hemingway's 'Ten Indians.'" *MidAmerica,* vol. 42, 2015, pp. 36–53.

———. "What to Make of Hemingway's 'Summer People.'" *The Hemingway Review,* vol. 34, no. 2, 2015, pp. 36–51.

Dearborn, Mary. *Ernest Hemingway: A Biography.* Knopf, 2017.

DeFalco, Joseph. *The Hero in Hemingway's Short Stories.* U of Pittsburgh P, 1963.

Donaldson, Scott. *By Force of Will: The Life and Art of Ernest Hemingway.* Penguin, 1977.

Dudley, Marc K. *Hemingway, Race, and Art: Bloodlines and the Color Line.* Kent State UP, 2012.

Fleming, Robert E. *The Face in the Mirror: Hemingway's Writers.* U of Alabama P, 1994.

Flora, Joseph M. *Ernest Hemingway: A Study of the Short Fiction.* Twayne, 1989.

———. *Hemingway's Nick Adams.* LSU Press, 1982.

Gajdusek, Robin. "Hemingway's Late Life Relationships with Birds." *Hemingway and the Natural World,* edited by Robert E. Fleming, U of Idaho P, 1999, pp. 175–87.

Grebstein, Sheldon Norman. *Hemingway's Craft.* Southern Illinois UP, 1973.

Grimes, Larry E. *The Religious Design of Hemingway's Early Fiction.* UMI Research P, 1985.

Hemingway, Ernest. *The Complete Short Stories of Ernest Hemingway: The Finca Vigía Edition.* Scribner's, 1987.

———. "The Dangerous Summer." *Life,* vol. 44, 5 Sept. 1960, pp. 78–109.

———. *A Farewell to Arms.* 1929. The Hemingway Library Edition, edited by Seán Hemingway, Scribner's, 2012.

———. *For Whom the Bell Tolls.* Scribner's, 1940.

———. *The Letters of Ernest Hemingway: Volume 2 (1923–1925).* Edited by Sandra Spanier, Albert J. DeFazio III, and Robert W. Trogdon. CUP, 2013.

———. *The Letters of Ernest Hemingway: Volume 4 (1929–1931).* Edited by Sandra Spanier and Miriam B. Mandel. CUP, 2017.

————. *The Letters of Ernest Hemingway: Volume 5 (1932–1934)*. Edited by Sandra Spanier and Miriam B. Mandel. CUP, 2020.

————. *The Nick Adams Stories*. Scribner's, 1972.

————. *The Short Stories of Ernest Hemingway: The Hemingway Library Edition*. Scribner's, 2017.

————. *The Sun Also Rises*. 1926. The Hemingway Library Edition, edited by Seán Hemingway, Scribner's, 2014.

————. *Winner Take Nothing*. Scribner's, 1933.

Hemingway, Leicester. *My Brother, Ernest Hemingway*. World, 1962.

Hendrickson, Paul. *Hemingway's Boat: Everything He Loved in Life, and Lost, 1934–1961*. Knopf, 2011.

Hovey, Richard B. *Hemingway: The Inward Terrain*. U of Washington P, 1968.

Johnston, Kenneth G. *The Tip of the Iceberg: Hemingway and the Short Story*. Penkeville, 1987.

Lamb, Robert Paul. *The Hemingway Short Story: A Study in Craft for Writers and Readers*. Louisiana State UP, 2013.

Lynn, Kenneth. *Hemingway*. Simon and Schuster, 1987.

McCann, Richard. "To Embrace or Kill: 'Fathers and Sons.'" *New Critical Approaches to the Short Stories of Ernest Hemingway*, edited by Jackson J. Benson, Duke UP, 1990, pp. 266–74.

McEwan, Ian. *On Chesil Beach*. Random House, 2007.

Mellow, James. *Hemingway: A Life Without Consequences*. Houghton-Mifflin, 1992.

Meredith, James Hughes. "Bird Hunting and Male Bonding in Hemingway's Fiction and Family." *Hemingway and the Natural World*, edited by Robert E. Fleming, U of Idaho P, 1999, pp. 189–201.

Meyers, Jeffrey. *Hemingway: A Biography*. Harper & Row, 1985.

Miller, Madelaine Hemingway. *Ernie: Hemingway's Sister "Sunny" Remembers*. Crown, 1975.

Moddelmog, Debra A. "Sex, Sexuality and Marriage." *Ernest Hemingway in Context*, edited by Debra A. Moddelmog and Suzanne del Gizzo, CUP, 2013, pp. 357–66.

Monteiro, George. *The Hemingway Short Story: A Critical Appreciation*. McFarland, 2017.

Montgomery, Constance Cappel. *Hemingway in Michigan*. Fleet, 1966.

Nakjavani, Erik. "The Fantasies of Omnipotence and Powerlessness: Commemoration in Hemingway's 'Fathers and Sons.'" *Hemingway: Up in Michigan Perspectives*, edited by Frederic J. Svoboda and Joseph J. Walmeir, Michigan State UP, 1995, pp. 91–101.

Oliver, Charles M. *Ernest Hemingway: A Literary Reference to His Life and Work*. Facts on File, 2007.

Paul, Steve. *Hemingway at Eighteen: The Pivotal Year That Launched an American Legend*. Chicago Review P, 2018.

Pottle, Russ. "Travel." *Ernest Hemingway in Context*, edited by Debra A. Moddelmog and Suzanne del Gizzo, CUP, 2013, pp. 367–77.

Reynolds, Michael. *Hemingway: The Homecoming*. Norton, 1992.

————. *Hemingway: The 1930s*. Norton, 1998.

————. *The Young Hemingway*. Norton, 1986.

St. John, Donald. "Hemingway and Prudence." *Connecticut Review*, vol. 5, 1972, pp. 78–84.

Sanford, Marcelline Hemingway. *At the Hemingways: A Family Portrait*. Little, Brown, 1962.

"Signor Caruso, Tenor, Arrested in Zoo." *New York Times*, 17 Nov. 1906, p. 1.

Smith, Paul. *A Reader's Guide to the Short Stories of Ernest Hemingway*. G. K. Hall, 1989.

————. "The Tenth Indian and the Thing Left Out." *Ernest Hemingway: The Writer in Context*, edited by James Nagel, U of Wisconsin P, 1984, pp. 53–74.

Strong, Amy. "Race and Ethnicity: American Indians." *Ernest Hemingway in Context,* edited by Debra A. Moddelmog and Suzanne del Gizzo, CUP, 2013, pp. 323–31.

Strong, Paul. "Gathering the Pieces and Filling in the Gaps: Hemingway's 'Fathers and Sons.'" *Studies in Short Fiction,* vol. 26, no. 1, 1989, pp. 49–58.

Waldhorn, Arthur. *A Reader's Guide to Ernest Hemingway.* Farrar, Strauss, 1972.

Whitlow, Roger. *Cassandra's Daughters: The Women in Hemingway.* Greenwood P, 1984.

Williams, Wirt. *The Tragic Art of Ernest Hemingway.* Louisiana State UP, 1981.

Young, Philip. *Ernest Hemingway: A Reconsideration.* Harcourt, 1966.

CONTRIBUTORS

Nicole J. Camastra (PhD, University of Georgia) serves as English Department head at the O'Neal School, a college preparatory school in North Carolina. She has published several essays on American writers including F. Scott Fitzgerald, William Faulkner, and Kate Chopin, and coedited *Elizabeth Madox Roberts: Essays of Discovery and Recovery* (2008).

Mark Cirino is professor and Melvin M. Peterson Endowed Chair of English at the University of Evansville (IN). He serves as the general editor for Kent State University Press's Reading Hemingway series, for which he wrote the volume on *Across the River and into the Trees* (2016).

Kirk Curnutt is professor and chair of English at Troy University. He is the coeditor with Suzanne del Gizzo of *The New Hemingway Studies* (2020) and the author of *Reading Hemingway's* To Have and Have Not (2017), *Coffee with Hemingway* (2007), and *Ernest Hemingway and the Expatriate Modernist Movement* (2000), among other works.

Donald A. Daiker, professor emeritus of English at Miami University in Oxford, Ohio, is coeditor, with John Beall, of *Hemingway's Combat Zones: War, Family, Self* (2019). His two dozen Hemingway essays and reviews have appeared in journals like *The Hemingway Review, MidAmerica,* and *The Fitzgerald/Hemingway Annual;* and in collections like *Hemingway and the Natural World* and *Hemingway's Short Stories.*

Suzanne del Gizzo is professor of English at Chestnut Hill College in Philadelphia and editor of *The Hemingway Review.* She has published more than twenty articles in scholarly journals and has coedited three books, most recently, *The New Hemingway Studies* with Kirk Curnutt, published by Cambridge University Press in 2020.

Carl Eby is professor of English at Appalachian State University and president of the Hemingway Society. He is author of *Hemingway's Fetishism: Psychoanalysis and the Mirror of Manhood* (1999) and coeditor of *Hemingway's Spain: Imagining the*

Spanish World (2016). He is the author of many essays on Hemingway, and he is currently working on a volume devoted to *The Garden of Eden* for KSUP's "Reading Hemingway" series.

Bryan Giemza is a writer and former Hemingway Fellow who believes in the power of the written word, as well as the power of public humanities for the common good. A faculty member of Texas Tech University's Honors College, he lives with his wife and two children in Lubbock and teaches courses in natural, human, and literary history.

Ryan Hediger is associate professor of English at Kent State University. His recent publications include *Homesickness: Of Trauma and the Longing for Place in a Changing Environment* (2019). He coedited *Animals and Agency* (2009), edited *Animals and War* (2013) and is currently editing an essay collection on labor norms in the Anthropocene titled "Planet Work."

Verna Kale is assistant research professor in English at the Pennsylvania State University and associate editor of the Cambridge edition of *The Letters of Ernest Hemingway*. She has published a critical biography, *Ernest Hemingway*, and is editor of *Teaching Hemingway and Gender*.

Alberto Lena holds a PhD in American studies from Exeter University. He is currently working as civil servant at the Department of Education in Castilla y Leon (Spain). He is the author of essays on Francis F. Coppola, Benjamin Franklin, F. Scott Fitzgerald, John Dos Passos, Alfred Hitchcock, Ernest Hemingway, and Thornton Wilder.

Krista Quesenberry is a visiting assistant professor of English at Albion College. Her recent work centers on identity in American life-writing of the twentieth and twenty-first centuries, especially memoir, graphic narratives, and archives. She has been affiliated with the Hemingway Letters Project since 2011 and has been published in *Life Writing, The Journal of Graphic Novels and Comics,* and *The Hemingway Review*.

Robert W. Trogdon is professor of English at Kent State University. He is the author of *The Lousy Racket: Hemingway, Scribners and the Business of Literature* (2007) and coeditor on the first three volumes of the *Letters of Ernest Hemingway*. Trogdon most recently edited Hemingway's *The Sun Also Rises & Other Writings, 1918–1926* for the Library of America.

Susan Vandagriff is assistant professor and scholarly communications librarian at University of Colorado Colorado Springs. She presented at the 2016 Hemingway Conference and has been published in *The Hemingway Review*.

Boris Vejdovsky, PhD, is *Maître d'enseignement et de Recherche I* (associate professor) at the University of Lausanne, Switzerland. He is the author of *Ideas of Order: Ethics and Topos in American Literature* (Tübingen Franke, 2009) and of *Ernest Hemingway, la vie, et ailleurs* (Cedex Michel Lafon, 2011). The latter was translated into six languages, including American and British editions titled *Hemingway: A Life in Pictures.*

INDEX

Venice, Italy, 77, 110, 120, 150, 199
"Very Short Story, A" (Hemingway, short story), 271, 279, 282, 287; anaesthetic in, 182, 245
Veterans' Bureau, 223
"Veteran Visits the Old Front, A" (Hemingway), 110, 117
Vevey, Switzerland, 147, 153, 154, 158, 159, 165
Villa, Pancho, 262
Villon, François, 225
"Visiting Team, The" (Hemingway), 103
Vonnegut, Kurt, 193

Wagner, Robert, 27
Waldhorn, Arthur, 204, 270
Walker, Robert, 24
Walloon Lake, Michigan, 276
Walpole, Hugh, 287
Walsh, Ernest, 79
Waste Land, The (Eliot), 83, 86, 114
Watts, Emily Stipes, 35, 45
Watts, Mary Stanbery, 11
"Way You'll Never Be, A" (Hemingway, short story), 7, 10, 83, 182
Wertenbaker, Charles, 85
What We Talk About When We Talk About Love (Carver), 12
White, Gilbert, 189
Whitehead, John, 18
Whitlow, Roger, 282, 284, 285
"Who Murdered the Vets?" (Hemingway), 16
Williams, William Carlos, 149
Williams, Wirt, 204, 261, 270
Wilson, Edmund, 6, 84, 274
Wilson, Sir Andrew Talbot, 119
Wilson, Sir Henry, 119

Wimsatt, William K., 11
"Wine of Wyoming" (Hemingway, short story), 140, 240, 271, 290
Wisteria Island, 16
Wolfe, Tom, 187
Woolf, Alfred, 75
Woolf, Herbert Morris, 75
Woolf, Leonard, 75
Woolf, Samuel, 75
Woolf, Virginia, 75
Works Project Administration, 16
World War I: All Quiet on the Western Front and, 188; damage to France in, 210; damage to San Donà in, 120; deaths in, 197; Eden, Anthony, in, 108; Generals Die in Bed and, 200; Hemingway's experience during, 186; horrors of, 193, 209; memorial museum of, 112; naturalist writers predating, 189; Paris Peace Conference following, 166; propaganda in, 103; rum and ether in, 109; Savoia as cry in, 113; as setting for Hemingway's fiction, 110, 111, 179; Thompson's history of, 112; Wilson, Sir Henry, and, 119 (see also Battle of the Piave); "Wine of Wyoming," as background of, 209, 210, 211, 218, 223
Wyatt, David, 239, 242, 243

Yellowstone County, 248
Yellowstone Valley, 253
Young, Neil, 12
Young, Philip, 13, 119, 271; The Nick Adams Stories and, 101, 176, 208, 287

Zaragoza, Spain, 35, 36, 40, 46, 47
Zenson di Piave, Italy, 101, 120
Zola, Émile, 50, 66